Also by Norbert Elias

THE HISTORY OF MANNERS
POWER AND CIVILITY

THE·COURT
·SOCIETY·

THE · COURT
· SOCIETY ·

NORBERT ELIAS

Translated by Edmund Jephcott

PANTHEON BOOKS, NEW YORK

Library of Congress Cataloging in Publication Data

Elias, Norbert.
The court society.
Translation of: Die höfische Gesellschaft.
Includes bibliographical references and index.
1. Aristocracy.   I. Title.
HT647.E5313 1983   305.5′2   83-4236
ISBN 0-394-53282-1
ISBN 0-394-71604-3 (pbk.)

Contents

I   Introduction: sociology and history   1

II   Preliminary notes on the problems to be studied   35

III   The structure of dwellings as an indicator of social structure   41

IV   Characteristics of the court-aristocratic figuration   66

V   Etiquette and ceremony: conduct and sentiment of human beings as functions of the power structure of their society   78

VI   The bonding of kings through etiquette and status chances   117

VII   The sociogenesis and development of French court society as functions of power shifts in society at large   146

VIII   On the sociogenesis of aristocratic romanticism in the process of courtization   214

IX   On the sociogenesis of the French Revolution   268

Appendix 1 On the notion that there can be a state without structural conflicts   276

Appendix 2 On the position of the intendant in the estate management of the court aristocracy, with particular reference to the economic ethos of the court aristocracy   284

Index   295

THE·COURT
·SOCIETY·

·I·

Introduction:
sociology and history

1. The princely court of the *ancien régime* and the social formations associated with it are a rich field for sociological study. In the
countries of the *ancien régime* where the sovereign ruled almost
without intervention by assemblies of the estates, i.e. in countries
with absolutist rule, the princely court still combined two distinct
functions as it had done at earlier stages of the development of the
state when centralization was less complete: it was both the first
household of the extended royal family, and the central organ of the
entire state administration, the government. The personal and professional duties and relationships of the ruling princes and their
assistants were not yet as sharply differentiated and specialized as
later in the industrial nation states. In the latter, organs of public
control in the form of parliaments, press, jurisdiction or parties increasingly imposed a separation of private and public concerns on
even the most powerful people in the state. In dynastic societies with
their court elites, a considerable overlap of personal and official
interests was still taken for granted. The idea that they could or
should be separated emerged only here and there, and in a
rudimentary form. It was not a normal official or professional ethos,
but arose, if at all, from obligation towards, or fear of, someone
more powerful. Family ties and rivalries, personal friendships and
enmities were normal components of governmental and of all official
affairs. Sociological studies of court society therefore throw into
relief a particular aspect of an earlier stage in the development of
European states.

Of course, it was not only in the evolution of European societies
that courts and court societies were central to the state. Conquering
societies, or societies threatened by conquest, in the pre-industrial
period, where populations already differentiated in terms of function
were ruled from one centre over large areas, generally showed a
strong tendency to concentrate power in a single social position, that

1

of the monarch. And wherever this was the case — in the centrally governed empires of Antiquity, in China, in India as in the pre-revolutionary France of more recent times, the monarch's court and court society formed a powerful and prestigious elite.

The princely court and the society belonging to it are therefore specific figurations of people that are no less in need of elucidation than cities or factories. Historical studies and documentation on individual courts exist in profusion. But there is a lack of sociological studies. However much sociologists have concerned themselves with feudal or industrial societies, court society, which at least in European history arises from the former and issues in the latter, has been almost completely neglected.

2. The rise of court society is undoubtedly connected to the advancing centralization of state power, to the growing monopolization of the two decisive sources of the power of any central ruler, the revenue derived from society as a whole which we call 'taxes', and military and police power. But the fundamental question raised by this social dynamic, the question how and why, in a particular phase of state formation, a social position emerges which concentrates an extraordinary degree of power in the hands of a single person, has seldom been posed and remains unanswered. A certain reorganization of the perceptions is needed if we are to see the significance of this question. It involves a switch from the historical to the sociological perspective. The former throws light on particular individuals, in this case individual kings, while the latter illuminates social positions, in this case the development of the royal position. It may be observed again and again in societies at this stage of development, in dynastic societies, that a particular occupant of this autocratic-monarchical position, or perhaps even a whole dynasty, may be killed or violently removed from the throne without the character of society as a dynastic state ruled by autocratic rulers or their representatives being altered in the slightest. Usually the deposed king is replaced by another king, the expelled dynasty by another dynasty. It is only with the growing industrialization and urbanization of societies that, somewhat unevenly, there is a reduction in this regular process by which a dethroned king or disempowered dynasty is sooner or later replaced by another hereditary central lord with an equal abundance of power. The question how the figuration of interdependent people was constituted that made it not only possible but apparently necessary for many thousands of people to be ruled without restriction by a single family for hundreds or thousands of years is, therefore, one of

the central problems with which a sociological study of court society is confronted. But in raising the question how it was possible at a particular stage in the development of states for the social position of the absolute monarch, which we denote by the word 'emperor' or 'king', to re-establish itself constantly, we tacitly also raise the question why this position is approaching extinction in our own day.

3. The following studies are concerned in detail only with court society in a very specific epoch. But a sociological investigation of social formations in this particular epoch would be meaningless if we were to lose sight of the fact that court societies are to be found for a long period in the development of many states, and that the task of a sociological study of a particular court society includes the evolving of models that make it possible to compare different court societies. The question just raised — how certain figurations of interdependent people made it possible for individuals with a small circle of helpers to maintain themselves and their dynasties in more or less unrestricted power over an overwhelmingly larger number of subjects for long periods — this question itself indicates that the study of a single court society can contribute to the clarification of broader sociological questions of social dynamics. As will emerge, the power of the individual ruler was by no means so unrestricted or absolute, even in the age of so-called 'absolutism', as this term suggests. Even Louis XIV, the *Roi Soleil*, who is often taken as the supreme example of the omnipotent absolute monarch, proves on closer scrutiny to be an individual who was enmeshed through his position as king in a specific network of interdependences. He could preserve his power only by a carefully calculated strategy which was governed by the peculiar structure of court society in the narrow sense, and more broadly by society at large. Without a sociological analysis of the specific strategy whereby a ruler like Louis XIV maintained the constantly threatened elbow-room and manoeuvrability of the royal position, and without elaborating a model of the specific social structure which made this strategy both possible and necessary for the individual ruler's survival, the behaviour of such rulers would remain incomprehensible and inexplicable.

This makes the relationship between the sociologist's and the historian's standpoints somewhat clearer. In conjunction with a sociological study, which owing to prevailing habits of thought can easily be misunderstood as an historical one, such clarification may be helpful. Historical investigation is directed, as is emphasized often enough, primarily at unique and unrepeated sequences of events. If it concerns itself with the French court in the seventeenth and eight-

eenth centuries, the actions and character-traits of particular individuals, especially the kings, are at the centre of its interest.

4. A systematic investigation of problems of the type indicated in
the preceding discussions, problems concerning the social function of
the king, the structure of the court in French society in the seventeenth and eighteenth centuries, transcends the plane of the 'unique
and unrepeated' events with which historiography has been concerned hitherto. The historian's failure to undertake a systematic
study of social positions such as the monarchy, and therefore of the
strategies and scope for decision imposed on the individual king by
his position, leads to a peculiar narrowing of the historical
perspective. As a result, what is called history often looks like an
accumulation of discrete actions by individual people. As the level on
which people are interconnected and interdependent, of the long-
term, recurring structures and processes to which such concepts as
'state' or 'estates', and 'feudal', 'court' or 'industrial' society refer,
usually lies beyond or, at best, in the margins of the traditional field
of historical study, the isolated, unrepeated data placed at the centre
of such study lack any systematic or verifiable framework of
reference. The connections between particular phenomena are often
left to arbitrary interpretation and speculation. This is why history,
as currently understood, provides no real continuity of research.
Ideas on the connections between events come and go. But in the
end, one seems just as correct and just as unprovable as another. As
Ranke pointed out long ago:

> History is always being rewritten. . . . Each period takes it over and
> stamps it with its dominant slant of thought. Praise and blame are ap-
> portioned accordingly. All this drags on until the matter itself
> becomes unrecognizable. Then nothing can help except a return to the
> original evidence. But would we study it at all without the impulse of
> the present? . . . Is a completely true history possible?[1]

5. The word 'history' is always being used both for what is written
about and for the writing itself. The confusion is great. At first sight
'history' may seem a clear and unproblematical concept. On closer
examination, we find how many open questions are concealed behind
the apparently simple word. What is written about, the object of
research, is neither true nor false; only what is written about it, the
result of research, can be true or false. The question, rather, is what

---

[1] L. von Ranke, diaries 1831–49, in *Das politische Gespräch und andre Schriften zur
Wissenschaftlehre* (Halle, 1925), p. 52.

the object of historical study actually is. What is the 'matter', which according to Ranke is often made unrecognizable by all the praise and blame of historians?

Ranke himself knew no other answer to this pressing question than to refer back to the original evidence, the contemporary sources. This insistence on the study of sources, on careful documentation, was a major contribution.[2] It gave an immense impulse to the whole of historical research. Without him it would be impossible in many areas to advance to the sociological plane at all.

But precisely when the importance of careful documentation as the basis of historiography is moved into the foreground, the question of the purpose and object of historical research is raised all the more clearly. For are the documents, the original sources of information, the substance of history?

They are, it appears, the only reliable thing. Everything else that the historian has to offer is, it could be argued, interpretation. These interpretations often differ widely in different generations. They depend on the changing trend of contemporary interests, and the attendant praise and blame of historians. Ranke pointed to the heart of the problem: the historian apportions praise and blame. He not only

---

[2] It may be of interest in this connection to point to the recognition accorded to the scholarship of German historians a few years ago by one of the most eminent English historians, Prof. A. W. Southern, in his Inaugural Lecture: *The Shape and Substance of Academic History* (Oxford, 1961), pp. 15ff: 'In his Inaugural Lecture of 1867 Stubbs had spoken with confidence of the "good time coming" in historical studies with a historical school built ". . . on the abundant collected and arranged materials now in course of publication". He foresaw a time not far ahead when history could cease to be a mere task for children, or an instrument "to qualify men to make effective speeches to ignorant hearers, and to indite brilliant articles for people who only read periodicals", and become a thing "loved and cultivated for its own sake", entailing a "widespread historical training which will make imposture futile and adulteration unprofitable".

'What had gone wrong with this vision? To put it bluntly, England had not kept pace with Germany and was falling every year further behind. In 1867 Stubbs had been aware, but not I think very keenly aware, of the great work of the editors of the *Monumenta Germaniae Historica*; and, after all, he could reflect, England had its own Record Publications, and its own Rolls Series in which more than seventy volumes had been published in the ten years between 1857 and 1867. In view of this record, Stubbs may be excused for not having understood in 1867 that the situation in England was quite different from that in Germany. By 1877, still more by 1884, he could not fail to mark the difference. In England the flow of printed sources had fallen off; many deficiencies in the scholarship of those already published had been disclosed. In Germany not only had the work of publication gone on apace, and at a conspicuously higher level of scholarship than in England — a painful difference which would be even more marked if Stubbs's own publications were removed — but the work of the German editors was being supplemented every year by a more and more formidable array of monographs. It is fashionable now to sneer at these monuments of Teutonic diligence, but no serious scholar will feel inclined to sneer; and to anyone who saw it happen, it must have appeared the most prodigious event in the history of scholarship. There had never been anything like it before.'

carefully communicates the contents of the documents, but evaluates them. He distributes light and shade according to his own judgement, but often enough as if the distribution were self-evident, in accordance with the ideals and the underlying view of the world to which he subscribes among the factions of his time. Contemporary circumstances decide how he sees 'history', and even what he sees as 'history'. He makes his selection from the events of the past in the light of what he approves or disapproves in the present.

This is clearly what Ranke is alluding to by saying that the 'matter' itself is obscured by 'praise and blame'. And so it has fundamentally remained. The meticulousness of documentation, the reliability of references to historical sources and the overall knowledge of these sources have increased considerably. This provides a certain — one might say the only — justification for calling historiography scientific. But the historical sources are fragments. Historians attempt to reconstruct the connections between events on the basis of these fragmentary remnants. But while the references to sources are verifiable, the assembly and interpretation of the fragments are left largely to the discretion of the individual researcher. He lacks the firm framework which gives research in more mature disciplines models for connecting events, called hypotheses and theories, the development of which is in constant touch with the growth of detailed knowledge in the field. Thanks to this contact, the questions posed in these more mature disciplines, the selection of particular data and the development of comprehensive models, have a high degree of autonomy in face of the polarized value-judgements which have their roots in disputes outside scholarship. In historiography these outside factions and ideals with which the individual researcher identifies himself in his own society, determine to a considerable extent what he brings to light from the sources and what he leaves in the shadow, and how he relates it together. This procedure reminds us of the way people build houses of their own in the style of their own time from the ruins of buildings from earlier periods. This is the main reason why, as Ranke put it, 'history is constantly being rewritten'. Each generation selects debris from the past and assembles it in accordance with its own ideals and values into houses of its own kind.

6. It is in this lack of autonomy of historiography in face of the tensions and conflicts within the societies in which 'history' is produced and consumed, that the main reason for the rudimentary or quasi-scientific character of the greater part of present-day historiography is to be sought. This lack of autonomy gives rise to

one of the decisive features distinguishing historiography from more mature disciplines: it lacks the specific continuity of development which is the hallmark of research in such disciplines. In the latter, not only does the amount and exactitude of detailed information grow in the course of generations, but in close touch with it the scope and certainty of the connecting frameworks are likewise developed. In the former, in historiography, there is certainly a continuous growth of particular knowledge, but there is no continuity of growth on the plane of a unifying framework. In the older and more mature disciplines the significance of earlier hypotheses and theories on the nature of connections, whether in a specialized field, or in the universe as a whole, is preserved as a step on the way to later hypotheses and theories, because these later steps would not have been possible without the earlier ones. While later theories go beyond them, the significance of earlier steps remains as a link in the unbroken chain of research. Without Newton, Einstein cannot be completely understood. The continuous progress of scholarship does not necessarily consign the comprehensive models of earlier stages to the wastepaper basket, and indeed, it does so less often the more secure and autonomous the progress of scholarship has become. In the realm of historiography it is still far more the rule than the exception for the efforts of researchers who worked three or more generations ago to lie as dead books in the libraries. But it would arouse misunderstanding if we did not add that here the difference between history and sociology is at best one of degree. In both, short-lived values and ideals originating in the conflicts of the time often serve as substitutes for more autonomous theories, for models of relationships, which can be tested and revised as new knowledge is acquired. But sociological research differs from historical research at least in understanding that the posing and selecting of individual questions is subject to the heteronomous caprice of the individual researcher or the conventional beliefs of groups of researchers, unless there is at least an attempt to develop models that are in constant touch with the growth of knowledge and uninfluenced by the fluctuating controversies of the time, and are thus more adequate and autonomous than their predecessors. In historiography, as far as one can see, there is not even an effort in this direction, nor any understanding that if more autonomous models and theories are not developed, the very selection of data from the abundant documentation is dictated by short-lived and unverifiable research conventions. One can see the importance of models as determinants of the selection of problems from the composition of the present book. In keeping with the unquestioned traditional models that govern the evaluation and selection of problems in the discipline of history, many of the problems with which these sociological studies are concerned, and likewise the documentation needed to investigate them, play at most a marginal role in history as such. A study of the ground plan of palaces or details of court etiquette, for example, may seem like curiosities if measured by the yardstick of the historian. But it emerges that the layout of the accommodation and the whole architectonic structure in which families of a certain society lived give both a reliable and a verifiable insight into the basic form of the marriage relationship characteristic of people in this society, and beyond that, into their relationship with other people in the framework of social life. Court etiquette which, by the values of bourgeois-industrial societies, may well seem something quite unimportant, something merely 'external' and perhaps even ridiculous, proves, if one respects the autonomy of the structure of court society, an extremely sensitive and reliable instrument for measuring the prestige value of an individual within the social network.

By and large it can be said that the mere selection of court society as the object of study jars on the prevalent popular scheme of values which often influences historical research. In the present period of social development, dynastic rulers and their courts are becoming less and less significant. They are among the moribund social formations of our day. As far as they still exist at all in developed countries, they have lost much of their earlier power and prestige. As compared to the time of their apogee, the court societies of our day are mere epigones. The representatives of rising social formations usually regard these remnants of a past era with mixed feelings.

It is understandable that this negative evaluation helps to obstruct the view of court society as a social form with a character no less distinct and individual than, for example, the feudal elites or the party elites of industrial societies. The latter may receive more attention today because they are social types belonging to the present, in which most people are interested. The former, the feudal elites, are quite prominent in historical and sociological studies perhaps because they can be considered dispassionately from a distance as ancestors and antitheses of present formations. Feudal social forms appear as something long extinct; they do not arouse defensive attitudes, and are sometimes even romantically idealized. The realization that court society has specific structural features that can be ascertained whether one approves them or not, is made more difficult by the survival of residues of this social formation in our own time. Towards the disempowered court elite descended from what were once the most powerful formations in many European states, the rising elites of industrial nation states have preserved a negative, defensive attitude that echoes the struggles of earlier days. Here, too, the values and affects of society at large impinge on the selection of what is regarded as historically or sociologically relevant and what is not. The study and even the concept of court society still suffer from this kind of popular evaluation.

It is by no means easy to show what is meant by saying that a conscious effort is needed to secure greater autonomy for the selection and formulation of sociological problems — whether they relate to the present or the past — in face of popular valuations that are taken for granted and therefore untested. But this is one example. If it is our task to enlarge the understanding of the various ways in which individual people are interconnected, then all the figurations formed by human beings, all social groupings, are equivalent. We return here in a somewhat broader sense to the insight expressed by Ranke when he said that all periods of history are fundamentally of equal value. He too tried in his own way to point out that those exploring human relationships are denied access to their subject if they allow themselves to be guided by the preconceived values of their own time and social group. One simply cannot imagine any social formation, whether large or small, whether long past or still present, the objective investigation of which could contribute more or less than any other to our understanding of the way in which people are connected together in all their situations, in thinking as in feeling, in hating as in loving, in action as in inaction. The variability of these human connections is so great that, at least while our knowledge remains as limited and fragmentary as it is, one cannot conceive of an objective study of a hitherto unexplored human figuration and its evolution that would not bring new understanding of the human universe and of ourselves.

7. In a discussion of the relationship between historiography and sociology, therefore, the frequently mentioned problem of the uniqueness of historical events plays a central part. The idea that the uniqueness and unrepeatability of events is a distinguishing characteristic of human history, the object of historical research, frequently goes hand in hand with the notion that this 'uniqueness' is rooted in the nature of the object, regardless of all the value-judgements of the researchers. But this is by no means the case. The fact that what is currently studied as history is generally regarded as a collection of individual data, has its origin in the belief that events, which are unique and unrepeatable, constitute the essential reality of

the process being studied. It originates, in other words, in a specific valuation which can easily seem self-evident. But it is perhaps better to examine this belief, to see how far it is justified.

For unrepeatable and unique phenomena are by no means confined to the sequences of events that historians take as the object of their studies. Such phenomena exist everywhere. Not only is each human being, each human feeling, each action and each experience of a person unique, but each bat and bacillus. Every extinct animal species is unique. The Saurians will not return. In the same sense *Homo sapiens*, the human species as a whole, is unique. And the same can be said of each speck of dust, of our sun, the Milky Way and of every other formation: they come, they go, and when they have gone they do not return.

The problem of uniqueness and unrepeatability is therefore more complex than it appears in discussions of the theory of science. There are different degrees of uniqueness and unrepeatability, and what is unique and unrepeatable on one level can be seen on another as repetition, a return of the never-changing. Our unique sun, the unrepeatable, slowly changing Earth on which we live, appear to the fleeting generations as eternally recurring forms. As for the unique human species, individual human beings are themselves repetitions of an unchanging form, and what differs between people now appears as a variation of the ever-recurring basic pattern.

But it is precisely this variation, this uniqueness of the individual in the framework of a constantly recurring basic pattern, to which in certain societies, and within these societies in certain branches of research, a particularly high value is attached. This valuation is itself connected with the special structure of our society and in particular with its high degree of differentiation and individualization. It is this which finds expression in the historiography of this society. The explanation is complex, and it is unnecessary here to pursue this extensive network of connections in detail. However apt or inapt the historical theory may be that places only the unique and individual aspects of the historical process in the foreground, what is certain is that in this emphasis a specific, socially engendered form of human consciousness is reflected. Not only do people value in themselves what they actually perceive to be distinctive and unique; in accordance with a specific social tendency ingrained in the individual, people also normally regard it as an ideal to develop their social community into something as unique and unrepeatable as possible. The attention to specific unique and unrepeated features in the course of events, which largely determines the theory and practice of historical research, would be unthinkable without the special value attached to the uniqueness and unrepeatability of individuals in those societies in which this kind of history is written.

The question to which we must therefore address ourselves is that of the relative heteronomy or autonomy of this kind of valuation as applied to the sequence of events studied by 'history'. Is the theoretical guiding idea of historiography, which gives greater importance to the unrepeated and unique features of the process, especially of individual people and their actions, a product of unprejudiced critical analysis and therefore object-adequate? Or is it the result of an ideological manipulation whereby their specific social conditioning causes historians to project short-lived extraneous values and ideals on to the process to be studied?

It would be simple if these questions could be answered by a mere 'either/or', by 'yes' or 'no'. The difficulty is that in the history of human societies — and, as will be discussed in more detail later, 'history' is always concerned with the development of particular human societies — unrepeated and individual aspects of the process are connected to recurring social aspects in a way that necessitates careful study and cannot be reduced to a simple formula. This is not the case in non-human, animal societies.

8. How and why unique, individual aspects play a special part in the history of human societies can be seen by even a cursory comparison with the history of animal societies. If we are to see the problem in the correct light, such a comparison is almost indispensable. The relationships, the interdependences between ants, bees, termites and other social insects, the structure of their societies can, as long as the species stays the same, be repeated over many thousands of years without any change. This is so because the social forms, the relationships and mutual dependences, are largely anchored in the biological structure of the organisms. Leaving aside minimal variations, the social structures of social insects and, with slight differences of degree, of all other animals that form specific social figurations, change only when their biological organization changes. It is one of the specific peculiarities of societies formed by human beings that their structure, the form of individual interdependences, can change without a change in the biological organization of human beings. The individual representatives of the species *Homo sapiens* can form societies of the most diverse kinds without the species itself changing. In other words, the biological constitution of the species makes it possible for the nature of its social life to develop without the species developing. The transition from the *ancien régime* to the early indus-

trial regime of the nineteenth century, the change from a primarily agrarian village society to a more urbanized one, was the expression of a social, not a biological development.

The whole discussion of the relationship between sociology and history is impeded by the fact that up to now even scholarly studies have generally neglected to define clearly both the difference and the relationship between biological evolution, social development and history. There were no doubt biological, evolutionary changes in the social relationships and structures of our forbears. We know little about this side of the evolution of hominids, possibly because bio-sociological problems of this kind receive little attention from specialists in human pre-history. But the changes in human social life that come within the view of historians and sociologists take place within the framework of one and the same biological species. Whether we are concerned with the social and historical relationships of the ancient Sumerians and Egyptians, of the Chinese and Indians, the Yoruba and Ashanti, or of the Americans, Russians and French, we are always dealing with people of the nature of *Homo sapiens*. The fact that in this case changes in the structure of the social life of individual organisms take place without changes in the biological, innate and hereditary constitution of the organism itself, is explained finally by the fact that the behaviour of these human beings is governed to a far greater extent than that of any other organism known to us by the experience of the individual organism, by individual learning and, indeed, *must* be so governed. This innate and hereditary biological peculiarity of the human constitution, the dependence of behaviour on the experience of the individual from childhood on, is therefore the reason why human societies, unlike ant societies, have what we call 'history' or, with a different emphasis, 'social development'.

How much the development of human societies, social development, differs from biological evolution is shown by the fact that the former, unlike the latter, can in a certain respect be reversed. Despite the jokes one may read on the subject, we can be certain on the basis of existing biological knowledge that the species *Homo sapiens* can certainly become extinct, but cannot revert to a species of ape or reptile. When the ancestors of whales evolved from land animals to water creatures, they did not become fishes but remained mammals. By contrast it is quite possible that highly concentrated nation states could disintegrate and the descendants of their inhabitants live as simple nomadic tribes. This is what is meant by saying that the figurations formed by bees and ants are to a high degree genetically fixed while those of human beings are comparatively free in this respect. Change in human figurations is very closely bound up with the possibility of transmitting experiences gathered in one generation to subsequent generations as acquired social knowledge. This continuous social accumulation of knowledge plays a part in the changing of human society. But the continuity of the collection and transmission of knowledge can be broken. The increase in knowledge does not bring about a genetic change in the human race. Socially accumulated experiences can be lost.

9. Clarification of such fundamental matters is needed if we are to understand the relationship between the repeatable and the non-repeatable aspects of social change. As can be seen, the sequences denoted by terms such as 'biological evolution', 'social development' and 'history' form three distinct but inseparable layers in a process encompassing the whole of mankind, the speed of change being different at each level. Measured by the length and rate of change of an individual human life, social developments often take place so slowly that they seem to stand still. It is possible that the social figurations formed by people change so little for a number of generations that they are regarded by those involved as immutable social forms. Thus, for a long period in the development of European society, people are embraced over and over again by the figuration 'knight – page – priest – bondsman'. Today, and for a number of generations past in the developed industrial societies, people are repeatedly found in relationships such as 'worker – employee – manager' or 'higher – middle – lower official'. The functional interdependence of these and all the other positions in a particular society entails, as can be seen, a certain exclusivity. Knight and bondsman would scarcely fit into an industrial figuration.

Each of the individuals making up such figurations is unique and unrepeatable. But the figuration itself can be preserved relatively unchanged over many generations. Thus, figurations that are almost identical or, at any rate, only very slightly changed, can be formed by different, more quickly changing individuals. Seen from the perspective of the quickly changing, unique and unrepeatable individual, the figurations formed by these individuals appear as recurring phenomena that are more or less unchangeable.

It would be a misunderstanding of this state of affairs to interpret the conceptual models of such figurations as artificial structures imposed by the investigator on the people being observed. This is roughly what Max Weber meant when he referred to his models of certain slowly evolving figurations as 'ideal types'. The models of the bureaucracy, the city, the state or capitalist society that he attempted to develop, did not refer to figurations that he introduced into his material merely to bring order into something disordered. These figurations are just as real as the individual people forming them. What still seems difficult to grasp today is the fact that these figurations formed by people can have a slower rate of transformation than the individual people forming them.

The relation between the rate of change of social figurations to that of biological phenomena is similar. Seen from the standpoint of the former, the latter change so slowly that evolution appears to be standing still. We have here, therefore, an image of mankind as a river with three currents running at different speeds. Seen in isolation the phenomena in each of these streams are unique and unrepeatable. But in the context of the differing rates of change, phenomena in a slower current are apt, from the position of a faster current, to seem immutable, eternally recurrent. In biological chronology ten thousand years is a very short period. The changes that have taken place in the biological constitution of the species *Homo sapiens* in the last ten thousand years are relatively slight. In social chronology ten thousand years is a very considerable period. The changes in social organization that have taken place in many areas of mankind over the last ten thousand years are, comparatively, enormous. In this period, in many societies, villages grew into towns, towns into city states, city states into territorial states, into greater or lesser dynastic states and finally into industrial nation states; and the rate of change in these series has accelerated considerably. But in individual chronology, in terms of the rate at which children grow into old men and women, long-term social developments still take place very slowly. This is the reason why they are not often perceived as what they are, as structured developments of social figurations, but rather, the individual lifespan being taken as the framework of reference, as static 'social systems'.

10. In the discipline we call history today, there is perhaps not sufficient consideration of whether and how far a chronology based on the length and rate of change of individual life is a suitable framework of reference for the investigation of long-term social developments. The individual takes himself for granted as the measure of all things. This has been done in the mainstream of historiography up to now more or less consciously and consistently. The observing lens is applied primarily to changes that take place through individual people, or are believed to be attributable to individual people as their causes.

In the development of history itself this concentration on sharply outlined individuals has a very close connection with a specific social distribution of power. This should not be entirely forgotten. The attention of historians was frequently focused above all on people who were regarded as particularly significant as individuals by virtue of their achievements for a particular state or group. These were, first of all, people in very powerful social positions — emperors, kings, princes, dukes and other members of royal houses. Through their power positions they did indeed stand out from the mass very clearly for the historian as individuals. Thanks to their social positions their scope for action, compared to that of other people, was large, and their individual peculiarities prominent. They were unique and unrepeatable. The habit of thinking in terms of the reigns of individual kings and speaking, for example, of 'Prussia under Frederick the Great' or the 'Age of Louis XIV' has survived until today as a sensible way of dividing up the course of history.

It is similar with other people in positions of power, such as the great army leaders whose victories or defeats were of major importance for the 'history' of a certain social entity, or ministers and other assistants of ruling princes to whom societies owe new institutions or who resisted innovation. As power shifted in the societies themselves, this emphasis in historiography also shifted in the course of time. Beside the individuals belonging to powerful or prestigious elites, less clearly defined and powerful groups of people were included in the field of historical study. But in the historians' more general perception of their own activity, the individual person as such, and particularly the individual distinguished by power or achievement, nevertheless retained his position as the primary framework of reference in interpreting the connections between events and as a symbol of their uniqueness. Even when a political historiography that focused on rulers or powerful elites was slowly extended to include economic, intellectual, religious, artistic and other social aspects of the development of a society, historiography nevertheless remained strongly orientated towards relatively individualized elites. With few exceptions such as economic and social history, the individual works and deeds of people belonging to particular social elites are still usually chosen as an historical framework of reference, without the sociological problems of the formation of such elites becoming part of the study. Questions of strategy in selecting problems and evidence are still by and large ignored in discussions of the nature of historiography. Such discussions are often content to refer to the magnitude of the individual's achievement as such, and to the single individual as the source of the great achievement which cannot be further explained. Here, with the individual, the search for the explanations of events seems to reach its goal. The problem that has been set seems solved, once an individual author has been found for a certain historical phenomenon. Any loose ends that are left behind are treated like other historical phenomena that cannot be explained by reference to great, nameable individuals, as a somewhat blurred background. But if the final explanation of historical connections is sought in this way in something mysterious and not further explainable, in the secret of an 'individuality in itself', it is difficult to avoid interpreting the high social value of a person, his achievements, characteristics and utterances, automatically as the personal value and greatness of that particular individual. The simplest example of this is seen in the epithet 'the Great' applied to hereditary kings. What is said later in this study on Louis XIV illustrates this problem. It still happens that historians and teachers accept persons designated as great by a particular social tradition at face value. Too easily in the writing of history a conventional and therefore scientifically unreliable and untested scale of values is applied when assessing human greatness. In ignorance of the social structures which give an individual person his opportunity for achievement, people without particular personal merit are presented as great and vice versa.

Historians are apt to say that they are not concerned with societies but with individuals. But on closer inspection we find that historiography is not so much concerned with individuals as such as with individuals who play a part in and for societies of a particular kind. We can go further and say that it is interested in these individuals *because* they play a part in social entities of one kind or another. It would of course be possible to include in historiography the 'history' of a dog, a flower-bed or a person selected at random. Everyone has his 'history'. But when 'historical research' is spoken of, the word 'history' is used in a very specific sense. Its framework of reference is ultimately formed by the social entities that are considered especially important. There is always a hierarchical scale of values which decides which of these historical entities is more or less important as a framework. The historical studies whose social framework of reference is a particular city within a state generally rank lower than those whose framework is an entire state. At the top of this scale of values at present we doubtless find the nation states. Their history today provides the main framework for selecting individuals and historical problems central to historical research. One does not usually reflect on why the history of social units such as

'Germany', 'Russia' or the 'United States' serves at present as the primary framework for selecting individuals who are placed in the foreground of historial research as 'historical figures'. And yet there is no tradition of research within which the connections between the actions and achievements of the individual actors of history and the structure of the societies within which they attain significance are systematically investigated. If this were done, it would not be difficult to show how often the selection of the individuals on whose fate or actions the attention of historians is focused is bound up with their membership of specific minorities, of rising, ruling or declining elite groups in particular societies. At least in all hierarchical societies the individual's 'opportunity for great achievements' that attracts the eye of the historian depended for a long period on his belonging to specific elite groups or the possibility of gaining access to them. Without a sociological analysis that takes account of the structure of such elites, the greatness and merit of historical figures can scarcely be judged.

11. The court society which is the subject of this book is an elite formation of this kind. In this study there are a number of examples illustrating what has just been said. Individuals who in the reign of Louis XIV did not belong to court society, or have access to it, had relatively little chance of proving and fulfilling their individual potential by achievements that would be deemed of importance on the traditional scale of historical values. Through a more detailed study of such an elite, moreover, it can be very reliably shown in what way its structure gave or denied individual people their opportunities for achievement and fulfilment. The Duc de Saint-Simon, for example, through his specific social position as a member of the high aristocracy but not of the royal house itself, was denied access by the strategy of Louis XIV not only to government posts but to all positions of official or political power. These were precisely the positions for which he strove throughout his life. It was in this direction, as a statesman, politician or governor, that he hoped above all to find fulfilment. In such positions he expected great achievements of himself. As this possibility was closed to him by his position in the power structure at court as long as Louis XIV lived, he tried to find fulfilment, aside from his involvement in court intrigues, through literary activity in the form matching the custom and taste of the court aristocracy, the writing of memoirs recording court life in its details. Excluded from political power he passed into history, as we say, through his achievements as a memoirist. Neither the development of his individuality nor his attitude as a writer can be

understood without reference to a sociological model of court society and without knowledge of the development of his social position within its structure.

The traditional debate on the role of the individual in history sometimes starts from the assumption that the antithesis between historians who concentrate on 'individual phenomena' on one hand, and on 'social phenomena' on the other, is irreconcilable and inevitable. But this antinomy is in fact quite unreal. It can only be explained in the context of two political-philosophical traditions, one of which presents 'society' as something extra-individual and the other the 'individual' as something extra-social. Both conceptions are fictitious, as can be seen here. Court society is not a phenomenon that exists outside the individuals forming it; the individuals forming it, whether king or valet, do not exist outside the society which they form together. The term 'figuration' serves to express this situation. Traditional linguistic usage makes it difficult to speak of individuals together forming societies, or of societies composed of individuals, although this is precisely what is actually observable. By using somewhat less loaded words, it becomes possible to express what can actually be observed clearly and unequivocally. This is the case when we say that individual people together form figurations of different kinds or that societies are nothing other than figurations of interdependent people. In this connection the concept of the 'system' is often used today. But as long as social systems are not thought of in a similar way as systems of people, this term remains nebulous and unreal.

12. If we look back and ask once more whether the view that unrepeatable and unique aspects of the process called 'history' constitute its essence is founded in the nature of this process itself or is an ideologically conditioned, extraneous evaluation imposed on this process by historians, we find that the preceding discussion has taken us some way towards an answer. It would be better to say that in the interpretation of 'history' as a complex of unique events both object-oriented and ideological valuations play a part. A comprehensive analysis of this amalgam of autonomous and heteronomous valuations would be a very large undertaking. We must be content to clarify a few aspects of this question by pointing to problems that play a part in the following study.

The court of Louis XIV was unique. Louis XIV himself was a single, unrepeatable phenomenon. But the social position he occupied, that of king, was not unique, or at any rate not in the sense that its temporary occupant was. There were kings before Louis XIV and there were kings after Louis XIV. They were all kings, but their persons were different.

Kings like Louis XIV have a scope for unique, unrepeatable experiences and behaviour which is extraordinarily wide. That is the first thing that, in Louis XIV's case, can be said about the reality of his uniqueness and unrepeatability. As compared to people in other social positions, Louis XIV's scope for individualization was especially large because he was a king.

But the king's scope for individualization was also especially large in another sense: because he was a human being. That is the second thing that can be said about this scope. As compared to non-human organisms, each human being has an extraordinarily large opportunity for the individualization of his own unique existence. Even in the simplest human societies known to us, the single organism's opportunity for individualization is very much greater than in the most complex non-human animal societies.

If historians focus their attention on the plane of the many-layered human universe on which that which differs between people, their individuality, plays a special part, if they try to show the contribution of individual persons and their unique gifts and behaviour to events that were of importance in the history of certain societies, these efforts may therefore be entirely appropriate. For differences in the individual elaborations of the repeatable basic biological structure of human beings can indeed play a greater or lesser part in the changes in societies which we call their 'history', the importance of their role depending on the structure of the society in question. Thus a historian writing on the period of Louis XIV, for example, can rightly point out how much the splendour of his court, and more broadly, French policy under his rule, owed to the specific gifts and also the specific limitations, in short to the unique individuality, of the king.

But the study would be inadequate if it were to stop at this point. Without a systematic examination of the royal position as such, as one of the positions making up the figurations of the court and of French society, the relationship between the individual person and the social position of the king cannot be understood. The former developed within the latter, which in its turn was in a process of development and change both within the narrower structure of the court elite and in the broader one of French society as a whole. It is not necessary here to pursue in detail the connections between the personal development of the king and the social development of the royal position, but the conceptual clarification to which this model of the king's development contributes is of importance. The concepts 'individual' and 'society' are often used as if they referred to two different substances at rest. These terms can easily give the impression that they denote not only different objects, but objects existing in absolute isolation from one another. But in reality it is to processes that these words refer, processes that can be distinguished but not separated. The king's personal development and that of his position go hand in hand. Since the latter possesses a specific elasticity, it can be steered, up to a certain point, by the personal development of its occupant. But through its interdependence with other positions in the total social structure to which it belongs, each social position, even that of the absolutist monarch, combines with its flexibility an extraordinary autonomy, as compared to the strength of its individual occupant. Very firm limits are set to his scope for action by the structure of his position, limits which, exactly like the elasticity of a steel spring, make themselves more strongly felt the more he stretches and tests the flexibility of his social position by his individual behaviour. While on one hand the occupant's personal development therefore influences within certain limits that of his position, on the other the development of his social position as a direct representative of society as a whole influences the personal development of the occupant.

We can already see at this point how incomplete and unclarified is the hypothesis of the uniqueness and unrepeatability of the object of historical study. Considered purely as a person, Louis XIV was unique and unrepeatable. But the 'pure person', the 'individual in himself', is a product of the philosophical imagination no less artificial than the 'thing in itself'. The development of the social positions through which an individual passes from his childhood on, is not unique and unrepeatable in the same sense as the individual who passes through them. As the development of the royal position moves at a different rate from that of its successive occupants, as this position could survive the demise of one occupant and be transferred to another, it had, as compared to an individual, the character of a repeatable phenomenon, or at least one that was not unique in the same sense. Historical research can therefore only appear in the traditional way as a discipline concerned solely with unique and individual phenomena, as long as it excludes sociological problems such as this from its field of enquiry. As we can see, the understanding of the uniqueness even of a king remains fragmentary and uncertain without a study of the royal position which is not unique and individual in the same sense.

Moreover, modalities like uniqueness and repeatability are only symptoms of structural peculiarities of the sequence of events to which these terms refer. If one penetrates the layer of the unique and individual events to the more comprehensive layer which includes the social positions and figurations of people, one opens the way to a type of problem that is concealed from a view restricted to individualistic historical problems.

With the aid of a systematic study of figurations it can be shown, for example, that even at the time of Louis XIV a man in the position of the king ruled by no means 'absolutely', if we mean by this that his actions and power were subject to no limits. The notion of the 'absolute ruler' gives a false impression, as we shall see. Considered from this point of view, the study of the social position of an absolutist monarch contributes to the understanding of broader problems, to which reference has already been made: how is it possible that an individual man is able to maintain his position as a ruler, deciding directly or indirectly for good or ill the fate of hundreds of thousands and perhaps millions of people, and the wide scope for decision that his position confers, for long periods? Which development in a structure composed of interdependent people, which figuration of human beings allows the formation of a central position with the particularly great freedom of decision that we call 'absolutism' or 'autocratic rule'? Under what conditions are social positions of monopoly rule formed that confer on their incumbents far greater powers than other social positions? Why really do hundreds of thousands of people, not only in crisis situations but as part of the normal routine of social life, obey a single man? And in the case of kings, not only a single man during his lifetime, but perhaps his son and grandson, in short the members of a particular family for several generations?

13. The sociology of power has found its most fruitful treatment so far in the work of Max Weber. His wide-ranging discussions[3] provide a store of sociological insight that has not nearly been exhausted. However, his approach, compared to that adopted here, was extensive, not intensive. He attempted to evolve models — 'ideal types' in his own terminology — that were reached through careful comparison of the largest possible number of phenomena of a certain type known to historians at the time. In consequence he adduced a huge volume of material when constructing a model of the type of rule which includes the one discussed here. It is to be found in his study of 'patrimonialism'. In his terms the form of rule studied here

[3] Max Weber, *Wirtschaft und Gesellschaft* (Tübingen, 1922), section 3 [trans. as *Economy and Society*].

could perhaps be classified as a traditional form of rule between patrimonialism and sultanism,[4] or as one of the 'highly centralized patrimonial bureaucracies'[5] of which he rightly says that unlike feudalism they are very often characterized by the importance of a factor frequently overlooked by scholarship: trade.

But precisely because Weber tried to assimilate such an extraordinary volume of data, the model of what he called patrimonialism is very loosely constructed. It threatens to crumble in his hands. As a basis for further work it has proved by and large less fruitful than his more solidly constructed model of charismatic rule. In this we have a model of the crisis form of monopoly rule. It refers to the type of ruler who tries to assert himself against existing routine and firmly established power groups with the help of other groups that, usually, were previously outsiders. The central group of absolutist monopoly rule that is studied here constitutes in many respects the antithesis of charismatic leadership. The model which is developed relates to a monopoly rule that has become firmly established. The material on which it is based is far more limited than that used by Max Weber in elaborating his models of traditional, non-charismatic types of rule. As against the extensive use of evidence, an intensive examination of a single regime seemed to offer many advantages in constructing a sociological model of non-charismatic rule. In such a study we can establish in detail which distribution of power and which specific routines enable a single person to maintain himself throughout his life in the always risky position of a powerful autocrat. The model of the royal mechanism, as developed here, forms the centrepiece of the answer given by this study to the questions posed earlier concerning the conditions of such rule.

But if we are to avoid theoretical aridity it is necessary to show, with the aid of detailed studies and examples, how this mechanism of competing power groups functions in practice; we must attempt to observe it directly at work. This has been done here. To understand how even the routine of getting up in the morning and going to bed at night could serve a king as instruments of power, is no less important for a sociological understanding of this type of 'routinized' monopoly rule than it is for a more general insight into the structure of the 'royal mechanism'. It is only through such paradigmatic details that we can gain a concrete picture of what has been previously formulated theoretically. For sociological theories which are not borne out by empirical work are useless. They hardly deserve the status of

[4] *Ibid.*, pp. 133ff., 628ff.
[5] *Ibid.*, p. 740.

theories. For example, only this practical basis gives us a deeper understanding of the ever-present danger, the element of risk integral to even the most powerful autocracy, and of the institutional measures by which the ruler and his central group, often without consciously realizing it, seek to counter this risk. Only once we are aware of this situation does it become possible to elucidate the relationship between the position of a king predetermined by the particular figuration of the time, and a king's personality as it develops within this position. And only then do we have enough firm ground under our feet to find out how much a model of routinized autocracy established in this way can contribute to an understanding of other social phenomena of a similar kind — for example, what light does this model of royal monopoly rule in a pre-industrial dynastic state throw on dictatorial rule in an industrialized nation state? In the study of despotic rule up to now, as we know, attention has been focused primarily on the person of the ruler, precisely because a particular person is here endowed by his social position with an extraordinary degree of power. Even in scholarly studies, the main if not the only explanation of the nature of a regime and its fate is sought often enough in the personal characteristics of the ruler. It may help in this broader context, too, to evolve a more precise model of monopoly rule enabling us to understand better how and why, even within the framework of an extremely powerful social position, the limits of its flexibility and of the scope for action of its occupant are incessantly felt. Like other social positions, that of a monopoly ruler demands a very carefully judged strategy of behaviour if the occupant is to secure the throne and its power for himself and his family over a long period. Just because the flexibility of this position and the scope for decisions it confers are particularly large, the possibility of error, rashness and derailment, which could in the long run lead to a reduction of power, is particularly acute. A tightrope-walker's confidence and skill are needed, with all the temptations such a position offers its occupant, if he is permanently to avoid steps that would reduce his power. Only in conjunction with an analysis of the development and structure of a position as such, can we obtain a clearer picture of the part played in its development and exploitation by the special qualities of its particular occupant. Only then is it possible to find a way out of the labyrinth of heteronomous valuations in which discussion tends to lose itself as long as praise and censure of the person of the ruler take the place of an explanation of the system of rule. In this sense, therefore, a study of the ruling elite of a particular autocratic regime, provided it aims consistently at autonomy of valuations, can be of use as a basic model for other studies of the relation between the dynamics of position and the dynamics of individuality. In the case of Louis XIV it is very clear how far he succeeded in matching his individual steps and inclinations to the conditions of the royal position with a very specific aim, to preserve and optimize the power attaching to it. However we may define the 'greatness' of Louis XIV, the relationship between greatness of power and of person remains unclear until the convergence or divergence between individual inclinations and goals and the demands of the royal position have been examined.

14. In other words, we obtain not only an incomplete but a distorted picture of the historical process if we stop short at seeking the origin of the splendour characterizing the reign of Louis XIV, or of the royal court and the policies of the French state, in the unique and unrepeatable individuality of particular persons. The ideological element in the emphasis on unique and unrepeated factors as the essential matter of history lies, among other things, in the fact that what is at most a partial view of a limited area is presented as an overall view of history, as history itself. Even the traditional idea of the individuality of the single human being that underlies the historiography concerned with individualities contains assumptions which require examination. This idea presents a being standing completely alone, an isolated rather than just a single human being, a closed rather than an open system. What are actually observed are people who develop in and through relations to other people. By contrast, the individualistic historical tradition postulates individuals who are ultimately without relation. Like many present-day notions, the historiography concerned primarily with 'individuals in themselves' obviously suffers from a fear that an approach based on the idea of people dependent on others and on whom others depend — and whose interdependence can be determined by investigation — could reduce or even extinguish the unique value of the individual human being. But this idea is itself connected to the erroneous belief that the word 'individual' refers to aspects of people existing outside their relations to one another, outside 'society', while the word 'society' refers to something existing outside individuals, such as a 'system of roles' or a 'system of actions'.

This general conceptual elucidation of the relations between the individuality and the position of the king, in conjunction with the detailed studies of this relation to be found in what follows, may contribute to replacing the dichotomous image that still plays a predominant part in the current usage of the words 'individual' and 'society', by concepts which are in closer touch with observable facts.

What was said above shows the direction to be taken by this study. The problem cannot be approached by assuming that the individual Louis XIV was something that developed independently of the social positions which he occupied first as heir to the throne and then as king; nor can it be approached by assuming that the development of these social positions was totally independent of their occupant. But the social plane of this development involves a process of a different order of magnitude, and on a different time scale, to the individual plane. As compared to the rate of change of the individual royal person, the social royal position appears as something evolving more slowly. The latter is a phenomenon of different magnitude to the former because it is part of a figuration made up of hundreds of thousands of people. The autonomy of his social position sets limits to the individual power of even the mightiest monopoly ruler. If the development of the former is viewed from a great distance, it is not difficult to see that it too, like the development of the French state to which it belongs, has its unique and unrepeatable aspects. The lack of attention in historical studies to both the difference and the relationship between the individual people with their relatively quick rate of change and the much more slowly changing figurations formed by these people, is a symptom of the ideological factors that encroach on historiography.

15. The one-sidedness of the assumption that the stratum of unique events, and especially the unique actions, decisions and characteristics of individuals, are the most important aspects of the process studied by historians, is apparent from the fact that historians themselves, in the practice of their work, hardly ever confine themselves strictly to the depiction of such events and actions. As a framework in selecting individual events they can never do without concepts related to the more slow-moving social stratum of the historical process. Such concepts can be relatively factual, as in matters such as economic development, migration of populations, government, bureaucracy and other state institutions, or with social entities like Germany and France, or they may be more speculative, as in discussion of, for example, the 'spirit of the age of Goethe', the 'life and times of the Kaiser', the 'social background of National Socialism', or the 'social milieu of the court'. The role and structure of social phenomena usually remain unclarified in the framework of historiography because the relationship of individual and society has itself not been clarified. The elucidation of the latter is obstructed by

pre-existing and untested value-judgements which guide the historian in selecting and interpreting his subject matter.

In keeping with this, social phenomena, the figurations formed by individuals, are treated in many, though no longer all, historical studies as a kind of backdrop before which apparently isolated individuals act as the real causes of historical events. It is this structure of historical perception, the stress on unique events and individual historical figures as a sharply defined foreground against social phenomena as a relatively unstructured background, that particularly impedes the clarification of the relationship between historical research and sociology. It is the task of sociology to bring the unstructured background of much previous historical research into the foreground and to make it accessible to systematic research as a structured weft of individuals and their actions. This change of perspective does not, as is sometimes asserted, rob individual people of their character and value as individuals. But they no longer appear as isolated people, each totally independent of the others. They are no longer seen as completely hermetic systems, each of which harbours the ultimate explanation of this or that socio-historical event. In the analysis of figurations, individuals present themselves far more as they may be observed, as open, mutually related sub-systems, linked by interdependences of the most widely differing kind through which they form specific figurations. Even those who, by specific social standards, are the greatest, the most powerful people, have their place as links in these chains of dependence. Even in their case we cannot understand their position, the way they reached it and their achievements attained within the scope permitted by it, if we do not subject these figurations themselves to careful scholarly analysis rather than treating them as an unstructured background. The fact that the figurations formed by people often change far more slowly than the people forming them, and that therefore younger people can take up the positions vacated by older ones; the fact, in short, that the same or similar figurations can frequently be formed over an extended period by different individuals, makes it appear as if these figurations have a kind of 'existence' outside individuals. Bound up with this optical illusion is the use of the terms 'society' and 'individual' whereby these appear as two separate objects made of different substances. But if we adjust our conceptual models more exactly to what we can actually observe, we find that the situation itself is simple enough and can be formulated quite unambiguously: the individuals who here and now form a specific social figuration can disappear and give way to others but, no matter how they change, the society, the figuration itself, is always formed by individuals. Figurations have a relative independence of particular individuals, but not of individuals as such.

The self-image of some historians makes it appear as if they are concerned in their work exclusively with individuals without figurations, with people wholly independent of others. The self-image of many sociologists makes it appear as if they are concerned exclusively with figurations without individuals, societies or 'systems' wholly independent of individual people. As we have seen, both approaches, and the self-images underlying them, lead their practitioners astray. On closer examination we find that both disciplines are merely directing their attention to different strata or levels of one and the same historical process.

The forms taken by the sequence of events on these two planes differ in many respects. Consequently the conceptual categories and methods of research used to elucidate them need a certain specialization. But as these planes themselves are absolutely inseparable, specialization without co-ordination would mean a misdirection of research and a squandering of human energies.

Efforts to achieve a more fruitful co-ordination of historical and sociological work currently still founder on the fact that there is no unified theoretical framework to which both sociological and historical research can refer. Without such a framework one can easily give the impression of trying to reduce work on one plane to that on the other. But what has been said in this introduction on the relationship between the two disciplines is a first step towards such a theoretical framework, which could be expected to bring about a considerable long-term re-orientation of these two unrelated specialized disciplines, but by no means the end of their specialization.

It might be said that such an undertaking, in conjunction with a limited sociological investigation, places too much emphasis on fundamental theoretical questions. The original impulse to write it came from the editors of this series, who felt with undoubted justification that given the present state of thought and knowledge, the sociological study of a period which is past and therefore labelled 'historical' requires a clarification of the relationship between sociological and historical research. And, as will perhaps be seen, it turned out to be very useful to couple a fairly limited empirical study to fundamental theoretical considerations. Relationships between the details of the empirical study can be far more fully understood if their theoretical significance is seen, and theoretical trains of thought can be better assimilated if empirical data to which they refer are to hand.

But the purpose of an introduction sets fairly narrow limits to these ideas on sociology and history. It would certainly be worthwhile to take account of the various types of historical and sociological research in their relationships to one another. It must be enough here to pick out a few basic problems of historical research which are of especial importance through their relationship to the problems of sociology. Discussion of them shows how and why sociological studies are re-orientating those of historical research as understood up to now. It may be useful by way of summary to pick out three points from the argument of this introduction that are of importance for a better collaboration between disciplines and deserve more detailed attention.

16. Historical studies often suffer from heteronomy in their valuations. The distinction between what seems important to the researcher by the scale of values of his own time, and especially on the basis of his own ideals, and what is important in the context of the period being studied — for example, what ranked high or low in the values of the people alive then — is often very blurred. The historian's personal scale of values conditioned by his time usually has the upper hand. It largely determines the kind of questions he asks and his selection of evidence. Sociological investigation demands a stricter curbing of the personal feelings and ideals of the researcher or, in other words, a greater autonomy of valuations. In both fields researchers are stopped in their tracks by a quagmire of uncertainties if they uncritically apply political, religious or related valuations of their own society to the period being studied, instead of respecting the specific ties, and, in particular, the specific scale of values existing within the societies being studied, when selecting and investigating problems.

In this study there are many examples of this kind of subordination of present-day values to those of the social formation which is the object of our study. The choice of subject in concerning ourselves with court society is itself, as has already been mentioned, one example. In terms of the prevalent political and social values of our time, court society is a social formation whose market-value is low. Accordingly, systematic studies on princely courts rank low in the hierarchy of historical topics. In current sociological attempts at classifying the various types of society, court society hardly figures at all. But considered from the standpoint of the objective of research, the study of events and their connections, courts and court societies as a specific kind of human figuration certainly have no less importance than other elite formations, such as parliaments and political parties, which are paid a great deal of attention on account of their topicality.

The same is true of lesser phenomena characteristic of court societies. Ceremony and etiquette have a relatively low place in the valuations of bourgeois societies. Accordingly, there is a lack of systematic studies of such phenomena. But in court societies they are considered very important. One can scarcely hope to understand the structure of such societies and of the individuals forming them, if one is unable to subordinate one's own scale of values to the one that was accepted then. If one does so, one is immediately confronted with the question why the people of this other social formation attach high significance to traditions of ceremony and etiquette, and what significance these phenomena have in the structure of such a society. If such questions are raised, if, in other words, the autonomy of the object of research is clearly and consistently respected in the initial posing of questions, it is not difficult to determine the function of etiquette and ceremony within the structure of this different type of society. They prove to be, among other things, important instruments of rule and the distribution of power. Through studying them we gain access to structural problems of court society and of the individuals forming it that would remain closed to an approach based on heteronomous valuations.

17. The second point concerns basic ideas on the independence and dependence of people. Without its always being clearly expressed, there is a certain tendency to see, in the kind of historical research centrally concerned with uniqueness and individuality, evidence of the ultimate independence and freedom of the individual, while a sociology concerned with societies is seen as testifying to the individual's ultimate dependence and determinacy. But this interpretation of the two disciplines and their relationship eludes scholarly investigation. It is based on assumptions derived from general philosophical, political and religious conceptions external to science. For in using words like 'freedom' and 'determinacy' in this sense, one is not seeking to pose an open question that can be decided one way or the other by systematic research, but is using the words as symbols for preconceived convictions. How large the scope for decision of a king or a slave actually is can be demonstrated, if one takes the trouble, by careful empirical investigation, and the same is true of the network of dependences surrounding an individual person. In talking of the 'freedom' or 'determinacy' of man as such, one is embarking on a level of discussion which operates with

assertions that are not accessible to any confirmation or refutation by systematic scientific work, or by a systematic testing of empirical evidence. Despite this unscientific character, convictions of this kind play no small part in the intellectual foundations of history and in discussions of its relation to sociology. The historian who focuses his attention on closed individuals as the primary framework of reference, frequently does so with the idea that he is breaking a lance for the freedom of the individual; the sociologist's attempt to elucidate social connections is apt to appear to the former as a negation of freedom, as an undertaking that threatens to extinguish human individuality.

Such considerations are understandable as long as one believes that scientific problems can be posed and solved on the basis of metaphysical or political preconceptions. But if one does so, the problems remain in reality insoluble. The decision has been taken before the investigation begins. If one is prepared to approach such problems through two-pronged investigations on the theoretical and empirical planes in closest touch with one another, rather than on the basis of preconceived dogmatic positions, the question one is aiming at with words such as 'freedom' and 'determinacy', poses itself in a different way.

What has been said up to now in this introduction, together with some of the empirical studies that follow, shows how the question poses itself. Not even a man as powerful as Louis XIV was free in any absolute sense of the word. No more was he 'absolutely determined'. If we refer to empirical data, a formulation of the problem in terms of an antithesis between absolute freedom and absolute determinacy — such as the use of these words introduces into discussions of the relationship of history to sociology — becomes untenable. We need far more finely differentiated theoretical models if we are to pose the problem in a way that gives better access to factual connections that can be proved by evidence.

As has already been seen, the problem that then confronts us has at its centre the network of dependence within which scope for individual decision opens to the individual, and which at the same time sets limits to his possible decisions. The conceptualization of this state of affairs is difficult above all because many of our forms of thought and existing concepts are concerned merely to express relationships between inanimate physical phenomena. If the problem of human interdependence is posed in traditional form as the problem of absolute determinism or absolute 'freedom', we are really still moving on a plane of discussion on which modes of thought appropriate to the observation of simple physical processes stand opposed to isomorphous metaphysical ways of thinking. Representatives of one side treat man simply as a physical body of the same kind as a billiard ball and maintain that his behaviour is causally determined in exactly the same way as a billiard ball when it is set in motion by collision with another ball. The spokesmen of the other side basically say only something negative. They say that the behaviour of the individual is *not* determined in the same way as that of a billiard ball; it is *not* causally determined on the pattern of the classical conception of physical causality. This statement at once leads on to the idea that at each moment of his life man is absolutely free and the utterly independent master of his decisions. But this idea is not less fictitious than the opposed one that a person has absolutely no scope for decision, that he is 'determined' like a billiard ball in motion.

In pursuing the problems that arise in sociological and historical research, we are as little helped by concepts derived from physical relationships as by the traditionally opposed metaphysical concepts. We realize the inadequacies of this type of concept for the clarification of sociological and historical problems at once if we attempt to express the fact, for example, that in many cases the 'freedom' of one individual is a factor in the 'determinacy' of another. While non-scientific, metaphysico-philosophical discussion normally takes man as such as its starting point, as if there were only a single human being in the world, a scientific discussion of 'freedom' and 'determinacy' which aims at more than mere assertions can start only from what is actually observable: a multiplicity of people who are more or less dependent on one another and at the same time more or less autonomous in their relationships to one another. As long as a person lives and is healthy, he possesses, even as a prisoner, even as a slave, a degree of autonomy, a scope for action within which he can and must take decisions. But even the autonomy of the mightiest king has fixed limits; even he is enmeshed in a net of dependence the structure of which can be determined with a high degree of precision. In conjunction with empirical observations of this kind we arrive at a model that takes account of the multiplicity of individuals as one of the basic facts affecting considerations on man as such. On this basis it can easily be shown that the enlargement of the scope for action of a certain individual or group of individuals can entail the reduction of the scope of action or the 'freedom' of other individuals. Thus, for example, the increase in the power of the French kings or their representatives in the seventeenth century meant a reduction in the freedom of the French nobility. Assertions of this kind can be proved and tested. Assertions of the absolute freedom or absolute determinacy of man are untestable speculations scarcely deserving serious discussion.

It must be enough here to indicate briefly the methodological approach by which the non-scientific discussion of the 'freedom' or 'determinacy' of *man*, which underlies discussions of the relation of history to sociology, is converted into a scientific discussion of the relative autonomy and the relative dependence of people in their relationships to one another. The structure of interdependence binding individuals to one another is accessible, in the case of each individual person as in that of whole groups of people, to a progressive empirical investigation. Such an investigation can arrive at conclusions that can be represented in the form of an interdependence-model, a figuration-model. It is only with the aid of such models that we can examine and, to an extent, explain the scope for decision of an individual within his chain of dependences, the sphere of his autonomy and the strategy governing his behaviour. This revised way of posing the question also throws into sharper relief the non-scientific, ideological character of the notion that historical research concerned with individual phenomena is the standard-bearer of the freedom of man, while sociology concerned with social phenomena is the standard-bearer of determinism.

One of the tasks to which the following studies attempt to make a contribution is the elaboration of figuration-models through which the scope for action and the dependence of individuals become more accessible to empirical investigation. These studies are concerned in part to explore the interdependence of the individuals forming court society and to show in a number of specific cases, particularly that of Louis XIV, how an individual uses the latitude given to him by his position within a specific figuration, in the strategy of his personal behaviour.

The sociological theory that evolved in the course of these and other studies differs markedly, as can be seen, from the currently prevalent type of sociological theory whose most prominent representative is Talcott Parsons. It must be enough here to allow the two-pronged development of ideas on the theoretical and empirical levels to speak for itself. Even without explicit discussion it shows clearly enough how and why the sociological approach is brought into closer touch with the empirical task of sociology if we advance from a sociological theory of actions and systems which, like that of Talcott Parsons, both implies and leaves unbridged an imaginary gulf between individual and society, to a sociological theory of figurations which transcends the notion of such a gulf.

With regard to historical research another point deserves mention by way of summary. We said earlier that some historians, by starting from the idea that the process they are investigating consists of an accumulation of basically unconnected actions of individual people, tend to see sociologically relevant phenomena as an unstructured background. The sociological study of court society is an example of a re-orientation in the way of posing the problem, of selecting evidence and, indeed, in the whole way of perceiving that becomes necessary if such background phenomena of traditional historical research are brought into the foreground as structured phenomena. To be sure, the Versailles court and the social life of the courtiers are treated often enough in historical studies. But historical depictions do not usually go beyond an accumulation of details. What sociologists are aiming at when they speak of social structures and processes often seems to historians the artificial product of the sociological imagination. Empirical sociological studies like this one provide an opportunity to test this idea. Within historical research today strong tendencies are making themselves felt which seek to bring into view, beside the stratum of the human universe that we see when studying the actions of single short-lived individuals, the more slowly flowing layer of figurations formed by individuals. But there is as yet no theoretical foundation for this enlargement of historical and social vision, partly because historians themselves often believe they can do without explicit theoretical foundations in their work. It is unlikely that, in the long term, the complementing of the historical by the sociological method of work can be stopped. But it is relatively unimportant whether this enlargement of historical perspective takes place through the efforts of specialist sociologists or historians, or through a collaboration of the two.

18. The third point that can be picked out in conclusion is very closely related to the other two. We started by raising the question of which peculiarities of historiography up to now are responsible for the fact that history is constantly being rewritten. The answer pointed to the difference between the high standard and accuracy of historical documentation of details on one hand, and the far lower standard of historical interpretations of the connections between these details on the other. The store of certain knowledge of historical detail is growing, but the growth in certain knowledge of connections between details is not keeping pace. As there is for traditional historians no sure basis for representing historical

connections, this is very largely left to the whim of the scholar. The gaps in the knowledge of the connections between well-documented details are filled over and again by interpretations determined by the short-lived values and ideals of the historians. These values and ideals change with attitudes to the great controversial questions of the time. History is constantly being rewritten because the historian's way of seeing the connection between the details documented merely reflects his attitude to the extra-scientific issues of the day.

The urgency of the task of ensuring that socio-historical research should attain the continuous progress from one generation to the next which characterizes scientific work in other fields, and without which this work loses much of its significance, scarcely needs mentioning. What has been said here may be enough to show that without the curbing of short-lived values and ideals, in short without the replacement of the prevalent heteronomous valuations by autonomous ones in the investigation of historical connections, efforts to achieve greater continuity in research can hardly be successful.

It can therefore be useful to test sociological models of long-term processes from this point of view, for example those of the civilizing process and state formation,[6] or models of specific figurations within such processes, for example, the model of court society. They all spring from a concern to track down the connections inherent in the subject matter itself. They are an attempt to elaborate sociological models of connections in which the autonomy of the subject matter is not obscured by the preconceived values and transient ideals of the researcher. They do not lay claim to being the definitive models, the last word on the processes and figurations studied. No theory or model in any field of research can claim to be absolutely definitive. And in this case we are certainly at a beginning rather than a conclusion. They are models that can be further developed irrespective of fluctuations in the extra-scientific ideals of the researchers, provided that in the machinery of research itself an attempt is made to hold these alien values in check, giving precedence to the elucidation of connections as they really were. To be sure, this restraint on the part of researchers cannot be achieved if the times are too restless, the tensions too great, the conflicts too inflamed. But if the fears of crisis and the reciprocal threats of people over the coming generations are not too great, we see no reason why history, through the opening of a new, sociological dimension, should not in the course of time be assured the continuous development it lacks today.

[6] N. Elias, *The Civilizing Process* (Oxford, 1982), vol. 2, pp. 98–100ff.

·II·

Preliminary notes on the problems
to be studied

1. The princely court of the *ancien régime* sets the sociologist no fewer problems than any other social formation — such as feudal society or the city — which has already been accorded detailed sociological investigation. At such a 'court' hundreds and often thousands of people were bound together in one place by peculiar restraints which they and outsiders applied to each other and to themselves, as servants, advisers and companions of kings who believed they ruled their countries with absolute power and on whose will the fate of all these people, their rank, their financial support, their rise and fall, depended within certain limits. A more or less fixed hierarchy, a precise etiquette bound them together. The necessity of asserting themselves within such a figuration gave them all a special stamp, that of court people. What was the structure of the social field at the centre of which such a figuration could form? What distribution of power, which socially instilled needs, which relationships of dependence brought it about that people in this social field constantly converged over generations in this figuration, as a court, as court society? What demands were transmitted from the structure of court society to those who wished to rise or merely to survive within it? These, roughly sketched, are some of the questions which the social formation of the court and court society in the *ancien régime* pose for the sociologist.

2. It was not simply the free will of the court people that held them together at court and which, after their fathers and mothers, united the sons and daughters in this manner. Nor was it the brilliant inspiration of a single person, for example the king, which gave this form to the human community. From the Renaissance on the courts gained increasing importance in almost every European country, and even if the French court, above all that of Louis XIV, was exemplary of the detailed arrangements of the European courts of the seventeenth and

eighteenth centuries, the 'court' of this period was itself the expression of a very specific social constellation and no more planned or intended by any single person or group than — to name other typical figurations at random — the Church, the city, the factory or bureaucracy. No more than we can understand the structure of our own Western society and the national social unit composing it without studying the process whereby more and more people crystallized out of the social field in the form of 'cities', no more can we understand the preceding epoch without explaining from the social structure characteristic of it what produced the 'court', what, in other words, constantly brought and held together people of this social field in the figuration of the court and court society.

3. Within every social field there are representative and less representative, central and less central organs. The town, for example, and above all the large city, is one of the most representative organs of our own society. In our social field it represents the matrix with by far the most far-reaching influence; even the inhabitants of country districts cannot escape its effects however hard they try. The most influential human types in our society either come from the city or at least have received its stamp. In this sense, therefore, urban people are representative of our society. The 'princely court' as a special organ within the city — as far as it still exists — no doubt still has, in Western Europe, above all in England, some influence in modifying the imprint of the city, but is hardly representative, like the city itself, of the social field of the West today. It is precisely this representative and central significance that the court had for most Western European countries in the seventeenth and eighteenth centuries. In this period it was not the 'city' but the 'court' and court society which were the centre with by far the most widespread influence. The town, as was said in the *ancien régime*, merely 'aped' the court.[1] This is particularly true of the French court.[2] An after-effect of the bourgeois opposition to the court, as was mentioned in the Introduction, frequently obstructs our

---

[1] Cf. '*Tableau du siècle' par un auteur connu* (Saint-Cyr) (Geneva, 1759), p. 132: 'La Ville est, dit-on, le singe de la Cour.'

[2] 'Court' has a meaning which changes with the period to which it is applied. In what follows, it refers to the princely court, in keeping with the usage of the time. However, if we were not concerned primarily with France, but also with Germany, a characteristic reservation would need to be made. For in Germany, above all in the western part, the households of more lowly members of the aristocracy, e.g. counts, had a court character in some respects; and as in Germany not all power was concentrated in *one* princely court, these petty court formations down to the households of the landed gentry had a very different social and cultural importance than did similar formations in France.

view of the representativeness of the courts and court society in the
preceding centuries, and prevents a study of its structure that is free
of irritation and resentment, an observation of its functioning
which is as free of emotional reactions as 'village', 'factory', 'horde',
'guild' or any other figuration formed by people.

Characteristic of this rather emotional approach to the court is the
view of Franz Oppenheimer, which will be quoted here because it
contains in very definite form a widespread and typical judgement on
the court of the *ancien régime*:

> The pre-capitalist, very opulent and very extravagant courts, above all
> those of the English Stuarts and the French Bourbons, but to a lesser
> extent the German and Slavonic dynasties too, were over-abundantly
> endowed, thanks to their extensive domanial possessions and the
> tributes from their 'crown peasants' flowing from them, with all the
> means of crude enjoyment. But they desired the means of satisfying
> refined tastes and perverse luxury, and were therefore interested firstly
> in fostering a flourishing trade within the country, and secondly in ob-
> taining the cash needed to maintain the court in its refined splendour,
> to feed the noble parasites who had no other source of income than
> their pensions, and not least to conduct the endless wars in which the
> need for glory, dynastic family interests and confessional superstitions
> entangled with empires. [3]

This is the essence of what Oppenheimer sees of the 'court' as a
social formation in his work that aspires to embrace the whole wealth
of social forms. In this judgement, as far as it refers to France, there
is nothing in the facts presented, apart from seeing the tributes from
crown peasants as the primary basis of the Bourbon royal court, [4]
that is actually wrong. But the perspective from which the judgement
and evaluation of these facts are made completely obscures the context which produced them and in which alone they can be
understood.

Max Weber saw somewhat further when he said: '"Luxury" in the
sense of a rejection of the purposive-rational orientation of con-

---

[3] *System der Soziologie* (Jena, 1924), vol. 3, 2, 1, p. 922.
[4] At the time of the first Bourbons income from domanial possessions, as compared to that
from other sources, above all taxes for the maintenance of the royal household, played only a
very insignificant part. Substantial parts of the old domanial possessions had been disposed of
by the kings in the wars and emergencies of the sixteenth and even the fifteenth centuries. Sully
and after him Richelieu often complained about this. Both tried in vain to buy back the royal
domain. Cf. Marion, *Dictionnaire des institutions au XVIIième et XVIIIième siècles* (Paris,
1923), art. 'Domaine'.

sumption is, to the feudal ruling class, not something "superfluous", but one of the means of its social self-assertion.'[5]

But in this brief remark Max Weber has merely indicated one of the problems of the court. To test the correctness of this view and to bring the problem posed in it some steps towards a conclusion is one of the objectives of this study.

4. We tend to assign importance to the functional aspects of earlier epochs which play a particular part in the present. In this way we often ask first of all about the economic views and arrangements of the court epoch; from this perspective it is called the epoch of mercantilism. We ask about its state structure, and from this perspective we call it the epoch of absolutism. We ask about its system of rule and its bureaucracy and from this standpoint we call it an epoch of patrimonialism. These are all categories which are of particular importance in our own society. But would a section cut through our society really touch on the decisive structural lines of the past epoch? Is it not rather the case that there are rising and falling planes of integration, so that a plane which is not especially relevant to us was once perhaps central, and, conversely, a stratum central today was once peripheral?

Max Weber makes his section through the *ancien régime* primarily at the level of the bureaucracy, so that for him the phenomenon of the bureaucracy, and the mode of rule expressed in the different types of bureaucracy, always overshadow the phenomenon of the court. In this way he contributes many illuminating facts and details on the structure of court rule and court society; but the 'court' itself is not among the types of social formations that he expressly discusses.[6]

5. Where the court is directly viewed as a social phenomenon, it is one aspect above all that interests researchers of our society: its luxury. This is a phenomenon which is important and characteristic, but which highlights only a particularly conspicuous difference between the behaviour of court people and that normal today, and tends to distract from the social structure of the court as a whole, which alone can make the isolated phenomenon of luxury comprehensible.

---

[5] Max Weber, *Wirtschaft und Gesellschaft* (Tübingen, 1922), p. 750. His way of posing the problem — and it is no more than this — went beyond that of Thorstein Veblen, who has the merit in his *Theory of the Leisure Class* (1899) of having dealt — no doubt for the first time — with problems of status-orientated consumption as sociological problems.

[6] The index of *Economy and Society* contains only a reference to 'court justice' relating to a quite different period.

In other words, while it is sometimes possible today to investigate the structure of a simple tribe, for example, as an autonomous figuration of people, and largely to exclude one's own value-judgements in doing so, such detachment is much more difficult in the case of formations closer to us and classified as 'historical', the more so because the prevalent form of historical research leaves the prestige of heteronomous valuations unquestioned.

This observation should not be misunderstood. It is not meant as a 'reproach' but seeks only to lay bare the immanent structure of the process of research, which reveals the autonomy of its subject matter only very slowly and against inevitable resistances.

Moreover, the heteronomous view is not necessarily unfruitful. Sombart, for example, for whom the phenomenon of the court is relevant in connection with the rise of modern capitalism precisely through its quality as a 'centre of luxury', formulates the general problem of the court very trenchantly. The section he devotes to the courts, headed: 'The princely courts as centres of the spread of luxury', begins with the following ideas:

> An important consequence and, in its turn, a decisive cause of the transformations undergone by the state constitution and army at the end of the Middle Ages, is the emergence of large princely courts in the sense in which we use the word today. The predecessors and models of these later developments are here, as in so many areas, the high dignitaries of the Church. Perhaps Avignon was the first modern 'court' because it was here that two groups of people first came together continuously and set the tone who were in the succeeding centuries to form what was called court society: noblemen without any other calling than to serve the court, and beautiful women 'souvent distinguées par les manières et l'esprit' who really set their stamp on life at the court.
>
> . . . With the courts of the Popes the other princes of Italy competed. But of decisive importance for the history of the court was the emergence of a modern court in the much larger and more powerful France, which from the end of the sixteenth century and throughout the next two centuries became the undisputed teacher in all matters concerning court life. [7]

This short survey, very useful for the purposes of this study, gives at least an indication of what the social formation of the court signified and of the problems it poses: at a certain stage in the

[7] W. Sombart, *Der moderne Kapitalismus*, 5th edn (Munich and Leipzig, 1922), vol. 1, 2, pp. 720 – 21.

development of European societies individuals are bound together in
the form of courts and thereby given a specific stamp. What held
them together and what stamped them in just this way?

This human stamp was one of the most important ancestors of the
one prevalent today. As a central figuration of that stage of development, which after a long struggle gave way abruptly or gradually to a
professional-bourgeois-urban-industrial stage, this aristocratic court
society developed a civilizing and cultural physiognomy which was
taken over by professional-bourgeois society partly as a heritage and
partly as an antithesis and, preserved in this way, was further
developed. By studying the structure of court society and seeking to
understand one of the last great non-bourgeois figurations of the
West, therefore, we indirectly gain increased understanding of our
own professional-bourgeois, urban-industrial society.

·III·

The structure of dwellings as
an indicator of social structure

1. What we refer to as the 'court' of the *ancien régime* is, to begin with, nothing other than the vastly extended house and household of the French kings and their dependents, with all the people belonging to them. The expenses for the court, for this whole enormous household of the king, are to be found in the list of expenditure of the French kingdom as a whole under the characteristic heading *Maisons Royales*.[1] It is important to realize this at the outset in order to see the line of development leading to this elaboration of the royal household. The court of the *ancien régime* is a highly differentiated descendant of the patriarchal form of rule whose 'embryo is to be sought in the authority of the master of the house within a domestic community'.[2]

The kings' authority as masters of the house within their court has its correlative in the patrimonial character of the court state, i.e. the state whose central organ is the king's household in the extended sense, that is, the 'court'.

Where the prince organizes his political power . . . on the same principles as his domestic authority [writes Max Weber[3]], we speak of a patrimonial state formation. The majority of the great Continental empires up to the threshold of the modern age and even, to an extent, in the modern age, have had a pronounced patrimonial character.

The patrimonial administration was originally fitted to the needs of a purely personal, largely private household. The attainment of

---

[1] B. Forbonnais, *Recherches et considérations sur les finances de France*, 6 vols (Liège, 1758), where a number of these lists are printed.
[2] M. Weber, *Wirtschaft und Gesellschaft* (Tübingen, 1922), p. 679.
[3] *Ibid.*, p. 684.

'political' rule, i.e. the rule of *one* master of the house over others[4] who are not subject to his domestic authority means, sociologically speaking, the assimilation to domestic authority of power relationships differing from it in degree and content but not in structure.

This aspect, too, must be understood when the court is called, as it was earlier, the 'representative organ' of the social field of the *ancien régime*. The king's rule over the country was nothing other than an extension of and addition to the prince's rule over his household. What Louis XIV, who marked both the culmination and the turning point of this development, attempted, was to organize his country as his personal property, as an enlargement of the household. This can only be understood if we realize that the court represented for him — perhaps more than for kings who had fought their enemies personally at the head of an army — his primary and most direct sphere of activity, the country being only a secondary and indirect one.

Everything that came from the king's wider possessions, from the realm, had to pass through the filter of the court before it could reach him; through the same filter everything from the king had to pass before it reached the country. Even the most absolute monarch could exert an influence on his country only through the mediation of the people living at the court. Thus the court and court life were the place of origin of the whole experience, the whole understanding of men and the world, of the absolute monarchs of the *ancien régime*. Thus the sociology of the court is at the same time a sociology of the monarchy.

Of course, this primary sphere of action of the kings, the court, did not remain untouched by the gradual enlargement and the increasing greatness of the royal domain. The necessity that existed for the king at the end of this development to rule the whole country from his house and through his household understandably transformed this

---

[4] Quite in keeping with this formulation of Max Weber's, if perhaps with some overgeneralization, M. von Boehn, *Frankreich im 18.Jahrhundert*, (Berlin, n.d.), p. 46, writes: 'Every Frenchman saw in his King the head of his own family. . . . Among the nobility and the high bureaucracy no marriage could be concluded without the prior agreement of the King. To neglect this step would have been to make oneself guilty of rebellion. The King could even arrange marriages without or against the will of the parents. His will was enough in some cases to make any resistance impossible.' 'Everyone', writes Rétif de la Bretonne shortly before the Revolution, 'considers the King as a very personal acquaintance.' Cf. also La Bruyère, *Les Caractères*, 'Du souverain ou de la république': 'To call a king "father of the people" is less to praise him than to call him by his name or to define him.' That king rules well . . . 'who makes a court, and even a whole realm, like a single family perfectly united under the same head.'

household, the *Maison du Roi*.[5] The conspicuous product of this interaction between the size of the country and the size of the royal
household is the *château*, the court of Versailles, within which the
most personal actions of the kings always had the ceremonial
character of state actions, just as outside it each state action took on
the character of a personal action of the king.

2. Not all the social units or integrating forms of men are at the
same time units of accommodation. But they can all be characterized
by certain types of spatial arrangement. For they are always units of
interrelated *people*; and even if the nature of these relations cannot
be expressed solely by spatial categories, they are, at any rate, *also*
expressible through spatial categories. For every kind of 'being
together' of people has a corresponding arrangement of space, *where*
the people belonging together actually are or can be together, if not
as a whole then at least in small units. And so the precipitate of a
social unit in terms of space and indeed, more narrowly, in terms of
rooms, is a tangible and — in the literal sense — visible representation of its special nature. In this sense the kind of accommodation
of court people gives sure and very graphic access to an understanding of certain social relationships characteristic of court society.

The accommodation of court people is characterized first of all by
the fact that all or at least a significant part of them had lodgings in
the king's house, in the Château of Versailles, and a residence, i.e. an
hôtel, in the city of Paris. The country houses that most of them also
owned can in this connection be disregarded.

The Château of Versailles, the outer receptacle of the French court
as the dwelling place both of the court nobility and of the king, cannot be understood in isolation. It forms the tip of a society articu-
lated hierarchically in all its manifestations. One must see how the
court nobility live at home to understand how the king lives and how
the nobility live with him. The town residences of the nobility, the
hôtels, show in a fairly clear and simple form the sociologically
relevant needs of this society with respect to accommodation which,
multiplied, telescoped together and complicated by the special

---

[5] To give a preliminary survey of this development which will be discussed later in more detail,
an article by Marmontel (*Encyclopédie*, art. 'Grands') summarizes it as follows: 'In former
times France formed a very ill-combined federal government incessantly at war with itself.
After Louis XIV, all these co-states had been united into one. But the great vassals still conserved in their domain the authority that they had had under the first sovereigns, and the
governors who had taken the place of these sovereigns assumed their power. These two parties
opposed the authority of the monarch with obstacles that had to be overcome: the gentlest and
therefore the wisest means was to attract to the court those who, far off . . . and surrounded by
people accustomed to obeying them, had become so redoubtable.'

governmental and representative functions of the kings, also determine the structure of the royal palace which is to house the society as a whole.

3. The building in which the court nobility of the *ancien régime* lived was called, according to the rank of its owner and therefore its size, an *hôtel* or a *palais*. The *Encyclopédie*[6] reproduces the ground plan of such an *hôtel*.[7] The explanations of it given there and the accompanying article complete the picture we gain of the functions of its individual parts and rooms. What of all this is sociologically relevant?

We see before us a building the parts of which are grouped around a large rectangular court. Towards the street one of the short sides of the court is formed by a colonnade closed to the outside, at the centre of which the broad *porche* forms both the entrance and a passage for carriages. To the right and left along both wings of the building the colonnade is continued to the central building on the other short side, so that one can always reach this from the entrance without getting wet. This central building, behind and beside which the large garden stretches, contains the reception rooms; in the adjoining part of both wings the *appartements privés* are located. Behind them, separated from the main garden on one side by a large gallery and on the other by bathing and toilet rooms, there are two smaller flower gardens. In the parts of the wings closer to the street, finally, are the stables, kitchens, servants' quarters and storerooms. They are grouped on both sides around a small courtyard called a *basse-cour*, which is separated by parts of the building from the small flower gardens below the windows of the *appartements privés*. In the vicinity of these small courtyards where a part of the kitchen work is done, where visitors' coaches are parked between stalls after their owners have alighted at the staircase of the central building in the great court, the life of the *domestiques* is lived.

It is, as we can see, a curious form of town dwelling that the court people created in their *hôtels*. They are town houses, but we still sense in their structure a connection with the country manor house. But while the estate residence is still present, of all its functions it has retained only its approach and its prestigious appearance. The

---

[6] Diderot and D'Alembert, *Encyclopédie ou Dictionnaire raisonné des sciences etc.* is quoted throughout in the Geneva edition of 1777ff.

[7] *Enc.*, 'Recueil de Planches', vol. 2, section 'Architecture', plate 23. The plan reproduced there is the work of Blondel, a royal architect. To be sure, not all the *hôtels* of the eighteenth century followed this plan in detail, yet a plan of this kind, regarded as exemplary, is useful to us; it shows how an experienced architect conceived the optimal solution of these accommodation needs.

stables, storerooms and servants' quarters are still there, but they have merged with the manor house, and of the surrounding nature only the gardens are left.

This relationship of the *hôtel* to the country manor has symptomatic importance.[8] Certainly, the court people are town-dwellers, and to an extent town life sets its stamp on them. But their bond to the town is less strong than that of the professional citizens. Most of them still possess one or more country seats. From them they normally have not only their name but a large part of their income, and they retreat there from time to time.

Their society is always the same, but the locality changes. Now they live in Paris, now they move with the king to Versailles, to Marly or one of his other *châteaux*, now they make their home at one of their own country houses or live as guests at the estate of one of their friends. This peculiar situation — a firm link to their society which represents their real homeland, together with a relatively changeable locale — not least determined their character and that of their houses. Everything about the latter — and this will shortly be discussed again — points to their close links with this society; hardly anything about them, perhaps only the compression of different complexes into a single whole, points to a functional link with the town. Hardly anything would need to be altered if this house were erected in the country. Its owners are involved in the structure of the city solely as consumers, if we disregard their involvement in Parisian court society. This consumption, given enough servants, could normally be almost as well satisfied in the country. At most, the still greater luxury points to the city.

4. The interchangeability of locale was, of course, directly connected to the fact that these lords and ladies commanded a large body of servants. These servants, from the intendant and the *maîtres d'hôtel*, who were responsible for the management of income, the order and comfort of the household, the supervision of the other personnel, down to the coachmen and lackeys who looked after transport, were the precondition of this specific and limited mobility. It gave the court people the freedom demanded by the by no means always easy tasks with which life at the itinerant court and among court society presented them.

The court people themselves do not talk much about these serving hands that bear them. The *domestiques* live, as it were, behind the scenes of the great theatre of court life; and so in what follows we

---

[8] Cf. Jombert, *Architecture moderne* (Paris, 1728), pp. 43ff.

shall not have much to say about them. But here, in considering the house in which the court aristocracy live, we must start by looking behind the scenes.

What we see when observing the life and bustle around the two *basses-cours*[9] is an abundance of personnel and a differentiation of services which are very characteristic of both the refined taste and the high domestic standards of this society. There is the house intendent[10] who deals with all business matters for the lord and lady. There is the *maître d'hôtel* who supervises the personnel and, for example, announces when the table is laid. There is, to mention a particularly characteristic example, not only a large kitchen, a smaller *garde-manger* in which the perishable dessert meats, particularly fowl, are locked,[11] but also an *office* with special ovens and appliances, supervised by a *chef d'office* to be distinguished from the *chef de cuisine*, where, among other things, the stewed fruit, jams and fine pastries are prepared; another oven beside it, which gives a specially gentle heat, serves for the production of biscuits, *gâteaux* and other dry pastries; adjoining this is a *laboratoire d'office* where ice is prepared and, as the *Encyclopédie* says, 'other works which would give off humidity in the preceding rooms'.[12] Next to it there is a room with particularly good locks, the *office paré*, where, under the supervision of the *officier d'office* who also has to oversee the laying of the table, the silver is kept. Sometimes the master of the house has lunch here with his friends.

---

[9] '*Basse-cour* . . . this, in a town building, is a courtyard separated from the main court, around which are the buildings to be used as coach-houses, stables or in which are located the kitchens, offices, servants' quarters, etc. The *basses-cours* must have entrances to the outside, so that their service can be carried on conveniently and *without being perceived from the masters' apartments or from the main court*' (author's italics), *Enc.*, art. 'Basse-cour'. Whereas in classes and societies where the lady of the house has the function of housewife, or where the masters wish to maintain direct control of the domestic personnel, the servants' quarters are situated in such a way that more or less constant supervision is not difficult, here the separation of the servants' rooms, above all the kitchens, from the masters' quarters, is a characteristic expression of the fact that the masters wished to have as little contact as possible with these affairs relegated behind the scenes. The court lady is not a housewife. This complete isolation of the kitchens from her sphere of supervision shows it. An opposite example will make the situation even more visible. A sixteenth-century writer (Olivier de Serres, *Théâtre d'agriculture*, ch. 5: 'Dessin du bastiment champestre', vol. 1, p. 21) describes the arrangement of a noble's house in the country as follows: 'Your kitchen will be placed on the first floor of the house on a level with and close to your dining-room, from which you will enter your bedroom; in this way, through the door of the dining-room and the bedroom where you often are, those who are in the kitchen, *will be under observation and the idleness, shouting, blasphemies, larcenies of servants and serving maids will be suppressed*.'
[10] Cf. Appendix 2, pp. 284ff.
[11] Cf. *Enc.*, art. 'Garde-manger'.
[12] *Enc.*, art. 'Office'.

For other reasons, too, it is worth illustrating by an example the specialization in what was succinctly called the *bouche*, i.e. everything to do with eating and drinking. For what took up only one or two rooms in the household of a *grand seigneur* was allocated a whole apartment in the *Maison du Roi*, and to head such a department of the king's *bouche*, e.g. the *fruterie* where fruits of all kinds were prepared for the table, the *sommellerie* or the *paneterie* where wine and bread were kept, guarded and distributed, was a sought-after and highly paid court office. In this way almost everything to be found on a large scale in the king's residence is present on a smaller scale in that of the *grand seigneur*. Not even the Swiss Guards are missing. A small room near the entrance on one side and the stables and coach-houses on the other provides the *logement des Suisses*.[13] But, of course it was not always genuine Swiss whom the individual nobleman appointed to guard his house. Often enough they were satisfied to put Swiss uniforms on their lackeys.[14]

5. While the rooms for such domestic activities as have just been described, and for the servants concerned with them, are carefully segregated from the living and reception rooms, nevertheless the way the whole structure of court society rests on a broad stratum of servants is directly expressed in the layout of the masters' rooms themselves. From the entrance each of the various living or reception apartments is approached through one or more antechambers. They are to be found before the bedrooms of the lord and lady of the house, before the state bedroom as before the *salle de compagnie*. This room, the antechamber, is the symbol of good court society in the *ancien régime*. Here, in constant readiness, the liveried or non-liveried lackeys and servants await the commands of their masters. Hardly anything better characterizes the latter's attitude to their servants than a remark which makes up almost half a short article which the *Encyclopédie* devotes to the antechamber: 'As the first antechamber is intended only for the *livrée*', we read, 'fireplaces are seldom used here. One is content to place stoves before them to protect all parts of an apartment from the cold air which the constant opening of the doors between the entrance and the masters' rooms lets in.'

[13] If one looks for them, occasional incidental references to servants can, of course, be found in literature. The Swiss Guard who, as commanded, has either to admit guests or turn them away, is mentioned several times, for example, in Lauzun, 'Pariser Gespräche', in Blei, *Geist des Rokoko* (Munich, 1923), pp. 51, 55.
[14] Cf. A. Schulz, *Das häusliche Leben der europäischen Völker* (Munich and Berlin, 1903), p. 60.

We should not forget, in reading such passages, that to the aristocratic nucleus which made up the *monde* of the eighteenth century, the idea that all people regardless of social rank were 'equal' in any definite sense was entirely alien. The *Encyclopédie*, which was already much closer to such ideas, does stress in its article on the *domestique* that there were no longer any slaves in France, and that servants, too, should not be regarded as slaves but as 'free people'.

But even it justifies, for example, the established law whereby theft from a house was punished by death.[15] In other words, it justifies rationally what from the standpoint of the *grands seigneurs* was a consequence of their belief in the self-evident inequality of the social classes and so in no need of rational explanation. This belief did not need to express itself in bad treatment of the servants. It could also find expression in a kind of intimacy towards some of them. But what was always present in it was the ineradicable distance, the deepseated feeling that they were concerned with a different race, with the 'common people' — a phrase used by the *Encyclopédie* itself — in this army of men and women who filled their households and whose constant presence gave the situation of court people a quite different form and atmosphere to our own. And this arrangement of rooms which provides for at least one antechamber to each of the masters' rooms, is thus an expression of the *co-existence of constant spatial proximity and constant social distance, of intimate contact in one stratum and the strictest aloofness in the other*.[16]

This peculiar kind of relationship, though modified in a specific way that will be described in more detail later, is to be found on another level of the social hierarchy in the king's house. Here, the

---

[15] 'Domestic theft is punished more severely than other theft because it contains a horrible abuse of confidence and because the masters are obliged to leave many things in their hands.' Voltaire, in a book that appeared later, *Prix de la justice et de l'humanité* (1777), castigated the barbarity whereby people could be killed for a trivial offence solely because it involved domestic theft. Where such contempt of the *domestique* can lead even in Voltaire's own intimate circle is shown very clearly by an incident described by his secretary Longchamp, a former servant of his mistress, the Marquise de Châtelet, in his memoirs: the Marquise showed herself naked before him in her bathroom in a way that caused him the utmost embarrassment, while she scolded him with total unconcern for not pouring the hot water properly. Brandes, who quotes this passage in his book on Voltaire (German translation, Berlin, n.d., vol. 1, pp. 340–41), comments in this as follows: 'She is not embarrassed to show herself without clothes before a lackey; she did not consider him as a man in relation to herself as a woman.' A very specific aspect of the behaviour of court people can be explained in connection with this. Permanent command of a stratum of people whose thoughts were totally indifferent to the ruling class allowed the people of this class to show themselves naked before other people, for example when dressing or undressing, but also in the bath and even when performing other intimate functions, with far less concern than is the case in a society without this broad substratum of servants. The nobility show themselves in this way before their servants and the king before the nobility.

grands seigneurs and *grandes dames* who, as masters on a lower level, confine their inferiors to the antechamber, now stand in their turn as servants in the antechamber and await the summons of their master, the king.

6. There is in each of the two wings of the *hôtel* adjoining the parts overlooking the *basses-cours*, an *appartement privé*, one for the lord and one for the lady of the house. One is on the left and the other on the right of the main court. Both apartments are built almost identically; the two bedrooms are exactly opposite each other. But they are separated by the whole width of the court. And the occupants cannot see each other from the windows; for the window frontage of both — to avoid the noise of the coaches frequently arriving and departing, the *Encyclopédie* supposes[17] — open on to the flower gardens at the rear. Both the lord and the lady have, connecting to their bedrooms, their own cabinets in which, while or after dressing, they can receive visitors, with their own antechamber adjoining this and of course their own wardrobe.

The position of man and wife in this society could scarcely be more succinctly or clearly characterized than by this equal but wholly separate disposition of their private apartments. We meet here with a form of marriage and family that perhaps deserves greater attention in sociological theories of the family.

'How does she get on with her husband?' the new servant asks the lady's chambermaid.[18]

'Oh, very well at the moment,' is the answer. 'He is a bit pedantic, but ambitious. She has a lot of friends. They don't go to the same social gatherings; they see each other very little and live very decently together.'

This is, of course, an individual case; not every man in this society is ambitious and pedantic, not every lady has many friends. Yet something very typical of the structure of this society is visible here. The society is so spacious that man and wife can have different circles of acquaintances. The scope for married people to lead their own

[16] If there was a second antechamber before the masters' rooms, it was for people 'above the common' (*Enc.*, art. 'Domestique'), i.e. above the servants. But by this we should not understand guests of similar rank to the masters of the house. These latter are led, when visiting the lord's private rooms, either into the bedroom itself or a cabinet between the antechamber and the bedroom, or, when visiting the reception rooms, into the *salon* following the antechamber. The kind of people who gathered in the antechamber to the bedroom of a rich lord, and when there were two, some in the first and some in the second, according to rank, is shown by an account from the life of Mme d'Epinay (Thirion, *La vie privée des financiers*, 1895, p. 306).

[17] *Enc.*, art. 'Appartement'.

[18] Duc de Lauzun, 'Pariser Gespräche', in Blei, *op. cit.*

lives is in this respect, and certainly not only in this one, entirely different from that in a more spatially confined society.

On the other hand, certain contacts between the spouses are demanded by decorum, convention and the need to keep up public appearances. The minimum of contact required by society places limits, in certain areas, on the independent lives of both partners. The general nature of the demands which the *grand seigneur* has to make on his wife becomes apparent, for example, when the lord referred to by the chambermaid in the dialogue just quoted comes to his wife's apartment in the late morning while she is still asleep and gives the following message to the maid: 'Tell her that we have a week's mourning for Mme de Saucourt and ask her to visit my mother who is ill. I am going to Versailles. I will be back tomorrow or the day after.'

The duty towards society — and the visit to the sick mother-in-law is a part of this — and more broadly the maintenance of the reputation and honour of the 'house', this was left in common when other individual affinities were lost and when the lack of affection between the partners caused them to make use of their freedom. [19]

The publicly sanctioned relationship between man and woman finds its expression in professional-bourgeois society in the formation and the concept of the 'family'. In the seigniorial society of the *ancien régime* it is expressed in the concept of the 'house'. Not only do people speak of the 'House of France' to denote the unity of the royal line over generations, but each of the *grand seigneurs* speaks of his own 'house'. In the usage of the *ancien régime*, the term 'family' is more or less restricted to the upper bourgeoisie, that of the 'house' to the king and high aristocracy. The *Encyclopédie* notes this difference in the linguistic usage of different classes with, as may be understood, strong censure. [20] What is involved, as we have seen, is not merely a *façon de parler* but a reality, an actual difference in the form taken by the socially sanctioned sexual relationship in the high nobility and in the upper bourgoisie. [21] This cannot be explored in detail here. It must be enough to point out that in reality 'family life' in the sense used in bourgeois society is no part of the objectives of a marriage for the court aristocracy. Rather, the primary object of

---

[19] Cf. *Enc.*, art. 'Mariage (droit naturel)', which expressly states in one place that through marriage the wife attains 'à la liberté'.

[20] Cf. *Enc.*, art. 'Famille, maison'.

[21] It must be admitted that to an extent the former coloured the latter, so that the definitions of the terms *maison* and *famille* throughout the *ancien régime* do not coincide necessarily with those of the real types of the seignorial marriage in the style of the 'house', and spatially confined, closely knit bourgeois family life.

marriages in this circle is to secure a continuation of the 'house' which is in keeping with the rank of the husband and which increases the prestige and connections of the present representatives of the house to the utmost. It is in this context that the relationship between the lord and lady of the house must be understood. What society watches over, above all, is the relationship of these two people as outward representatives of a house; for the rest, they may love each other or not, be faithful to each other or not, their relations can be as devoid of personal contact as is allowed by their duty as joint representatives. On personal matters social control is lax and weak. The layout of the lord's and lady's private apartments represents in its way the optimum arrangement, given the accommodational needs arising from this court type of marriage — to which the bourgeois term 'family' can hardly be applied.

7. In forming a mental picture of the domestic space occupied by the great lords and ladies of the *ancien régime*, we see in it a structural aspect of the *network of relationships* of which they are a part. The special nature of their relationship to their servants is expressed in the separateness of the rooms surrounding the *basse-cour*, and of the antechamber. The particular relationship between husband and wife is expressed in the characteristic distance between their *appartements privés*. And finally, the nature of their involvement in the network of society is represented in the layout of the reception rooms. That these take up the main and central part of the ground floor, which is given over to social purposes — a larger area than both the *appartements privés* together — is in itself a symbol of the importance which their relation to their society has in the lives of these people. The centre of gravity of their existence lies here.

The reception rooms are divided in two. At their centre, rising to include the second floor and usually decorated with Corinthian columns, the main *salon* is generally to be found, the centre of social life for the court aristocracy. The visitor alights from his coach at the outside staircase in front of the main building, passes through a large rectangular hall and from there reaches the large, circular *salon*. On one side of this, reached from the hall by their own entrance, are the rooms of the *appartement de société*, principally the antechamber and the cloakroom; then comes a *salle de compagnie*, a small, more intimate oval *salon*, a dining room next to which is the buffet, and so on. On the other side of the main *salon* is the *appartement de parade*, including smaller ceremonial *salons* and cabinets, and then, connecting to one *salon*, a large gallery extending far beyond the adjoining wing and separating the main garden from the smaller flower garden. In addition, this ceremonial apartment includes bedrooms of state with all their appurtenances.

This division of the reception rooms into two has a quite specific social function. The *appartement de société* is intended for the more intimate circle of the lord and, above all, the lady. Here, especially in the afternoon, they receive the people who come to keep them company. These rooms, adapted for comfort rather than display, are the scene of the more intimate social life, not unduly bound by etiquette, that we know as *salon* society from the history of the eighteenth century.

The ceremonial apartment, on the other hand, is the symbol of the peculiarly public posture which the great figures of the *ancien régime* adopted even when they were not performing official functions. Here, usually in the late morning, they receive the official visits of people of equal and higher rank; here they perform all the 'business' of court life which brings them into contact with court people outside their intimate circle; here they receive visits as representatives of their 'houses'. The state bedroom with its own antechamber and cabinet serves for receiving high guests who are to be especially honoured; here the lady, representing the 'house', receives official visits on special occasions, for example after a confinement, from the *lit de parade*. And the intrusion of many aspects of what we consider private life into the public, social sphere that is visible here as at many other points, is very characteristic of the structure of the lives of these people. Without it, the differentiation of the reception rooms into an *appartement de société*, and an *appartement de parade* could not be fully understood. High rank, and the attendant obligation to keep up appearances, give social life, for example a visit, a seriousness and weight, in the lives of these people without professions, that in professional-bourgeois society attaches only to business or professional visits, hardly to 'private' ones. The professional visits of bourgeois classes — including, of course, 'private visits' directly serving professional purposes — derive their character from their connection with money-earning, career, the maintenance or enhancement of one's professional-social position. The differentiation of the court reception rooms into one apartment for relatively intimate social intercourse and another for official social life is in some degree analogous to the division between private living rooms and professional offices within bourgeois society. This differentiation makes quite tangible a state of affairs that will be discussed frequently and in greater detail later; if the structure of the social life of the court people of the *ancien régime* is judged by the structure and divisions of professional-bourgeois life, then the whole of court life falls within the 'private' sphere. But this kind of definition gives a distorted picture. As court aristocrats had no professional life in our sense, the distinction between professional and private life is inapplicable. But the need to maintain and improve their social position imposes on these people obligations no less strict and compulsions no less powerful than the ones acting on modern people as a result of analogous tendencies in professional life.

This gives social life at court and within court society a characteristic double face. On one hand it has the function of our own private life, to provide relaxation, amusement, conversation. At the same time it has the function of our professional life, to be the direct instrument of one's career, the medium of one's rise or fall, the fulfilment of social demands and pressures which are experienced as duties. Depending on the occasion, one face may be more strongly accentuated than the other; the former is more easily blocked out than the latter. This double face finds expression in the differentiation of the reception rooms. In gatherings in the *appartement de société* amusement and conversation will be more prominent, but the more official side is not absent. But at those functions for which the ceremonial rooms are opened, the public character of the lord, the maintenance of the interests and prestige of his house, are in the foreground.

8. At the end of the *ancien régime* the Duc de Croy said once: 'Ce sont les maisons qui ont écrasé la plupart des grandes familles.' (It was their houses that crushed the majority of the great families.)[22]

That people should ruin themselves for the sake of their houses is incomprehensible unless we understand that in this seignioral society the size and splendour of a house are not primarily the expression of wealth but of rank and status. The physical appearance of the house in space symbolizes, for the *grand seigneur* and the whole of this society, the rank and importance of his 'house' in time, that is, the significance of his family over generations and therefore himself as its living representative.

High rank entails the duty to own and display an appropriate house. What appears as extravagance from the standpoint of the bourgeois economic ethic — 'if he was running into debt why did he not reduce his expenses?' — is in reality the expression of the seigniorial ethos of rank. This ethos grows out of the structure and activity of court society, and is at the same time a precondition for the continuance of this activity. It is not freely chosen.

[22] Cf. D'Avenel, *Histoire de la fortune française* (Paris, 1927), p. 302.

This can already be seen from the terms used to denote the different types of houses. A merchant's house was not called an *hôtel*. *Hôtel* is the term for houses of the higher court aristocracy. It is probable that in the course of the eighteenth century this term was somewhat extended to include, for example, the houses of rich tax farmers. All the same, the *Encyclopédie* still states quite clearly: 'Dwellings take different names according to the different estates of those occupying them. We speak of *la maison* of a bourgeois, *l'hôtel* of a noble, *le palais* of a prince or a king.'[23]

Palais, for example, was reserved expressly for the residence of the king and the princes. The term was also used for the seats of the higher courts, because they formed, in a sense, branches of the royal residences, and finally it had become usual to call the residences of high ecclesiastics *palais*.

'Apart from these,' says the *Encyclopédie*, 'no person, no matter what his rank may be, may affix the name "Palais" to the gateway of his house.'[24]

9. But corresponding to this differentiation of terms according to estates there was, of course, a difference in the houses themselves. A consideration of this difference gives us a view of the more general structure of this society. The great mass of town dwellings was made up of so-called *maisons particulières*.[25] This term is revealing: the translation 'private houses' does not adequately render the social character of these houses. Today the concept 'private' is not solely, but primarily, an antithesis of the concept 'professional'. The residence of even a high official would be called a 'private house' if it belonged to him personally and if its rooms were not used for his profession, i.e. as offices. In the *ancien régime*, by contrast, it was precisely the great mass of professional people whose houses were called *maisons particulières*, even when, indeed, especially when, they were used for professional purposes. They were called by this name to distinguish them from the residences of those strata that were distinguished not by a profession in our sense but primarily by their high status, that is, the nobles, the clerics, the magistrature or *robe* and finally the financiers, i.e. the tax farmers.

This sense of the difference between the professional classes and the estates finds clear expression, moreover, in the linguistic usage of the time: to become a cleric or an officer, to enter the *robe* or

---

[23] Cf. *Enc.*, art. 'Hôtel'.
[24] Cf. *Enc.*, art. 'Palais'.
[25] This description, together with the following material, is based on the *Enc.*, 'Recueil de Planches', vol. 2, 'Architecture'.

finance,[26] according to a writer of the 1750s,[27] is 'to take an *estate*'. 'The other functions of citizens, that is to say the most useful ones, are content with the humiliating name of profession or trade.'

This remark shows quite clearly how, below the layer of estates and at first despised by these but then gradually rising, professional strata are gaining substance. The people of the society of estates, and especially those of the leading court circle, above all the princes and 'great ones', lead a more or less 'public'[28] life in their own understanding of the term, i.e. a life in 'society' or the *monde*. This is really the 'public sphere' of the *ancien régime*. Whoever lies outside it leads a *vie particulière*.

Seen from the standpoint of court society the people of the professional strata are outsiders. They exist in the margin of the *monde* — the word is revealing — in the margin of the 'great world'. They are little people. Their houses lack the public, ostentatious character of the *hôtels* and palaces. They are private houses without significance, like their occupants.

Corresponding to their different social functions is the different way the houses are built.[29]

Within their specific tradition the court people develop an extraordinarily sensitive feeling for the status and importance that should be attributed to a person in society on the basis of his bearing, speech, manner or appearance. The intense scrutiny of each manifestation of a person, including his house, to determine whether or not he is respecting the traditional boundaries proper to his place within the social hierarchy, and to assess everything relating to him in terms of its social valency, its prestige value, springs directly from the mechanism of absolute rule in the court society and the hierarchical structure of the society centred around the king and the court. This sensitivity forms in the ruling class as an instrument of self-assertion and defence against the pressure from those of lower rank. Accordingly, these people experience many things that we would be in-

---

[26] That finance, the tax farmers and their retinue, should be included among the estates would be surprising today only if we adopted a wrong perspective. The primary endeavour of financiers was to attain rank and social prestige and, if possible, a noble title for themselves or at least the next generation, and to lead a noble life, i.e. one determined primarily by considerations of prestige. This is of importance in showing that possession of capital or, more precisely, of money need not be automatically connected with a 'capitalist' outlook or mode of life. It depends on the overall structure of a society which goals rising middle-class families hope to attain and can attain by the acquisition of capital.

[27] Dangeul, *Remarques sur les avantages et les désavantages de la France* (1754), p. 72.

[28] On *particulier* as antithesis to *public*, cf. *Enc.*, art. 'Particulier'.

[29] For plans of the different types of houses, mentioned here only for cross-reference, cf. Jombert, *op.cit.*

clined to dismiss as trivial or superficial with an intensity that we have largely lost. This will be seen again and again. An act of sociological reflection is needed on our part in order to make visible the social tensions and pressures underlying this concern for, and often conflicts over, 'trivial' and 'superficial' matters.

In this respect the description given by the *Encyclopédie* of the houses of the different estates and groups is very revealing. The basic principles of the lowest type of houses already mentioned, those of the professional classes, are defined as follows: 'symmetry, solidity, convenience and economy'. The social character of these principles for the construction of apartments for small artisans and tradesmen is easily overlooked, since they correspond fairly exactly to what is now broadly required for *every* house.[30] But the fact that at that time they were referred to expressly as criteria for the houses of the lowest classes, and that *économie* in particular is mentioned only in relation to these lower classes, is significant in two ways. First, it illuminates the development of domestic architecture in general; second, it supports the observation, for which much other evidence can be found, that economy had little bearing on the architectural style of the court-absolutist upper classes. It is not mentioned among them. The lowest social classes did not need to keep up appearances, they had no real obligations regarding status. For this reason they give priority to building characteristics which, while they need not be absent for the others, are entirely eclipsed by display and prestige. Utilitarian values such as convenience and solidity thus become quite unashamedly the main architectural concern of these classes. The need for economy becomes quite apparent in the outward appearance of the houses.

[30] Within the development of society there are rising and falling cultural forms and ideas. Here we have an example of a rise of cultural forms over a long period. That it is functionally linked to the rise of professional and mass classes is easily recognized. Economy, comfort, symmetry and solidity have established themselves with these classes as predominant features of houses, but to do so they had to find preference over the kind of houses that were reserved to the upper class and of which the *cinq ordres d'architecture* (cf. p. 73, n.31) are particularly characteristic. This traditional manner of ornamenting houses to indicate social distinction, prestige and ostentation was naturally not without influence on the appearance of the houses of the lower classes even in the *ancien régime*. Transformed and simplified, this style of facade design constantly percolated downwards. The struggle between these two tendencies, economy and ostentation, continued up to our day even if the representative character of the old ornamentation slowly faded. It was kept alive by the fact that, following after the aristocratic classes and partly in conjunction with them, successive waves of bourgeois make use, in their desire for social distinction and prestige, of the style evolved by the upper class of the *ancien régime*, though with particular modifications (particularly in France; in Germany styles from other epochs play an additional role). At the same time the need for economy arising from the conditions of the broad professional classes generated other styles. The conflict between economy and ostentatious ornamentation was one of the roots of the *Kitsch* style in architecture.

10. In all other groups, however, and the more so the higher their rank, the obligation to put on an appearance corresponding to one's rank, and to express through one's house the estate to which one belongs, moves further and further into the foreground. As regards houses, prestige value eclipses purely utilitarian values. The estate ethos, the instrument of self-assertion in the upper classes, has precedence over the economic ethos which is at first an instrument of advancement in the lower classes.

These connections, which have been only provisionally formulated here and will be enlarged on as the structure of this society as a whole is elucidated, become still clearer when we see the attributes attached by social custom to the next group of houses, although they are still bourgeois houses.

The next highest group in the hierarchy of houses is the *maisons particulières* built by rich bourgeois as their permanent residences. These houses 'should have a character derived neither from the beauty of the *hôtels* nor from the simplicity of ordinary houses (i.e. the previous group). The "orders of architecture"[31] should never play any part in their decoration, despite the opulence of those who have them built.'

How clearly the thinking in terms of estates, and particularly the highest estates of the *ancien régimes*, emerges here! The size and ornamentation of a house are made dependent not on the wealth of its owner but solely on his social rank and the visible show which this requires.[32]

If we look at the structure of such a house,[33] we find by and large the same elements as in the *hôtel*. The domestic architecture of the aristocracy as the authoritative class in all questions of styles of living is the model for that of the upper bourgeoisie. But all the dimensions are reduced. The courts and above all the two *basses-cours* are quite small; the rooms for domestic services surrounding them are of a correspondingly reduced size; kitchen, a larder and a small office are there, nothing else. The apartments of the master and mistress of the house have moved quite close together, both a symbol and a condi-

[31] The *ancien régime* knew of five such *ordres d'architecture*: the Ionic, the Doric, the Corinthian, a variant of the Corinthian called *l'ordre composite*, and the Tuscan. The expressive content of these styles in regard to different social classes is defined very exactly (*Enc.*, art. 'Ordres').

[32] How it happens that such views are put forward in the *Encyclopédie* cannot be explained in this context. But it can be pointed out that there is a whole number of articles in the *Encyclopédie* in which the differentiation of the estates is described and affirmed as something entirely self-explanatory (e.g. article on 'Noblesse'), even though there is usually some ideological reinterpretation.

[33] Plans can be found in the *Encyclopédie*, 'Recueil de Planches', plates 25 and 26.

tioning factor of the relative spatial confinement of bourgeois marriage as compared to the spaciousness of marriage for the court-aristocracy. But it is above all the society rooms that have shrunk. Characteristically, the ceremonial apartment is entirely absent. The circular *salon* is there but smaller and limited to one storey; adjoining it on one side is a longish room combining the functions of a cabinet and of a gallery, on the second a small boudoir, on the third a *salle de compagnie*. The antechamber to it also functions as a dining room for the family. When it is used for the latter purpose, the servants are sent into the entrance hall. These are the only social rooms to be found in these houses.

11. The difference in structure between bourgeois and aristocratic society that emerges here is very revealing. In the life of court people social life occupies a quite different space and time than in that of professional-bourgeois people. The number of people that a court person must receive at his house is larger; the number of people whom the professional bourgeois[34] must meet with socially, i.e. privately, is smaller. The former expends a far greater amount of time on social intercourse than the latter. The mesh of direct relationships is tighter in his case, the social contacts more numerous, the *immediate* ties to society greater than for the professional bourgeois for whom contacts *mediated* through profession, money or goods have overwhelming priority.

Chronologically, this situation lasted until the 1760s and 1770s. At that time the social and economic rise of professional groups became steadily more visible, while large sections of the nobility became increasingly impoverished. But legally, as well as in the consciousness of the different groups and in social life, the dividing walls remain very strong.

Which attributes are considered appropriate in the *monde* to distinguish the *hôtels*, 'les demeurs des grandseigneurs'? 'The character of their decoration', says the *Encyclopédie*,[35] 'requires a beauty fitting the birth and rank of the persons who have them built; nevertheless they should never exhibit the magnificence reserved for the palaces of kings.' Cultural forms that we usually perceive purely aesthetically, as variants of a certain style, are perceived by their contemporaries also as the finely shaded expressions of social qualities.

---

[34] In this description we can disregard the intermediate strata such as financiers and the *robe* which, although bourgeois, imitated and sometimes surpassed the nobility in their style of life. To understand these intermediate strata it is necessary first to understand the example set by court strata.
[35] Cf. *Enc.*, 'Recueil de Planches', vol. 2, 'Architecture', pt. 5.

Each of these *hôtels* is originally built for a quite specific client, a particular 'house'; and the architects take pains in the form and ornamentation of the *hôtel* to make the social status of its occupants directly visible.

The residence of a prince who leads an army, we read, of a cardinal, of a *premier magistrat*, i.e. the holder of one of the high offices in the judiciary, and finally of a *ministre éclairé* entrusted with government, must have a quite different appearance from that of a mere marshall of France or a bishop or a *président à mortier*, that is, men of lower rank within the hierarchies of nobility, clerics, *robe* and pen. All these, as persons 'who, not holding the same rank in society, should have habitations fitted out so as to mark the superiority or inferiority of the different orders of the state'.

The residences of princes are called *palais* or, more exactly, second-class *palais* (measured by the royal palaces); those of the others merely *de grands hôtels*. But for both types the ornamentation must reflect their social function:

> For the dwelling places of the military, a martial character should predominate, announced by straight lines, by filled-in sections approximately equal to the spaces, and by an architecture which has its source in the Doric order.
>
> For the house of a man of the Church a less severe character will be chosen, announced by the disposition of the principal parts, by a fitting repose and a restrained style that is never belied by a frivolity of ornamentation. [36]
>
> Finally, for the house of a magistrate, one should adopt a character revealed by its formal arrangement, the distribution of its parts, which are the only means of showing unequivocally from the outside of a building the worth, piety and urbanity of its occupants.
>
> For the rest, we repeat that one should always remember to avoid in these different styles the grandeur and magnificence proper to the palaces of kings. [37]

12. One cannot understand the structure of a society unless one is able to see it simultaneously from the they-perspective and from the we-perspective. At present, the only method by which a high degree

---

[36] This characterization, which is pursued in greater detail in the *Encyclopédie*, is supported by particular examples of known Parisian *hôtels*. An example of the *hôtel d'un militaire* is the Hôtel de Soubise, later the Palais des Archives in the Rue Vieille du Temple. In the same street we find, as an example of the *hôtel* of a family in which high ecclesiastical honours were hereditary, the *Hôtel de Rohan*, built at the beginning of the eighteenth century for the Archbishop of Strasbourg, Armand de Rohan, by Delamair, the architect of the Hôtel de Soubise.

of certainty can be obtained from the they-perspective often appears to be the quantifying one, the counting of heads, the use of statistical instruments. As can be seen, there are other ways. They are particularly needed when we are attempting to define figurations that elude what is often taken to be *the* scientific approach, namely their disintegration by analysis into atoms, particular actions, opinions, variables, or whatever else may constitute them.

The study of the way court people arranged and experienced their houses, their own 'image', is an example of a figuration-analysis conducted simultaneously from the they-perspective and the we-perspective. The social canon of house design or, expressed traditionally, the 'object-oriented' aspect of the house design of court people, is the starting point. It is distinguishable, but wholly inseparable, from the 'subject-oriented' aspects of house design, the way the groups concerned themselves experience and explain the layout of their houses.

Considered in this way, a study of the shaping of house and living space in court society affords a first, limited insight into the social structure with which we are concerned. We see it from both the they-perspective and the we-perspective, as a figuration of other people whom we call 'they'; at the same time we see how these people themselves see it, how they see themselves when they say 'we'.

It is a society of hierarchically ordered estates. But this absolutist society of estates is distinguished from the preceding medieval one by the fact that the representatives of the monarchy have gained clear

[37] In the bourgeois-capitalist world of the nineteenth century, too, objects of use take on representative and prestige functions. But the primary things to be represented in the estates society of the *ancien régime* are, as we have said, the rank and status uniting the individual explicitly with a number of other people, with a larger or smaller stratum or group. The new member has to adapt to the slowly changing, traditional forms of expression of his group. The groups or castes as a whole are the real bestowers of prestige; what a particular style in a person's property is intended to express in the widest sense is therefore his membership of this or that group within the estates, his place on a particular rung of the hierarchy, his share of its rights and prestige. In professional bourgeois society, above all in the late nineteenth century, however, what is primarily to be represented is wealth and especially the wealth of a *single* family. Without going further into this important distinction here, we will juxtapose the above description to one relating to a bourgeois period; in it a complex situation is perhaps slightly oversimplified, but in this context it gives a valuable picture of the change in the meaning and form of social ostentation and the desire for prestige.

From Ernst Heilborn, *Zwischen Zwei Revolutionen*, vol. 2, pp. 127–28: 'To know how Frau Jenny Treibel looks we must glance at the little Maltese dog sitting with her in the coach. The value of this little dog stems less from its charming appearance or pleasing qualities than from the knowledge that it is very expensive. This is the ostentation of Frau Jenny Treibel: whether or not the effect is ridiculous or impressive, it is enough that it should be expensive. The money that Frau Jenny Treibel spends on herself, her clothes, her dinners, her surroundings, determines her social value. . . . A division of labour has been effected, the husband's task being to earn money, the wife's to put on a display.'

preponderance over the estates. The rather fluctuating distribution of power in medieval society has given way to a more stable one. That the king's power far exceeds that of the nobles, the high clergy and the high administration is now beyond doubt. It finds symbolic expression in the fact that no other person is in a position, or would dare, to build himself a house that approached or even surpassed that of the king in size, splendour or ornamentation. After the other members of the royal house come the three leading cadres, the high nobility of the sword, the high clergy, and the body of high judicial and administrative officials. All these are hierarchically ordered internally. Below them, likewise in hierarchical order, come the middle and lower strata of each of the three cadres. Somewhat out of line with this formation come the financiers, bourgeois who have become very rich. Among their most prominent representatives are the tax farmers and other men who finance state enterprises.

The 'Third Estate' is no longer really an estate at all but a collection of different professional groups whose social structure coincides less and less with its designation from above as an 'estate'. This 'estate' includes as its lowest stratum the *peuple* — peasants, tenant farmers, artisans, workers, lackeys and other servants. But it also includes — we should think of the twofold division of the *maisons particulières* that corresponds at least approximately to this — a whole spectrum of middle bourgeois strata, 'merchants, manufacturers, lawyers, attorneys and doctors, actors, teachers or priests, officials, employees and clerks'. From the Third Estate leading groups rise to approach the *noblesse d'épée* — the holders of high office in the judiciary and administration, the tax farmers and the literary bourgeois intelligentsia. These three groups also represent the three main avenues of advancement open to the bourgeoisie in the society of estates. The upper magistrature has long laid claim to equal status to the nobility of the sword. The tax farmers must be content to outshine it in external appearance. The *Encyclopédie* places the upper magistrature on a level with the nobility of birth and also with the upper clergy. [38] In terms of power the high courts, above all the parliaments, can to an extent hold their own, from the death of Louis XIV onwards, with the nobility and the clergy. But within the absolutist power structure they still form a kind of moderate opposition. They struggle for the power and prestige of their social cadre; but they are never fully recognized. Legally they remain, despite all their privileges — if we leave aside the leading families ennobled under Louis XIV — the representatives of a bourgeois

[38] Cf. *Enc.*, art. 'Noblesse d'épée'.

stratum. Afterwards their leading group forms a special branch of the nobility, the *noblesse de robe* which, despite its increasing power, never loses its special character as a nobility of officials. In social life, too, the houses of the *robe*, at least in the capital with which we are solely concerned here, do not play the same role as those of the court aristocracy. The latter, both obliged and inclined to conviviality by their nature as an estate, are the real core of 'good court society', of the *monde*, of *bonne compagnie*, through the entire *ancien régime* until shortly before the Revolution. This good society consists of a network of social circles with the high court nobility as its central, most prestigious and influential group. More in the margin of 'good society' are the financial circles. Apart from a few cross-connections such as the *salon* of its president, *Hénault*, the magistrature, the chief proponent of Jansenism which was never seriously accepted in court society, maintains a social life of its own in Paris. [39]

Any other bourgeois frequenting the *monde* in the eighteenth century, above all representatives of the bourgeois intelligentsia, do so as a rule as guests rather than hosts, and this is certainly not without importance for the structure of this society. It is in *hôtels* and not bourgeois houses that these people meet and fulfil their convivial needs, and that the qualities are produced which hold together, make visible and seal off to the world below the various elements composing the *monde*: a shared *savoir-vivre* and wit, a delicacy of manners and a highly developed taste. Through such immediately perceptible characteristics the members of the *monde* stand out from the mass of other people. In conjunction with them the specific consciousness of prestige and public display is developed in the *monde* that has already been shown to be the main factor shaping the design of houses. 'Good society', write the Goncourts in discussing the largest and most influential *salon* of the eighteenth century, that of the Maréchale de Luxembourg, [40] 'was a kind of association of both sexes the goal of which was to distinguish itself from bad society, from vulgar associations, from provincial society, by means of the perfection of pleasing forms, by refinement, courtesy, delicacy of manners, by the art of consideration and good breeding. . . . Appearance and behaviour, gestures and etiquette were exactly fixed by "good society".'

13. An elaborate cultivation of outward appearances as an instru-

[39] Material on this and what follows is primarily from E. and J. de Goncourt, *La femme au XVIIIe siècle* (Paris, 1877), and V. du Bled, *La société française du XVIe au XXe siècle*, vol. 5 (Paris, 1900).
[40] *Op.cit.* vol. 1.

ment of social differentiation, the display of rank through outward form, is characteristic not only of the houses but of the whole shaping of court life. The sensitivity of these people to connections between social rank and the shaping of their visible environment including their own gestures, is both a product and an expression of their social situation.

> To be sure [says the *Encyclopédie* in describing their houses] the rank of the persons for whom they are built is the source of the different expressive forms. But how can one attain to them without frequenting the *monde*, where one learns to distinguish all the requirements and the style of this or that building which suits this or that owner? . . . It cannot be doubted that by frequenting good society one gains a sense of what is fitting; one learns to observe good manners; one acquires judgement. There the ability to order one's ideas is born; one acquires purity of taste and a positive knowledge of the character appropriate to each building.

The attitude that finds expression in such ideas points to one of the underlying antimonies of this society. What in retrospect generally appears as luxury to us today is, as Max Weber recognized, anything but superfluous in a society so constructed. Veblen termed this luxury 'conspicuous consumption'. In a society in which every outward manifestation of a person has special significance, expenditure on prestige and display is for the upper classes a necessity which they cannot avoid. They are an indispensable instrument in maintaining their social position, especially when — as is actually the case in this court society — all members of the society are involved in a ceaseless struggle for status and prestige.

A duke must build his house in such a way as to tell the world: I am a duke and not merely a count. The same applies to every aspect of his public appearance. He cannot allow another to appear more ducal than himself. He must make sure that in official social life he has precedence before a count. If he had a country to rule, he would always enjoy superiority over the count through his real function, the size of the area he controls. To express this superiority in social life would then be important but not essential; for he would realize himself not only here. But in this absolutist society of estates the various noble ranks have hardly any corresponding governmental functions. It is by and large titles that the king awards. Even if they are linked to land ownership, this represents a source of income rather than an area of power. For the king alone rules in the land. Thus the most real way of asserting one's rank is by documenting it through an appropriate social appearance. The compulsion to display one's rank is unremitting. If the money to do so is lacking, rank, and therefore the social existence of its possessor, has very little reality. A duke who does not live as a duke has to live, who can no longer properly fulfil the social duties of a duke, is hardly a duke any longer.

From this we can see the peculiar predicament in the light of which the economic affairs of a *grand seigneur* are to be understood. The merchant, to maintain his social existence, must match his expenses to his income. The *grand seigneur* of the *ancien régime*, to maintain his social existence, must match his expenses to the requirements of his rank. The axiom *Noblesse oblige* in its original meaning represents an ethos quite different from the economically orientated ethos of professional-bourgeois classes. The contradiction within the social existence of this court aristocracy, all the more perceptible the more the French economy develops into a network of people practising rational economics, lies in the fact that while their expenses are dictated by their rank and obligations within society, their income is not.

This situation is further aggravated for the nobility throughout the eighteenth century by increasing competition from rising bourgeois strata, above all the financiers, as regards outward appearances and style of life. Not for nothing are these new classes counted among the estates rather than the professional strata. Not for nothing does 'to go into finance' mean *prendre un état*. The financiers have more or less assimilated the estates' forms of thinking and behaviour. *Their* estate, too, though once lacking in tradition, now requires appropriate display. Here, just as in the magistrature, we are in fact concerned not with professional-bourgeois but with estate-bourgeois strata. It should also be noted that at least the upper part of the magistrature is largely made up of families whose rise out of the professional-bourgeois classes took place in the course of the seventeenth century, and who kept themselves apart as an estate from that time on, whereas the financial families of whom we hear in the eighteenth century achieved their rise almost without exception in that century. But even from their behaviour it is apparent that motivation[41] by rank, honour and prestige is more important than motiv-

---

[41] The Abbé Coyer, in his treatise *Noblesse commerçante*, proposes to relieve the distress of the nobility by opening professional and commercial activities to them. In discussing this suggestion he says (*Développement et défense du système de la Noblesse commerçante* (Amsterdam, 1757), pp. 136–37): 'Those among us who are frightened by the idea of a

ation by economic 'interest', although of course mixtures between the two sometimes form.

The desire to stand out, to distinguish oneself socially from those who do not belong, finds its linguistic expression in terms like *valeur*, *considération*, *se distinguer*,[42] and in many others which, used as a matter of course, are both a shibboleth of membership and proof of respect for the same social ideals. The terms themselves, like the attitudes and values they symbolize, sooner or later pass into the rising bourgeois families seeking assimilation into bourgeois society, the financiers. In their circles, too, *économie* and *intérêt* lose their primacy; within one or two generations they are replaced by motivation through 'honour', the desire for distinction and prestige.[43]

But the style of life of the financiers has a retroactive effect on that of the *grands seigneurs*. The whip of fashion, now wielded by the former as well, is also felt by the latter. To ignore it always means to forfeit prestige. At the same time prices are going up;[44] while the nobility's income from rents remains the same, their need of money increases.[45]

---

commercial nobility examine with M. de Montesquieu the principle of monarchies, honour, this honour of prejudice, father of valour. A principle that would be destroyed, they say, by an entirely contrary principle to be found in commerce, that of interest.' One can see how consciously the different motivations of the professional classes and the estates were experienced in the *ancien régime*.

[42] Even today there is an echo of these values in expressions like 'a distinguished man'; but the strict meaning of 'distinction' as an expression of social rank is only faintly heard, and the meaning relating to an external appearance formerly inseparable from social rank has moved into the foreground [especially in German].

[43] 'Since the Third Estate has grown rich, many commoners have become people of the *monde*. The successors of Samuel Bernard are no longer Turcarets but Paris-Duverneys, Saint-James's, Labordes, refined, cultivated in heart and mind, tactful, versed in literature, philosophy, good manners, *giving receptions, knowing how to receive visitors*. Give or take a nuance we find the same society in their houses as in that of a *grandseigneur*. Their sons throw money out of the window just as elegantly as the young duke with whom they take supper.' Taine, *Les origines*, 'Ancien régime', vol. 2, ch. 3, 3, p. 173.

[44] Henry Sée, *Französische Wirtschaftsgeschichte* (Jena, 1930), p. 170.

[45] On the increasing impoverishment of the nobility, cf. de Tocqueville, *L'ancien régime*, ch. 8. He quotes a complaint by a nobleman in 1755: 'Despite its privileges the nobility is being ruined and is daily losing importance, while the Third Estate is seizing control of wealth.'

·IV·

Characteristics of the court-aristocratic figuration

1. As can be seen, the network of interwoven factors in which the social existence of a non-working class is enmeshed is no less compelling or inescapable than the entanglement that can lead a working class to ruin. This is the situation that finds expression in the dictum of the Duc de Croy: 'It is their houses that have crushed the majority of the great families.'

The special figuration that breeds such an attitude, requiring it for its own continuation, has been only faintly indicated in the foregoing. But the specific attitude that arises from being enmeshed in this court society has already emerged somewhat more clearly from the layer of heteronomous evaluations stemming from the professional-bourgeois economic ethos that conceals it. This economic ethos is not something self-explanatory. People do not act automatically according to its commands, regardless of the society they live in, provided only that they can think 'rationally' or 'logically'. The divergence of the attitude of the court aristocracy to financial income and expense from the professional-bourgeois one is not to be explained simply by assuming an accidental accumulation of personal faults or vices in individuals; it does not involve an epidemic of caprice or an impairment of foresight and self-control in the individuals concerned. We have to do here with a different social system of norms and values, whose commands individuals can escape only if they renounce contact with their social circle and membership of their social group. These norms cannot be explained by a secret buried in the breasts of large numbers of individual people; they are explainable only in the context of the specific figuration formed by these individuals and the specific interdependences binding them together.

2. On one hand we have the social ethos of the professional bourgeoisie, whose norms oblige the single family to subordinate ex-

penses to income and, where possible, to keep present consumption below the level of income so that the difference can be invested in savings in the hope of increased future income. In this case the security of the position already attained by the family and, still more, the attainment of higher status and prestige, depend on the ability of the individual, in his income – expenditure strategy, to subordinate his short-term inclinations as a consumer to the saving-for-future-profits ethos. From this professional-bourgeois canon of behaviour that of prestige consumption diverges. In societies in which the status-consumption ethos predominates, the mere preservation of the existing social position of the family, not to speak of an increase in social prestige, depends on the ability to make the cost of maintaining one's household and one's expenditure match one's social rank, the status one possesses or aspires to. Anyone who cannot maintain an appearance befitting his rank loses the respect of his society. In the incessant race for status and prestige he falls behind his rivals and runs the risk of being both ruined and eliminated from the social life of his status group. This obligation to spend on a scale befitting one's rank demands an education in the use of money that differs from bourgeois conceptions. We find a paradigmatic expression of this social ethos in an action of the Duc de Richelieu related by Taine.[1] He gives his son a purse full of money so that he can learn to spend it like a *grand seigneur*, and when the young man brings the money back his father throws the purse out of the window before his eyes. This is socialization in keeping with a social tradition that imprints on the individual the duty imposed on him by his rank to be prodigal. In the mouths of court aristocrats the term *économie*, meaning the subordination of expenditure to income and a systematic limitation of consumption in the interests of saving, has a somewhat contemptuous nuance until far into the eighteenth century and even beyond the Revolution. It symbolizes the virtue of small people. Veblen, as we can see, is hindered in his study of 'conspicuous consumption' by an uncritical use of bourgeois values as criteria for economic behaviour in other societies. He thereby blocks his own way to a sociological analysis of prestige consumption. He has no clear perception of the social compulsions underlying it.

Types of prestige consumption are to be found in many societies. One example is the institution of Potlatch in a number of tribes on the north-west coast of North America, the Tlingit, Haida, Kwakiutl,

[1] Cf. H. Taine, *Les origines*, 'Ancien régime', vol. 1, ch. 2, 2.

and some others. The status, rank and prestige of a family and the associated social privileges are, according to this custom, periodically put to the test by the enforcement of very high expenditure in the form of great feasts or rich presents made above all to rivals for status and prestige, and in other ways. As in France, there were in England in the seventeenth and eighteenth centuries periods of violent competition for status and prestige within the upper class, manifested, for example, in the construction of 'stately homes', to use the current term. Of course, in England the king and court did not constitute a power centre overshadowing all others. The English upper classes therefore did not have a court character to the same degree as the French. The social barriers between the nobility and leading groups of the bourgeoisie, the consolidation of which, in France, Louis XIV always saw as crucial to the preservation of his own power, were lower and more fragmentary in England. The specifically English stratum of rich bourgeois landowners, the gentry, took a no less eager part in competitive prestige building and status-consumption than did the leading aristocratic families. And likewise there was a whole number of such families which ruined themselves in this way.

Considered from a distance, the ruin of families in such cases can appear simply as the personal failure of particular families, and to an extent, of course, this is also the case. If someone loses a race, it certainly means that he personally cannot race as well as his rivals. But races are set up in such a way that, unless there is a dead-heat, there are necessarily losers. Upper classes with a status-consumption ethos and strong competition for status are set up in such a way that there is always a number of families in the course of being ruined.

3. Montesquieu created one of the earliest sociological models in Europe intended to explain the regularity with which noble families within his field of observation were ruined. He presents this decline of families of the nobility of the sword as a phase in the circulation of families within the estates. He proceeds from two assumptions that are revealing with regard both to the structure of his society and to his own membership of an estate. He assumes that the legal and other barriers separating the different social elites of his society will remain untouched. In his opinion the differences between the leading cadres within the estates of French society, as between the estates themselves, cannot and should not be obliterated. But at the same time he sees that within this firm framework of estates and their elites there is a continuous circulation of rising and declining families.

One of the most important barriers dividing the two noble formations of French society, that of the sword and that of the *robe*, from the mass of the people is the legal prohibition to engage in any commercial enterprise. To increase one's income in such a way is regarded as dishonourable and incurs the loss of title and rank. Montesquieu considers this prohibition a useful and quite indispensable institution for an absolute monarchy. This arrangement, he argues, gives each of the leading groups a special kind of social reward different to that of every other. This is precisely what spurs them on:

> The reward of tax farmers is wealth, and wealth rewards itself. Fame and honour are the rewards of that nobility which knows, sees and feels nothing other than fame and honour. Respect and esteem are the reward of the high judicial and administrative officials who find nothing in their path but work followed by work, and who watch day and night over the welfare of the realm. [2]

From such remarks we can see fairly clearly where Montesquieu himself stands. He belongs to the last-named group, the *robe*. The rivalry between this nobility of officials and the nobility of the sword is quite apparent in his description. He can seldom prevent himself from speaking of the nobility of the sword without inserting an ironic comment. But compared to other remarks made by spokesmen of the two rival noble formations about each other, Montesquieu's are very moderate. Few people saw as clearly as he that the regularity with which families of the nobility of the sword were ruined was not a result simply of personal weaknesses but of their social situation and especially their social system of values.

He remarks first of all how wrong it would be to abolish the rule forbidding the nobility to enrich themselves by trade. To do this would be to deprive merchants of the main incentive they have to earn large amounts of money: the more successful they are as merchants, the greater is their chance of leaving the commercial estate and buying themselves a title. Once their wealth enables them to rise into the nobility of officials, their families might later be able to rise even further to the nobility of the sword. If this happens they are soon forced to reduce their capital by expenditure befitting their estate. For the nobility of the sword, says Montesquieu with a slightly ironic undertone, are people who are always thinking about how to make a fortune but who think at the same time what a pity it is to increase their wealth without at once starting to squander it. This is the

---

[2] Montesquieu, *Esprit des Lois*, bk. 13, ch. 20.

section of the nation which uses the basic capital of its property to serve the nation. When a family has ruined itself in this way it gives place to another which soon begins likewise to consume its capital. Thus closes, in Montesquieu's model, the circle leading from rich bourgeois families who have risen into the aristocracy, to impoverished noble families whose members must perhaps finally earn their living by working and who, deprived of their rank and their pride, fall back into the bourgeoisie, 'the people'. The model simplifies the actual state of affairs, but it throws light on the combination of firm barriers between the hierarchically ordered estates and their elites, and a certain degree of social mobility that enables individual families to rise or fall from one estate and one elite to another.

4. This combination of rigidity and mobility of social stratification cannot be understood unless we remember that, in the form observed by Montesquieu, it is an integral part of the absolutist mechanism of government in France. In his youth Louis XIV had had first-hand experience of how dangerous it can be for the king's position if elites of the estates, above all the nobility of the sword and the high judicial and administrative officials, overcome their mutual dislike and make common cause against him. Perhaps he had also learned from the experience of the English kings who owed the precariousness of their position largely to the combined resistance of noble and bourgeois groups. At any rate, the reinforcement of the existing differences and rivalry between the estates, especially between their elites and, within them, between the different rungs of the hierarchies, was one of his fixed maxims as a ruler. It is quite obvious, as will be shown more exactly, that these differences and petty jealousies between the most powerful elite groups in the realm were among the basic preconditions for the abundance of power held by the kings and denoted by the term 'absolutist'.[3]

The long reign of Louis XIV contributed much to the process whereby the specific accentuation that the differences between the estates, and other social distinctions, received through their constant exploitation by the king as instruments of power, become perceptible in the ideas and feelings of the groups themselves as an essential part of their own convictions. Owing to the keen competition for status and prestige rooted in the convictions, values and ideals of the king's subjects, tensions and jealousies between the different estates and ranks, and especially between the rival leading groups, constantly reproduce themselves in heightened form like a freewheeling machine, even when, after Louis XIV's death, their constant

[3] Cf. Appendix 1, p. 276.

manipulation gives way to far less systematic control. As in other cases, the habituation of whole groups to attitudes first imposed, or at least strengthened, by their dependence on others who dominate them, plays a major part in the routinization of tensions and conflicts.

What has been said of the differences and conflicts between elites of the estates, applies no less to the social mobility which, despite all the rivalry, leads from one stratum to another. This, too, the rise and fall of families within the stratified society, is determined first by social factors; that is, it is not created by the king or other individuals. Like the social stratification by estates, the rise and fall of families is first and foremost a manifestation of the immanent dynamic of this figuration. But when the balance of power within the whole figuration shifts after a series of struggles between the representatives of the estates and the kings in the latter's favour, as is the case in France in the seventeenth century, the king has the chance of controlling social mobility in the interests of the royal position or simply his own interests and inclinations. Louis XIV does this quite deliberately.[4] After his death the exploitation of such opportunities becomes a kind of routine; towards the end it is again somewhat more influenced by the internal power struggles of court and other elite formations.

As long as the power and scope of the royal position are large enough, at least the kings and their representatives are able to control the social rise of families as they think fit by distributing titles to rich bourgeois families. As they, too, are especially bound by the ethos of status-consumption, they frequently take advantage of their right to ennoble as a source of income appropriate to their rank.

Just as social rise can be controlled from the royal position in such a figuration, so, within certain limits, can social decline. By his personal favour the king can alleviate or prevent the impoverishment of a noble family. He can come to the family's help by awarding a court office, or a military or diplomatic post. He can make available to them one of the livings at his disposal. He can simply give them a financial present, as in the form of a pension. The king's favour is thus one of the most important opportunities open to families of the nobility of the sword to counteract the vicious circle of enforced ostentation at the cost of their capital. It is understandable that people were unwilling to mar this opportunity by behaviour disagreeable to the king. The king brings his subjects to a point where, as Montesquieu once put it, they think *comme il veut*. If we

[4] Cf. D. Ogg, *Louis XIV* (London, 1967), p. 140.

study the network of dependence in which the king and his subjects are enmeshed, it is not difficult to understand how this is possible.

5. Likewise, the meaning that court buildings and their design have in the eyes of the society that produced them emerges only when they are seen in the context of the specific mesh of interdependence in which their owners and their circle were woven. Understanding of this mesh is impeded today by the fact that in developed industrial society it has become possible to enjoy high social status and prestige without the need to prove this status constantly by extravagant display. Social pressures towards status-consumption have certainly not disappeared. Much that is said here about court society sharpens our awareness of parallels in industrial societies and helps us to formulate structural similarities and differences. A social pressure towards conspicuous consumption and rivalry for prestige leading to the display of expensive status symbols can certainly be observed in the upper strata of industrial society. The decisive difference is that here the consumption and display are considerably more privatized than in court-absolutist societies. Their link to the central power struggles in industrial societies is far looser. They are not built directly into the power mechanism and hardly serve any longer as instruments of rule. Consequently, the social pressure towards these practices is far less strong; it is no longer as inescapable as in court society.

It is, therefore, one of the most distinctive structural features of industrial societies, and from the standpoint of preceding societies one of the most novel and surprising, that in them even the groups with the highest income save and invest a part of their revenue, so that, unless they make mistakes, they become constantly richer whether or not they wish to do so. The rich and powerful members of court societies usually used their whole income on conspicuous consumption. The lessening in the compulsion towards display even among the most affluent elite groups of industrial societies has become of decisive importance in the development of domestic architecture, dress and artistic taste in general. Moreover, the mighty and rich in these societies not only save like the less wealthy and powerful, but they even work like them as well. One could say that in some respects the rich live today as the poor did earlier, and the poor like the rich.

6. In pre-industrial societies the most respected wealth was that which had not been earned by work, that is, inherited wealth, primarily rent from inherited land. Not work as such but work for the sake of earning money, like the wealth so earned, had a low place in the values of court strata of pre-industrial societies. This was very

emphatically the case in the most influential court society of the seventeenth and eighteenth centuries, the French. When Montesquieu observes that many families of the nobility of the sword live on their capital, this means first of all that they sell land, then perhaps jewels and other inherited valuables to pay debts. Their income from rent diminishes, but the compulsion to display gives them no honourable way to limit their consumption. They contract more debts, sell more land, their income falls further. To increase it by participating in lucrative commercial enterprises is both legally forbidden and personally degrading. It is equally degrading to reduce expenditure on household or display. The competitive pressure for status, prestige and power in this society is no less strong than competition for capital and economic power in industrial societies. Apart from inheritances, rich marriages and favours from the king or other great courtiers, loans are the means most readily available to people in this position to maintain their accustomed status-consumption in the short term when their income falls. Without them a family inevitably falls behind in the incessant race for status, forfeiting self-respect and the respect of others. As we have said, in many cases only the favour of the king can save indebted noble families from total ruin.

Not all the families in court society go into decline. What percentage do so cannot now be said. What is essential in this context is not the number, although this has its significance, but the structure of interdependence that exerts pressure on the people of this society. The threat of foundering is felt even when a family is successfully shooting the rapids. There is an abundance of positions at court, in the diplomatic corps, in the army, in the Church, that are reserved for members of families of the nobility of the sword. Membership of court society or connections with people who frequent the court are in many cases conditions of access to such positions. They assure an income, but at the same time entail obligations to display. And in the end individual noble families, particularly those whose rank is beyond doubt, break the taboo on involvement in large industrial enterprises. Smaller business ventures remain disreputable. As an introduction to the problems of an elite formation that differs in several respects from the more familiar formations of industrial society, this short survey of the network of interdependence in which people of this court society are enmeshed may be enough to begin with. It anticipates a good deal that — partly from other aspects — will be dealt with more thoroughly later. It may also serve as an introduction to the more detached way of thinking that is needed in seeking to understand the structure and experience of a different kind of society.

7. At first sight it may seem odd to choose a study of the structure of living accommodation as the starting point for a study of social interdependence. In particular, the linking of aristocratic house design and the absolutist structure of rule is perhaps unexpected. We are accustomed today to distinguish sharply between 'society' and 'the state', without always having a clear idea of the relationships that go with this conceptual distinction. We have grown used to the idea that social phenomena can be put into different conceptual pigeonholes without a need to enquire into their relationship to each other. We classify phenomena as political, economic, social, artistic and so on as if this were self-evident, usually without questioning the appropriateness of such classification to the facts observed, and without a clear picture of the relationship between the different classes. The matter-of-course way in which this classifying framework, which certainly has to do with professional specialization in industrial societies, is applied to societies at a different stage of differentiation, seriously impedes an understanding of the latter.

It detracts neither from the aesthetic enjoyment of court buildings nor from their artistic significance to reveal the social situation of court people and to point out the connections between social figuration and building style. The cross-connections between the power structure and the building style are revealingly characterized when the *Encyclopédie* states that no other palace may equal the royal one in ornamentation. As we saw, the distinction is repeated through all social ranks. It is expected that a family of the high court nobility that does not belong to the royal family will keep at a respectful distance from the residence of a prince of the blood as regards the appearance of its residence. The same applies, rung by rung, down to the lowest ranks. It depends on the actual distribution of power how far deviations from the norm, as in the case of a rich financier, can be tolerated. In societies more familiar to us, the interdependence between the general distribution of power in society and the different aspects of what we call 'private life', including house design, is relatively indirect. In court society the connection is far more immediately present to those involved. And as the differentiation between the 'public' and 'private' sides of a person has not advanced so far in court society as in present-day industrial societies, the sharper conceptual distinction between the 'public' and 'private' spheres of life that is taken for granted in industrial societies does not fit very well when applied to court people.

8. One gains a better understanding of the social connections encompassing one's own life by immersing oneself in the life of people in other societies. A study of court society reveals more clearly than is usually the case when we think only of our own society, that one's own values are a link in the chain of compulsions produced by the interdependence to which one is exposed. Philosophical and sociological theories often treat 'values' as something inexplicable, something 'ultimate' and 'absolute'. People, so it appears, decide in total freedom which values they will adopt. One no more enquires where the values that people can adopt come from than children ask where Father Christmas obtains his presents or the stork babies. It is also easy to overlook the limits and constraints imposed by the values one holds.

What has been said here on court society can make it easier to understand the connections between power and social structures and values. If one grows up in a society in which the possession of a title is rated higher than that of earned wealth, and in which membership of the royal court or even the privilege of access to the king's person — according to the existing power structure — ranks exceptionally high on the scale of social values, it is difficult to escape the compulsion to base one's personal goals on these social values and norms and to join in the competition for such opportunities, as far as the social position of one's family and one's own abilities allow. The goals one deems worthy of pursuing laboriously over long periods are never determined solely by the increase in satisfaction and value that each step taken towards them gives a person in his own eyes; they are also affected by confirmation of one's value or an increase in respect in the eyes of others. For a healthy person there can be no absolute zero-point in the relation between the image he has of his own value and of the values directing his efforts, and the confirmation or denial of his image through the behaviour of other people. This interdependence of the valuations of many individuals in a society makes it difficult if not impossible for a single person to seek fulfilment of his efforts in a way that has no chance of bringing him present or future rewards in the form of respect, recognition, love, admiration — in short, the confirmation or heightening of his value in the eyes of others. In other words, this interdependence of values reduces the chance of an individual growing up without such social values becoming a part of himself. The probability is slight that an individual could stand completely aloof, without participating in any way in the competition for opportunities that he thinks or feels are valued by others, without seeking fulfilment of his striving in a way that secures him an assurance of his value by the behaviour of others. Many — if by no means all — of the opportunities to the possession of which people of court society dedicated all the efforts of their lives, have since lost their lustre and meaning. How could people become excited over trivialities, one may ask, or devote their whole lives to attaining such futile goals? But although the lustre of many high values has faded with the power structure that gave them meaning, the situation of people in this society itself, and with it an understanding of the interdependence of values that implants in individuals the desire for such socially valued goals, can be vividly rekindled for people of another society by sociological study. One does not need to share the values of court people to understand that they formed part of the compulsions of their social existence, and that for most of these people it was difficult if not impossible to turn their backs on the competition for socially valued opportunities. In court society it was meaningful for a duke to be a duke, for a count to be a count, and for every bearer of court privilege to bear such privilege. Every threat to the privileged position of a single house, as to the system of privileges in general, was a threat to what gave value and meaning to the people of this society in their own eyes and in those of others around them whose opinions mattered to them. Every loss of privilege meant a loss of meaning and purpose. For this reason each of these people had to fulfil all the obligations regarding visible display that went with his position and privileges. Depending on one's rank in this many-runged society, there were polarities of values of the most divergent kinds. The whole system was full of tensions. It was shot through with the countless rivalries of people trying to preserve their position by marking it off from those below while at the same time improving it by reducing the demarcation from those above. Sparks flew on every side. But although groups of court intellectuals began to call into question the system of privilege itself, the mass of the privileged, as will be shown, were held fast by their figuration as a court society. While there were countless tensions and conflicts over particular prerogatives, a threat to privilege as such meant for most of the privileged a common threat to what gave their lives meaning and value. As in other societies, there were in French absolutist society enclaves for people who sought self-fulfilment in turning away from the competition for the central opportunities. Monasteries and some other positions in the Church offered such possibilities of withdrawal. But in their turn they usually opened the way to other forms of competition for status and prestige.

    9. Much that court people thought worthy of endeavour has paled

and seems almost worthless now. But by no means everything. Closely bound up with court values that have lost their meaning and lustre are others that have lost very little. They include a large number of works of art and literature that are characteristic of the special cultivation of taste in court society; they also include a large number of buildings. We understand the language of forms better if we also understand the type of compulsion to display and of aesthetic sensibility characteristic of this society in conjunction with status competition. Thus social phenomena that have not lost value are connected to others that have. In addition, the struggle of people with the constraints of their interdependence that emerges from an analysis of such a figuration never quite loses its significance, even though one's own constraints are of a different kind.

In accordance with an old philosophical tradition, views on human values are frequently classified in two groups that are normally understood as diametrically opposed. All value-judgements are thought to belong to one or the other. One has a choice merely between the ideas that all human values are 'relative' and that they are 'absolute'. But this simple antithesis hardly does justice to the observable facts. The fact that one is exploring the connections between the power structure and the social scale of values means no more than that one is pursuing facts that can be reliably recorded. It does not mean that one is advocating a complete relativism of values. Nor does this statement mean that one favours an absolutism of values. If we are trying to discover theoretical categories that will stand the test of further factual research, both these traditional philosophical classifications turn out to be crude simplifications. The problems that are encountered in the course of sociological research are far more complex and subtle than this simple antithesis suggests. The squandering of human life in the service of transitory values that are thought eternal at the time can be observed everywhere in the development of human society. But sometimes the sacrifices in the service of ephemeral values help to give rise to human works or human figurations of more lasting value. Only with the aid of comparative studies devoted to understanding devalued power structures and scales of values can we hope to attain a clearer picture of power structures and scales of values that have a chance of greater permanence.

·V·

Etiquette and ceremony: conduct and sentiment of human beings as functions of the power structure of their society

1. To understand the behaviour of the court aristocracy and the ethos of good society in the *ancien régime*, we need to have a picture of the structure of the court. But the relation of 'good society' to the court was not always the same.

The *monde* of the eighteenth century, measured by present-day social relationships, was an extraordinarily tightly knit social formation. But it was loose in comparison to the *monde* of the seventeenth century, and especially to good society in the reign of Louis XIV. For not only was the court the most important and influential centre of society at that time, but as Louis XIV, for reasons to be discussed, saw the fragmentation of social life, the formation of circles outside the court with displeasure — even though they could not be entirely avoided — convivial life was largely concentrated at the court itself.[1] By a gradual process this tight circle was loosened after his death.[2] Then the most eminent centres of social life were first of all the Palais Royal where the regent resided; the Temple where, in Louis XIV's time, the Grand Prior of Vendôme, heir of a bastard son of Henry IV, lived, apart from a period of banishment from 1706 to 1714, and after him the Duke of Conti; and a *château* of the Duc de Maine, one of the powerful bastard sons of Louis XIV, who, after the latter's death, competed for political power first with the Duke of Orléans and his wife from the great house of Condé who, as a princess of the

---

[1] Nevertheless, as we shall see, the French court does not conform in any way to what is usually understood by 'community' (*Gemeinschaft*). This does not mean, however, that it therefore fits the opposed category of 'society' (*Gesellschaft*).

[2] Cf. Taine, *Les origines*, 'Ancien régime', vol. 1, ch. 2, 1, p. 191: 'The monarchy produced the court, which produced polite society.'

blood, was of still higher rank than her husband. All these circles were nothing other than small courts.[3]

Under Louis XV the centre of gravity shifted to an extent from these palaces to the *hôtels*, the residences of non-princely court aristocrats.[4] This did not mean that the royal court lost its significance as the centre. In it all the threads of society ran together, from it the rank, reputation and even, to an extent, the income of court people continued to depend. The court merely shared its significance as a theatre of social life, a formative influence on convivial culture, more and more with aristocratic circles. Social life was slowly decentralized. It spread from the *hôtels* of the court nobility to those of the financiers. And it was at this stage of its development that the *monde* produced its well-known flowering of *salon* culture.

Under the feeble reign of Louis XVI, and with the growth of bourgeois wealth, the court further lost significance as a social centre.[5] Good society became looser still, but without its demarcations from the world below being entirely obliterated. They only become harder and harder to grasp in retrospect.[6] Until finally the storms of the Revolution shatter the whole structure. In its place a new good society forms during the Empire, with its centre first at the Napoleonic court; but owing to the changed conditions to which it owes its existence, this never equals the old one in elaboration and refinement. From now on the culture of social life and taste live on the heritage of the eighteenth century. The new tasks that must be performed lie in other spheres.

A number of lines can now be traced: the nobles' and financiers' *salon* of the eighteenth century is a descendant of the royal *salon* of the second half of the seventeenth. It is at the court of Louis XIV that the new court society is really formed. Here a process reaches

[3] Cf. E. and J. de Goncourt, *La femme au XVIIIe siècle* (Paris, 1877), ch. 2.

[4] This shift of the centre of gravity of good society from the royal palace to those of the princes, and from them to the *hôtels* of the high nobility and — at some distance — the rich bourgeoisie of the estates, also found expression in the style of good society. The transitions from Classicism to Rococo, from Rococo to the Louis XV style, correspond fairly exactly to this shift in the centre of gravity of court society.

[5] Under his reign some of the great court families, e.g. Rohan, Noailles, Montmorency, for the first time withdrew from the court. Cf. M. von Boehn, *Frankreich im 18. Jahrhundert* (Berlin, n.d.), p. 67.

[6] That they are still there can be felt in statements like the following, which also confirms some of what was said about the values and motivations of the *monde*. Necker as a minister gives a dazzling party: 'It happened', says a report of the time, 'that this celebration brought him more credit, favour and stability than all his financial operations. People only spoke for a day about his latest arrangement concerning the *vingtième*, while they are still talking at this moment of the party he gave.' *Correspondance secrète*, 5, p. 277, quoted by Taine, *op. cit.*, vol. 1, ch. 2, 2, p. 108.

culmination that has been long prepared: knights and the court epigones of knights finally become court people in the proper sense of the word, people whose social existence, and not infrequently their income, depend on their prestige, their standing at court and within court society.

2. We earlier reviewed the hierarchy of houses, the symbols of the social hierarchy, from the apartments to the *hôtels*. It remains to discuss the pinnacle of this hierarchy, the king's palace, the real centre of the court and of court society, and at the same time the building in which, more than all others, court people received the stamp that left its mark on the whole of Europe.

The royal palace received its most emphatic statement in a particular building, the Château of Versailles. After the *hôtels*, which under Louis XIV were only pendants of the royal palace before becoming centres of a more decentralized court life, we therefore have to elucidate sociologically at least a few aspects of the starting point of this movement, the Château of Versailles itself.

What we see when first looking at this building is something very peculiar; it is a complex of buildings that can hold many thousands of people. In terms of numbers, it could contain the population of a town. But these thousands do not live together here in the manner of citizens. It is not, as with the latter, individual families that form the social units around which the rooms are shaped and divided; this whole complex is both the king's house and, at least periodically, the quarters of court society as a whole. A section of this society had lodgings in the king's house permanently allocated to them. Louis XIV liked to see his nobles living in his house whenever he held court there, and he was pleased to be asked for a lodging at Versailles.[7] Above all the high nobility remained almost continuously at court, as the king wished, and often drove over daily from town *hôtels*: 'I shall hardly leave the court at all,' Saint-Simon says in one place, 'nor will Mme. de Saint-Simon.'[8] And Saint-Simon, we must remember, held no court office that might have bound him materially to the court.

The exact number of people who lived or could live at the Château of Versailles is difficult to ascertain. However, it is reported that in 1744 about 10,000 persons — including the servants — were accommodated in the Château;[9] this gives a rough picture of its size.

---

[7] Saint-Simon, in a summary of Louis XIV's life written after his death, said: 'He had countless apartments installed at Versailles, and he was flattered to be asked for one.' In the same passage he also refers to the 'immense buildings' that the king had erected at Versailles in the course of time.

[8] *Mémoires* (Paris, Delloye, 1843), vol. 17, ch. 35, p. 248.

[9] Boehn, *op. cit.*, p. 109.

Naturally, at such times it was crammed with people from cellars to roof.

In keeping with the uniform domestic needs and social customs in the court aristocracy, we find all the elements characteristic of the *hôtel* also present in the king's *château*. But just as they reappear in shrunken form in bourgeois houses, we find them here gigantically enlarged, raised, as it were, to a higher power, and not only for practical reasons but partly to demonstrate royal power and prestige. This applies first of all to the court in front of the Château. Of course, the king needed a larger court for the arrival of coaches than anyone else in the realm, because more people gathered at his house. But rather as the real use-value of a commodity, its immediate meaning and purpose, is eclipsed by its mediated meaning as a commodity worth so much money, here the direct social use-value of the court has its social prestige-value superimposed on it.

In describing the court appropriate to a large *hôtel* the *Encyclopédie* says that it was necessary to design a court 'which would indicate by its appearance the rank of the person who was to live there'.[10] This way of experiencing the front court where people arrived must be recalled when approaching the Versailles Château. *One* court is not enough to express the dignity and rank of the king, so there is, first, a broad *avant-cour*, which someone arriving from the west must walk or drive through and which resembles an open square rather than a courtyard in the more exact sense. Avenues on each side of it lead towards the Château, each flanked by a long east–west wing intended primarily for councillors and ministers. Then we come to the Château proper. The court area becomes narrower. One passes through a square courtyard which opens into a second, smaller one, both together forming the 'Cour Royal', and finally reaches a third, still narrower one, the Marble Court, which the central Château encloses on three sides. This middle part itself is so large that internally it forms four further small courts, two on the right and two on the left. And on the first floor of this middle Château lived the king and queen with their household. The greater part of the Cour Royal is formed by two narrow offshoots of the middle building, which join to the north and south the two massive wings of the Château. The northern one includes the Chapel and, separated by a small court, the Opera Chamber, the southern one rooms for the royal princes and the king's brother, and this whole building with its wings and courtyards, its hundreds of apartments, thousands of rooms, its large and

---

[10] *Enc.*, 'Recueil de Planches', vol. 2, 'Architecture', pt. 5, p. 25.

small corridors, now dark, now brightly lit, forms the external shell of the court and court society at least in the reign of Louis XIV.

3. It is always of some significance which aspect of living is given a special accent by being allocated a room or rooms at the centre of a house. This is especially true of the *ancien régime* where the upper class, above all the king, did not rent rooms already built and limited in size by rational calculation, but where needs, particularly that for prestige, determined expenditure and thus the shape of a building.

In this sense it is not without interest to note that the middle room on the first floor, from the windows of which one could overlook the whole approach in a straight line, the Marble Court, the Cour Royal, and in the distance the *avant-cour*, was the king's bedroom. Of course, this arrangement first expressed no more than a custom commonly found in the country seats of great lords. They, too, liked to use the middle room on the first floor as the bedroom.[11] The use of this arrangement in the Château may therefore be taken as an expression of how much the king felt himself to be the lord of the house in it; but, as was said earlier,[12] these functions — of king and lord of the house — merged in the case of Louis XIV to an extent which is at first almost unimaginable to us. The magnitude of his rule was reflected in his domestic functions. The king was, as it were, lord of the house throughout the land, and lord of the land even in his most seemingly private chambers. The form taken by the royal bedroom — and not only the *bed*room — is directly influenced by this. This room was, as is known, the theatre of a peculiar ritual hardly less solemn than a state ceremony. It reveals vividly how indissolubly the ruler's character as lord of the house merged with his function as king.

The ceremonies in Louis XIV's bedchamber are mentioned often enough. But it is not enough in this context to regard them as a curiosity, a dusty exhibit in an historical museum which surprises the onlooker only by its bizarreness. Our intention here is to bring them alive step by step so that we can understand through them the structure and functioning of the court figuration of which they are a segment, and so understand the characters and attitudes of the people who form this figuration and are formed by it.

As an example of the structure and the elaboration of court life we shall therefore now describe in detail, step by step, one of the ceremonies that took place in the king's bedchamber and which put into proper perspective both his significance in the narrower sense,

[11] Blondel, *De la distribution des maisons de plaisance* (Paris, 1737).
[12] See p. 6.

and this type of rule in the broader sense, just as one would today describe a work-process at a factory or legal procedures in an office, or the royal ritual of a simple tribe; this ceremony is the *levée*, the getting up of the king. [13]

4. Usually at eight o'clock, at any rate at a time decided by himself, the king is woken each morning by his first valet, who sleeps at the foot of the royal bed. The doors are opened by pages. [14] One of them has already notified the Lord Chamberlain [15] and the first Gentleman of the Bedchamber, a second the court kitchen [16] concerning the breakfast; a third stands in the doorway and admits only those lords who have the right to enter.

This right was very exactly graded. There were six different groups of people who were allowed to enter in turn. This was spoken of as the various *entrées*. First came the *Entrée familière*. Taking part were above all the illegitimate sons and grandchildren of the king (*Enfants de France*), princes and princesses of the blood, the first physician, the first surgeon, the first valet and page.

Then came the *Grande entrée*, consisting of the *grands officiers de la chambre et de la garderobe* [17] and the noble lords to whom the king had granted this honour. Then followed the *Première entrée* for the king's readers, the intendants for entertainment and festivities and others. After that came the *Entrée de la chambre* which included all the other *officiers de la chambre* together with the *grand-aumonier*, the ministers and secretaries of state, the *conseillers d'État*, the officers of the bodyguard, the Marshall of France and others. Admittance to the fifth *entrée* depended to a certain extent on the goodwill of the first Gentleman of the Bedchamber and, of course, on the king's favour. To this *entrée* belonged gentlemen and ladies of nobility who stood in such favour that the Gentleman of the Bedchamber admitted them; they thus had the advantage of approaching the king before all others. Finally there was a sixth form of entry, and this was the most sought-after of all. On this occasion, one did not enter through the main door of the bedroom but through a back door; this *entrée* was open to the sons of the king including il-

---

[13] On what follows cf. Marion, *Dictionnaire des institutions de la France au XVII et XVIII siècles* (Paris, 1923), article on 'Etiquette', and Saint-Simon, *Mémoires*, 1715.

[14] Saint-Simon describes this somewhat differently: he says that the doctor and, while she lived, the king's wet-nurse first came in to rub him down.

[15] The office of *grand chambellan* or lord chamberlain is one of the great court offices. Its occupant has supervision over all officers of the king's chamber; cf. *Enc.*, art, 'Chambellan'.

[16] The exact term for it is *bouche*, cf. also p. 47, and *Enc.*, art, 'Bouche'.

[17] All these court offices are purchasable; admittedly, the king's permission is needed and also, in the reign of Louis XIV, they are reserved exclusively for the nobility.

legitimate ones, together with their families and sons-in-law; and also, for example, to the powerful *surintendant des bâtiments*. To belong to this group was an expression of high favour; for the people included could enter the royal cabinets at any time when the king was not holding counsel or had begun a special task with his ministers, and they could remain in the room until the king went to mass and even when he was ill.

We can see that everything was very exactly regulated. The first two groups were admitted while the king was still in bed. The king wore a small wig; he never showed himself without a wig even when lying in bed. When he had got up and the Lord Chamberlain, with the first Gentleman of the Bedchamber, had laid out his robe, the next group was called, the *Première entrée*. When the king had put on his shoes he called the *officiers de la chambre* and the doors were opened for the next *entrée*. The king took his robe. The *maître de la garderobe* pulled his nightshirt by the right sleeve, the first servant of the wardrobe by the left; his dayshirt was brought by the Lord Chamberlain or one of the king's sons who happened to be present. The first valet held the right sleeve, the first servant of the wardrobe the left. Thus the king put on his shirt. Then he rose from his armchair and the *maître de la garderobe* helped him to fasten his shoes, buckled his dagger at his side, put on his coat, etc., etc. Once the king had finished dressing he prayed briefly while the first almoner, or in his absence another cleric, quietly said a prayer. Meanwhile the whole court was waiting in the great gallery on the garden side, that is, behind the king's bedroom, that ran the whole width of the middle part of the Château on the first floor.[18] Such was the *lever* of the king.

What is most striking in this is the minute exactitude of organization. But this was not, as we can see, rational organization in the modern sense, however precisely predetermined each part of it was, but a type of organization by which each act received a prestige-character symbolizing the distribution of power at the time. What are thought of usually, if not always, as secondary functions within the present social structure, were often primary functions there. The king used his most private acts to establish differences of rank and to distribute distinctions, favours or proofs of displeasure. This already indicates that etiquette had a major symbolic function in the struc-

---

[18] Analogous structures such as a very large terrace were very often found in the country seats of higher nobles. It is interesting to see how building custom was used here for the purposes of court etiquette. The gallery or terrace (cf. Blondel, *op. cit.*, p. 67), otherwise perhaps a place of relaxed conviviality, here also served as an antechamber for the court nobility; and its special size was used to assemble the whole court.

ture of this society and its form of government. It is necessary to proceed to other areas of court life to make this function visible, and to see its different roles for the king and for the nobility.

5. The attitude that was visible earlier in connection with the hierarchy of houses emerges still more clearly here. Now that it is seen operating in conjunction with the determining factor in this state-society, the king, at least the outlines of the social compulsions that brought about such an attitude begin to stand out. For the king to take off his nightshirt and put on his dayshirt was doubtless a necessary procedure; but in the social context it was at once invested with a different meaning. The king turned it into a privilege distinguishing those present from others. The Lord Chamberlain had the right to assist; it was precisely ordained that he should cede this right to a prince and to no one else;[19] and it was exactly the same with the right to be present at the *entrées*. This presence had none of the practical purposes that we first tend to suppose. But each act in the ceremony had an exactly graded prestige-value that was imparted to those present, and this prestige-value became to an extent self-evident. It became, like the size of the courtyard or the ornamentation of a noble's house, a *prestige-fetish*. It served as an indicator of the position of an individual within the balance of power between the courtiers, a balance controlled by the king and very precarious. The direct use-value of all these actions was more or less incidental. What gave them their gravity was solely the importance they conferred on those present within court society, the power, rank and dignity they expressed.

The fetish character of every act in the etiquette was clearly developed at the time of Louis XIV. But the connection with certain primary functions was still preserved. He was strong enough to intervene at any time to prevent a complete freewheeling of etiquette, the total submergence of the primary by the secondary functions.[20]

Later, however, this connection was loosened and the nature of acts of etiquette as prestige-fetishes emerged quite nakedly. Now the motive force that gave life to etiquette, reproducing it over and over again in this society, becomes particularly clear. Once the hierarchy of special rights within the etiquette was established, it was main-

[19] Cf. *Enc.*, art. 'Chambellan'.

[20] The reconstruction of such a ceremony at close quarters makes it easier, as we can see, to understand the meaning of this social phenomenon in the wider context of the power structure. In the ceremony at least three functional levels are fused into an indivisible functional complex: use-function, prestige-function and power or state function. The polarity postulated by Max Weber of purpose-rationality and value-rationality turns out not to be very applicable to such phenomena.

tained solely by the competition between the people enmeshed in it, each being understandably anxious to preserve any privilege, however trivial, and the power it conferred. So the mechanism perpetuated its own ghostly existence like an economy uncoupled from its purpose of providing the means of life. At the time of Louis XVI and Marie-Antoinette people lived under broadly the same etiquette as under Louis XIV. All those involved, from the king and queen to the nobles of various grades, had long borne it only against their will. We have enough testimonies to the extent to which, as it became detached from primary functions, it lost all dignity. Nevertheless it survived uncurtailed up to the Revolution. For to give it up would have meant — from the king down to his valet — to forfeit privilege, to lose power and prestige. How idle its functioning finally was, how the secondary power and prestige-functions in which the people were enmeshed finally overwhelmed the primary ones, is clearly shown by the following example:[21]

The queen's *levée* took a similar course to that of the king. The maid of honour had the right to pass the queen her chemise. The lady in waiting helped her put on her petticoat and dress. But if a princess of the royal family happened to be present, she had the right to put the chemise on the queen. On one occasion the queen had just been completely undressed by her ladies. Her chambermaid was holding the chemise and had just presented it to the maid of honour when the Duchess of Orléans came in. The maid of honour gave it back to the chambermaid who was about to pass it to the duchess when the higher-ranking Countess of Provence entered. The chemise now made its way back to the chambermaid, and the queen finally received it from the hands of the countess. She had had to stand the whole time in a state of nature, watching the ladies complimenting each other with her chemise. Certainly, Louis XIV would never have tolerated such subordination of the main purpose of etiquette. Nevertheless, the social and psychological structure that finally produced this freewheeling was already visible in his reign.

6. This structure merits closer investigation; for it illustrates peculiarities of the compulsions that interdependent people exert on each other within a figuration of a kind to be found in many other societies. Etiquette and ceremony increasingly became, as the above examples showed, a ghostly *perpetuum mobile* that continued to operate regardless of any direct use-value, being impelled, as by an inexhaustible motor, by the competition for status and power of the

---

[21] From an account by a chambermaid of Marie-Antoinette, Mme Campan, quoted by Boehn, *op. cit.*, p. 75.

people enmeshed in it — a competition both between themselves and with the mass of those excluded — and by their need for a clearly graded scale of prestige. In the last analysis this compelling struggle for ever-threatened power and prestige was the dominant factor that condemned all those involved to enact these burdensome ceremonies. No single person within the figuration was able to initiate a reform of the tradition. Every slightest attempt to reform, to change the precarious structure of tensions, inevitably entailed an upheaval, a reduction or even abolition of the rights of certain individuals and families. To jeopardize such privileges was, to the ruling class of this society, a kind of taboo. The attempt would be opposed by broad sections of the privileged who feared, perhaps not without justification, that the whole system of rule that gave them privilege would be threatened or would collapse if the slightest detail of the traditional order were altered. So everything remained as it was.

Undoubtedly the ceremonial was a burden to all concerned. 'One went only unwillingly to Court, and complained aloud when one had to,' the Countess Genlis records in the late eighteenth century.[22] But one went. The daughters of Louis XV had to attend the *couchée*, when the king took off his boots. They would quickly put on large, gold-embroidered crinolines over their indoor gowns, tie the prescribed long court train round their waists, hide the rest under a big taffeta coat and set off with their ladies in waiting, chamberlains and lackeys with torches, running to be in time, through the corridors of the Château to the king, to return in a wild chase a quarter of an hour later.[23] Etiquette was borne unwillingly, but it could not be breached from within, not only because the king demanded its preservation, but because the social existence of the people enmeshed in it was itself bound to it. When Marie-Antoinette began to tamper with the traditional rules of etiquette, it was the high nobility themselves who protested, as was only too understandable; but if it had hitherto been the prerogative of a duchess to be seated in the presence of the queen, it was deeply mortifying to duchesses to see others of lower rank likewise seated. And when the old Duc de Richelieu said to the king at the end of the *ancien régime*: 'Under Louis XIV one kept silent, under Louis XV one dared to whisper, under you one talks quite loudly',[24] it was not because he approved of this development but because he disapproved of it. The bursting of their chains would have meant, for the court nobles, the disintegra-

[22] *Ibid.*
[23] After Mme Campan, quoted by Boehn, *ibid.*, p. 73.
[24] *Ibid.*, p. 128.

tion of their status as an aristocracy. Of course, one could have said: 'I shall have no more part of this ceremony', and isolated nobles perhaps did so. But this also meant forfeiting privileges, losing power, and declining relatively to others. In short, it meant humiliation and, to an extent, self-immolation, unless the person concerned possessed other assurances of his value and pride, of his selfhood and identity, in his own eyes or in those of other people.

Within the court mechanism, one person's desire for status kept others vigilant. And once a stable balance of privileges had emerged, no one could break out without laying hands on these privileges, the basis of his whole personal and social existence.

The people thus enmeshed held each other fast in this situation, however grudgingly they bore it. Pressure from those of lower rank or less privileged forced the more favoured to maintain their advantages, and conversely the pressure from above compelled those on whom it weighed to escape it by emulation, forcing them too into the competition for status. Someone who had the right to attend the first *entrée* or to pass the king his shirt, looked down on and would not give way to someone who was only admitted to the third. The prince would not give way to the duke, the duke to the marquis, and all together as *noblesse* would and could not yield to those who were not nobles and had to pay taxes. One attitude fostered the other, and through pressure and counter-pressure the social mechanism achieved a certain equilibrium. It was in etiquette, visible to all, that this equilibrium was expressed. It signified for everyone yoked into it an assurance of his carefully graded social existence, though only a fragile assurance. For given the tensions by which this social system was both riddled and maintained, every link within it was incessantly exposed to attack by lower or almost equal-ranking competitors who, whether by performing services, through the king's favour or merely by clever tactics, sought to bring about shifts in etiquette and so in the order of rank.

A shift in the hierarchy that was not reflected in a change of etiquette could not occur. Conversely, the slightest change in people's position in etiquette meant a change in the order of rank at court and within court society. And for this reason each individual was hypersensitive to the slightest change in the mechanism, stood watch over the existing order, attentive to its finest nuances, unless he happened to be trying to change it to his own advantage. In this way, therefore, the court mechanism revolved in perpetual motion, fed by the need for prestige and the tensions which, once they were there, it endlessly renewed by its competitive process.

7. Louis XIV had certainly not created the mechanism of ceremonial. But thanks to certain opportunities open to his social function he had used, consolidated and extended it; and he did so from a standpoint that was significantly different from that of the nobility enmeshed in it. A concrete example of the way ceremonial functioned in his hands, supplementing the general description of a particular ceremony, may clarify its importance to the king. [25]

Saint-Simon, in connection with a conflict over rank, had resigned from military service. He informed the king that for reasons of health he regretfully could no longer serve. Louis XIV was not pleased. Saint-Simon found out in confidence that on receiving the news, he had said: 'One more who is abandoning us.'

Shortly afterwards Saint-Simon went back for the first time to the king's *couchée*. It was the custom at this event for a priest to hold a special chandelier, although the room was brightly lit. Each time, the king designated someone present to whom the priest had to give the chandelier. This was a mark of distinction. The procedure to be followed was exactly prescribed. 'One took off one's glove,' Saint-Simon writes, 'stepped forward, held the chandelier for a few moments while the king was lying down, and then returned it to the first valet.' Saint-Simon was understandably surprised when, that evening, despite his resignation from the army, the king appointed him to hold the chandelier.

'The king did so,' he comments, 'because he was vexed with me and did not want to show it. But that was the only thing I received from him for three years. In this time he used every opportunity to show me his disfavour. He did not speak to me, looked at me as if accidentally, never said a word to me about my resignation from the army.'

Louis XIV's attitude on this occasion is very revealing: etiquette here is not a ghostly perpetual motion machine controlled by no one; from the king's standpoint, it serves a clear purpose. He does not merely adhere to the traditional order of rank. Etiquette everywhere allows latitude that he uses as he thinks fit to determine even in small ways the reputations of people at court. He uses the psychological structure corresponding to the hierarchical-aristocratic social structure. He uses the competition for prestige to vary, by the exact degree of favour shown to them, the rank and standing of people at court, to suit his purposes as ruler, shifting the balance of tensions within the society as his need dictates. Etiquette is not yet petrified; in the

---

[25] Saint-Simon, *Memoiren* (1702), Stuttgart, 1814/15, vol. 1, pp. 142–43.

king's hands it is a highly flexible instrument of power.

In the earlier discussion of the court attitude to living space it clearly emerged with what care and deliberation, with what special calculations of prestige the shape and decoration of rooms were differentiated. The scene at the king's *couchée* described by Saint-Simon shows analogous behaviour in a different context. It also shows somewhat more clearly the function of this careful differentiation of all outward aspects of court society: the king is vexed but he does not fly into a rage, he does not discharge his anger directly in an affective outburst. He controls himself and expresses his relationship to Saint-Simon in a carefully measured attitude which reproduces the exact nuance that he thinks it desirable to express in this case. The minor distinction, combined with the slighting of Saint-Simon at other times, constitutes the graduated response to the latter's conduct. And this measured calculation of one's position in relation to others, this characteristic restraint of the affects, is typical of the attitude of the king and of court people in general.

8. What produces this attitude? Let us begin by attempting to find out what function the measured calculation of attitudes, the observation of nuances in the relationships of person to person, had for the bulk of court people.

They were all more or less dependent on the king. The smallest nuance in his behaviour towards them was therefore important to them; it was the visible indicator of their relation to him and their position within court society. But this dependence indirectly shaped the behaviour of court people towards each other.

Their rank within court society was, of course, determined first of all by that of their house, their official title. At the same time, however, permeating and modifying the official hierarchy, an actual order of rank which was far more finely shaded, uninstitutionalized and unstable established itself within court society. A courtier's position in this depended on the favour he enjoyed with the king, his power and importance within the field of court tensions. There was, for example, an institutional hierarchy among dukes, based primarily on the ancientness of their houses. This order was legally enshrined. But at the same time the duke of a younger house might currently enjoy higher esteem, through his relations to the king or his mistress or any other powerful group, than one from an older house. The real position of a person in the network of court society was always governed by both moments, official rank and actual power position, but the latter finally had greater influence on behaviour towards him. The position a person held in the court hierarchy was therefore ex-

tremely unstable. The actual esteem he had achieved forced him to
aspire to improve his official rank. Any such improvement necessarily meant a demotion of others, so that such aspirations unleashed
the only kind of conflict — apart from warlike deeds in the king's
service — which was still open to the court nobility, the struggle for
position within the court hierarchy.

One of the most interesting of these struggles was the one waged by
the Duke of Luxembourg against the sixteen dukes and peers of
France who were of older rank. Saint-Simon begins his account of
this struggle with the following words that graphically illustrate the
two sides of the court hierarchy just mentioned, and the way they interacted:[26] 'M. de Luxembourg, proud of his successes and the ap-
plause of the *monde* at his triumphs, believed himself strong enough
to move from the eighteenth rank of ancientness that he held among
his peers to the second, immediately behind M. d'Uzès.'

9. The actual order of rank within court society constantly fluc-
tuated. The balance within this society was, as we have said, very
precarious. Now small, almost imperceptible tremors, now large-
scale convulsions incessantly changed the positions of people and the
distance between them. To keep abreast of these upheavals was
vitally important to court people. For it was dangerous to be
discourteous to a person whose stock was rising. It was no less
dangerous to be unduly amiable to a person who was sinking in the
hierarchy, was close to disfavour; or one should only do so if it
served a particular purpose. A constant, precisely calculated
adjustment of behaviour towards everyone at court was therefore
indispensable. The behaviour one courtier judged appropriate to
another at a given time was for this other, as for observers, an exact
indicator of how high he currently stood in social opinion. And as an
individual's stock was identical to his social existence, the nuances of
behaviour by which people reciprocally expressed their opinion on it
took on extraordinary importance.

This whole bustle of activity had a certain resemblance to a stock
exchange. In it, too, a society actually present formed changing
assessments of value. But at a stock exchange what is at stake is the
value of commercial houses in the opinion of investors; at court it
was the value of the people present in each other's opinion. And
while at the former even the slightest fluctuation can be expressed in
figures, in the latter a person's value was expressed primarily in the
nuances of social intercourse. The gradations of domestic ornamen-

[26] *Ibid.*, ch. 16.

tation appropriate to the rank of a house's owner which, according to the *Encyclopédie*, could only be learned by frequenting good society, are crude — as is the division into estates itself — compared to the delicate shades of behaviour that were needed to express the actual order of rank at court at any time.

From such contexts one gains understanding of the specific type of rationality that formed in court circles. Like every type of rationality, this evolves in conjunction with particular constraints enforcing control of the affects. A social figuration within which an extensive transformation of external into internal compulsions takes place,[27] is a permanent condition for the production of forms of behaviour the distinctive feature of which we denote by the concept of 'rationality'. The complementary concepts of 'rationality' and 'irrationality' refer to the relative parts played by short-term affects and long-term conceptual models of observable reality in individual behaviour. The greater the importance of the latter in the unstable balance between affective and reality-orientated directives, the more 'rational' behaviour is — provided the control of the affective directives does not go too far. For pressure from and saturation by the affects is itself an integral component of human reality.

But the type of reality-orientated conceptual model involved in the control of human behaviour varies with the structure of social reality itself. Accordingly, the 'rationality' of court people is different from that of the professional bourgeoisie. On closer investigation it could be shown that the former is one of the early stages and pre-conditions of the latter. Common to both is a preponderance of longer-term reality-orientated considerations over momentary affects in the fluctuating balance of tensions controlling behaviour in particular social fields and situations. But in the bourgeois type of 'rational' behaviour-control, the calculation of financial gains and losses plays a primary role, while in the court aristocratic type the calculation is of gains and losses of prestige, finance and prestige respectively being the means to power in these societies. As we saw, in court circles a gain in prestige was sometimes bought with a financial loss. What appeared 'rational' and 'realistic' by court standards was thus 'irrational' and 'unrealistic' by bourgeois ones. Common to both was control of behaviour with a view to gaining power *as it was understood at the time, that is, in accordance with the figuration of people existing then.*

It must be enough to indicate the problem. It shows how inade-

---

[27] Cf. N. Elias, *The Civilizing Process* (Oxford, 1982), vol. 2, p. 239.

quate is a simple, absolute conceptual antithesis between two poles that leaves no room for a clear formulation of the many evolutionary constellations lying between the fictitious absolutes 'rational' and 'irrational'. Clearly, to do justice to the facts, far more refined and subtle concepts are needed; but they are not available.

Court 'rationality', if we may call it so, derived its specific character neither, like scientific rationality, from the endeavour to know and control extra-human natural phenomena, nor, like bourgeois rationality, from the calculated planning of strategy in the competition for economic power; it arose, as we saw, from the calculated planning of strategy in face of the possible gain or loss of status in the incessant competition for this kind of power.

Competitive struggles for prestige and status can be observed in many social formations; it may be that they are to be found in all societies. What is observed in court society has in this sense a paradigmatic value. It points to a social figuration that draws the individuals forming it into an especially intense and specialized competition for the power associated with status and prestige.

In face of such phenomena the attempt is often made to make do with explanations from individual psychology, for example by attributing an unusually strong 'urge to dominate' to the people concerned. But explanations of this type are, in their whole approach, inadequate here. The assumption underlying them, that in this society many individuals happened to come together who were endowed by nature with an especially strong desire to dominate, or with any other individual qualities that can explain the special nature of court competition for prestige, is one of the many attempts to explain something unexplained by something inexplicable.

We stand on firmer ground if, instead of a large number of separate individuals, we take the figuration formed by them as our starting point. Viewed from this standpoint, it is not difficult to understand the measured attitudes, the calculated gestures, the ever-present nuances of speech, in short the specific form of rationality that became second nature to the members of this society, that they exercised with effortless elegance and which, indeed, like the specific control of affects which its exercise demanded, was an indispensable instrument in the continuous competition for status and prestige.

10. We are apt to ask today: why were these people so beholden to external appearances, why so sensitive to what they regarded as the 'incorrect' behaviour of another, to the slightest infringement or threat to any outward privilege and, in a word, to what we regard as superficial? But this question, this assessment of what was centrally

important to court people as 'superficial', springs from a quite specific structure of social existence.

We can to some extent allow ourselves today to leave real social differences concealed, or at least undefined, because the relationships between people mediated by wealth and profession, and the resulting differentation of people, remain unambiguously real and effective even when not expressed directly in their public manifestations.

In particular, the financial opportunities open to a person need not appear too openly today because, in the course of functional democratization, the power of the less wealthy classes in relation to the more affluent has increased somewhat, as compared to the situation at the time of Louis XIV. But in court society social reality inhered directly in the rank and esteem granted to a person by his own society and, above all, by the king. A person with little or no standing in society was more or less worthless in his own eyes. In such a society the chance of preceding another, or sitting while he had to stand, or the depth of the bow with which one was greeted, the amiability of one's reception by others, and so on, were not mere externals — they are that only where money or profession are taken as the reality of social existence. They were literal documentations of social existence, notations of the place one currently occupied in the court hierarchy. To rise or fall in this hierarchy meant as much to the courtier as profit or loss to a businessman. And the agitation of a courtier over an impending rise or fall in his rank and prestige was no less intense than that of a merchant over an imminent loss of capital, of a manager or official over a threatening downturn in their career.

11. If we take a step further, the following connections come into view: in a social field where money and profession have become the main foundation of social existence, the individual's actual social environment is relatively interchangeable. The esteem he enjoys among the people with whom he has professional contact naturally plays a part, but he can to an extent always withdraw from it. Profession and money are relatively mobile foundations for existence. At least in professional bourgeois society they can be transplanted here or there. They are not unconditionally bound to a particular locale.

The foundations of court existence were quite different. Characteristics found to an extent in any 'good society' are developed here to the extreme. In any 'good society', that is, any society tending to isolate and distinguish itself from the surrounding social field, for example aristocratic or patrician society, the distinctive membership of 'good society' is a foundation of personal identity as of social existence. This varies in degree according to the nature of the 'good society'. Cohesion is less if a 'good society' emerges from a professional-bourgeois field, and greater with a court-aristocratic society. The structural pattern of 'good society', however, the formation of a 'class ethos' is, in varying degrees and with numerous modifications, discernible in them all. If, to obtain a sharply defined picture, we consider a noble 'good society', we see at once how far the individual is dependent on the opinion of the other members. He belongs to the 'good society', no matter what his title, only as long as the others *think* him a member. Social opinion, in other words, has a quite different meaning and function here than it has in a broad bourgeois society. It is the foundation of existence. A telling expression of the importance of social opinion in every 'good society' is the concept of 'honour' and its derivatives. Today, in accordance with the conditions of bourgeois society, it has been transformed and given new content. Originally, 'honour' was the expression of membership of noble society. One had honour as long as one was deemed a member by the society and so by one's own consciousness. To lose one's honour was to forfeit membership of 'good society'. One lost it through the judgement pronounced by social opinion in these rather closed circles, and sometimes by the verdict of special representatives in the form of a court of honour. They judged in terms of a specific noble ethos, central to which was the maintenance of everything that traditionally held the lower-ranking strata at a distance, such things being of self-evident value to the aristocracy.

If such a society refused to recognize a member, if he lost his 'honour', he lost a constitutive element of his personal identity. In reality a noble would often enough risk his life for his 'honour', losing it rather than forfeiting membership of his society, his distinction from the surrounding mass, without which his life, as long as the power of privileged society remained intact, was meaningless.

The 'opinion' that others had of an individual, therefore, often decided by no other means than withdrawal of status, exclusion, boycott, over life and death. The effect and reality possessed by the concerted opinion of members was as immediate as this. We are concerned here with a different type of social 'reality' than exists in bourgeois society. Even in 'good societies' within the latter, the threat of loss of status or membership has by no means lost all its effect. However, capital or professional opportunities can be preserved even if an individual member is ejected. In urban and, especially, big-city societies the individual also has possibilities of escape that deprive social control of much of the menacing authority it has in less mobile rural circles, and still more in the wholly inescapable court elite society of a state with absolute rule.[28] In the estimation of the court aristocracy, as we saw, ownership of capital was finally a means to an end. It was significant primarily as a condition for upholding a social 'reality', the centrepiece of which was distinction from the mass of people, status as members of a privileged class, and behaviour that stressed this distinction in all the situations of life, in short, nobility as a self-evident value.

But as property itself does not yet constitute a social 'reality' independent of the opinion of others, as the recognition of membership by others itself constitutes membership, people's opinion of each other and its expression in behaviour play a special role in this 'good society' as a formative and controlling instrument. For the same reason no member could escape the pressure of opinion without putting at risk his membership, his identity as part of an elite, which was central to his pride and his honour.

This is especially true when the members of a 'good society' are locally unified, as was the case with the French court nobility — unlike the French landed nobility who were thought of as backwoodsmen — and more broadly among the French court society which gathered in Paris or Versailles or wherever the king was residing.

It is true also — with certain restrictions — of 'good society' in England. The member families, the 'good' families of the nobility and of the wealthier bourgeois 'gentry', while usually spending part of the year at their country houses scattered across the country, resided for several months, during the 'season', in their town houses in London. This practice had begun intermittently in the early seventeenth century and become a regular institution by the eighteenth. Here, constituting with their wealth of personal contacts the 'good society' of the country, Society with a capital S, a market of opinion, they mutually passed muster and, in a constant round of social diversions interspersed with the great dramas of the inter-party parliamentary struggles, their individual market value, their reputations, their prestige, in a word their personal social power — in keeping with the code of 'good society' — were exalted, abased or lost. In accordance with the distribution of power in English Society, the court and court society did not by any means form *the* centre; it was at most one of the centres, of 'good society'. Often enough other great aristocratic

---

[28] As an example of a corresponding social formation on a working-class estate, cf. N. Elias and J. Scotson, *The Established and the Outsiders* (London, 1965).

houses outranked them as political and social centres. Parliament and the great drama of the parties within its Houses played a decisive role as an institution integrating the social elites in this political structure.

These connections between the power structure and the structure of noble society and, later, of 'good society', appear no less clearly in Germany. Following the shift of power away from the emperor and towards the territorial rulers, the German nobility did not coalesce to form either a unified, exemplary court society in the French sense, or 'Society' in the English. At least up to 1871, and really up to 1918, regional and local 'good societies', partly grouped around territorial courts and partly country circles of local lords, played a considerable role in German regions as institutions controlling the behaviour, the sense of belonging, and the honour of scattered individuals. In this they were supplemented by the officer corps of leading regiments and the socially prominent students' associations. But although German aristocratic society, compared to the French and English, was more various and chequered, the noble families of the Empire never entirely lost their sense of cohesion and distinction, nor their mutual assessment of status and prestige. But there was no central social elite formation, like the court society of France or Society in England, that might have served as a unifying mould of behaviour and a direct exchange of public opinion on the market value of members — apart from the high nobility which was small enough to permit fairly regular personal contacts across regional and territorial boundaries. Its place was filled mainly by strictly controlled registers of lineage, in book form, and by a kind of education that kept each generation exactly informed on the genealogy, the status in the extensive aristocratic hierarchy, and the current prestige-value of each member family — from the standpoint of their own rank and that of regional social opinion — and finally by numerous informal links between the closely knit regional noble societies. Moreover, the specific forms of exclusivity of many German noble groups, unlike those of Parisian court society or London Society, did not express themselves merely in a strict observance of internal distinctions, but often enough in a total self-encapsulation that excluded bourgeois people from normal social life. This exclusivity prevented the broad permeation of bourgeois circles by aristocratic forms of behaviour that can be observed for a time in both France and England. Only in certain relatively limited areas did upper bourgeois strata take over behaviour values from the nobility, for example a specific notion of 'honour' in the case of officers and students. The traditional denigration of the commercial acquisition of money and of town life was also passed from the nobility to the professional bourgeoisie by fixed forms of speech.

Finally, this heterogeneity of German elite 'good societies' is seen in the absence of a unified order of rank and status even in the urban bourgeois 'good societies'. There were and are many of these in Germany. Even with the rise of Berlin to imperial capital, no single urban 'good society' gained preponderance as the model and centre, membership of which conferred special prestige. Berlin society never had the same uniformity or the same precedence over provincial 'good societies' thát was possessed by London Society, in which elements of the country nobility, the court nobility and the landed and urban bourgeoisie came together. Most of the larger German towns developed, and still possess today, their own bourgeois 'good society'. Each has its own local hierarchy of rank and status. It is possible that an individual family might try to remove itself from one to another, say, from the 'good society' of Münster to the quite differently ordered one in Hamburg. But up to very recently, when this aspect of membership does seem to have changed somewhat, newcomers have usually been accepted only on probation. At any rate, they usually rank lower than the older 'good families'. For the 'age' of a family in terms of long membership and being known and respected is meritorious in any 'good society', a prestige-value that carries much weight in deciding the family's place in the internal hierarchy.

But even if the character and structure of the various 'good societies' in Germany were variable and often quite different, there are, or were until recently — certain uniform criteria of membership. One of the most characteristic of these was, and perhaps still is today, the ability to 'give satisfaction'. The concept of personal honour was first developed in noble circles with a powerful military tradition, an honour that had to be defended weapon in hand against other members of the same class, while non-members are ignored or — as once happened to Voltaire when he challenged a noble who had insulted him to a duel — soundly thrashed by one's servants. This concept of honour spread in Germany to bourgeois circles, particularly those of bourgeois officers and academics. All men, from the members of the high aristocracy down to the bourgeois student and old gentlemen of the corps, from students' *Burschenschaften* and other socially accepted associations to merchants, as long as they were reserve officers, were deemed capable of giving satisfaction. They could not be refused satisfaction by armed combat in case of an insult, no matter from which part of Germany they came. Membership of a 'good society', which in the case of the nobility could be easily checked, was proved for the bourgeois by membership of a certain regiment or association, which often also determined the choice of seconds. The disparateness of the many 'good societies' was here compensated by the fact that they all together formed a society of people capable of giving satisfaction, held together by a network of relatively well-known associations. It was sealed off from the mass of those below to whom one did not need to give satisfaction.

12. This short comparative excursus on differences between 'good societies' in different countries may suffice in this context to give the study of the court society of the *ancien régime* a wider radius of associations. As we can see, it is not here a question of whether or not one approves of the phenomenon of 'good society' or finds one 'good society' better than another. Value-judgements of this kind merely obstruct our view of the 'how' and 'why' of such phenomena. The latter is what concerns us here.

In addition, such comparisons make the particular inescapability of the situation of court people in face of prevalent opinion more easily understandable. In some other 'good societies' there is a degree of freedom to sidestep social opinion. But the court society of the *ancien régime* gave its members no such freedom. For there was no other entity which possessed or was able to confer comparable prestige. The courtier had no possibility of changing place, leaving Paris or Versailles and continuing his life elsewhere without loss of prestige or self-respect. Only in this one court society could its members preserve what gave them direction and purpose in their own eyes, their social existence as court people, their aloofness from all else, their prestige — the centre of their self-image and of their personal identity. *They went to court not only because they were dependent on the king; they remained dependent on the king because it was only by going to court and living within court society that they could preserve the distance from everything else on which their spiritual salvation, their prestige as court aristocrats, in short, their social existence and their personal identity depended.* Had they been concerned primarily with wealth, they could have reached their goal far better by pursuing a commercial or financial activity. But as they were concerned primarily with maintaining their elite character and their rank in court society, they could not escape going to court and forever depending *directly* on the king. Nor, consequently, did they have any possibility of escaping the pressure of court opinion. Just because they were inescapably tied to this society as long as they could not bear to renounce their social existence as aristocrats, the opinion of other court people, and the behaviour expressing it, had the extraordinary significance that has been discussed.

If it was the necessity of maintaining his distance from the outside world that fettered each court person to the court and propelled him into its bustle, within the society he was constantly driven on by the intense competition. In terms of its decisive motivation this was a competition for prestige. But, as the chances of gaining it were exactly graded in this hierarchical society, the competition was not for prestige as such but for *graduated* prestige or power. For the greater or lesser prestige a person enjoys within a figuration — his stock — is an expression of his weight in the multipolar equilibrium of tensions comprising it, his greater or lesser opportunity of influencing others or being subjected to their influence.

Everything that played any part in the relations between people became an opportunity for gaining prestige in this society. Rank, inherited office and the age of one's 'house' conferred prestige. The money one owned or received imparted prestige. The king's favour, influence with his mistress or the ministers, membership of a special clique, military achievements, wit, good manners, beauty of face and so on, all these endowed a person with prestige, combined in an individual and determined his place in the immanent order of rank of court society.

13. In this a peculiarity of the court way of evaluating and behaving is expressed, which Saint-Simon once defined as follows: what matters at court is not the thing itself but what it means in relation to certain people.[29] Again we see the meaning that etiquette and ceremonial had for the court nobility. This apparatus is apt to appear meaningless to us because we miss in it a practical use or purpose outside itself to which it relates, just as we tend to judge each person in terms of his objective function. But court society, as we have seen, put the emphasis in exactly the opposite place. While we like to objectify or reify everything personal, court people personify the objective; for it was always with people and their positions relative to each other that they were primarily concerned. In their etiquette, too, they did not come together for etiquette's sake. To enact their existence, to demonstrate their prestige, to distance themselves from lower-ranking people and have this distance recognized by the higher-ranking — all this was purpose enough in itself. But in etiquette this *distancing of oneself from others as an end in itself* finds its consum-

[29] 'On ne juge jamais des choses par ce qu'elles sont, mais par les personnes qu'elles regardent.' Saint-Simon, *Mémoires*, vol. 10, ch. 185.

mate expression. It constituted an action of court society within which the graduated opportunities of prestige it offered were assembled together. And the performers demonstrated that they were the holders of these opportunities, made visible the distancing relationship that both united them and distinguished them from each other, and so publicly certified the order of rank they accorded each other.

The practice of etiquette is, in other words, an exhibition of court society to itself. Each participant, above all the king, has his prestige and his relative power position confirmed by others. Social opinion, which constitutes the prestige of the individual, is expressed by reciprocal behaviour within a communal action according to certain rules. And in this communal action each individual's existential bond to society is directly visible. Without confirmation of one's prestige through behaviour, this prestige is nothing. The immense value attached to the demonstration of prestige and the observance of etiquette does not betray an attachment to externals, but to what was vitally important to individual identity.

But as each society always makes the finest and most elaborate distinctions in the sphere which for it is most vitally important, we find in court society a wealth and subtlety of nuances that is alien to a bourgeois society accustomed to making its distinctions in quite different spheres. The exactitude with which each ceremony is organized, the care with which the prestige-value of each step is weighed, matches the vital importance etiquette and behaviour have for court people.

It will be shown in the next section why the king subjected not only the nobles but himself to etiquette. The intention here is to make comprehensible the motivations and compulsions that caused the court nobility to bind themselves to etiquette and so to the court. The *primary* compulsion did not arise from the exercise of political functions; for such functions were largely blocked to the French nobility. Nor did it stem from the opportunities of gaining wealth available at court, for there were better opportunities elsewhere. The primary compulsion sprang from these people's need to assert their position as court aristocrats, in contra-distinction to the despised country nobility, to the nobility of office and to the people, and to maintain or increase the prestige they had once attained. A brief example will illustrate these ideas.

In an army camp the King of England, some Spanish grandees and a French prince have come together. The French prince is thoroughly displeased with the unceremonious manner of the Spaniards towards the English king. He decides to teach them a lesson. He invites them as guests with the king. They enter the rooms together and, to the guests' astonishment, see a table covered with dishes but laid for only one person. A single chair is present. The French prince asks the English king to be seated. The other guests have to remain standing and the French prince, standing behind the king's chair, is about to serve him. This is what French ceremonial required. The king ate alone, high nobles waited on him. Others stood at a proper distance. The English king protested, the Spaniards were furious at the affront. The host assured them that after the king had eaten in a fitting way, the other guests would find a well-laid table in another room. We understand that this prince desires the compulsion of etiquette; his abasement and distance vis-à-vis the king, which the latter as an Englishman does not demand, is for the Frenchman a confirmation of his own existence as a prince. He wishes to uphold etiquette, even where it is not imposed from above, because a failure to maintain his distance from the king threatens him with a failure by lower-ranking people to keep theirs from him.

14. One layer of the personal and social mesh in which court people live has now been removed. That this does not consist primarily of specialized economic interdependences has become clear, even though economic compulsions also impinge, of course, on the structure of court life. The desire for distance and prestige is not to be explained here by a desire for economic opportunities, even though it is made possible by a certain economic situation. The estate-ethos of court people is not a disguised economic ethos, but something different in nature. To exist in the lustre of aloofness and prestige, i.e. to exist as a court person, is, for a court person, an end in itself.

We find here an attitude the sociological analysis of which has a significance transcending our immediate theme. Of every fairly stable elite group, caste or social stratum that is exposed to pressure from below and often from above as well, it can be said — and will be stated explicitly here as a structural *regularity* of such units — that, to the people comprising it, their mere existence as members of an elite social unit is, partly or absolutely, a value and end in itself. The maintenance of distance thus becomes a decisive motor or matrix of their behaviour. The value of this existence needs no justification for the people involved, above all no utilitarian explanation. They do not seek a wider meaning transcending this existence. And wherever elitist tendencies are present in a society, the same phenomenon manifests itself.

The whole thinking of such elite units is determined by this structural law, this self-sufficiency of mere social existence, this unreflecting existentialism. The symbols or ideas in which such social units express the goals or motivation of their behaviour therefore always have the character of prestige-fetishes. They contain, concentrated within themselves, the whole prestige which this society lays claim to as an elite.

In this context if may be enough to refer once more to the symbol of 'honour' as a motive of action. The compulsion which it exerts is that which maintains its bearer's social distance. Honour is self-explanatory, transfiguring the existence of its bearer and needing no justification by anything outside itself. But elements of the estate ethos that we distinguish — by the example of court motivation through 'honour' or 'prestige' — from the economic ethos of bourgeois strata, can permeate the latter ethos under certain conditions. As soon as exclusive, elitist tendencies appear in bourgeois strata, they also express themselves in prestige symbols directed at maintaining the group's distance from others, while transfiguring its existence. In these symbols the group's existence is presented as an end in itself surrounded by its aura of prestige, even though in the case of bourgeois strata utilitarian values and economic interests mingle with the prestige-values. It is therefore of interest to examine the structure of court society from this point of view. For motivation by prestige, which appears today as one motivation among others and usually not as the primary one, still has total primacy in court society. Here the estate ethos is still quite distinct from the economic ethos of bourgeois strata.

Etiquette must also be understood, therefore, from contexts of this kind. It needs no utilitarian justification. *In it court society represents itself, each individual being distinguished from every other, all together distinguishing themselves from non-members, so that each individual and the group as a whole confirm their existence as a value in itself.*[30]

15. 'Life at Court is a serious, melancholy game, which requires us to draw up our pieces and batteries, form a plan, pursue it, parry that of our adversary, sometimes take risks and play capriciously; and

---

[30] As this section also constitutes a contribution to *the sociology of prestige*, reference will be made in conclusion to a book devoted likewise to prestige, Ludwig Leopold, *Prestige* (Berlin, 1916). The author approaches his subject from different assumptions and with different intentions, so that it could not be made use of in *this* context. As a general characterization of prestige, Leopold notes 'that it belongs to the world of feelings and manifests itself practically in acts of submission and in omissions'. The planes of the two studies do not intersect.

after all our dreams and measures we are in check, sometimes checkmate.'[31]

Life in court society was not peaceful. The number of people permanently and inescapably bound to one circle was large. They pressed on each other, struggled for prestige, for their place in the hierarchy. The affairs, intrigues, conflicts over rank and favour knew no end. Everyone depended on everyone else, and all on the king. Each could harm each. He who rode high today was cast down tomorrow. There was no security. Everyone had to seek alliances with others whose stock was high, avoid unnecessary enmities, fight unavoidable enemies with cold calculation, and scrupulously maintain towards all others the degree of distance befitting their status.[32]

In keeping with this structure, court society developed different aspects of its members from those of bourgeois industrial society. Some of them are enumerated below:

(i) The art of observing people

This is not 'psychology' in the scientific sense, but an ability, growing out of the necessities of life at court, to understand the make-up, motives, capacities and limits of other people. One must see how these people meticulously weigh the gestures and expressions of everyone else, carefully fathom the intention and meaning of each of their utterances.

One example in place of many:

'I soon noticed,' Saint-Simon writes of someone, 'that he was becoming cold; I followed his conduct towards me with my eye to avoid confusing what might be accidental in a man charged with delicate affairs with what I suspected. My suspicions became certainties that caused me to withdraw entirely from him while giving nothing away.'[33]

This courtly art of human observation is all the closer to reality because it never attempts to consider the individual person in isolation, as a being deriving his essential regularities and characteristics from within. Rather, the individual is always observed in court society in his social context, as a *person in relation to others*. Here, too,

[31] La Bruyère, *Caractères*, 'De la Cour'.
[32] 'Let a favourite observe himself very closely; for if he keeps me waiting less than usual in his antechamber, if his face is more open, less frowning, if he listens to me more willingly or accompanies me farther to the door, I shall think he is beginning to fall and I shall be right.' La Bruyère, *Caractères*, 'De la Cour'.
[33] Saint-Simon, *Mémoires*, vol. 18, ch. 31.

the completely social orientation of court people is manifested. But the art of human observation is applied not only to others but to the observer himself. A specific form of *self-observation* develops. 'Let a favourite observe himself closely,' as La Bruyère says.[34] This self-observation and the observation of other people are complementary. One would be pointless without the other. We are not concerned here with a religious self-observation that contemplates the inner self as an isolated being to discipline its hidden impulses, but with observation of oneself with a view to self-discipline in social life: 'A man who knows the court is master of his gestures, of his eyes and of his face; he is profound, impenetrable; he dissimulates bad offices, smiles at his enemies, controls his irritation, disguises his passions, belies his heart, speaks and acts against his feelings.'

Moreover, there is nothing here that might incline a person to deceive himself concerning his own motives. On the contrary. Just as he is forced to seek the true motives of others behind their controlled outward behaviour, just as he is lost if he is unable to unmask the affects and interests of his rivals behind their dispassionate facades, he must know his own passions if he is conceal them effectively. It was not only in the sphere of bourgeois-capitalist competition that the idea of egoism as a motive of human action was formed, but first of all in the competition at court, and from the latter came the first unveiled descriptions of the human affects in modern times. La Rochefoucauld's *Maxims* are one example.

Accompanying the act of observing people is that of *describing* them. Books and therefore writing had a quite different meaning for the courtier from that which they have for us. The court writer's intention was not to justify or causally explain the self by analysis or description. What was said above on the attitude of court people towards themselves applies here too. Description was a value in itself that neither needed nor allowed explanation or justification.

The court person expressed himself primarily in speech and in a particular kind of action, and his books, too, are nothing other than direct organs of social life,[35] a part of the conversations and social

---

[34] Cf. p. 134, n. 32.

[35] That the court-aristocracy was not fertile ground for literature and scholarship, which did not satisfy the demands of court life and the need for social distinction, is easily understood. The forms of literature and knowledge characteristic of court society match its specific needs and demands. They are above all memoirs, collections of letters, aphorisms ('maxims'), certain kinds of lyric poetry; i.e. literary forms that grow directly or indirectly out of the incessant conversation of society. In addition, after the mid-eighteenth century, there is a pursuit of certain forms of knowledge the possession of which could give the courtier a special reputation in

games or, like the majority of court memoirs, conversations prevented by the absence of a partner, for whatever reason. And so the attitude these people adopted in life is particularly well preserved in court books.

As the observation of people was a vital art for court people, it is understandable that the art of describing people is brought to a high pitch of perfection in court memoirs, letters and aphorisms.

The way opened for French writers and literature by these conditions was pursued in France, for reasons which cannot be studied here but were connected with the survival of a French 'good society' as a direct heir of court attitudes beyond the Revolution, by a number of writers up to very recent times. [36]

(ii) The art of dealing with people

The courtly art of observing people arises, as we have said, not from a delight in theorizing, but from the direct necessities of social

society and so an expectation of a court or diplomatic office. Thus the later Cardinal Bernis, for example, said in his memoirs (trans. by Konrad, Munich and Leipzig, 1917): 'The study of history, of happiness and morality [morality in court society is knowledge of the manners and character of people; expressions such as "French moralists of the seventeenth century" have this meaning] was from now on my only occupation; for I wanted *imperceptibly to accustom people to regarding me as serious, a man suited to affairs*' (in the diplomatic service). Also characteristic in this context is the following quotation from these memoirs of Cardinal Bernis, who himself came from an old seignorial family (cf. p. 57): 'It must be admitted that the *grandseigneurs* of today are less ignorant than those of the good old days. One even not infrequently meets a good writer among them; on the other hand, one used to find able commanders and astute ministers among the earlier ones, many of whom could hardly read or write. *It is not books that make great men, but events, nobility of soul and a sense of honour.*' Which forms of literature and scholarship were and were not germane to this society can be seen especially clearly from a letter like the following. It was written by Mme de Staal, the caustic and acute lady in waiting of the Duchess of Maine. One day Voltaire and his companion Mme du Châtelet arrive on a journey at Anet, the duchess's residence, late at night. They are found accommodation with some difficulty, but do not show themselves at all the next day. 'They arrived here,' Mme de Staal writes on 15 August 1747 to the Marquise du Deffant, 'at 10 o'clock last night. I doubt whether we shall see much of them today. One is writing about High Events [it was *The Century of Louis XV*], the other on Newton. They wish neither to play nor to go for walks. *To be sure, they are a pair of non-entities in a society with which their learned writings have no connection.*' And on 20 August 1747 Mme de Staal writes of Mme du Châtelet: 'She persists in only showing herself at night. Voltaire has written some *gallant verses* [including an "Epitre à Mme la duchesse du Maine sur la victoire remportée le 2 juillet à Laweld"] *which have slightly repaired the ill-effects of their unusual conduct.*' Learned writings have no connection with the life of this society. They keep people away from society, and this is improper. But 'gallant verses' have a place here. With them Voltaire atones for his and his companion's misconduct; this throws as much light on the sociology of Voltaire as on the forms of literature and learning characteristic of court-seignoral society which, unfortunately, cannot be given the interpretation they deserve here.

[36] But at least one line of development can be traced: from the human observation of Saint-Simon a straight line runs through Balzac, Flaubert and Maupassant to Marcel Proust, for whom 'good society' provided at once a sphere of life, a field of observation, and material for his book.

existence. The observation of people provided the foundation for dealing with them, and vice versa. One proved its worth in the other, and each fertilized the other. Therefore, the way in which one deals with a person is carefully calculated on the basis of one's purposes. An example may serve to illustrate this strategy. It concerns a conversation between Saint-Simon and the dauphin of the time, the grandson of Louis XIV.[37] Saint-Simon's concern was to show the future king the depreciation his caste, the dukes and peers, had to endure from above and below, from the princes of the blood and the king on one side and the ministers on the other.

Saint-Simon proceeds as follows:

> My main intention was to sound him on everything concerning our dignity. I therefore gently broke off any subject that led away from this goal, bringing the conversation back to all the different chapters of this theme. . . . I touched on the points where I had noticed him sensitive to such matters. . . .[38] I reminded him of the strange novelty of the Elector of Bavaria's pretensions with Monseigneur. . . . I suggested to him the natural thoughts on the extreme wrong that tolerance of these abuses did to the kings and their crown. . . . I showed him very clearly that the steps of this downfall were our own. . . .[39]
>
> I then came to the comparison with the Spanish grandees and the dukes and peers, which gave me a fine field. . . . Voyaging then to England, to the northern kings and throughout Europe, I showed without difficulty that France alone, of all the states of Europe, suffers in the person of its great ones what no other land has ever tolerated. . . . The Dauphin, actively attentive, appreciated all my reasons, frequently finished my arguments for me, was avidly impressed by all these truths. They were discussed in an agreeable and instructive way. . . . The Dauphin . . . was inflamed[40] . . . and groaned at the ignorance and lack of reflection of the King. I only touched on these diverse matters in presenting them in turn to the Dauphin. I then followed him, leaving him the pleasure of speaking, showing me that he was educated, and allowing him to persuade himself, to become heated while I observed his sentiments, his way of thinking and receiving impressions, in order to profit from this knowledge and so increase his conviction and indignation further. But having done this on

---

[37] Saint-Simon, *Mémoires*, vol. 18, ch. 106, pp. 11ff.

[38] In other words, he touched first on points where the dauphin's own interest is at stake.

[39] He shows the dauphin that his own interests and those of Saint-Simon's caste were damaged by the same opponents.

[40] How typical this approach is can be seen from the following maxim of Gratian in his Hand Oracle: 'The safety of prudence resides in inner moderation. The traps set for discretion are those calling for contradiction, explanation and sharp words that inflame.' From French translation by de la Houssaie (Paris, 1691), p. 217, Maxim 179.

every matter, I tried less to press the arguments and parentheses than to lead him on to other subjects, in order to show a moderation that might appeal to his reason, his justice, his conviction arrived at by himself, and his trust, and to have the time to sound him on all points, and to *impregnate him gently and thoroughly with my feelings and views on all these matters. . . .*

There is much in this conversation that is typical of the situation of the times: the noble in opposition seeks to form an alliance with the crown prince whose own position inclines him to an oppositional stance. The procedure is dangerous, particularly for Saint-Simon. He must carefully feel out the prince's attitude to see how far he can go. But the way he does so is also typical of the courtly way of dealing with people in general. Saint-Simon's account reveals the extraordinarily deliberate way he pursues his goal, and at the same time his pleasure in the art with which he performs the task. It shows clearly why it is those of relatively low rank who become masters of the tactics of conversation. As we said, he is the one most at risk in such a conversation. The prince can always break the rules of courtly conversation; he can, if he likes, break off the discussion and the relationship for any reason he chooses without losing much. For Saint-Simon, however, very much depends on the outcome of such a conversation, and it is therefore vitally important to him to proceed with an extreme control and deliberation that are not apparent to his interlocutor. In this situation a person whose inner concentration is revealed by outward tension is at a disadvantage. To lead one's higher-ranking interlocutor almost imperceptibly where one wishes is the prime requirement of this courtly manner of dealing with people. Gestures pointing directly or indirectly to one's own cleverness, which may at times be useful in conversation between relatively independent and equal-ranking people, for example businessmen or professional colleagues, are strictly prohibited here. 'Never speak of oneself,' one of Gratian's maxims is headed.[41] This reflects the necessity to be always aware not only of one's partner's general social situation and its implications for the conversation, but also of the changing relationship between the partners during the conversation. The art of what, with a characteristic narrowing of meaning, we call 'diplomacy' is thus cultivated in the everyday life of court society. The conversation of Saint-Simon with the dauphin is a revealing example. The qualities that are today required only from the external representatives of a country — though they are also increasingly

---

[41] *Ibid.*, Maxim 117.

needed in negotiations between large concerns or parties — are forcibly produced by hierarchical 'good society' in each of its members. The degree to which this happens depends on the society's structure.

This discussion of the courtly way of dealing with people also illuminates — for people from professional society and particularly for Germans — the emphasis on the 'how' rather than the 'what' of any procedure, both in court society and in the French society strongly influenced by it. The roots of this concern for 'externals' in the structure of this society were disclosed earlier. What we think of as 'external', as 'formalism', is nothing other than an expression of the primacy of the relationship of all things and events to the status or power of the *person* involved in relation to others. In this sense the behaviour quite inadequately termed 'formalism' turns out to be the opposite of the objectified or reified bourgeois attitude where the 'what' has primacy over the 'how', and where, at least ostensibly, the 'matter in hand' means everything, and the 'person', and therefore the 'form' of behaviour addressed to this person, mean very little.

Something similar, from a different aspect, is seen in the conversation between Saint-Simon and the dauphin. In this conversation Saint-Simon's tactics are always directed at securing greater influence and power by winning the trust and support of the dauphin. What appears to be the 'matter in hand', his complaint over the depreciation of his caste, is at the same time something highly 'personal'. But just because, for Saint-Simon, in keeping with the structure of court society, it is only possible to gain influence if he carefully analyses the person he is trying to influence — his interests and his own desire to wield influence — for these reasons the 'how' of behaviour takes on the special importance and elaboration it has here. The goal of this and similar conversations is never only an objective purpose, for example to sign an agreement, but it is always also to establish a certain relationship between the two partners. To this extent this way of dealing with people is never *only* a means to an end, but is always in part an end in itself. The form and tactics of the encounter[42] require a constant testing of the power-relationship between the partners

[42] Cf. Gratian, *op. cit.*, Maxim 14, 'La chose et la manière': 'The *substance* is not enough, circumstance also is needed. A poor manner spoils everything, disfigures even justice and reason. A fine manner, by contrast, adds to everything; it gilds a refusal, softens the bitterness that lies in truth, smooths the wrinkles of age. The "how" does much in all matters . . . the zeal of a minister, the valour of a captain, the learning of a man of letters, the power of a Prince are not enough, unless accompanied by this important formality. But there is no occupation where it is more necessary than in government. In superiors it is a great means of engaging loyalty to be more human than despotic. To see a Prince giving precedence to humanity is a double obligation to love him.'

which, if both their interests are satisfied, can become a relatively permanent relationship.

The bourgeois person, too, the businessman for example, has his tactics and his specific way of dealing with people. He is seldom concerned with the person as a whole to the same extent as the courtier. For the latter stands by and large in a lifelong relationship with every other member of his society. All these court people are, to a greater or lesser extent, depending on their place in court society, inescapably dependent on each other as friends, enemies or relatively neutral parties. They must therefore observe extreme caution at each encounter with each other. Prudence or reserve are dominant features in their dealings with each other. Because every relationship in this society is necessarily permanent, a single unconsidered utterance can have a permanent effect. Bourgeois people, by contrast, usually deal with each other over far more specific and short-lived purposes. The other person is of interest primarily in direct or indirect connection with a certain objective present at each meeting, and only secondarily as a person. The relationship comes quickly to an end if the material opportunities each offers to the other no longer seem favourable enough. In professional dealings between people, therefore, unlike court ones, the impermanence of the human relationship is of decisive importance. Permanent relationships are confined to private life. And, as we know, even the ostensibly indissoluble private relationships in bourgeois society are being increasingly encroached upon by the general impermanence and mutability of personal relationships within the professional sphere.

(iii) Court rationality (restraint of the affects for the sake of certain vital interests)

What is considered 'rational' depends at any time on the structure of society. What we reify as 'reason' comes into being whenever adaptation to a particular society and survival within it demand a specific foresight or calculation and therefore a constraint of short-term individual affects. The quantifying form of foresight or rationality constitutes only a special case of a more comprehensive phenomenon. That rationality is characteristic not only of Western bourgeois man was shown by Max Weber in his essays on the sociology of religion. What has not yet been stressed clearly enough, however, is that even in the West there have been and probably still are, beside bourgeois-capitalist rationality, other types of rationality born of different social necessities.

We come upon one of these non-bourgeois types of rationality in studying the court. A number of examples of specifically court rationality have already been given; the exact calculation of the degree and kind of decoration appropriate to a house, the structure of the *lever* and of etiquette in general, the king's self-possession towards Saint-Simon at the *coucher*, and so on. [43]

Why this attitude becomes important to court people is easily seen: affective outbursts are difficult to control and calculate. They reveal the true feelings of the person concerned to a degree that, because not calculated, can be damaging; they hand over trump cards to rivals for favour and prestige. Above all, they are a sign of weakness; and that is the position the court person fears most of all. *In this way the competition of court life enforces a curbing of the affects in favour of calculated and finely shaded behaviour in dealing with people.* The structure of social life within this figuration left relatively little room for spontaneous expressions of feeling. To make the dealings of people with each other calculable, as was shown above, an analogous means was used to that by which a work-process is made calculable in economic society: it was not left to tradition, chance or the whims of individuals. It was made independent of changing individualities and the fluctuations of their private personal relationships; it was organized and broken down into partial processes. Through organization it could be supervised and controlled; as everything always happened in the same way independently of the fluctuations of individuality, the whole was predictable; and by the division into partial processes it was possible to define exactly the prestige-value of every step in court society, like money-value in capitalist society. The intensive elaboration of etiquette, ceremony, taste, dress, manners and even conversation had the same function. Every detail here was an ever-ready instrument in the prestige struggle and this elaboration served not only for demonstrative display and the conquest of status and power, that is, external distancing, it also created graduated internal distances.

Bourgeois-industrial rationality is generated by the compulsion of the economic mesh; by it power-opportunities founded on private or public capital are made calculable. Court rationality is generated by the compulsion of the elite social mesh; by it people and prestige are made calculable as instruments of power.

16. The relationship between the social and personality structures that emerges here has far-reaching consequences which are outlined below.

---

[43] Cf. the quotation from La Bruyère on p. 104, n. 32.

The artistic style that we call 'Classicism' is an expression of the same attitude. The precise, cool and clear structuring, the careful calculation of effect and prestige, the absence of any uncalculated ornament, any scope for uncontrolled emotional release, all this reappears here. The same is true of the French Classical drama. First, it is an integral part of social life at court, not a leisure activity. The spectators sit on the stage, filling the background and sides. What is performed shows the same measured deliberation of structure that is characteristic of court life as a whole. Passions may be strong; passionate outbursts are frowned upon. It is not primarily the content of the play that matters — they are nearly all concerned with well-known material — but the delicacy of the way the protagonists master their fate, resolve their conflicts, just as in the court society exemplary for all upper classes the manner in which a person masters a situation was always of decisive importance. And in keeping with the general exclusion from court life of all actions that were not embodied in words, as conversation, what we find represented in French Classical drama, unlike the English, is not actions as such, but conversations and declamations about actions that are usually not seen by the audience.

This connection between court rationality and Classicism, which deserves to be treated in a separate study, is not seen only in France. In modified form it is no less true of German Classicism. The culture of Weimar is the only really significant court culture that Germans have produced in recent times. Here too we find, admittedly in the context of a quite different relationship of rising bourgeois strata to the court than in seventeenth-century France, a good many of the court characteristics we have referred to, at least as ideals: the serenity, the moderation of the affects, the calm and circumspection and not least the specific solemnity by which court people stood out from the mass. [44]

In addition, court rationality produces a number of counter-movements even within court society itself, attempts to emancipate 'feeling', which are always at the same time attempts to emancipate the individual from social pressure, but which in seventeenth-century France always end, outwardly at least, in defeat (for example, Mme Guyon, Fénélon, etc.). Through these counter-movements we see how important it is to find out how far the structure of a social field allows the free expression of 'feeling', in which direction this is chan-

[44] One needs only to compare the pre-courtly with the courtly Goethe to see these connections more clearly. However, we should not forget that Weimar was a very small and in some respects almost a bourgeois court.

nelled, and how far the emancipation of 'feeling' is punished by social downfall or at least degradation. For the latter is the case at court.

It will not be possible to understand Rousseau and his influence, the possibility of his success even within the *monde*, unless he is seen as expressing a reaction to court rationality and to the suppression of 'feeling' in court life. From this side, too, an exact analysis of the relaxation that took place during the eighteenth century in the *monde* illuminates the structural changes in certain psychological strata, though not in all, that made possible a degree of emancipation of spontaneous emotional impulses, accompanied by a theoretical assertion of the autonomy of 'feeling'.

Finally it should be pointed out that the conscious intellectual rationalism of the seventeenth and eighteenth centuries that we often refer to by the inexact term 'Enlightenment' is not solely to be understood in relation to bourgeois capitalist rationalism, since it has strong links to court rationality. These would be relatively easy to demonstrate in Leibniz, for example. But in Voltaire, too, these links with court rationality are not difficult to discern.

When we see some of the 'basic personality characteristics' or, as it is sometimes expressed, the 'spirit' of court people, emerging from the social figuration they form together; when we understand how they and their modes of expression developed most intensely and subtly in a quite different sphere and in a quite different direction to ours, because this sphere was of vital importance to them, something of the evolutionary curve leading from that human type to ours becomes visible, and what we have gained and lost in this transformation.

17. The forms of life and the possibilities of experience which the *ancien régime* harboured in its court and court society are as inaccessible to most members of industrial society as are the simpler societies with which ethnologists are concerned. As can be seen, it costs some effort merely to call them back in thought. Even the few Western courts of our own day are fundamentally different from the courts and court societies of the seventeenth and eighteenth centuries. They are organs of a bourgeois society. Nevertheless, many of the forms that the court society of those centuries imparted to people and their environment, whether it be furniture, pictures or clothes, forms of greeting or social etiquette, theatre, poetry or houses, live on in the nineteenth and twentieth centuries. But it was a peculiarly ghostly transformation that the heritage of court society underwent in the bourgeois age. This heritage was coarsened in a specific way by the

new mass society and emptied of its original meaning.[45]

For the court, and the 'good society' of the *ancien régime* centred around it, was the last relatively closed social formation in the West, the members of which did not work or calculate their affairs in rational economic terms. They were, if we may describe their mode of income in this way, essentially *rentier* formations. And their members not only had the time and inclination to cultivate spheres of life which in the nineteenth century, with the increasing differentiation of life into professional and private spheres under the pressure of rational economics, were relegated to private life; they were compelled by the necessities of court society to do so. For the members of the ruling stratum in the *ancien régime*, elegance of manner and good taste as prescribed by their mature social tradition were made possible by their *rentier* income and necessary by social convention and competition, if they were to be accepted and to prosper in their society.

The bourgeois people of the nineteenth century were shaped above all by the necessities of a profession demanding regulated work and subjection of the affects to routine. People's attitudes and relationships were now influenced primarily by their profession; here lay the centre of the compulsions which social interdependence exerted on the individual. Not only were the qualities and the forms of behaviour which society developed in its individual members changed by this, but most of the attitudes and relationships which in the *ancien régime* had been carefully moulded under the prevailing pressures now existed in a sphere which no longer lay at the formative centre of social influence. For those making up the *bonne compagnie* of the *ancien régime*, the tasteful arrangement of house and park, the more elegant or more intimate decoration of rooms according to fashion and social convention, or the refined cultivation of relations between men and women, were not only amusements enjoyed by individuals, but vital necessities of social life. Competence in these fields was a prerequisite for social esteem, which professional success brings today. Only by contemplating these non-working court people who lived on private means can we understand what the split in the new social life between the professional and private spheres has meant in terms of the make-up of later people, and the way the heritage from the preceding centuries has been assimilated. Almost everything that shaped court society in the seventeenth and eighteenth centuries, whether it be dance, the nuances of greeting, the

---

[45] Thus transformed, it became in many cases a basic element of the style of life that is commonly referred to — mistakenly, if in an entirely pejorative sense — by the term *Kitsch*.

forms of conviviality, the pictures decorating the houses, the gestures of courtship or the *lever* of a lady, all this moved more and more into the sphere of private life. It thereby ceased to be at the centre of the tendencies shaping society. Of course, the private life of bourgeois people was not untouched by social pressures. But it received the social moulding that imparts security and confidence only indirectly, from the sphere in which people were not primarily interrelated, the professional situation. The forms of behaviour imposed by professional life were subject to quite different constraints to those affecting private life. It was mainly these which were now moulded, cultivated and calculated.

The *bonne compagnie* centred around the court of the *ancien régime* developed in its members, like any other society, only certain aspects among the unlimited variety of possible human forms. Its members were, like all people, limited in their development — leaving aside individual limitations — by the factors specific to this social field. But this field not only limited them, but intensely encompassed their whole being. To express it quite simply, the people of this society did not stand for ten or twelve hours a day in the glare of public life and then withdraw to a more private sphere in which behaviour, while influenced by public, professional concerns, is formed above all by the impersonal statute book and a conscience shaped primarily by professional success and professional work.

Undoubtedly, such a division is already visible in the eighteenth century and among less influential classes even earlier, but in its fullest extent it became possible only within urban mass society. Only here could the individual, while remaining within the framework of social control, to an extent withdraw himself from it. At any rate, for the people of court society in the seventeenth and eighteenth centuries such a division, in the broadest sense of the word, did not yet exist. The success or failure of behaviour was not decided in the professional sphere, then influencing private life, but behaviour at any time and every day could decide a person's place in society, could mean social success or failure. And in this sense the formative tendencies of society extended equally to all spheres of human behaviour. It was in this sense that society encompassed the whole being of its members.

This peculiarity of the earlier society, to which we shall return frequently, is of equal importance in understanding the past and, by antithesis, the present. The slowly emerging character of bourgeois mass society contrasts sharply with it. *In it the professional sphere is the primary area in which social constraints and formative tendencies impinge on people.* The form of private life, certainly, is affected by its dependence on the professional situation. Nevertheless, individual behaviour here is not shaped with the same intensity as in court-aristocratic society, whose members had no 'professions' and knew no separation between professional and private spheres in the present-day sense. People in bourgeois mass society generally know very exactly how they have to behave within their professional spheres. The stamp of society is set primarily on professional behaviour. It is here that social pressures begin to act; but everything that is assigned to the sphere of private behaviour, whether it be domestic living, courtship or artistic taste, food or festivities, receives its decisive shaping no longer directly and autonomously from convivial life, but indirectly and often heteronomously, as a function of professional situations and interests. These may be the interests of those whose private lives they fill, or of those whose professional function is to fill the leisure time of others, and are usually a combination of these two tendencies. [46]

---

[46] In the more developed industrial societies professional time is slowly shortening and private time lengthening. It is perhaps too early to investigate what influence this shift is having on the make-up of people in general and on conscience in particular, or will have if it continues in the same direction. A preliminary study to a theory of leisure activity is to be found in N. Elias and E. Dunning, 'The Quest for Excitement in Leisure', *Society and Leisure*, no. 2, 1969.

·VI·

The bonding of kings through etiquette and status chances

1. If one is inclined at first sight to explain the sociology of etiquette by the dependence of the nobility on the prince, on closer inspection a more complex state of affairs emerges. The nobility's need for distinction, on which they depend for their existence, serves the king's need for power. The threatened elite group's desire for social distance is the point at which the king can exert leverage on them. The aristocracy's desire to survive and the king's task of governing interlock like the links of a chain encircling the nobility.

If a court person said: I care nothing for distinction, *considération*, *valeur*, *honneur*, and whatever else the symbols of prestige and distance were called, the chain was broken.

But the interlinking goes further. The king himself — for many reasons that will be discussed in detail — had an interest in maintaining the nobility as a distinguished and separate class. For the time being it may be enough to point out that he regarded himself as a 'nobleman', as the 'first noble'. It was said at court: 'Il est fou ou le roi n'est pas noble.' To let the nobility decay would have meant for the king to let the nobility of his own house decay. And this simultaneous distance from the nobility as its ruler and membership of the nobility as a nobleman determined both the king's place in etiquette and the importance he attached to it.

Everything that became visible in etiquette from the standpoint of the nobility reappears if we examine it from that of the king; distance as an aim in itself, rationality, a cultivation of nuances, control of the affects. But as seen by the king all this has a different purpose to the one described above. Etiquette for the king is an instrument not only of distancing but of power. Louis XIV expressed this very clearly in his memoirs (II, 15):

> Those people are gravely mistaken who imagine that all this is mere ceremony. The people over whom we rule, unable to see to the bottom

117

of things, usually judge by what they see from outside, and most often it is by precedence and rank that they measure their respect and obedience. As it is important to the public to be governed only by a single one, it also matters to it that the person performing this function should be so elevated above the others, that no-one can be confused or compared with him; and one cannot, without doing harm to the whole body of the state, deprive its head of the least mark of superiority distinguishing it from the limbs.

This, then, is the meaning of etiquette for Louis XIV himself. In power that may exist but is not visible in the appearance of the ruler the people do not believe. They must see in order to believe.[1] The more a prince distances himself, the greater will be the respect shown to him by the people.

For a court nobility which no longer has any governing functions, this distancing is an end in itself. It is the same for the king too; for he considers himself and his existence as the purpose of the state.

'Earlier,' wrote a member of the opposition,[2] 'one spoke only of the interests of the state, the needs of the state, the upholding of the state. Today it would be *lèse-majesté* to do so. The King has usurped the place of the state, the King is everything, the state nothing. He is the idol to which the provinces, the towns, finance, the great and the small — in short, everything — is sacrificed.'

As for his nobles, for Louis XIV his own existence as king is an end in itself. But this implies a monopoly of rule as one of his attributes. If on one hand, therefore, the king saw etiquette as a means to the end of ruling, ruling in its turn was finally a means to an end comprised by himself, his existence, his fame, his honour. The most visible expression of this total focusing of rule on the king's person and his elevation and distinction, is etiquette.

2. One cannot understand an instrument of power without considering the structure of the sphere for which it is intended. This gives rise to a particular task for the sociologist: the court must be studied as a structure of rule that prescribed, like any other, quite specific ways of ruling to the person wishing to control it. To be sure, the court was only a segment of the larger domain of the king. But it represented the central figuration in the whole structure of government, through the mediation of which the king controlled his wider dominion.

---

[1] We shall refer only in passing to the catholicity of this attitude, just as the important relationships between court and religious ritual in general cannot be discussed in the context of this study.

[2] Jurien, *Soupirs de la France esclave* (1691).

The task is, therefore, firstly to elucidate the structure of this primary sphere of the king's rule. We shall then have to answer the question how this court actually came into being in conjunction with the structure of the wider dominion, and why it reproduced itself over successive generations in the particular form it took.

The structure of a given system of rule, as a figuration of interdependent people, can be determined with almost the same rigour as that of a specific molecule by a scientist. This is not to assert any ontological identity between the objects of the physical sciences and of sociology. That question is not at issue here. The comparison serves only to clarify the objective of the sociologist. Any field of rule can be represented as a network of interdependent people and groups acting with or against each other in certain directions. As will be shown, different types of field of rule can be distinguished according to the direction of the pressure which the different groups exert on each other and the kind and strength of the interdependence of the people forming the system. How, therefore, should we define the court in this respect?

Within the court the king finds himself in a unique situation. Everyone else in it is exposed to pressure from below, from the sides and from above. The king alone feels no pressure from above. But the pressure from the ranks below him is certainly not inconsiderable. It would be intolerable, would hurl him into oblivion in a moment, if all the social groups, or even all the court groups below him, acted in the same direction against him.

But they do not act in the same direction. Through their interdependence, his subjects' potential for action is directed largely against each other, so that they cancel each other out in their effect on the king. In a broader sense that will be discussed later, this applies to the whole dominion. In a narrower sense it applies directly to the court as the king's primary sphere of influence and power. Here, not only does each individual, in a sense, compete with every other for prestige, but different groups struggle with each other. The princes and princesses of the blood compete with the legitimized bastards of the king, against whom the 'great ones', the dukes and peers, also struggle. As a separate group there are the ministers risen from the bourgeoisie, often from the *robe*. They too belong fully to the court; and they cannot survive unless they understand the unwritten laws of court life.

All these, and other groups as well, are, moreover, internally split. People of different groups and ranks combine. Certain dukes, ministers and princes form alliances, partly supported by their wives, against others. The dauphin's circle, and the king's mistress, all intervene, now here, now there in the shifting and complex balance of tensions.

3. This sets the king, as we can see, a very specific task as ruler: he must constantly ensure that the conflicting tendencies of court people act in his own favour:

'The king,' writes Saint-Simon, 'used the numerous festivities, walks and excursions as a reward or punishment for those who were or were not invited. As he realized that he did not have enough favours to dispense to make a permanent impression, he replaced real rewards by imaginary ones, by exciting jealousy, by petty everyday advantages, by his partiality. No-one was more inventive in this respect than he.'[3]

In this way the king 'divided and ruled'. But he did not only divide. What we can observe in him is an exact assessment of the power relationships at his court and a careful balancing of the tensions within it.

To show one line of his tactics, the king always protects and allies himself most readily with people who owe him everything and are nothing without him. The Duc d'Orléans, his nephew, the later regent, or his grandson the dauphin, amount to something even when not in his special favour. They are potential rivals. Likewise the Duc de Saint-Simon, to give another example, who was not exactly in disfavour with Louis XIV but never in special favour either, nonetheless carried a certain weight at court as a duke and peer. He quite consciously sought to ally himself with the heir to the throne, and when one died he sought support from the next.[4] 'The court being changed by the death of Monseigneur, for me it was a question of changing my behaviour towards the new Dauphin.'

That was *his* tactic. High nobility conferred a limited degree of independence of the king which should never be allowed to degenerate into open opposition. All the more strongly, therefore, did Louis XIV support himself on people who owed their place at court to him alone and would fall into total oblivion if he dropped them, above all his mistress, the ministers[5] and his bastard sons. He protected the latter above all, to the great vexation of the genuine nobility.

That, therefore, was one of the methods by which the king prevented a unification of court society against him and by which he promoted and maintained the desired tension-balance, the precondition of his rule. It is a peculiar type of field and form of rule

[3] Saint-Simon, *Memoiren*, vol. 2, p. 84.
[4] *Ibid.*, vol. 18, ch. 360, vol. 2.

that manifests itself here in the court, and analogously in the wider dominion of the absolute monarch. What is characteristic of this dominion is the exploitation of enmities between subjects to reduce their hostility towards, and increase their dependence on, their sole ruler, the king.

4. There are fields of rule with quite different structures and therefore of quite different types. Max Weber, in his types of rule, opposes the patrimonial form which includes the French absolute monarchy, to another that he calls the 'charismatic' form.[6] If the latter is observed in the same way as court rule above, we see that here too, at least insofar as it appears in the West and tends towards political rule, there is a primary sphere of influence of the ruler within a broader dominion. The relationship between these three factors, the ruler, an elite central group or groups and the broader dominion, is decisive for the structure and fate of charismatic rule.

It can no doubt be generally said that upheavals within the wider dominion, a more or less fundamental transformation or loss of the existing balance of tensions within it, is the precondition for the establishment of charismatic rule. This change and loss of equilibrium gives the bearer of charisma his decisive opportunity. At the same time it gives his rise its special character, so much stressed by Max Weber, as something diverging totally from everyday life.[7] Charismatic leadership is born of crisis. It has no permanence unless crisis, war and disturbance become normal in a society. For its rise, measured by the traditional processes of a given social organization, is extraordinary. The concealed or open upheaval within this organization, the shock to its structure, as a rule produces in the people who form the charismatic central group, a predisposition to become extraordinary themselves. But the task with which the future leader finds himself confronted, proving what Max Weber calls his

---

[5] From many examples of the situation of a minister, and also to illustrate how exactly the power position of each person was weighed and observed, cf. the following account (Saint-Simon, *Memoiren*, vol. 13, ch. 234, p. 111). One should also note how the important concept of *crédit* is used to express the stock of a person at court. Saint-Simon describes the struggle of court cliques against Chamillart, a minister of the king: 'Never', he writes of Chamillart, 'had he sought the good opinion of Monseigneur (the heir to the throne). The prince was intimidated beneath the weight of a father who, excessively jealous, never allowed him the least credit. Chamillart, wrongly believing that with the King and Mme. de Maintenon for him he needed no other support, and that, given the footing on which Monseigneur was with them, he would harm himself by doing the slightest thing for him, which, should it get back to them, would make them suspect he wanted to attach himself to him, paid no regard to the trifles that Monseigneur desired.'

[6] *Wirtschaft und Gesellschaft*, ch. 3, ¶9, p. 138.

[7] Cf. *ibid.*, p. 142: 'In its genuine form charismatic rule has a specifically extraordinary character.'

'charisma' precisely by performing it, is quite specific and clearly distinguishable from the task facing the absolutist ruler. As long as he and his supporters are still fighting their way up, he must more or less consciously direct the aims of all the people forming the central group of his rule *in one direction*, holding together a limited number of people within a generally disintegrating and unbalanced society in such a way that their combined pressure acts outwards on the wider dominion.

The absolute ruler, too, is surrounded by a central group, the court through whose mediation he rules, as the charismatic ruler rules through *his*. But the former's task is to maintain or constantly to re-establish both the tensions, and the balance between them, within a social field whose actual structure offers a good possibility of doing so. This applies to his wider dominion, but it also applies to the central group. Here, as shown above, he must carefully channel the tensions, cultivate petty jealousies and maintain, within the groups, a fragmentation in their aims and therefore in the pressure they exert. He must allow opposed pressures to interpenetrate each other and hold them in equilibrium; and this requires a high degree of calculation.

The situation is quite different for the ruler who is executor of a profound social upheaval or regrouping, the charismatic leader. Observing him during his rise to power one sees that, in his case, jealousies, rivalries and the tensions they produce are dangerous within the central group. They are doubtless always present. But they should not show themselves too clearly. They have to be suppressed. For what matters here, as we have said, is to direct the strength, the aims and thus the social pressure of all the people united in this group outwards, against the disturbed social field, against the wider dominion that is to be conquered. In the performing of this task lies the real secret of the form of leadership that Max Weber called charismatic. There must be a unity of interests in his central group, which is relatively small as compared to the rest of the social field, so that the arm of each of his followers acts as an extension of his own.

In the situation in which an aspiring charismatic leader finds himself, there is less scope for calculation because there is less predictability than in the field of absolutist rule. In human social affairs, an event is the more predictable for the protagonists the more stable the structure of the social field. The would-be charismatic leader borne up by an unstable or totally shattered balance, by contrast, is precisely the one who promises — as the new man, often but not always representing new social ideas as compared to the ones prevailing previously — to break through the established and predictable attitudes and motives of his social field. The same applies, to a certain degree, to the central group that carries him. Both together must venture into what to them is relatively incalculable. Thus their aims easily take on the character of 'faith'. They have to make use of means, attitudes or behaviour that are relatively untried. On close examination one will doubtless always be able to see where and how their behaviour and aims continue existing tendencies. However, risk is one of the structural features of their enterprise. They conceal from themselves the uncertainty and size of the risk, which might be unbearable if clearly contemplated, by faith in the special grace enjoyed by their leader, his 'charisma'. The overthrow of many of the established rules, precepts and forms of behaviour used by the previous rulers in varying degrees to control their subjects, confronts the charismatic group with a specific task. Command cannot be transmitted from the leader to the lower levels of leadership primarily through well-tried and firmly established channels, but only through the repeated personal sanctions of the leader or a small number of deputies, i.e. by creating a more or less personal and very direct relationship between the leader and the members of the central group.

All these people no doubt bear features of the class from which they come; such features always form part of personal character. But the relationships, the importance and, above all, the rise of people within the central group are not primarily determined by the social order of rank previously existing in the wider dominion, but by individual qualities that match the special task and situation of the central group. The possession of such qualities is therefore decisive in the selection of the leader; it influences his relationship to the other members of the group far more than any inherited or previously acquired social rank. Within the charismatic central group a new order of rank between the members is established. It is, admittedly, influenced to varying degrees by the social hierarchy of the wider dominion to be conquered. But selection within it follows different rules. In other words, the charismatic central group offers very specific *opportunities* of advancement.[8] People can command here who had no

---

[8] *Advancement* here can, of course, mean very different things. We are now concerned with a far more general sociological phenomenon than is suggested by the usual limitation of the term to elevation within professional bourgeois fields. The rescue of individuals or groups from a sinking class by transferring to a position that is not sinking, constitutes 'advancement' and, with specific modifications, produces certain traits typical of people rising in society. Rise or advancement in society therefore means any change within a social field which brings with it for the person or persons involved an opportunity of increasing their social prestige and self-confidence as compared to their starting point.

influence there. And not only that: mere membership of such a central group, even in the lowest positions, represents a rise for the people entering it from the surrounding field. They are elevated from the ordinary mass in the broader dominion to the smaller circle, which already means the elite, which feels itself special.

In conjunction with this function of the charismatic central group as a mechanism of advancement contrasting at least in part to the central court group as a mechanism of preservation and defence, there is a significant switch in the attitudes and character of the people rising in this way. The individual's identification with the social stratum or group in the wider dominion from which he comes, whether with village, town or tribe, with professional or estates group, grows weaker or disappears. It is replaced by a new identification with the charismatic central group in the foreground. In the feelings of its members it takes on the function of social homeland.

Alienation from the original group, which can naturally vary in degree, identification with a social formation that, again in varying ways and degrees, has the function of an advancement-mechanism for all those involved, and finally the common interest in performing the expansionist tasks of the group as well as the necessity of securing and perfecting its elite character, i.e. its not yet completed ascendancy over the forces in the surrounding area — all these are preconditions for the structure which most clearly distinguishes the charismatic central group from the court one. This structure entails the minimization, though not the disappearance, of internal tensions, and the concerted outward pressure of all members into the area to be penetrated, as long as the ascent to rule is not complete. All the more rapidly do the tensions become apparent once the goal is reached and rule established. [9]

In addition, the charismatic ruler, unlike a consolidated government, usually possesses no established administrative apparatus outside his central group. For this reason his personal power and individual superiority within the central group remain indispensable to the functioning of the apparatus. This defines the framework within which such a ruler must rule. As always, the structure of the central group, functionally related to the structure and situation of the social field as a whole, has a retroactive influence on the ruler. With this leader as the living incarnation of the group, the majority of its members identify as long as the hope and faith remain alive that he will lead them to their common goal or secure the position already

[9] Cf. Appendix 1.

reached on the way to it. Just as the court ruler manipulates the people in his central group through their need for social distance and competition for prestige and favour, the charismatic leader controls his central group during its rise through their need both to rise and, at the same time, to conceal the risk and the often dizzying fear aroused by it. The two types of leader therefore need quite different qualities to control their followers successfully. The former can construct an apparatus which considerably reduces his own risk and the necessity for extraordinary personal intervention. The latter, on the other hand, is constantly required to prove himself directly in action and to take repeated incalculable risks. There is no position within the charismatic central group, not even that of leader, no hierarchy, ceremony or ritual, that is not determined by the group's orientation towards a common goal, and that could not be endangered and changed in the uncertain pursuit of that goal. Each mechanism used by the charismatic leader to control the group takes its primary meaning from this. Even though the need to manipulate the central group by balancing the tensions between factions and persons within it, a need which occupies the foreground in the stabilized rule of an autocratic monarch, is certainly not entirely absent from unstabilized charismatic rule, it here plays only a secondary role. In the total figuration there are no stabilized groups that can hold each other in equilibrium over long periods. A well-calculated long-term strategy for manipulating people is less important than unpredictable daring and readiness to leap in the dark, coupled with the intuitive belief that this is really a leap into the light. Indeed, one can say that this absolute conviction in the midst of social upheaval and general uncertainty, of his own ability always to take the decisions that will finally prove right — a conviction that is neither open to nor seems to need any rational justification — is one of the most basic attitudes of the charismatic leader and one that needs closer investigation. Each of them is riding on thin ice. If he reaches the other side, there are many historians who, showing the common inclination to equate success with personal greatness, will credit him with an extraordinary gift of doing the right thing in difficult situations. If the ice breaks, drowning him and his followers, he is likely to pass into history as an unsuccessful adventurer. The ability of such people to transmit to others their unshakeable belief in their own gift of taking correct decisions, is one of the means by which the central group is cemented together despite all the rivalries and conflicts of interest. This ability and this conviction are the real substance of the belief in his charisma. Success in mastering incalculable crises legitimizes the ruler as 'charismatic' in the eyes of the central group and the subjects in the wider dominion. And the 'charismatic' character of the leader and his followers is maintained only as long as such crisis situations constantly recur or can be created. Often they are created artificially simply because the tasks of a consolidated rule require other gifts than those that arise on the way to consolidation.

The leader must therefore master the tasks with which he is constantly confronted very much from his own inner resources. An encounter with the lowest member of his central group can become a trial for him. No etiquette, no social aura, no apparatus can protect or help him. His individual strength and personal inventiveness must prove him superior, legitimize him as leader, over and over again.

5. The situation was quite different for Louis XIV, who can be contrasted with the *arriviste* type of monopoly ruler as a very marked example of the conserving ruler. In his way Louis XIV is undoubtedly one of the 'great men' of Western history, whose influence has been exceptionally far-reaching. But his personal resources, his individual gifts were by no means outstanding. They were mediocre rather than great. This apparent paradox leads to the centre of the problem.

What we call 'great men' are, briefly, men who by successfully solving certain problems posed by their social situation have achieved a very far-reaching effect, whether briefly but intensely at one period of their lives, or throughout their lives, or even after their deaths. The more far-reaching their effect, usually but not always in terms of space and historical time, the greater appears the person who produced it.

The paradox mentioned just now in connection with the 'greatness' of Louis XIV points to a curious circumstance: there are situations in which the most important tasks are not those which can be solved by people with qualities that we romanticize somewhat as originality or creativity, people distinguished by extraordinary drive and activity, but by people of steady and placid mediocrity. Such was the situation of Louis XIV. His task as a ruler has already been sketched. Unlike the *arriviste* charismatic ruler, he had to prevent the social pressure of his subjects, especially his elite, from acting in a single direction.

6. In his youth Louis XIV had experienced an attempt to overthrow the existing order at the expense of his house, the time of the *Fronde*. At that time attacks by almost every group were aimed in the same direction, against the representatives of the monarchy. This unity disintegrated relatively quickly. When Louis XIV came of age

and ascended the throne, the rule of absolute monarchy had been re-established. Louis XIV inherited his power. The task he took on was therefore not to conquer and create, but to secure and consolidate, or at most to extend the existing structure. He had to supervise and keep alive the tensions between the different estates and classes. An innovating genius might well have foundered on this task; he might have guided the machinery wrongly and destroyed the figuration that favoured him. Louis XIV was not an innovator and did not need to be: 'Had he been indolent or sporadic, the conflicts of the institutions between themselves would have plunged the monarchy into anarchy, as happened a century later; had he been a man of genius and vigour, the slow, complex machine would have made him impatient, he would have broken it. He was calm and regular; not rich in inner resources, he needed the ideas of others.'[10]

His intelligence, according to Saint-Simon, was below average. That may be an exaggeration, but it certainly was not outstanding.

In addition, his whole education, including that of his intellect, had been rather neglected. The disturbed times when he was young had given his preceptors, above all Mazarin, little leisure to worry about his education. 'He was often heard to speak bitterly of this time; he even told how one evening he had been found in the basin of a fountain in the garden of the Palais Royal where he had fallen. He was hardly taught to read or write and remained so ignorant that he knew nothing of the best-known events in history.'[11] Louis XIV himself once said: 'One feels bitter grief at not knowing things that all others have mastered.'[12]

Nevertheless he was undoubtedly one of the greatest kings and most influential men in Western history. He was not only equal to his specific task of defending and extending an important power position that he had inherited, he was made for it. And as he performed it to perfection, he acted in fundamental accord with all those who in some way shared the splendour of his rule, even if they were in many respects oppressed by it: 'The great power and authority of Louis XIV come from the conformity of his person with the spirit of his time.'[13]

It is interesting to see how he himself formulates his task as ruler as being in exact agreement with his own needs and inclinations:

---

[10] Lavisse, *Louis XIV. La Fronde. Le Roi. Colbert*, Histoire de France (Paris, 1905), vol. 7, 1, p. 157.
[11] Saint-Simon, *Memoiren*, vol. 2, p. 69.
[12] Lavisse, *op. cit.*, p. 125.
[13] *Ibid.*, p. 134.

You need not believe [he once said to his son] that affairs of state are like the prickly and obscure problems of science that have perhaps bored you. The task of kings consists chiefly in exercising good sense, which always acts of its own accord and without effort . . . everything that is most necessary for this task is at the same time pleasant; for it consists, in a word, my son, in keeping one's eyes open on the whole world, incessantly learning the news from every province and every nation, finding out the secrets of every court, the whims and weaknesses of every prince and every foreign minister, informing oneself on an endless number of matters of which we are believed ignorant and, likewise, seeing in our own surroundings what is most carefully concealed from us, discovering each of the views and thoughts of our own courtiers.[14]

This ruler, in other words, was possessed by curiosity to know everything that went on in his immediate surroundings and in the wider world. To discover their hidden driving forces was to him a kind of sport from which he gained extraordinary satisfaction. But it was also one of the most important tasks arising from his social function as a ruler. Incidentally, one sees in this description how, from the ruler's perspective, the whole world appeared as an extended court, to be manipulated in the manner of the court.

That 'ruling' is a complex activity, and that the manipulation of people is one of the most important functions in this activity, has already been stressed. It is a central function of both charismatic, conquering rule, and of the defensive, conserving rule of Louis XIV.

The *kind* of manipulation practised, however, is very different. Louis XIV's words to his son indicate how the conserving ruler practised it: by an exact calculation of the passions, weaknesses, errors, secrets and interests of everyone. A way of thinking focused on the person, admittedly the 'person in a situation', referred to above as a characteristic feature of court people in general, is found here in the king. If, for the other court people who are exposed to pressure on all sides, such thinking serves as an instrument in the struggle for prestige — 'he who has ambitions must be well informed'[15] — for the king who is exposed to pressure only from below, it is an instrument of rule.

The conquering ruler must rely largely on the inner loyalty of the people within his central group. He can do so because their interests coincide very largely with his own. The pressure he necessarily exerts on them is relieved by the meaning and purpose, visible to all his

[14] *Ibid.*, p. 130.
[15] Saint-Simon, *Memoiren*, vol. 1, p. 156.

followers, that come from success in their common action within the wider dominion.

The conserving ruler in the situation of Louis XIV, living under the pressure of a possible threat from below, cannot count to the same extent on the loyal support of his followers. For the pressure he must exert to maintain his rule finds no relief in communal outwardly directed actions, at least as long as there are no wars. For him, therefore, the observation and supervision of people is indispensable in defending his rule. Louis XIV performed this task with an intensity that reflected his enjoyment of it. This has already been seen from his stated doctrine. The example of his practice will show still more clearly how the human observation characteristic both of the court aristocracy and the court king is aimed, on the king's side, directly *against* the nobility and serves to control it:

> The King's curiosity to know what went on around him constantly increased; he instructed his first valet and the governor of Versailles to engage a number of Swiss in his service. These received the royal livery, were responsible only to those just named and had the secret commission to frequent the corridors and passages, courts and gardens by day and night, morning and evening, to hide, observe people, follow them, see where they went and when they returned, overhear their conversations and report exactly on everything.[16]

That the observation of tensions and discord between his subjects is especially important to a conserving king in the situation of Louis XIV scarcely needs to be stressed after what has been said on the structure of this kind of dominion. The unification of his subjects threatened the king's existence. All the same, it is interesting to see how consciously he understood this task, encouraging and even creating breaches and tensions between people in both large and small matters.

> You must [he told his son] divide your confidence among several. The jealousy of one holds the ambition of the others in check. But although they hate each other, they have common interests and can therefore come to an agreement to deceive their lord. He must therefore obtain information from outside the close circle of his advisers and maintain permanent contact with people who have access to important information within the state.[17]

---

[16] *Ibid.*, p. 167.
[17] Lavisse, *op. cit.*, p. 158.

7. It is a peculiar form of activity to which the need for security drives this ruler. His attitude could be described as 'passive', measured by the far more active one of the conquering, charismatic leader. But 'active' and 'passive' are concepts which do not do justice to this complex social reality. The conquering leader himself drives his central group to action. In his absence the activity of his group is often broken. The conserving ruler is carried by the jealousy, antitheses and tensions within the social field that created his function; *he needs only to regulate these tensions and to create organizations which both maintain the tensions and differences and facilitate their supervision.*

Such a mechanism of regulation, consolidation and supervision — one among others — is the court and its etiquette as understood by the king. We spoke earlier of a social *perpetuum mobile* within the *ancien régime*. This is again seen very clearly in the contrast with charismatic rule. The central group of the latter decays more quickly the stronger are the tensions arising within it, since it is then less able to perform *its* task. The central group of internally defensive rule, which is not concerned with action and conquest, but with mutual defence and distancing, perpetuates itself — and the king's wide scope for decisions — through the opposed ambitions of the subjects as long as these can be held in check by the king. From the circle of rivals for prestige — if we may put it somewhat epigrammatically — now one steps forward to whisper into the king's ear how he can harm another, and then a second to tell him how he can harm the first; so it goes on in a circle. But the king decides, and in deciding against a particular person or group he has all the others on his side, as long as he does not disturb the entire system.

Here, therefore, a lively imagination was not needed in the ruler. Once the system had been established, what Louis XIV himself called *bon sens* and possessed himself to a high degree, was quite enough to regulate it and maintain it in equilibrium. *Above all, however, it was possible for the ruler within this social mechanism to achieve large-scale effects by a relatively small expenditure of personal energy.* The energy was generated in the *perpetuum mobile* driven by competition — 'la jalousie de l'un sert de frein à l'ambition des autres', to use the king's own words — and the king needs only to channel it. The machinery functioned like a power-station within which the movement of a lever by the controller released many times the force he had himself exerted.

The charismatic leader always confronts people directly, urging them on, intervening actively, pushing through his own ideas. A ruler like Louis XIV always had to be approached. Something was proposed to him; something was requested of him; and when he had listened to the arguments and counter-arguments of various people seeking his favour, he decided. Energy was, as it were, conducted into him; he kept his distance and made use of it. He needed no great ideas of his own and he had none; the ideas of others flowed to him and he made use of them:

> No-one knew as well as he how to sell his words, his smile, even his glances. Everything in him was valuable because he created differences, and his majesty was enhanced by the sparseness of his words. If he turned to someone, asked him a question, made an insignificant remark, the eyes of all present were turned on this person. It was a distinction that was talked of and increased prestige . . . no-one else was ever so polite by nature; no-one paid so much attention to differences of age, status and merit, both in his answers — when he said something more than his 'I shall see' — and in his behaviour.[18]

Jealousies whirl around the king, maintaining the social balance. The king plays on them like an artist. His chief interest in this, apart from simply keeping it in motion, was in being able clearly to overlook the human machinery he had to control, which undoubtedly contained within it a good deal of explosive material. This tendency to supervise and predict at each moment the workings of the machinery of rule is another characteristic of the conserving form of rule. While the charismatic ruler cannot protect himself from the unpredictable, the whole life of Louis XIV was built up in such a way that nothing new or unforeseeable, apart from illness or death, should reach the king. It is this difference in the entire figuration, not simply a peculiarity of particular persons, that is referred to when speaking of the 'rationality' of this absolutist form of rule and the 'irrationality' of the charismatic form: 'With an almanac and a watch one could tell, three hundred leagues away, what he was doing,' said Saint-Simon of Louis XIV.[19]

Every step of both the king and his entourage was predetermined. Every action by a person influenced the others.

8. Everyone within the chains of interdependence was concerned for reasons of prestige to ensure that others performed their steps according to precept. Thus everyone automatically controlled everyone else. Any 'stepping out of line' injured and disadvantaged others. It

[18] Saint-Simon, *Memoiren*, vol. 2, p. 86.
[19] Lavisse, *op. cit.*, p. 124.

was therefore extremely difficult if not impossible for the individual to break out. If no such organization, etiquette and ceremony had existed, the individual would have been able to stay away for periods at will; there would have been larger scope for his initiative. But the court etiquette not only subjected the movements of each individual very largely to the control of the ruler; it made the many hundreds of courtiers visible at the same time, acting as a kind of signalling device that publicly registered any self-will, any outburst or mistake by an individual, since this impinged on the prestige-claims of others, and were therefore reported through all the intermediate links to the king.

In face of so 'functional' a structure, the distinction between rationality of value and of function loses its clarity. The mechanism of etiquette was highly 'functional' in conserving and securing the king's rule. In this sense it too was a 'purpose-rational' organization, not less so, at any rate, than the instruments of power produced by societies competing for money and professional opportunities. In both cases, though perhaps more nakedly in the former, 'rule' is for its bearer an end and value in itself, or is at least based on values that seem self-explanatory. In this sense the instruments that secure this 'rule' are both 'purpose-rational' and 'value-rational'.

The position of the king, as it had evolved in the social field of the *ancien régime*, liberated the powers of its occupant in a special way. Not only did money flow to the occupant of this position — for example, in the form of taxes or revenues from the sale of offices — without his needing to engage in any professional activity, but he was the recipient of other social energies more difficult to quantify, in the form of the human powers that were at his disposal without any formal agreement. He had control of these not only, but mainly, because the structure of social interdependence gave them to him, rather than because the king seized them from the social field by his own activity. Moreover, all this human potential at the king's disposal in what his contemporaries themselves called *la mécanique*,[20] was organized in such a way that it acted as an amplifier of the king's energies, so that if the king merely lifted a finger or spoke a word, far greater energies were set in motion within the social field than he had used himself. For this reason his own energies, however great or small they might be, were liberated to an exceptional degree.

9. In the case of Louis XV, who took over royal power in an entirely secure condition, having personally experienced no direct

---

[20] E.g. Saint-Simon, quoted by Lavisse, *op. cit.*, p. 149.

threat to it and therefore lacking the permanent exertion of will his predecessor had shown in exercising power, a large part of these liberated energies were dispensed in pursuit of pleasures and amusements intended to dissipate the aimlessness and boredom so often characteristic of the second generation of ruling classes, a boredom produced precisely by this liberation of their energies.

For Louis XIV, by contrast, the maintenance of power was still a demanding task. The threat to his position had lessened in the course of his reign and the really decisive moment had occurred before it began. But as he had known the danger as a young man, the preservation of his function as ruler was a far more immediate concern for him than for Louis XV.

What was said above on the ideas and interests of court people and conserving classes in general, applies particularly to him: he had a goal, but not one outside himself, not a future goal. In a rather more limited context he once wrote: 'Beware of hope, a bad guide.'[21] That also applied in this broader context: he was a summit. He had a position without hope. So the goal he gave the energies liberated by his position was to secure, defend and above all to glorify his present existence: 'Louis XIV — and this is visible from his first words and his first gestures onwards — places quite simply in himself the principle and the purpose of things. . . . If he uttered the words *L'État c'est moi* he merely wanted to say: "It is I, Louis, talking to you".'[22]

If we regard Louis XIV as a creator of the modern state we should realize, if this view is not to be entirely misleading, that in his own motivation the state as an end in itself played absolutely no part. That his activity contributed to the development of France as a strongly centralized state is beyond doubt. At the same time we should remember the observation of Jurieu quoted earlier: 'The King has taken the place of the state, the King is everything, the state nothing.'[23] Saint-Simon, who sometimes has something of a Whig about him and at any rate is always secretly in opposition, once said in praise of the dauphin and as an explicit polemic against the attitude of Louis XIV: 'The great and sublime maxim that kings are made for peoples and not peoples for kings, was so deeply imprinted in his soul that it had made luxury and war odious to him.'

The 'state' as a value in itself is here a thoroughly subversive idea. Opposing it as Louis XIV's motivation, and therefore a decisive impulse in the policies and actions of France in his reign, is the king's

[21] Lavisse, *op. cit.*, p. 122.
[22] *Ibid.*, p. 131.
[23] Marion, *Dictionnaire*, art. 'Etat'.

own claim to prestige, his desire not only to possess power over others but to see it constantly recognized publicly in the words and gestures of others and so doubly assured. Even for Louis XIV we find the public confirmation and symbolization of power becoming a value in its own right. Symbols of power take on a life of their own and the character of prestige-fetishes. The prestige-fetish that best expresses the self-justifying character of the king's existence is the idea of *gloire*.

This prestige-fetish has remained an intermittently powerful influence on French politics up to the present day. But it has been transferred to the nation or to people who believed they embodied it. It is, moreover, closely coupled to economic, utilitarian motives. For Louis XIV himself, the prestige motive had absolute priority over other kinds of motivation for the reasons that have been given. Without his always noticing it, economic factors no doubt often influence the direction of his actions. But the course of events cannot be properly understood if we ignore the fact that this social structure encouraged the ruler to place prestige far above financial considerations, and to consider the latter as accessories of the former.

Louis XIV's foreign and domestic policies remain incomprehensible if one overlooks this connection between the structure of his self-image — his *gloire* as an end in itself — and the structure of his social position as ruler. In this respect, too, the opportunities and tasks presented by his position interacted closely with his personal inclination. That he particularly exploited the opportunities offered by his position to increase the glory and prestige of the king — himself — and that his personal inclinations lay in the same direction, is a decisive condition for what may be called his greatness as a king. He was not distinguished by intelligence or imagination or creativity, but by the serious and conscientious way he sought throughout his life and in every act to represent his ideal of the greatness, dignity and glory of the king of France through his own behaviour.

He occupied the royal position at a stage in the social development of France that allowed him to express his personal desire for *reputation* and *gloire* to an extraordinary degree. As a result, those of his subjects who counted most in the play of forces, the members of the social elite, the upper classes who were themselves strongly impelled by the desire for prestige, found magnified in their king what they felt on a smaller scale within themselves.

They understood him; and at least in part, at least for a time, they identified themselves with the splendour that his reign spread about it, felt their prestige increased by his.

10. A modern historian[24] has said with regard to Louis XIV's monarchy that in French eyes 'absolute monarchy was not only the solution to the question of the best government, it was also a grace, a providential help: to idealize and adore herself in royalty was for France a need. Already absolute in law, royalty became absolute in fact, by a sort of universal consent that long remained the essential political dogma of the nation.'

This is certainly a generalization of a far more partial phenomenon. For one thing, this identification of subjects with king lasted only as long as there were visible successes, and as long as social distress was not too oppressive. But above all this idealizing account conceals the ambivalence characteristic of the attitude of many of his subjects towards the king. For it was in the nature of the structure of this social field that, on one hand, almost all the groups of subjects identified with the king, seeing in him their ally in the struggle against the rest, but that they lived, on the other, in a state of constant tension with the king, and whether they expressed it or not, were inwardly opposed to him.

With this important reservation one can say that the above-mentioned agreement[25] between the king's person and the aims of the upper classes had its root in their common primary motivation, that of prestige. One must hear the king himself speak to understand the full significance of this kind of motivation:

> The love of *gloire* surpasses all the others in my soul. . . . The ardour of my age and the violent desire I had to increase my reputation gave me a strong passion for action, but I felt from that time on that the love of *gloire* has the same delicacy and, if I may put it thus, the same timidities as the more tender passions. . . . I found myself held back and pressed forward almost equally by one and the same desire for *gloire*.[26]

He conducts wars because the rank of conqueror is the most 'noble' and sublime of all titles, because a king must wage wars by virtue of his function and his destiny. 'And when he makes peace,

[24] Lavisse, *op. cit.*, pp. 134–35.
[25] *Ibid.*, p. 134.
[26] *Ibid.*, pp. 134–35.

Louis XIV announces that fatherly love for his subjects has gained the upper hand over his own *gloire*.'

Glory for the king was what honour was to the nobles. But the glorification of his own social existence, his claim to prestige, surpassed those of all others in his realm in magnitude and intensity in the same proportion as did his power. The king's need not only to exert his power but to demonstrate it constantly through symbolic actions, to see it ceaselessly reflected in triumphs over others, in the subservience of others — precisely this is *gloire* — refers beyond itself to the strength of the tensions that he had to manipulate with the utmost vigilance if he wanted to keep and use his power.

11. This immense need for domination and for glorification of his own existence as king, distinguishing him conspicuously from all others, in its turn placed chains on him that drew him inexorably into the social mechanism. The question was raised earlier why the king enmeshed not only his nobility but himself in the apparatus of etiquette and ceremony. It was, as we have seen, the king's ideal both to rule and to display himself as ruler in each of his acts. An understanding of the conditions both of his autocracy and, at the same time, of the permeation of his thinking and feeling by the need for prestige and self-display, in short, by the ideals of the court aristocracy to which he belonged, enables us to answer the question why the king became enmeshed. He could not subject other people to ceremony and display as means of power without subjecting himself to them as well.

The interdependences of people and the compulsions arising from them always find one of their focal points in certain social needs and ideals. The kind of entrapment this leads to varies with the kind of social needs which lead to dependence on others.

How the nobility's need for prestige and social distance gave the king the means of harnessing them to the court apparatus has been shown. We now see how the coercion of this apparatus reacted on the king. After the death of Cardinal Mazarin, Louis XIV wanted to rule himself, to hold all the strands of power in his own hands and share the glory of ruling with no other person. How strongly his attitude was influenced by the situation of his predecessor can be seen from the fact that throughout his life he held to the maxim that he would never admit a cleric to his council. He would give no one the chance of becoming a second Richelieu. Perhaps the most difficult moment of his life, from his own point of view, was when after Mazarin's death he declared that he would appoint no new *premier ministre* but would henceforth rule himself. He himself said later of his debut as king: 'In my heart preferring to all things and to life itself a high reputation if I could obtain it, but realizing at the same time that my first steps would either lay its foundations or deprive me for ever of even a hope of it. . . .' [27]

But once he had taken this step, he was the prisoner of his position as a king who not only rules but reigns, finding himself constrained by the task that he had taken on for the sake of a *haute réputation*. From now on no one else could help him to control and supervise the people around him. He himself could no longer make his actions dependent on whims or chance meetings. To keep the rule over his country firmly in his hands he had to organize himself, keep himself firmly in hand. Just as he tried to turn his country and particularly his central group, the court, into a clearly visible and calculable organization, he had to subject his own life to a clear and calculated order. Without the latter the former could not function; without the latter the former would have been meaningless.

If the 'state' had confronted the king as a social entity with a meaning and value of its own, it might have been possible for him in his own life to separate activity directed towards the state from that which concerned only himself. But as the state had for him no meaning and value in itself, as the prestige motivation in this society made the glorification of the king the real end in itself, as finally everything, the people, the court and even his family, had to elevate the king, there was in his life no separation between state and private actions. He was the master and thus the meaning of the whole, he ruled his land as father of the house and his house as father of the land. The king's desire and need to display himself as king penetrated, we have said, his most private actions. His getting up and going to bed, his love-making were actions just as important and carefully organized as the signing of a state treaty; they all served equally to maintain his personal rule and his *réputation*.

12. The greater his sphere of power was and the more directly everyone at court depended on him, the greater was the number of people who sought to approach him. He liked and desired this congestion of people; it too glorified his existence. But he was lost if he could not organize it. Each gesture, utterance and step he made was for the supplicants of utmost importance in terms of prestige. As the monopoly supplier of opportunities sought by a disproportionately large number of competitors, he had to calculate and organize very carefully the distribution of these opportunities, and with them

[27] *Ibid.*, p. 139.

himself, if he was not to lose control over this agitated situation.

Had his dominion been smaller, for example, as big as that of the medieval kings of France who had allowed their vassals to retain the function of rulers over large areas, and therefore independent power and standing, its demands on him would have been smaller also. A small area is relatively easy to supervise and the number of people coming from it with requests to the king can never be very great. The larger the dominion, the larger is the number of those pressing around the king whom he must always confront as one individual; the greater therefore is the pressure on the ruler, provided, of course, that he continues to try to control the larger dominion in the traditional way, as a single lord of the house for the whole land. With the pressure, the exertion demanded of him by his function also increases. The larger the country and the greater the *réputation* of the ruler, the greater are the compulsions to which he is exposed. Etiquette and ceremony, to which all his steps are bound and which amid the onrush of supplicants exactly define the distance which he must keep from them and they from him, are therefore instruments of power, expressions of the compulsion which rule exerts on the ruler.

'A king lacks nothing except the sweetness of a private life,' says La Bruyère.[28] After the need to maintain the power of his position unimpaired, it is above all through his need for *gloire* that this pressure to organize his whole life acts on the king. Driven by it, Louis XIV was perhaps the last to involve his life totally with the function of king in accordance with the old tradition whereby the functions of lord of the house and lord of the land were not clearly distinguished. The layout and function of his bedroom, the starting point of this chapter, is a symbol of this. The king had hardly anything in his *château* at Versailles that could be called an *appartement privé*. When he wanted to get away from the pressure of etiquette at Versailles he would go to Marly or another of his country *châteaux* where the ceremony was less oppressive than at Versailles, though oppressive enough by our standards.

Louis XV, however, following the trend of relaxation that has been mentioned before, left Louis XIV's bedroom and had his *appartment privé* installed in a more intimate and less ostentatious suite of rooms on one side of the Marble Court. Traces of the gradual differentiation between state and king, which culminated in the state or

---

[28] *Caractères*, p. 128, ch. 'Du Souverain et de la République'.

nation as an end in itself and its highest director as a functionary with a public and a private life, began to appear.

13. Louis XIV's position as king is a good example of the possible conjunction of two phenomena which, considered purely philosophically, without regard to empirical observations, might seem completely irreconcilable: the magnitude of his scope for decisions — often conceived as 'individual freedom' — and the magnitude of his bondage, his dependence on others, the constraints acting on him. In his case these were two aspects of the same phenomenon.

The abundance of power which his position made available to him could only be maintained by a carefully calculated manipulation of the complex, multipolar balance of tensions within his narrower and broader dominion. Etiquette and ceremonial were among the instruments he used to organize and maintain the distance between all the groups and persons in court society, including his own person, and so to preserve the balance within the elite central group. They were certainly not the only instruments available to him for this purpose. Without other means of power that are discussed in more detail elsewhere,[29] above all, control of the army and the whole state revenue, the mastery of court society through etiquette and ceremony could not have survived long. But without his adroit manipulation of these court instruments, the king would easily have fallen under the control of one of the rival groups or persons and so lost part of his control of the basic monopolies of physical force and taxation.

This constraint on the most powerful people in the highest positions in large organizations is a very general phenomenon. But when we speak of large organizations today, we too easily associate the term exclusively with industrial concerns. We forget that the figurations referred to by the term 'state' include a whole series of large organizations which existed before industrial concerns came into being within the framework of some state organizations. The lesser importance attached to state organizations as compared to industrial organizations in current studies of organizational problems is no doubt connected with the different ways the two are classified. 'States' are conceived as political phenomena while industrial enterprises are classified as economic phenomena. In the study of political and historical phenomena the investigation of types of organization at present plays only a small part. Whatever the reason for this may

---

[29] The problems of the monopolies of power and taxation as instruments of rule are treated at greater length in N. Elias, *The Civilizing Process* (Oxford, 1982), vol. 2, pp. 104ff.

be, one can learn a great deal about states of various types by considering them simply as organizations and trying to understand their structure and how they function. Such an approach may allow us to see rather more clearly the problem that confronted Louis XIV. It is a problem that preoccupies any single person who has the controlling position in a large organization: how can a single man permanently retain control over the enormous organization? At the present stage of social development the directors of the few large organizations that are actually controlled by a single person, for example, industrial concerns, have a wide range of impersonal methods of control at their disposal. The rank and powers of the various functionaries are partly laid down in written rules and precepts. Written documents, apart from their other functions, have the function of control. For they make it possible to check with a high degree of accuracy what happened in a particular case and who took the decision. In addition, in the majority of large organizations, there are specialist controllers whose primary task is to check what is happening within the organization and so to relieve the pressure on the controller at the top.

Despite their formal organizational framework based on written contracts and documents, which was developed only in rudimentary form in the state of Louis XIV, there are in many organizations of our time, even industrial and commercial ones, rivalries for status, fluctuations in the balance between groups, exploitation of internal rivalries by superiors, and other phenomena that have emerged in the study of court society. But as the main regulation of human relationships in large organisations is formalized in a highly impersonal manner, such phenomena usually have a more or less unofficial and informal character today. In court society we therefore find quite openly and on a large scale many phenomena that exist below the surface of highly bureaucratized organizations.

14. We cannot leave the problems of the entanglement of so powerful a ruler as Louis XIV without adding a few words on the fundamental importance of such studies. To the everyday way of thinking it seems that the ruled depend on the rulers, and not the rulers on the ruled. It is not easy to understand that the social position of a ruler such as a king arises from the division of functions and the interdependence within society in exactly the same way as that of an engineer or a doctor. Acute observers situated close to a ruler, like Saint-Simon in the case of Louis XIV, often see how the ruler's dependence influences his decisions. But from a greater distance rulers often appear the free and independent authors of their deci-

sions and actions. In historiography this fiction finds expression in the widespread tendency to use rulers such as Louis XIV or Frederick the Great and Bismarck as the final explanations of historical events, without sketching the mesh of dependence, as was done here in a limited way for Louis XIV, that provides the framework and scope for their decisions. In this way the rulers or even the members of small power elites are often represented to their subjects as symbols of individual freedom, and history itself as a collection of the actions of such individuals.

In sociology related ideas currently find expression in theories of action or interaction which are based — tacitly or overtly — on the idea that the starting point of all social investigations are free individuals, the absolutely independent masters of their own decisions and actions, who 'interact' as such. If an approach based on such a theory of action fails to make headway in solving sociological problems, it is supplemented by a system theory. While an action theory is usually based on the idea of the single individual outside a social system, a system theory usually rests on the idea of a social system outside single individuals.

The preceding studies of the court and, particularly, of the position of a single person, the king, are able to mitigate the difficulties one encounters when trying to tackle such theoretical problems without empirical reference points, because in this case it is possible to relate all the theoretical ideas directly to empirical facts.

A princely court, a court society, is a formation consisting of many individual people. Such a formation can certainly be called a 'system'. But it is not very easy to bring the use of this word into close touch with the phenomenon it refers to in sociological research. It does not sound very convincing to speak of a 'system of people'. For this reason the concept of the figuration is used here instead. One can say: 'A court is a figuration of individual people' without doing violence to the words. This somewhat reduces the difficulty that has led with a certain regularity, in the history of sociology up to now, to inconclusive contests between theoreticians who focus attention on individuals as such and others who concentrate on society as such.

In addition, the concept of a figuration has the advantage that, unlike that of 'system', it arouses the expectation neither of something closed on itself nor of immanent harmony. The term 'figuration' is neutral. It can refer to harmonious, peaceful and friendly relationships between people, as well as to tense and hostile relationships. Court society is full of tensions, but this does not detract from its character as a specific figuration of people.

Does this bring the problem of the relationship between individual and society closer to a solution? A few more steps in the argument are needed to show at least the beginning of a solution. As was indicated at the outset, figurations formed by people have the peculiarity that, with few exceptions, they can continue to exist even when all the individuals who formed them at a certain time have died and been replaced by others. So there was a French court under Louis XIV just as there was under Louis XV. The latter was formed by individuals different from the former. But one figuration passed over into the other in a continuous coming and going of members. In what sense can one say that in both cases we are concerned with a specific figuration to which the same term can be applied — the figuration of a 'court', and a 'court society'? What entitles us, despite the change in individual members, and despite certain changes in the figuration itself referred to as the 'development of the court', to speak in both cases of a 'court' and a 'court society'? What is it in such cases that, despite all the changes, really remains the same?

At first sight one might perhaps be satisfied with the answer that while the individual members change, the relationships between them do not. But this answer takes us only half-way. The concept of 'relationship' can be easily interpreted as something that depends solely on this or that individual person. But the relationships of the courtiers to each other or the relationships between the king and courtiers of different rank, infinitely diverse as the individual variations may have been, were finally determined by specific conditions which were for individual people, including the king, unalterable.

The conceptual difficulty that we encounter here arises from the fact that these conditions are often understood as something existing outside individual people, as when one speaks of 'economic', 'social' or 'cultural' conditions. On closer examination we find that what binds people together in a particular formation and often allows the formation to survive over several generations — with certain developmental changes — are specific forms of mutual dependence between the individuals or, to use a technical term, specific interdependences. The preceding analysis of interdependence has shown that such bonds are by no means always of a harmonious and peaceful kind. One can be just as dependent on rivals and opponents as on friends and allies. Multipolar balances of tensions such as emerge from a study of court society are characteristic of many interdependences: they are to be found in all complex societies. Long-term changes in them and in some cases the disintegration of a traditional equilibrium and its replacement by a new one — all these processes can be precisely analysed.

This is the situation that is obscured by an uncritical use of terms such as 'social conditions', *Zeitgeist*, *milieu* and many others like them. Even the concept of 'interaction' in its present usage does not do justice to the observable data. Like that of 'action', the meaning of 'inter-action' is by no means so obvious and unambiguous as it may seem at first sight. Just as the former suggests that the nature and direction of actions are to be explained solely by the initiative of the individual who acts, the latter conveys the impression of something arising solely from the initiative of two originally independent individuals — an *ego* and an *alter*, an 'I' and an 'other' — or from the meeting of a number of originally independent individuals.

The preceding discussions show clearly enough why theories of action and interaction are of relatively little use to empirical sociological research. They are based on the same image of man which tacitly underlies many historical studies in the classical manner, an image of single human beings each of whom is ultimately absolutely independent of all others — an individual-in-himself, a *homo clausus*.

The sociological theory of interdependence which has been the guiding thread in the preceding discussions and which in its turn has been given precision and clarity by such discussions, adheres more closely to the facts. It takes its starting point from the observation that each human being from childhood on belongs to a multiplicity of interdependent people. Within the mesh of interdependence into which he is born, his relative autonomy as an individual responsible for his own decisions develops and affirms itself to varying degrees and according to varying patterns. If in investigating socio-historical problems one does not go beyond the actions and decisions of individual people, as if they could be understood without reference to the dependence of these individuals and to the mesh of interdependence that they form with others, one denies oneself access to precisely the aspects of human relationships that provide the firm framework of their 'inter-action'. The analysis of the network of interdependence of a king as powerful as Louis XIV is a good example of the degree of certainty that can be attained by an analysis of interdependence. What has been said up to now — to reiterate — constitutes a model of this mesh of interdependence that is capable of and needs verification. But such analysis of figurations puts socio-historical research on to a track on which a greater continuity of research is possible. The connections that it brings to light are not determined by the preconceived ideals of the researcher. To perceive them and elaborate them clearly one must frequently disregard one's own ideals. If we were not concerned with people, we could say that we are here advancing to the thing itself. The interdependence of a king and his courtiers are data that can be discovered but not invented.

By demonstrating human interdependence, does one deny human beings their 'freedom'?

We cannot know what the word 'freedom' means, as generally used, until we better understand the compulsions that people exert on each other and, above all, the socially moulded needs of people for each other which make them interdependent. The concepts currently at our disposal in discussing such questions, particularly the concept of 'freedom' itself, are too inexact to express clearly what we see when we observe people — ourselves — in their actual dealings with each other.

A powerful king, through the opportunities open to him, has greater scope for decision than any of his subjects. In this sense one might say that he is more free than any of his subjects. The preceding study shows very clearly that a powerful ruler may indeed be called 'more free' in this sense, but is certainly not 'free' if 'free' means the same as 'independent of other people'. Nothing better characterizes the problem of human interdependence than the fact that each act of a ruler, while perhaps coming closest to the ideal picture of an individual act based on free decision, makes the ruler dependent on the ruled through being directed at other people who could either oppose it or at least not respond in the expected way. This is what the concept of interdependence expresses. As in a game of chess, each relatively independent act by an individual represents a move on the social chessboard which produces a counter-move by another individual — or frequently, in reality, by many other individuals — which limits the independence of the first and demonstrates his dependence. Every living person with some degree of mental health, even a slave, even a prisoner in chains, has a degree of autonomy or, if one prefers the more dramatic term, of freedom. The fact that even prisoners possess a degree of autonomy is sometimes romantically idealized as proving the metaphysical freedom of man. But the idea of an absolute freedom of the individual transcending all ties to other human beings is no doubt significant mainly in that it flatters people's sentiments. If we leave aside all metaphysical or philosophical speculation on the 'problem of freedom' that cannot be confirmed by reference to observable phenomena, we find ourselves confronted by the fact that while different degrees of independence or, to express it differently, of power can be observed in the relations of people to each other, there is no absolute zero-point of one or the other. Moreover, it is usually the case that a relatively independent action by one person calls into question the relative independence of another; it changes the constantly shifting balance of tensions between people. One can predict with a fair degree of certainty that in the next phase of development, thinking and enquiring people will increasingly turn away from the use of absolute and ossified antitheses such as 'freedom' and 'determinism' and towards problems of balance.

In saying this, however, we are addressing ourselves to problems that lie outside the scope of this book. What has been said up to now must be enough to indicate that the concepts of 'freedom' and 'determinacy' as used in traditional debates on such absolute alternatives are too coarse to be of further value in the investigation of observable human phenomena. The tradition that dominates such debates holds fast to a highly artificial and therefore unusable assumption. It places at the centre of the problem an isolated individual who is apparently absolutely independent of all other people. It is the freedom or determinacy of this artificial product of human fantasy that is then discussed. The discussion can only be removed from the half-light of such collective fantasies if it is placed on a sociological basis — if, in other words, we take as our starting point not the assumption of an absolutely independent isolated human being, but what can actually be observed, a multiplicity of interdependent people forming specific figurations such as the court. This approach removes the barrier that so often divides the discussion of theoretical from that of empirical problems today. A detailed study of a single society, as we can see, provides material for investigating the more general theoretical problem of the relative dependence and independence of individual people in their relations to each other, and this latter problem in its turn helps to clarify the former. The questions that arise in a sociological study of a powerful ruler are particularly fruitful in this context. If instead of two diametrically opposed concepts like freedom and determinacy, problems of degree and equilibrium are made the centre of study, it emerges that the problem of freedom and the problem of the actual distribution of power among people are more closely related than it usually appears.

·VII·

The sociogenesis and development of French court society as functions of power shifts in society at large

1. Every form of rule is the precipitate of a social conflict — it consolidates the distribution of power corresponding to its outcome. The moment of consolidation, the point of social development reached at the inception of a regime, therefore has a determining influence on its specific form and its subsequent fate. So Prussian absolutism, for example, which took a firm shape considerably later than the French, and incorporated its feudal nobility much later, was able to create an institutional framework for which the preconditions were lacking not only in France but in the whole Western world at the time of the birth of the French absolutist regime.

The formation of these two absolutist structures was preceded by conflicts between the kings and the feudal nobility. In both, the nobility lost their relative political independence, but what the French kings were able and wished to do with their newly won power in the seventeenth century was different from what the Prussian kings were to do with it in the eighteenth. A phenomenon that can often be observed in history is apparent here: a country which has developed later in a particular respect develops more mature structures in response to institutional problems than one that was previously ahead of it. Much of what Frederick II was able to develop in his country, for example the kind of bureaucracy and administration that he introduced, had its counterpart in France only after the Revolution and Napoleon. These in their turn were able to solve problems in France that Prussia, and then Germany, could only solve a good deal later. It is of the highest importance for the fate and the 'physiognomy' of nations, at what time — and that always also means in what way — the social problems that recur in all the major countries of the West are generated and solved. The kings were in no way exempted from this development. It dictated their problems and tasks, which were then deflected by their nature in this or that direction, being stifled by it here and brought to fruition there. They too, like all other individuals, were exposed to the compulsions that have their origin in the phenomenon of human interdependence. Even their unlimited power was an expression and consequence of this.

2. There is, of course, a strong temptation to treat them as people standing outside the fate and network of society because they do not seem to belong directly to any of the social strata of their people. At least, one is inclined to understand their motives and the general tendency of their actions largely in terms of their personal dispositions. Certainly, in earlier times their position within the social field, their chances of asserting their personal inclinations, in short, the way they were enmeshed in the social whole, was often very unusual. But in their own special way they too were enmeshed. Even a king or a succession of kings always stood within a particular social tradition. Whether they were great or small, the way they behaved, the type of motivation and goals they had was always shaped by a specific social career, by their relation to certain social strata and generations. Some of them, such as Napoleon I or Frederick II of Prussia, as executors of a social upheaval or a transformation of the state and thus as rulers during a breakdown of traditions, were ambiguous in their kind of motivation and behaviour, while others were unambiguous. Among the unambiguous leaders are the French kings of the *ancien régime* who were and remain, by their behaviour, their motivation, their ethos, court aristocrats, representatives of a social stratum that one can only refer to negatively and colourlessly as a class without earned income, a non-working class, because the bourgeois language of our time has attached derogatory overtones to its positive characteristics.

That the French king felt himself to be a nobleman, *le premier Gentilhomme*,[1] and stated that he was shaped in his actions and thoughts by the aristocratic attitudes with which he was brought up, is a phenomenon that cannot be completely understood unless we trace the origins and development of the French monarchy from early times through the Middle Ages. This cannot be done in the present context. What is important here is to understand that in France there was a strong and uninterrupted tradition of aristocratic culture throughout the whole Middle Ages up to modern times, unlike the situation in many German countries. The king, needing the company

---

[1] Lemonnier, *La France sous Charles VIII, Louis XII et Francois Ier* (Paris, 1903), p. 244.

of like-minded people for the fulfilment of the tradition of which he was a link, was therefore bound more strongly by them than the kings of countries in which there was a sharper break between the Middle Ages and the modern period, or in which aristocratic culture was less richly developed.

3. No less important, however, is a second circumstance, connected with this, which is easily overlooked. For centuries, up to the time of Henry IV, and even up to that of Louis XIV, the French kings had been engaged in an unresolved conflict, if not with the nobility as a whole — parts of it had always fought on their side — at least with the high nobility and their followers. And the whole shape of aristocratic culture was necessarily transformed as the kings came closer to victory and as this culture, losing its previous variety, became centred in *one* place, Paris, and on *one* social organ, the *royal court*. However, the kings who had played such a part in the transformation of this aristocratic culture were in their turn affected by it in the most extreme way. They never stood outside the nobility as the bourgeoisie did later. Of the latter it can be said with some justice that it gradually discarded aristocratic culture as its model, so that finally it no longer understood aristocratic attitudes and overran the nobility from outside as the bearer of its own non-aristocratic convictions. But what was brought about by the establishment of the absolute monarchy and by the subjugation of the great and petty nobility by the French kings in the sixteenth and seventeenth centuries was no more than a gradual shift of the centre of gravity within one and the same social stratum.

From a nobility scattered across the whole country, a court nobility centred around the king grew as the central, influential power. And just as the majority of the nobility were transformed from knights into court *seigneurs* and *grands seigneurs*, the kings too were transformed in the same way. Francis I was still a knightly king, *le roi chevalier*.[2] He was fond of tournaments and hunting; war for him was a splendid knightly game in which he put his life at stake. For this was required by chivalrous-aristocratic convention, by his honour, and he felt himself bound as king by this law of knightly behaviour like every other knight.

The case was still similar with Henry IV who, when a Huguenot leader and a great vassal of the kings of France, on receiving the news that their opponents were preparing for war, offered to settle the matter by personal combat with the enemy leader, the Duc de Guise:

---

[2] On this and what follows see Lemonnier, *op. cit.*, p. 188.

'Inequality of rank shall not deter me.'[3] One against one, two against two, ten against ten or twenty against twenty, they would fight with the weapons that were customary in an affair of honour between knights. Thus he spoke. After attaining power he embodied the transition between the late-chivalrous type of king and the court-aristocratic type that was to find its first perfect representative in Louis XIV, who no longer, like Henry IV, rode into battle at the head of his nobles. He had his wars fought more and more by generals with paid troops, and even if he occasionally exposed himself to fire, he was hardly accustomed to physical warfare. Tournaments too, under Louis XIV, entirely lost their character as personal, man-to-man combat. They became a kind of court game. And if we are looking for an example of how much the king had now become a court aristocrat in his behaviour, but how much, at the same time, his person carried a special weight within court society that distanced him from the others, we might consider this picture of a knightly game that took place in 1662 under Louis XIV:

> There were five quadrilles each wearing different colours and representing different nations: Romans, Persians, Turks, Moors, Russians, each under a leader of the highest rank. The King led the first troop representing Romans; his device was the sun dispersing clouds. Of the knights following him the first bore a mirror reflecting the rays of the sun on his shield, the next a laurel branch, this tree being sacred to the sun, the third an eagle with its eyes turned towards the sun. . . .[4]

'If it were not a game,' says Ranke, 'it would border on idolatory. All the devices of the first troop have the same meaning; those of the others hint at it. It is as if they all renounce being anything in themselves; *they all have being only in relation to the king*.'

This game is a symbol. If we consider it not for its own sake but in relation to the development of the balance of power, and compare the attitude of Louis XIV with Henry IV's when issuing his challenge, we can see clearly what it means to say that Henry IV was the last knightly king while Louis XIV was a court-aristocratic king. Even as kings, both belonged to aristocratic society in their whole outlook, their behaviour and motivation. This society was an inseparable part of their existence. But the importance of the two kings within their societies was different. In the case of Henry IV, the

---

[3] Cf. Ranke, *Französische Geschichte* (Leipzig, 1876/77), 4th edn, vol. 1, bk. 6, ch. 1.
[4] Pelisson, *Histoire de Louis XIV*, 1, 26, quoted by Ranke, *op. cit.*, vol. 3, bk. 12, ch. 3, p. 204.

king's power in relation to the nobility, while greater than that of any preceding king, was less than Louis XIV's. He was not yet so preponderant as the latter nor, therefore, so distanced from his nobles.

4. Louis XIV, while living amidst court society, had become its only centre to a greater extent than any of his predecessors. The balance of forces between the king and the noble society to which he belonged had been totally displaced. Between him and the rest of the nobility there was now an immense distance. Nevertheless, this was a distance within one and the same social stratum. What is paradigmatically expressed in this knightly game is true of the whole position of Louis XIV within the court nobility, and of his attitude towards it: this nobility was his society. He belonged to it and needed it. But at the same time he distanced himself from it to the same degree as his power position raised him above all the other nobles.

In Louis XIV's behaviour towards the court nobility, therefore, two tendencies are always intertwined. These determine the position of the nobility within the power structure and, embodied in and constantly reproduced by the institutions, remain characteristic of his successors up to the end of the regime. First, there is a tendency to establish and secure the absolute personal power of the king by institutions of all kinds against the claims of the great and petty nobility; second, there is a tendency to preserve the nobility as an estate dependent on and serving the king. but distinct from all other classes and with its own specific culture, this being the only adequate society for the king.

This ambivalent attitude of the king towards the nobility, which from now on was of decisive importance in shaping that class, did not express the personal whim of a single ruler but was enforced by the situation that had slowly developed in the course of the sixteenth century. This development gave rise to a specific figuration in which the nobility was deprived of the foundation of its social position and eminence together with a major part of its economic power, while the kings were given huge new opportunities arising from their function. The kings were bound to the nobility by origin and culture; through the social development of France they moved further and further from the position of a *primus inter pares* to a power position that left all the other nobles in their realm far behind. The solution to the conflicts arising from this simultaneous participation and pre-eminence was provided by the court.

There had been a conflict between the nobility and the monarchy in France for a long time. Its causes up to the seventeenth century can be disregarded in this context. This conflict was finally decided in the seventeenth century in the monarchy's favour. The fact and the extent of this victory were determined by circumstances that lay largely outside the will, ability and power of particular French kings. That the crown went to Henry IV after the religious wars may have depended on personal gifts and relatively accidental constellations. But that the power position of the kings in relation to the nobility had shifted to an extraordinary degree in the kings' favour and was to do so still more in the future, was the result of social shifts that lay outside the power of the kings or of any individual person or group. These gave the kings important opportunities — which, of course, were exploited or not according to their individual gifts — while they shook the foundations of the nobility's existence.

6. The upheavals in the social structure of the West that took place in the course of the sixteenth century were certainly hardly less important than those that manifested themselves at the end of the eighteenth century. Undoubtedly, the inflow of precious metals from overseas and the increased circulation of currency resulting from it sooner or later, in all the countries of the West, though in very different ways, was not the only cause of the upheavals in the sixteenth century. But it can be said that the inflow of precious metals acted as a catalyst. The downpour of gold and silver brought to life many seeds that had been planted during the development of Western societies, which without this rain would probably have grown far more slowly or withered away. On the other hand the flood of precious metals would hardly have occurred had not the development of European societies itself reached a stage at which it needed and could make use of currency. In the case of France, the connections between the increase in money circulation and the direction taken by the social upheavals of this time have been clearly shown.[5]

The first result of the increase in the money supply was extreme inflation. On a contemporary estimate the purchasing power of money fell to a quarter.[6] Prices rose accordingly. Moveable wealth increased. Even though land remained the firm basis of wealth, it became increasingly usual to keep a considerable sum in cash at one's house. This devaluation of money had very different consequences for different strata of the people. These connections cannot be more concisely or clearly depicted than in the following passage. From about 1540 on,

[5] On this and what follows cf. H. Sée, *Französische Wirtschaftsgeschichte*, (Jena, 1930), vol. 1, pp. 118ff., and Lemonnier, *op. cit.*, p. 266, where a detailed bibliography can be found.
[6] Mariéjol, *Henri IV et Louis XIII* (Paris, 1905), p. 2.

the Tours *livre* fell continuously and prices imperceptibly rose. Some consequences of this phenomenon can already be discerned in the reign of Francis I: a rise in farm rents and in the value of land, and conversely a reduction in fixed revenues such as taxes. . . . The results were disagreeable neither for agriculture nor for industrialists or merchants who could raise their prices proportionally. They were painful for those at the top and at the bottom, for the landed aristocracy and the workers. . . . The lords and nobles sought court and government functions; the bourgeois administrative posts or offices. The former congregated around the king, the latter spread into salaried employment. This started the movement that carried everything towards a regime of absolutism, centralization, aristocracy, bureaucracy.[7]

Leaving aside the importance of this process for other classes, for a major part of the French nobility the devaluation of money shook if it did not destroy the basis of their economic existence. They drew fixed rent from their land. As prices rose continuously, the income they received through agreements no longer met their needs. At the end of the religious wars the majority of nobles were head-over-heels in debt. In many cases creditors expropriated them. The greater part of landed property changed hands at this time. And at least a part of the aristocracy displaced from their land in this way came to the court to seek a new existence. We can see how social destiny here narrowed the opportunities open to a whole class, and thus their power position, their social prestige, their distance from other classes.

7. If we include the king among the nobility we can say that by virtue of his function he was the only noble in the land whose economic base, whose power position, whose social distance were not reduced by this process but actually increased.

Originally the revenue from his land had been the main income of the king as of all nobles. This had long since changed. Taxes and other payments that he skimmed off from the wealth of his subjects had taken on increasing importance in the king's revenue. So the king who owns and distributes land gradually becomes a king who owns and distributes money.

The late-chivalrous kings of the sixteenth century are transitional types. The court monarchy of the seventeenth and eighteenth centuries is, economically speaking, a monarchy founded on money income. So that while the nobility of the late sixteenth and early seventeenth centuries, who lived essentially on their land and scarcely played any part in the commercial movements of their time, were im-

---

[7] Lemonnier, *op. cit.*, p. 269.

poverished by the devaluation of money, the king's income through many channels, particularly taxes and the sale of offices, increased not only in proportion to the devaluation of money but far in excess of it, owing to the increasing wealth of certain taxable classes. This constantly increasing income that the kings received through their special position in the total figuration of society, with its growing urbanization and commercialization, was one of the decisive conditions of their increase in power. By distributing money to those serving their regime they created the governmental apparatus. It should not be overlooked here that this royal income, unlike that of merchants and artisans, was not the result of activity in a salaried profession, but was paid to the king from the earned income of professional classes through paid functionaries. It was one of the king's functions to control these functionaries, to co-ordinate their activity and to take decisions at the highest level. From this point of view, too, it can be said with good reason that the kings were the only members of the noble class who were given increased opportunities by this change in the figuration. For the kings were able to retain the important aspects of their seigniorial character; they did not need to become involved in any professional activity and yet could increase their income from the growing wealth of their land.

While the king rose the rest of the nobility fell; that is the shift of equilibrium that was referred to earlier. And the distance which Louis XIV maintained between himself and the nobility, which he very consciously elaborated in etiquette, for example, was not simply 'created' by himself personally, but generated by this whole social development which furnished the social function of the monarch with immense opportunities while reducing those of the remaining nobility.

Not less significant for the fate of the nobles was the change in warfare that came about in the same period. The relatively great weight of the medieval nobility in the balance of tensions between it and the central rulers rested not least on the latter's heavy dependence on their nobility in all military undertakings. These nobles had to meet the main part of the costs of their military equipment themselves — for the armour, horses and weapons for themselves and their followers — from the surplus income from their land or from the proceeds of plunder. If they did not follow their lord's call to battle, or if, as sometimes happened, they left the army after the time prescribed by tradition and withdrew to their estates, castles and courts, in the end only a penal expedition could bring them back into line. But such an expedition or even the threat of it was only effective if the central lord commanded a sufficiently impressive troop of warriors. And command of such a troop in turn depended on how far he could rely on parts of his warrior nobility.

In the course of the sixteenth century changes in military technique that had been long prepared and were also partly connected to the growth in money circulation became increasingly perceptible. The following quotation points to a number of important structural features of the transitional period:

> In the French armies of the sixteenth century the most diverse elements mingled. Only in emergencies, and then without much success or military value, were the feudal nobility called to arms. The old feudal army had in reality ceased to exist. The nobles capable of bearing arms rather joined the companies of heavy horsemen, the orderly companies, that were summed up by the term *gendarmerie*. The *gensdarmes* provided their own horses and costly armour; the less wealthy were included in the companies as mounted marksmen. . . . For their brave cavalry charges as well as their personal services the warriors, with their honour and education, were indispensable to the generals. But the future no longer belonged to this military type. Sharply distinguished from the heavy knightly cavalry, far below it in rank, developed the light cavalry founded more and more on modern firearms. . . . The whole form of the army rested on the hired soldier.

In the balance between the bulk of the warrior nobility and the ruling princes preponderance shifts in the latter's favour in the military sphere too. Their increasing income allows them to hire troops for their wars. Commanders who are also entrepreneurs equip armies recruited from the lower classes. In place of gifts of land, or fiefs, by which military services were paid for in earlier, less monetarized and commercialized phases of social development, money, *la solde*, increasingly becomes the dominant form of payment. Princes hire mercenaries or soldiers. The word itself contains an echo from this earlier phase of development. This considerably reduced their dependence on the feudal nobility but increased their dependence on money sources and the extensive network of which they were part. The shift of the military centre of gravity from armies recruited from the upper classes to armies recruited mainly from the lower strata was further promoted by the development of firearms. Even earlier, weapons such as crossbows were traditionally the weapons of peasant and other non-noble troops. In the battles of the chivalrous armies they played the role of auxiliary troops, partly because the armour of knights and horses reduced the effect of the bolts. But with the development of firearms, against which armour offered no protection, the social balance tilted away from the old warrior nobility. The whole development of states that made it possible for princes to switch to paid armies in their wars favoured the development of firearms for the foot soldiers and was favoured by them.

In the future it will be possible, with the aid of systematic studies of interdependence and shifts of balance, to summarize this kind of transformation of a figuration in more exact and comprehensive models than is possible or necessary within this framework. It is enough here to point out that both the increase in the money which the central rulers received through their social position with the accompanying reduction in the traditional income of the landed nobility, and the increasing military importance of mercenary armies carrying firearms with the accompanying decline of traditional knightly warfare, reduced the central rulers' dependence on his nobility while increasing the nobility's dependence on the central ruler. The shift in the balance of power between nobility and king cannot be formulated as if it had its beginning in a single sphere of social development. The expansion of trade cannot be understood without the increased state protection of trade routes and increasing legal protection for merchants, and vice versa. Without sufficient troops kings could not expect a secure income from taxation, nor would they have the troops without the income.

8. Numerous problems are raised by the transition from one distribution of power, one balance of forces to the other. A few further remarks may help to fill out the picture somewhat. The kings' distribution of land in a barter economy, and of money pensions in a money economy, founded two very different kinds of relationships. The first placed the enfiefed nobles spatially at a distance from the king. As long as the use of credit was difficult and undeveloped it was never easy to stay away from one's own land for long periods. Even during campaigns, and as late as the battles that led to Henry IV's victory, nobles quickly left the army if no victory, no plunder were to be expected, and returned home. [8]

Money distributed by the king, however, made it possible, and often compulsory, to stay in his proximity. If land and rent paid in kind tended to make knights stay at home, land as a source of money rent allowed them to stay away. And money income such as pensions or presents disbursed directly by the king, which could be renewed by constant favour but withdrawn by disfavour, exerted strong pressure

[8] Cf. Ranke, *op. cit.*, bk. 6, ch. 2, p. 368.

in the direction of permanent residence at his house, compelled people to buy the king's good opinion by repeated personal services. Thus the kind of dependence enforced by the payment of rent in kind on one hand, and the distribution of salaries, pensions and gifts on the other, were different. The former permitted greater independence than the latter. For, on his estate, no matter what it was like, the nobleman was still a little king, and when he was once enfiefed he was fairly secure. At any rate it was not very easy to withdraw the fief; a constant seeking of the king's favour was not needed to maintain possession of the gift.

Money gifts, however, had to be constantly enticed anew from the royal treasury. Pensions were more quickly and easily withdrawn than land and rent in kind that existed far from the royal residence. In this sense the people dependent on money incomes from the king lived on more uncertain ground than those who had received land.

The favour of kings manifested in money presented a greater risk for those dependent on it, raised them and cast them down more rapidly in society and so produced more mobile and complex human attitudes and physiognomies than favour expressing itself in land. And the dependence of the recipients of favour on the king was greater, more visible, more immediate than that of the landed nobles.

The courtly king distributing money or pensions, with all his personal moods, actions and feelings, directly and permanently surrounded by suitors, had power over a wider circle of people than any feudal king. His money gathered people to him.

We therefore have good reason to juxtapose the king who gave land to the king who gave money; for one royal type emerged directly and gradually from the other whose behaviour was continued in him.

In other words, we cannot understand the attitude of the money-giving French kings to their nobility if we do not realize that it grew out of the traditional attitude of the highest liege lord towards his feudal vassals. The old bonds between king and nobility which are expressed when, for example, the king calls himself the *premier Gentilhomme* or when the nobility feels itself to be the *vraie force active, le corps vivant du pays*,[9] the king's traditional obligation to preserve his nobles and the nobility's to serve the king — none of these was extinguished. If we consider the *pension* economy of the *ancien régime* we should not forget that in it the old feudal relationship is still present, though transformed by the court. One of the basic constituents of the attitude of the courtly kings and nobility to each other

[9] Lemonnier, *op. cit.*, p. 244.

was that it had grown out of the old feudal interdependence of the chivalrous kings and their vassals and followers.

But the feudal ethos was originally founded on a more equally balanced mutual dependence of the partners. Wherever this dependence was small, as with the great vassals, the ethos and its obligations were readily violated. The vassals needed the feudal prince as a co-ordinating commander, as the owner or distributor of conquered land, and the liege lord needed his followers and vassals as warriors and deputies to defend or increase his possessions, as fighters in his wars and feuds. In addition, the king originally needed the rest of the nobility — apart from the fact that they provided his companions on hunts, at tournaments and social pleasures as well as the warriors in his battles — because it was only from them, even if in the form of clerics, that he could draw his advisers. From his group of warriors, to begin with, came the more or less independent administrators of the king's land, who levied taxes and imposed law. Given such an extensive dependence on the nobility and such an intertwining of mutual interests, the distance between the kings and the other nobility could not take on the same dimensions as later.

In the course of time the central rulers increasingly overshadowed the rest of the nobility. They were able to increase their power at the expense of the nobles partly because they were able to use people from the other estate which was slowly emerging, the bourgeoisie, for tasks which had previously been reserved for the nobility and high ecclesiastics. In France they succeeded in expelling the nobility from almost all these functions and in replacing them by people who had risen from the *roture*. By the end of the sixteenth century the major part of the judiciary, the administration and even the majority of ministerial functions were in their hands.

9. What now remained to make the nobility necessary to the king? This is a crucial question; for even though the feudal relationship was continued in modified form in the court relationship of king and nobility, the old ethos and obligations could scarcely have survived given the unequal positions of the two parties in the new money economy, if the impoverished nobles had only needed the king for survival while he no longer needed them as a special and irreplaceable estate. Why, then, did the king still need the nobility?

This question immediately leads us to a much larger one: every institution is the product of a quite specific distribution of power in the balance formed by interdependent groups of people. It is produced not only *once*, by this constellation, but over and over again as a figuration that outlives many individual people for a certain period.

We must therefore explain the *social production and reproduction of the distribution of power* with regard to the court of the *ancien régime*. The question raised before, of the nobility's dependence on the king and the king's on the nobility, a mutual dependence embodied in the court, is only another formulation of the problem of the social production and reproduction of the court. For just as the social institution of a factory, for example, cannot be understood until it has been related to the structure of the social field producing it, so that the mutual dependence of workers and factory owners can be understood, the same applies to the social institution of the court. It can only be understood once we have stated the *formula of need*, i.e. the nature and degree of the interdependence which first bound together and then held together the various people and groups forming the court.

Only then does the court appear before us as it really was, no longer a fortuitous historical grouping to which the question 'why' cannot be applied, but a figuration of people from certain strata that was constantly reproduced in this form because it offered the people forming it satisfaction of the various needs that were constantly reproduced in them.

From the court of the Capetians, above all that of Louis IX (1226–70), there is a continuous line of development to the courts of Francis I, Louis XIV and his successors. The survival of the court tradition in France from the thirteenth to the eighteenth centuries, despite fundamental changes in the social structure, was one of the most important preconditions for the refinement of court culture in France and for the formation of a specifically 'French' tradition. Within this development there is a decisive turning point in the fifteenth and sixteenth centuries. Whereas previously, in gradually diminishing numbers, the great vassals had had their courts like the king, [10] so that the king's court had been only the first and not always even the richest, most brilliant or most influential, during these centuries, with increasing royal power, it gradually became the predominant centre. From the nobility's standpoint this development meant their transformation from an agrarian feudal class into a court nobility. If we try to pinpoint the moment when this change became visible more exactly, we are led above all to the reign of Francis I.

10. Francis I, as has been mentioned, represented a transition between the chivalrous and courtly types of king with perhaps an inclination towards the former rather than the latter.

[10] A more detailed study of this process can be found in N. Elias, *The Civilizing Process* (Oxford, 1982), vol. 2, pp. 117 ff.

Just because he was a transitional type, it is difficult and, in this context, impossible to elucidate the structure of his court in detail. But as a starting point for a study of the mature form of the court characterized by the king's control of the distribution of money, we shall briefly mention a few structural elements of the transitional courts of the sixteenth century.

'The sixteenth century,' writes a French historian,[11] 'saw the birth of something new in France: aristocratic society. The nobility definitively replaces feudality, and this is a revolution.'

It was indeed a kind of revolution, and as far as the nobility was concerned it was not merely a transformation but a complete rebuilding. Under Francis I there were certainly still a few large fiefs; but he tolerated no independence and his bourgeois *baillis*, his law courts staffed by plebeians, the parliaments, increasingly displaced the feudal administration and jurisdiction.

At the same time Francis I built up, beside the land-owning nobility with its hierarchy of fiefs, a new titular nobility extending from the simple noblemen to the princes and peers of France. These noble titles bestowed by the king were still linked to land-ownership and ground rent, but the rank they conferred no longer depended solely on that traditionally associated with a certain piece of land. It represented a distinction bestowed by the king and less and less linked to governmental functions. The king did not respect the tradition associated with land, breaking it at will.[12] It was above all military services that the king rewarded in this way. Exceptional opportunities were therefore open to the *homines novi*, to warriors. Partly beside and partly within the old nobility a new noble hierarchy was formed within which status depended far more on the title bestowed by the king and the pension going with it than on tradition. The effects on the structure of the nobility were very soon seen. As early as the second half of the sixteenth century almost all the names of the aristocracy are new names.

As before, therefore, the nobility was a military estate. The king needed it above all in this form. But his growing power enabled him to undertake what with reference to a later period would be called 'rationalization', enlightened reform: he broke with tradition and began to reconstruct the nobility in keeping with his purposes as ruler.

The growing financial power available to him can be seen in the sharp increase in royal expenditure for presents, pensions, salaries,

---

[11] Lemonnier, *op. cit.*, p. 243.
[12] Material on this and what follows can be found in Lemonnier, *op. cit.*, pp. 244ff.

and so on, as compared to that of his predecessors. Admittedly he already operates the deficit economy so characteristic of later French kings. The reserves accumulated for the war treasury are used up all too quickly and there are constant attempts to tap new sources of money by raising taxes, selling offices, and so on. But all this only shows how more and more powers became available to the king through the development of the social field and of his position within it.

As a result, more and more people flooded to the court. It is characteristic of the transitional character of this period, when new forms were only beginning to be imposed on the development of society, that at least in the first half of the reign of Francis I there was no building large enough or good enough to hold the growing court. That the container for this growing court with its money economy had constantly to be renewed and extended until finally the Château of Versailles, a symbol of both culmination and stagnation, is large enough to contain all further development, throws much light on the correspondence between the development of the royal court and of society as a whole. At this stage in the development of states, the royal court is the highest centre of integration in society. The tasks of integration increase earlier or later with the growing differentiation of functions that takes place in the course of this development. It is therefore possible in a sense to read off the increase in the general division of labour within a society from the growth of the royal court — allowing, of course, for the specific distribution of power within dynastic societies.

It is also characteristic of the situation of the court in the transitional period that the people who gather here, while living in more direct and constant dependence on the king than earlier, are still basically knights and warriors and not, as later, courtiers who occasionally go to war. The period is full of wars, military expeditions and their vicissitudes. We should think only of Francis I's imprisonment. So the court always had something of the army camp about it.

There was, in addition, another factor that had considerable importance: the larger the court became, the more difficult it was to supply it in one place for any length of time.

Attempts have been made to explain the rise of early capitalist cities from the concentration of large groups of consumers at the courts of princes or kings.[13] But in such contexts we see to what ex-

[13] W. Sombart, in *Luxus und Kapitalismus* (Leipzig, 1913), ch. 2, drew attention to the existence and significance of large consumer strata in the seventeenth and eighteenth centuries. According to him towns are primarily concentrations of consumer strata and above all of court consumers. His view is based partly on the urban theories of Cantillon from whom he makes

tent, in illuminating social processes, an explanation of a particular fact by a *single* cause is always a partial explanation. Unilinear cause-and-effect relationships are an inadequate type of explanation here. The task of explanation lies in revealing interdependences through which the development of a single social formation is seen as part of the development of the whole network of functions within society. The growth of the court consumer stratum and the accompanying growth of the early capitalist town do not stand alone in a single causal relationship; they are functions of a change in the structure of the total figuration. Only in conjunction with progress in the exchange of money and commodities accompanying the expansion of trade, the commercialization of the social field, was it possible to keep a large number of people *permanently* together in one place the immediate environment of which was understandably insufficient to support such large numbers. In addition, the revenue of landowners must have taken on the character of direct or indirect money pensions, and the money economy must have been given certain secure forms if a section of the landowners were to sever themselves from their land and take up permanent residence far from it, in the town. In other words, the formation of the court consumer stratum is part of a more comprehensive movement.

Furthermore, the more unified the administration, the larger the area from which the king drew his income, the larger this income through increasing commercialization and more efficient civil and military administration, the larger could the consumer society become that lived and profited directly or indirectly from the king's income and property; and the greater would be the advantage to the town in which the king's income from the whole country was brought together. It is in this context that the form of the court in the transitional period must be understood. Until some way into the seventeenth century it was not very firmly bound to a particular place. Paris was the king's capital, but other cities competed with it in importance. Absolute centralization, the emergence of a *single* aristocratic society and thus the elaboration of a single exemplary human type, was only beginning. The royal court was still peripatetic,[14] it travelled from castle to castle. On horses and mules

the following quotation: 'If a prince or seigneur . . . settles down in a place he finds agreeable, and if several other seigneurs take up residence nearby in order to see each other frequently and enjoy agreeable society, this place will become a town. . . .'

[14] An analogous account relating to Henry II's reign can be found in L. E. Marks, *Gaspard von Coligny* (Stuttgart, 1892), vol. 1, 1, pp. 159–60: 'With several thousand followers, thousands of horses, the court travels throughout the Empire, visiting the castles of the king and the great nobles, and towns — on which it places a heavy burden.'

the king, the great lords and ladies, with their whole following, journeyed about. A long convoy of carts, carriages and servants of all kinds followed, and even the furniture, the carpets and utensils accompanied the court on its pilgrimage.

In this way the arteries connecting provincial life with the court, rural life with the town, were not as constricted as they became later, even though this constriction was gradually making itself felt in the permanent residence of large sections of the nobility at the court. A process of distancing is taking place. But the constant movement of the court prevents the distances from becoming petrified.

The basic structure of court departments and offices is already the same as under Louis XIV, even if everything is on a smaller scale. A *Grand Maître de l'Hôtel* has supervision of all the offices in the royal household. He, like the Grand Equerry, the Grand Chamberlain, the Grand Cupbearer and other incumbents of the great court offices, are powerful people not only at court but in the realm too. How far the nobility is growing into the king's household in this process can be seen above all from the fact that under Francis I it becomes customary for the king and the princes of the blood to be served by nobles even as regards lower functions such as that of valet.[15] Nevertheless, all relationships are in a state of flux in this period. The hierarchy of court people is more unstable, and the inheritance of offices is diminishing. Thus the mobility of the court and its military mode of life do not leave much scope for the formation of an inescapable etiquette.

One tendency which is of great importance for later developments, however, emerges very clearly in Francis I's reign. The distance separating those who belong to the court from those who do not takes on ever-increasing importance within the social field. The more insignificant the traditional functions of vassal and knight become — functions which previously maintained the distance between the nobility and other classes — the more distance and prestige attaches to the function of 'belonging to the court'.[16] The dividing line that is drawn between people and groups in this way also passes through the nobility itself. A part of the old nobility passes into the new aristocracy formed on the basis of belonging or not belonging to the court; another part does not gain access to this new, exclusive group. At the same time, a number of bourgeois people succeed in

---

[15] 'De ces temps (de Francois Ier), les rois et les grands princes du sang se servoient de gentils-hommes pour valletz de la Chambre, ainsi que je l'ai ouy dire à force anciens.' Brantôme, quoted by Lemonnier, *op. cit.*, p. 207.

[16] Lemonnier, *op. cit.*, p. 211.

entering this group and rising within it. In this way the nobility is reconstituted in this period on the basis of a different principle of social distance than previously.

The co-existence and overlap of these two forms of distance, through inherited feudal or professional functions, and through membership of the court, is of the greatest importance for the social structure of the *ancien régime*. The criterion of membership of the court finds expression in the existence of a court and non-court nobility, and later in the existence of a court bourgeoisie, or at least one existing in close proximity to court society and imitating it, and a non-court professional bourgeoisie.

'The seigneurs of the French kings were, to begin with, not merely advisers but legislators.'[17] That the power of the kings in relation to the nobility then grew *quite gradually and continuously* in France from about the time of Philip IV onwards, if with some fluctuations; that, under Francis I, in the period we call the Renaissance, and then under Henry IV in the seventeenth century, what had been long prepared was merely consummated — this was one of the decisive reasons why much of the medieval–feudal order was preserved and continued in the court order, while being transformed in the process. The nobles' governmental rights, the voice of the Estates General in decisions, were suppressed gradually, not abruptly, by the king.[18] And the decisive role played in this by the kings' 'free access to the wealth of their subjects through their independence of the estates' assemblies'[19] can be felt if we compare the situation of Francis I, who was virtually independent of the estates' agreement, with that of Charles V, which was more difficult in this respect.

Then, in the sixteenth century, there was a kind of reaction. The assemblies of the estates were called more frequently, and the struggles between them and the king became more violent.[20] The social background of the French religious wars is relatively difficult to understand in the absence of a detailed sociological study that is as yet lacking. The difficulty arises in particular because, apart from the actual religious differences between groups, there are, interwoven with them in the most diverse ways, struggles between cliques of the

[17] Koser, 'Die Epochen der absoluten Monarchie in der neueren Geschichte', *Historische Zeitschrift* (Munich–Leipzig, 1889), vol. 61.
[18] 'The direct and fatal cause . . . was the gradual and incessant transformation of feudality, the imperceptible but constant diminution of the seigneurs' power and the immense development of royal power.' Callery, 'Les premiers Etats généraux', *Revue des questions historiques* (1881), p. 87.
[19] N. Baumgarten, *Karl V*, 2, 3, quoted by Koser, *op. cit.*, p. 225.
[20] Koser, *op. cit.*, p. 260.

great families for the crown, struggles of the aristocracy impoverished by the money economy for a new foothold, and at the same
time, both among parts of the nobility and above all in urban strata,
powerful tendencies seeking to preserve or re-establish the rights and
freedoms of the estates. [21]

But however that may be, if we say that at the end of the religious
wars, with the victory of Henry IV, the absolute monarchy's victory
over all opposed social classes, including the nobility, was also decided, it should not be overlooked that while this formulation fairly
accurately states the results of these conflicts, the battlefronts in
them and the intentions of the antagonists were by no means as
unambiguous as it suggests. As so often, the words make it appear as
if what emerged afterwards was identical to what was actually desired
by the people and groups involved. Individual people are seen as the
planners, creators and causes of what in reality can only be
understood in terms of the total social network of people and their
wishes, the constellation of the social field as a whole, and the opportunities it gave individual groups and people.

11. Henry IV was originally a great vassal of the king of France, a
kind of prince, and it is unlikely that in this position he favoured the
idea of suppressing all the great vassals in the interests of the French
kings. Then, when he had become king, without possessing the king's
actual power, particularly his financial power, it was precisely he
who, characteristically at the head of a chivalrous army of nobles *in
the old style*, [22] fought against armies of mercenaries sent partly by
the King of Spain, partly by the Pope. He himself would at first have
been quite unable to pay a mercenary army of any strength from his
own means; and so the man who was finally to open the way to the
absolute power of the monarchy, particularly over the nobility, won
his victory with the aid of this same nobility, at the head of a noble

---

[21] Cf. Ranke, *Französische Geschichte*, bk. 6, ch. 3. 'The goal of the towns was the freedom
of the German Imperial cities.'
[22] Cf. Delbrück, *Geschichte der Kriegskunst* (Berlin, 1926), pt. 4, p. 258. 'The Huguenot wars
do not advance French military techniques and even have a retrogressive effect. A civil war
rests on the supporters the parties can find within the country, who come and go more or less at
will. The passionate partisanship necessary to ignite a civil war, which is particularly intense in
religious wars, produced in the Huguenot wars a peculiar late flowering of chivalry. The nobles
went into battle on their own impulse and served without payment. They fought bravely, but
the reverse side of chivalry was also noticeable: when Alexander of Parma had terrified Paris in
1590, he manoeuvred and avoided battle. Then Henry IV's army, that consisted mainly of
noble volunteers, finally dispersed without having done anything. In the end it was only
money, he said, that distinguished him and the prince of Parma. With better finances he too
would have been able to keep his army in the field. The silver of Potosi, Ranke observes, was
needed to develop the spirit of standing armies in Europe. There is no doubt that the American
precious metal helped the Spaniards considerably.'

army. He was, admittedly, supported by external powers who sent him money and troops, and by circumstances such as the death of Gregory XIV, as well as by dissent among his enemies.

It can be said with justice that at the end of the religious wars the struggle between monarchy and nobility was really decided, the way to absolute monarchy open. But apart from the social movements already mentioned that favoured the expansion of the king's power and gave him the means to extend and secure his rule, these last religious wars showed a further aspect of the social constellation that gradually gave the function of king such great preponderance over the representatives of all other functions. For in these wars a Catholic, Royalist nobility fought side by side with Protestants from all classes in Henry IV's camp, against other sections of the nobility who were allied to the Catholic towns, the clergy, the King of Spain and the Pope.

Henry IV's contemporaries themselves in many cases saw only that he was fighting at the head of the nobility and that his opponents, apart from rival noble families, were above all urban bodies and sections of the clergy. The fronts were certainly not entirely clear. For there were also Protestant towns which supported Henry IV. It is equally certain that on his side, that of the Protestants, there was also the Catholic–Royalist nobility, a moderate Catholic nobility sharply opposed to the strict Catholic groups on the other side; for their camp had produced the regicide, the murderer of Henry III, and in their camp he was revered.

As always in such cases, a great variety of motives will have drawn together the majority of the nobles on this side. At least one of the most tangible of these motives — which brought the majority of nobles into conflict with the Catholic clergy — deserves mention here, particularly as it does not generally receive sufficient attention.

Francis I had secured control, by a concordat, over a large section of the church livings in France. He thereby gained possession of funds, following the decay of the kings' domanial possessions, with which he could again richly reward nobles who served him. Thus a good part of the French nobility became beneficiaries of church wealth, exactly as, on the other side of the Channel, a section of the English nobility acquired land expropriated from the Church as a result of similar measures by Henry VIII. In both cases the king's actions brought a not inconsiderable section of the nobility into conflict with the clergy. It would be interesting to trace the connections which in England in the course of time brought a substantial part of the citizens of the capital into the camp opposing the old Church, while in France it was precisely the capital that was 'worth a Mass'. But it will be enough here to limit our attention to the problem of the nobility.

The expropriation of church livings by Francis I and their use as rewards for services rendered to the king, created a situation which contained the seed of long-lasting conflicts of interest between the nobility and the clergy.

Brantôme has described this situation and these conflicts of interest so vividly that it is worth quoting his accounts at length and without commentary on this question.

> What primarily induced King Francis to conclude the concordat with the Pope to abolish all elections to bishoprics, abbeys and priories, and to confer the right of nomination on himself, was partly the grave abuses that had crept into the elections, and partly the King's wish to obtain new sources of rewards for his nobility, for which the income from the Crown estates and taxes was insufficient, being entirely used up by the heavy costs of war. He considered it better, at all events, to reward men who had served him well with fat livings, than to leave these to idle monks, people, he said, who were good for nothing except drinking, eating, carousing, gaming or, at best, twisting gut strings, making mouse-traps and catching birds.
>
> I must note at this point that for some time, particularly after the foundation of the Ligue, certain conscientious people, or rather astute flatterers, had begun to complain shrilly about the nobles who owned Church estates. These, they said, did not belong rightfully to them but to the clergy, and this was a grievous error and offence which weighed heavily on the King's conscience.
>
> This might have had some substance if such Church estates had belonged wholly and really to the nobles who occupied them. But as it is, what harm does it do these cantankerous fellows . . . if after maintaining the abbot, the monks, the poor, paying the capital tenth and other taxes to the King, the nobles enjoy the surplus, a trifle, mere crumbs falling from the master's (the King's) table, the better to serve him.[23]

In another place Brantôme says: 'I have heard several percipient persons express their amazement at how a crowd of nobles could join the Ligue in France, for had it had the upper hand there can be no doubt that the clergy would have robbed them of the Church estates.'[24]

[23] Quoted from Brantôme's biographical fragments in *Allgemeine Sammlung Historischer Memoiren*, ed. Friedrich Schiller (Jena, 1797), vol. 13, section 2, p. 193.
[24] *Ibid.*, p. 197.

There we have, in somewhat forthright terms, one of the reasons why the majority of the nobles opposed the 'sacred Ligue'. The majority on the other side, apart from the clergy, consisted above all of the towns, with Paris at their head, which had grown immensely in the sixteenth century and was now slowly beginning to play, with its various bourgeois corporations, a special role in the history of France. There were, of course, nobles in this camp too. Above all, the strict Catholic party was headed by men from the great families who were pretenders to the throne. But for obvious reasons the 'Great Ones' of France hardly ever formed a united front. This small group of competing families, headed by the princes of the blood and therefore the nobles dependent on them, allied themselves as the need arose with other great social powers in the land to be carried up by them. It is enough that the social structure underlying these conflicts should be indicated here. For it is not without significance in understanding why this system, the French social field, despite all the disturbances, resistance and conflicts during these centuries, tended constantly and increasingly towards a balance centred on an absolute monarchy.

What we find in the conflicts of the sixteenth and seventeenth centuries are, generally speaking, on one side 'bourgeois corporations' that have become rich and numerous, and therefore powerful and confident enough vigorously to oppose the power of the nobles, but not strong enough to claim power for themselves. On the other side we find a nobility that is still strong enough to defy the rising bourgeois strata, but too weak, particularly economically, to establish its own power over them. In this constellation it is decisive that the nobility have already lost their administrative and judicial functions and that, thanks to these functions, rich and therefore powerful bourgeois corporations headed by the parliaments have formed as a kind of upper class of the bourgeoisie. So the nobility, with their shrinking financial basis, needed the kings in order to resist the pressure from bourgeois strata with their growing wealth, and the bourgeois corporations needed the kings to protect them against the threats, the presumption and the one-sided privileges of a still semi-chivalrous nobility. A figuration with a balance of forces of this kind, in which two estates held each other more or less in an equilibrium in which neither group was able to attain permanent preponderance over the other, gave the legitimate king, who was apparently equidistant from all groups, the chance to appear as a peacemaker bringing the weary warriors the respite they all longed for. This was indeed Henry IV's function to the highest degree. It, too, contributed decisively to his victory. The king appeared over and again as the ally and helper of each class or corporation against the threats from other groups which they could not master on their own.

12. What was set out earlier with regard to the central group of the absolute monarch, his primary sphere of activity, the court, therefore applies with appropriate modifications to his broader dominion as well: he ruled because and as long as the great social groups of the bourgeoisie and the nobility held each other in balance while maintaining an intense rivalry for power. It will be necessary to ascertain whether this is a sociological regularity that applies to court absolutism in general. If that were the case it would mean, in brief, the following: the opportunities of the prince within a social field organized in estates grow when the actual social power which — in conjunction with the advancing money economy — accrues to bourgeois groups on one hand and noble groups on the other through their social functions is so constituted that none of the classes or groups competing for supremacy can attain lasting preponderance. The prince rules, and rules so absolutely, because each of the competing groups needs him in their conflicts with the others, and because he can play one off against the other. The fact that he belongs by origin to one of the two partners, the nobility, has considerable influence on the structure of the court as on other matters. But because he can base himself on bourgeois groups on some issues, becoming less and less a *primus inter pares*, he distances himself from the nobility; because on other issues he can find support in the noble groups, he distances himself from the bourgeoisie. And so he maintains himself as the distanced ruler in a way very similar to what was seen earlier within the court, by carefully supervising and maintaining the balance of tensions between the estates and groups within his dominion.

Whether or not it can be demonstrated for other countries, therefore, this structure can be established without difficulty in the case of France. We hardly need to mention that the enumeration of the opportunities offered to the kings by their social field, which they were able to exploit in establishing their power, in no way detracts from the greatness and achievements of individual kings, if such an enumeration were not constantly misunderstood as a denial of the value of personality. The situation is, on the contrary, such that we can only really understand the greatness of the person if we are aware of the networks and entanglements in and through which he acts and thinks. In connection with this royal function of balancing a tension-filled social field, a peculiarity in the attitude of the French upper

classes towards the king can be understood, namely their ambivalence, which becomes the more perceptible the more independent
the kings become in their control of all state revenue through their
situation as arbitrators.

Each of these strata, the leading group of the bourgeoisie, the
parliaments, no less than the leading noble group, the hierarchy of
the court nobility, would gladly have limited the king's power on
their side. And attempts, or at least a suppressed inclination, to do so
are present throughout the entire *ancien régime*, though they seldom
emerge openly under Louis XIV. But each of these strata also needed
the strength and power of the legitimate kings to protect and maintain their own positions against the numerous threats and en-
croachments by other groups to which they were exposed in these
times of increasing interdependence. So it happens that on occasions
numerous noble groups ally themselves with the parliaments against
the king's representatives, as at the time of the *Fronde*. But they
always stay together only briefly, for very soon they fear the growing
power of their momentary allies more than that of the kings, and join
forces in one form or another with them or their representatives once
again. This typically ambivalent attitude, and the conflict situation it
implies, therefore make possible brief alliances between the various
leading groups against the monarchy. In such alliances the mass of
the bourgeoisie, up to the Revolution, nearly always plays the more
or less passive part of a tool for the purposes of one of the elite
groups. The alliances then break up in the way described. From the
days of the religious wars up to the pre-revolutionary period, this was
one of the constant patterns, despite all the changes and shifts in the
social balance, in this phase of the figuration's evolution.

13. In addition, neither the bourgeoisie nor the nobility and still
less the clergy — whose attitude in this play of forces must be the
subject of a separate analysis — was internally unified. For example,
the parliaments — which in the seventeenth century had been a
leading plebeian group but by the eighteenth were already an intermediate stratum between the nobility and the bourgeoisie, the
noblesse de robe — often made use of the mass of the populace and,
when it served their purposes, protected traditional rights, particularly those of the urban guild corporations. But, unlike many towns,
they had no special interest in the old order of the estates, nor, above
all, in convoking the Estates General. For they themselves claimed to
represent the nation, to have the right to object in its name to royal
decrees that seemed illegal. On occasion, they would refuse to
register such decrees, which deprived them of legal force, justifying

this by their origin in the old Royal Council (*Conseil du Roi*), and considering themselves superior to the Estates General. But at the same time, through their privileges, through the offices they had purchased or which their property represented, they were intimately connected with the king's rule. In face of attempts by other strata, particularly the nobility, to abolish the purchasability of offices and therefore the foundation of their existence, they depended on the king's help, just as they did when unrest among the populace, to which they themselves contributed a good deal, as in the case of the *Fronde*, exceeded a certain level and threatened their own property.

> The members of the Parliament sometimes make a noise moving their curule chairs, but they have no desire to die on them, struck by barbarian hands. These fathers of the nation always remember at the last moment that they are also fathers of families and that healthy bourgeois tradition requires that they should not leave the capital that they received from their ancestors diminished to their children. And so the conflict between the King and the Robe takes on an acrimonious character which sometimes goes as far as prison but stops short at their purses. [25]

It was just because both the official prestige and the purses — that is to say, the appropriated livings — of the high gentlemen of the *robe* were very closely bound up with the traditional rule of the king, that the parliaments and the whole *noblesse de robe* developed the ambivalent attitude towards the king that has been mentioned. They wanted to have their share of power and therefore to limit the power of the king, but they also needed a powerful king because their existence and offices were founded on his rule. As a result, their conflicts with the king, as long as his power overshadowed that of all other classes, take a typical course: 'Deliberation by the Assembly of the Chambers, decree by the Council, i.e. the King, which overrules the deliberation, resistance by the *Compagnie*, angry outbursts from the Prince, bitterness, regret and finally the obedience of the rebels.' [26] This refers to the seventeenth century. Later, as the power position of the kings gradually weakens in relation to other groups in the social field, the monarchy, which previously subdued and moderated the tensions and claims of these groups, becomes itself a figure in the game needing alliances with other groups. In the course of the eighteenth century, therefore, these typical conflicts take a dif-

---

[25] Charles Normand, *La bourgeoisie française au XVII siècle* (Paris, 1908), p. 249.
[26] *Ibid.*, p. 264.

ferent course: they end increasingly with the victory of the parliament. The latter's whole attitude, however, is that characteristic of a wealthy intermediate stratum with several fronts: against the nobility, the clergy and sometimes the populace they need a strong king, against the king they often make use of the populace and sometimes ally themselves with the nobility, above all the high nobility — with which this class has common ground in that, unlike the mass of the nobility, it has no direct interests as an estate. Towards the clergy, as long as they do not come from its own circle, and above all towards the Jesuits, its attitude is utterly implacable.

This may give an example of the strengths of the rivals risen from the bourgeoisie with which the nobility of the sword, already deprived of almost all administrative functions and the entire higher jurisdiction, had to contend. We also see clearly why and how much this nobility needed the king, and we understand how the kings were able to build and secure their rule on the basis of social groups that held each other more or less in check, until they themselves became more and more directly entwined in the tensions and the interplay of the different groups.

14. Like the Third Estate, the nobility itself was split into different groups; this enormously complicated the situation, multiplying the fronts and possibilities of alliances. The provincial and rural nobility, who from the religious wars to the Revolution hardly played the role of a political power elite any longer, can be disregarded here.

What was significant was the difference between the situation of the high nobility, e.g. the princes and dukes, the so-called 'great ones' (*grands*),[27] and that of the majority of the court nobility. For

[27] The expression *grands*, a standard term in the framework of the French society of the *ancien régime*, needs some further explanation, as there was no exactly equivalent social group in German society in the *ancien régime*. The absence of such a group is not without importance concerning the structural differences between the balance of social forces in the two countries. If we look in the German noble hierarchy for a group whose place corresponds roughly to that of the *grands* in the French, we find, above all, the rulers of petty principalities. But this already reveals the extraordinary structural difference between the two societies.

Elizabeth Charlotte of the Palatinate, who by marriage was removed from a German princely court to the French royal court, has left behind some observations that vividly illuminate this difference. She wrote (paraphrased by Ranke, *Französische Geschichte* (Leipzig, 1877) 4th edn, vol. 4, p. 230), for example, 'that between what in Germany and in France was called a "duke", she perceived an immense difference. In the former the word referred to born princes and free lords, in the latter only to a rank bestowed by the government (i.e. by the king) . . .

'Even the Princes of the Blood, for all their pretensions, she placed far below the German princes. For even the great Condé was married to a niece of Cardinal Richelieu, the Prince de Conty to the niece of Cardinal Mazarin, both of whom were of anything but high birth. People boasted of greatness in these houses, but did not know what greatness was. A *German* prince had a far better feeling for it, having no bourgeois relations and being nobody's *subject*.'

It is not often fully realized how much the peculiar tradition of the German nobility, which

on one hand these *grands* were, within the noble hierarchy, especially close to the king. To an extent his relations formed their centre; and it was no part of their intentions to undermine the authority and power of the king in relation to other strata, thereby weakening their own privileged position in the realm. Their own standing was far too closely bound up with the king's for this.

But on the other hand, just because they were especially close to the king, these 'great ones' were particularly jealous of his power, and disposed to deplore their enforced subjection to him, their inclusion in the category of *subjects* which equated them, in this regard, to everyone else.

Marmontel, in the article in the *Encyclopédie* devoted to the *grands*, depicts this group's peculiar position between two fronts very clearly though with some ideological embellishment. After speaking of the state as a machine that can only be kept in motion by an exact combination of all its parts — an image frequently used in the eighteenth century and one in close accord to this analysis — he describes the situation of the *grands* as follows:

Although the first subjects, they are slaves if the state becomes

---

placed heavy social penalties on marriage by a noble to a socially inferior, bourgeois girl (a tradition which lived on in bourgeoisified form in the National Socialist order of the family, in the punishing of marriages between a bourgeoisie regarded as a racial nobility with girls from groups regarded as socially inferior), was bound up with the fragmentation of the German Empire into numerous independent territorial states. In the course of state integration, of the increasing centralization of the central monopolies which played a decisive part in the formation of a unified state, the governmental functions of the territorial rulers withered away in France, as in England. Noble titles such as prince, duke and others were now significant only in referring to the inherited rank of a family. And even a prince — in relation to the king — was a 'subject'. The preservation of differences and barriers between nobility and bourgeoisie therefore finally lay in the hands of the king. In Germany the nobility maintained these differences and barriers far more on their own initiative. The dishonour, suspicion, derision and disadvantages that were heaped on a noble who married below his rank or had a 'blemish' in his family tree, could not, therefore, be made good by royal favour or other opportunities. Social opinion in this respect in Germany, in conjunction with the rivalries between noble families of all ranks, was far more implacable than in France. Naturally, 'misalliances' occurred, and the taboo applied far more severely to marriages of sons than of daughters. But through education from childhood on the condemnation of marriage between noble and bourgeois, of 'impure blood', deeply permeated the system of emotive value-judgements.

As so often, people of lower social rank took over the values of their social superiors even when they reflected dishonour on themselves. Thus broad sections of the upper bourgeoisie in Germany adopted these aristocratic values as their own. It will be an interesting task of future sociologists to observe how long a tradition of values which, as in this case, maintains sharp differences of social rank, can survive within a social structure in which it no longer has any proper function.

The situation of the French nobility cannot be understood unless we realize that the maintenance of barriers between the different noble ranks and between nobility and bourgeoisie has a different structure from that in Germany.

despotic; they fall back into the crowd if it becomes republican. They therefore hold to the prince on account of their superiority to the people, and to the people on account of their dependence on the prince. . . . Thus the *grands* are attached to the monarchist constitution by interest and by duty, two indissoluble bonds.

At the same time these same *grands* were especially dangerous to the king. For from this circle, and from it alone, his rivals could come. Indeed, as late as the reign of Louis XVI there was a plan in these circles to force the king to abdicate and to replace him by one of his relations. And even though, in the course of the eighteenth century, the kings again drew their ministers from the lower and middle nobility, it was an unquestioned tradition of the regime from Louis XIV on, and one that was very seldom broken, to deny these *grands* any access, even unofficial, to government, as far as was possible. This too is an example of the tensions and divisions existing within the nobility itself.

The ambition of the grands [says the *Encyclopédie* in one place] seems to lie in the direction of an aristocracy; but even if the 'people' allowed itself to be led in this direction, the simple nobility would oppose it, at least if they were not assured a share of authority. In this case, however, the *grands* would have twenty thousand of their own kind in place of *one* lord, so that they would never agree to such a solution. For ambition to rule, which alone causes revolutions, undoubtedly suffers less acutely under the domination of a single one than under equality with a large number.[28]

These alternatives graphically illustrate the social and psychological aspects of the figuration of tensions, as seen from the standpoint of the *grands*. The king's 'superiority' guarantees their distance from those below. Any conflict with the king forces them to seek allies below them, and their pride is offended by the necessity of placing themselves on the same level as their social inferiors. The desire for aloofness and superiority, for maintaining their exclusive existence, forces them into an ambivalent situation shot through with repulsions and attractions both from above and from below from which there is no escape.

There is another factor which further complicates the situation of the *grands*: their circle is so small and so closely linked to royal rule that its members do not really uphold the interests of their estate, the nobility as a whole, even though they may occasionally place

[28] *Enc.*, art. 'Grand' (philos., moral., polit.).

themselves at the head of such interests or, to win allies, make temporary concessions to the estates as the regent did. Basically, however, everyone in this small circle, in which each sees a direct competitor in almost every other, acts in his own personal interest, i.e. the interests of his 'house'. The group of the *grands* was, in fact, always split into hostile, rival houses and factions. As the great vassals of the kings had done earlier, each of them, at least up to the time of Louis XIV and more clandestinely under his successors, wanted at least a share of power if not the crown itself.

But precisely when one of the *grands* made a bid in this direction, it was revealed with particular clarity how this social field always restored its own balance, centred on the legitimate king. The basic structure always returned, a precarious balance of the many strata and groups within this social field, none of which had a sufficient power basis to establish its own rule against all the others and against the king.

Every usurper therefore succumbed to the same entanglement among the various groups and fronts. The stronger he became, the stronger grew the common front of all the rest. And the legitimate king, or the legitimate heir, had an immense advantage over him: his legitimacy. For this distanced him in the consciousness of each of the groups and strata not only from themselves but from all the others, so predestining him to function as the stabilizer of the otherwise precarious equilibrium.

Characteristic of this situation is the fate of one of the most important members of this class, the great Condé. When Mazarin ruled and Louis XIV was still a minor, the most disparate groups gathered together, for a period and for the last time before the definitive stabilization of the absolute monarchy, for a joint attack on its omnipotence, represented by the minister. The parliaments, the noble estate, urban corporations, men from the high nobility, all attempted to take advantage of the monarchy's weak moment, the queen's regency exercised by the cardinal, for their own purposes. But this rising by the *Fronde* showed exactly the picture which has just been mentioned: groups form an alliance against the minister representing the king. Parts of the alliance negotiate with the minister, leave the alliance, fight against their former allies, and then partly rejoin their side. Each of these groups wants to diminish the king's power, but each fears at the same time that it might increase the power of another. Prince Louis II of Condé is one of the most important figures in this game. What he wants, at first quite independently of the *Fronde* as such, is quite clear. He wants his share in the power of the state monopolies. In October 1649 he demands 'that without his prior knowledge and advice no high position shall be filled either at court or in the war, either in internal or in external affairs; that his servants and friends should be considered when vacancies occur; that in no matter should a decision be taken without his authorization.'[29] Mazarin first promises to fulfil this demand, but then allies himself with Condé's opponents. For the sake of appearances, he writes the prince a letter as late as 16 January 1650 solemnly pledging that he will never sever himself from him, and asking for his protection. On 18 January he has him arrested.

At this point, however, the situation is quite quickly reversed. Fear of Mazarin gains the upper hand on every side. Other *grands*, fearing they might meet the same fate as Condé, the parliament, the assembly of the noble estates in Paris, all press for the release of the prince. On 18 February he returns to Paris. Ranke, as always incomparably clear in describing particular situations, depicts the position to which the prince returns as follows:

> The entire situation has changed. It seemed to depend only on Condé to take possession of the position he had sought a year before as the first man in the land. . . . But to exert great authority one must depend only on oneself. Condé was fettered by a thousand considerations. The friendship he had promised the most aristocratic of the *Frondeurs* burdened him like a hard duty.[30] . . . Master neither of parliament nor of the ministry, uncertain of the Duke of Orleans, agreeing neither with the nobility nor with the clergy, what great act was open to him?[31]

[29] Document printed in Champellion's edition of the memoirs of Condé. Collection de Michard, 2, p. 205; quoted by Ranke, *op. cit.*, bk. 2, ch. 4.

[30] From this situation there is once again a way open for agreement with certain sides of the court. The court and court society were, if not the battlefield, at least the place behind the scenes where alliances were prepared and individual factions staked their claims before they were put into practice. This is true from the time of Louis XIV on; and it is in this context that we must understand d'Argenson, for example, in his diary of the year 1736 that was published later, in 1787, with the title *Loisirs d'un ministre*. After praising his outstanding gifts in war, his instinct for military technique, his courage and presence of mind in the most glowing terms, he writes of the great Condé: 'This hero in war was at court and in affairs a very mediocre politician. He had no idea how to seize his opportunity at the right time.' When he wrote down these observations the courtier d'Argenson, whose greatest ambition was to become a minister, understandably failed to see the compelling nature of the entanglements in which the prince was caught. From everything he has been told about the prince he understands only that he was successful in war but not in court intrigues. This again points to the connection between what is generally regarded as part of the character of courtiers, their devious manoeuvring, with the figuration they formed. Their character was nurtured by the struggles of the many groups living in one place (cf. ch. 3, parts 1 and 12, pp. 52–4 and 77–80). No military art could help someone who had not also mastered court arts and politics.

[31] *Ibid.*, bk. 2, ch. 4.

It would be possible on closer analysis to demonstrate a similar situation to the one besetting this man and the faction supporting him, in the case of most of the other groups and corporations forming the *Fronde*. Characteristic of this whole situation with its multiplicity of possible alliances in which everyone carefully observed everyone else to make sure he did not grow too strong, is the passage (from Aubery) also quoted by Ranke in which we read: 'The prince had reserved the right to be someone's friend or enemy as their conduct demanded. . . .'

One can read in Ranke, whose admirable account has scarcely been surpassed in its essential features by more recent French research, how the prince, through new alliances both internally and with the Spaniards, and favoured by the common hostility of almost all strata to Mazarin, again wins the upper hand; how, courageous and smiled on by the fortunes of war, he defeats the royal army in the suburb of Saint-Antoine, how the citizens of Paris willingly open the gates to him and how, at the very moment when he is about to establish his rule, giving his friends and supporters the leading posts,[32] the citizens' fear of his excessive power immediately gains the upper hand. The desire to curtail the over-mighty power of the king, which Mazarin had made particularly hated, is eclipsed, as the prince's power grows, by fear of a threat to the position guaranteed up to now by the legitimate monarchy, of changes in the established order. The citizens finally drop their ally. Then gradually a balance of forces between the social groups in the country is re-established under the definitive rule of the legitimate king.

The structure of these conflicts, and of the figurations whose oscillations they represent, has therefore been confirmed from a particular aspect in the way described above: groups and corporations form alliances, but each fears that the other might gain too much power. Each feels threatened by each increase in the power of every other, and this fragmentation of France into strata and groups none of which was able on its own to win clear preponderance over the others, makes them all more or less dependent on the king as the social peacemaker, the only guarantor of peace and relative security from the threats of rivals. If this tension between social groups of

---

[32] Ranke, *op. cit.*, bk. 2, ch. 5, p. 108, characterizes the typical aspects in this course of events: 'The great majority of property owners permit the overthrow of a regime which they feel to be burdensome without taking direct part in the victory of its opponent. No sooner has the latter attained power and revealed his own equally burdensome demands, than the time for a return to the old order has arrived. From the sympathies then aroused restorations are made.' This pattern, however, does not fit the present case of the *Fronde* very exactly. As may be seen, there are other, perhaps more fundamental structural lines that determine its fate.

roughly equal power gave the French monarch his immense opportunity, the growing income he received from the country and his control of an army paid with this income and which directly and indirectly secured its regular flow from society, made it possible for
him to take advantage of the balance of forces and secure the wide
scope enjoyed by his rule.

15. 'Louis XIV,' writes Ranke, 'had the good luck, like Henry IV,
to return as the country's liberator from an *unlawful* power which
oppressed everyone and satisfied few or none.'

It was not only luck. Within this social field a usurper of power
would only have had a chance of success if either a major power shift
in the relations between social forces had already taken place, and he
had taken power as the charismatic leader of the stratum which had
just grown strong, or if he himself had been so superior to the king in
money and therefore in troops that he was not only able to defeat the
king's army decisively, but to break the resistance of all the groups
interested in the existing equilibrium. If neither were the case, the
probability that the figuration that had developed by that time would
revert once again to its previous balance was very great. The new
wielder of power would have had to appear as unlawful, i.e. a threat
to the existing balance; in face of the legitimate king, even one
discredited by unpopular representatives, his chances were therefore
slight.

This shows us a particular aspect of the sociological importance of
a king's legitimacy in this figuration of people. As we know,
hereditary succession to the throne has often been rejected because it
makes descent and not ability the principle for selecting a ruler. From
a sociological point of view, this way of selecting the ruler in the old
France still heavily bound by tradition, certainly had a specific function. In this field with its unstable balance between the higher,
politically active strata, it provided a certain guarantee that the king
was interested in maintaining the existing order. In addition it
assured each of the leading groups that he was not too one-sidedly
bound to the interests of an opposing group since, unlike a usurper,
he had not needed to seek allies among the conflicting social groups
in order to come to power. The lawful origin of the kings *distanced
them equally from all the social groups in the country*. It is not even
important whether this was actually the case. What mattered was that
the legitimacy of the king's blood removed him, in the consciousness
of the various strata and in his own, from the tensions attaching to
the other groups. Since, in a field where the strata and groups are
more or less in balance, none of them either tolerates a ruler coming

from another or — if they are upper classes [33] — desires the overthrow of the established order or prolonged disturbances, the 'legality' of the king's birth appears to all groups finally as a guarantee that he is not under obligation to other groups for his instatement, or one-sidedly involved in their interests. If the situation of Henry IV or Louis XIV is compared — as a kind of antithesis — to that of the regent [34] who stood on the borderline of legitimacy, the logic of events that arises from the specific multipolar equilibrium of this figuration will everywhere be seen. The more uncertain the legitimacy, the more remote the kinship of the new ruler to his predecessor, the greater is the compulsion on him to secure his rule through alliances with individual groups, and the greater, therefore, is the threat to others and to the existing balance.

At the same time, however, this figuration exerted a pressure on the king, once he had attained power, in the direction expected by the various groups, compelling him to give none of them advantages which would give them too much power in relation to the others. For just because his rule was founded on the fragile equilibrium between groups holding each other in check, any increase in the power of one would have endangered his own rule as much as the position of the others, and so the whole existing figuration. In this sense, therefore, the kings were extremely interested in maintaining the existing, constantly oscillating balance of forces. They may have been especially bound to the nobility by origin and culture. But they could no longer grant it a pre-eminence that endangered equilibrium within the state, any more than they could to the bourgeois corporations, if they wished to safeguard the foundations of their own power. To preserve the balance in their realm they had to preserve the nobility, but they had equally to distance themselves from it. Here, therefore, we have reached a point which is of great importance in understanding the relations between king and nobility, and in answering the question why the king preserved the nobility — which also explains the function of the nobility in this realm.

16. The notion that the relationships between strata and groups in

[33] The 'politically active' groups in France in the *ancien régime*, at least up to 1750 and to a considerable extent up to the Revolution, were conservative elite groups, that is, above all, the leading groups in the pyramids of the estates of the bourgeoisie, the nobility and the clergy. How far reformist groups such as the leading encyclopedists had influence on the affairs of state remains to be investigated.

[34] The sentence with which Ranke opens his account of the regency of the Duke of Orleans at once reveals the pattern described above: 'But not without concessions in favour of those who had helped him by their decisions, did the Duke attain the highest position.' Ranke, *op. cit.*, vol. 4, p. 323.

a social field are generally unambiguous, that, for example, hostility between them is predominant and history is therefore a history of class struggles, proves on clear examination to be, while not incorrect, certainly one-sided. Ambivalent relations between social strata in one and the same state, their oscillation between mutual dependence and mutual hostility, especially in multi-layered figurations where most groups have several fronts, are far more frequent than has been demonstrated until now. The *ancien régime* was riddled with such ambivalent relationships. One cannot understand it without introducing this or a similar category. The attitudes of the nobility to the king, of the politically active bourgeoisie and the *noblesse de robe* to the king, were ambivalent, as were the relations between the nobility and the bourgeoisie themselves. One of the most interesting problems of the *ancien régime* is how, in the course of a peculiar transformation of the bourgeoisie, this ambivalent attitude to the nobility finally became, in a particular situation, the unambiguous hostility of parts of the bourgeoisie towards the nobility, the king and other parts of the bourgeoisie. No less ambivalent, however, was the attitude of the kings themselves to the social classes, above all the nobility. For just because the nobility was socially close to the king, closer than all the other strata of the people, just because the king was always a man of the nobility, to maintain the distance between king and nobility was both difficult and important. The nobility was particularly dangerous to the king, and the closer a group within the noble hierarchy was to the king, the more it threatened him. We have already pointed out that the *grands seigneurs*, the peers and above all the princes of the blood, not only showed an inclination to restrict the king's power like the rest of the noble estates and the elites of the bourgeois pyramid, but that between them, the descendants of earlier great vassals or kings, and the reigning king there was a latent rivalry. If on one hand the kings belonged to the nobility, felt and acted as nobles and needed the nobility as an integrating element in their dominion — if for all these reasons they were concerned to preserve it, on the other its existence meant a latent threat to their rule, from which they had constantly to defend themselves. This ambivalent relation of the king to the nobility therefore provides the foundation — and also the explanation — of the peculiar form which the court nobility took on in the *ancien régime*. The provincial nobility, as already mentioned, no longer played any part as a political factor.

17. Why the king needed the nobility has been stated. He needed them, subjectively and by tradition, both to provide his company and

to serve him. The fact that the nobility rendered him even the most personal services distanced the king from all the other people in his realm. Even the military and diplomatic functions of the nobles were finally no more than derivatives of such court functions. He needed them, from the objective standpoint, as a counterweight to the other strata in his realm. The annihilation of the nobility, the abolition of the distance separating them from the bourgeoisie, the bourgeoisi-fication of the nobility would have so far displaced the centre of gravity of this figuration, so greatly increased the power of the bourgeois strata, and made the kings so dependent on this class that they, perhaps without always realizing exactly what this balance in their realm meant for their own social position, strictly maintained the distinctions between estates and so preserved the nobility as a distinct class in its own right.

But if the kings needed the nobility and therefore preserved it, they had to do so in a way which minimized the threat it posed to their rule. A long and very gradual development had prepared the final solution to this problem. First, with the aid of a bourgeois royal bureaucracy, the kings expelled the nobility from almost all posts in the higher judiciary and administration. In this way the powerful stratum of the *robe* came into being, which counterbalanced the nobility in actual power if not in social esteem. In this process the kings showed a persistent tendency to fill all the power positions in their dominion with persons lacking a following or relations and dependent solely on them. So the bulk of the nobility in the sixteenth century was thrown back on its function as knights and landowners. With the slow expansion of the money economy and the upheavals which this brought about above all in the value of money and in army reform, this basis was violently shaken. It was this above all which drove a good part of the nobility to the court, binding it to the king in a new form. The kings were able to take advantage of this oppor-tunity. This is the only context in which the formula of the 'victory of the monarchy over the nobility' has any meaning. Seen from the standpoint of the final result, one can say that the struggle between monarchy and nobility was really decided at the end of the religious wars, and that by and large the way to 'absolute' monarchy was then opened. That the struggle between nobility and monarchy was not conducted unambiguously as such by the conflicting parties has already been said.

But the fact that Henry IV opened the way to absolute monarchy at the head of a noble army is not without significance in understand-ing the relation between nobility and king in this monarchy. Leaving aside the nobility's dependence on the king and the king's on the nobility within the new order, there were traditional bonds linking them. This ethos, while it could not have been maintained without mutual dependence, nevertheless carried weight as a tradition. It was never quite extinguished in the France of the *ancien régime*, but was gradually transformed about the period of Henry IV from its feudal to its court shape. The social organ which maintained these two functions of dependence and distance in accordance with the new power relationships established after the religious wars, was the court, in the form it took on definitively under Louis XIV. Through the court a good part of the nobility was from now on deprived of all independence while being provided for and maintained in constant dependence on the king.

The double face of the court as an instrument through which the king simultaneously dominated and supported the nobility as an aristocracy, corresponds exactly to the ambivalent character of the relationship existing between nobility and king. But the court did not attain this double function at one stroke, through the inspiration of an individual king. It slowly developed in this direction hand in hand with the transformation of the real power position of nobility and kings, until Louis XIV finally seized the opportunity presented to him and very consciously developed the court into an instrument of rule in the double sense of providing for and subduing the nobility. It will be enough to show in broad outline how the court was formed to this end.

18. Under Henry IV and even under Louis XIII the court offices, like the majority of military appointments, had the character typical of all offices in seigniorial absolutism: they were purchasable and therefore the property of their incumbent. This applies even to the position of *gouverneur*, the military commanders of the separate regions of the realm. That the incumbents could in certain cases only exercise their office with the king's permission, that in others they were quite simply allocated by the king's favour, can be taken for granted. The two methods of filling posts, through purchase or through the king's grace and favour, were intermingled. But the former slowly became predominant, and since the majority of nobles could in no way compete with the bourgeoisie in financial wealth, the Third Estate, or at least families coming from it and only recently ennobled, slowly but visibly occupied these posts as well. Only the great noble families still had enough income, partly through the size of their estates and partly through pensions paid to them by the king, to hold their own to some extent.[35] A disposition to help the nobility in

this situation is unmistakable in Henry IV as in Louis XIII and Richelieu. They all needed to keep the nobility away from political power, but they also needed to preserve it as a social factor.

After the murder of his predecessor Henry IV was, to begin with, entirely dependent on the nobility. In this situation he started — under pressure from his supporters — by swearing a royal oath, a written pact which contained among other things the following undertaking:

> We promise him service and obedience upon the oath that he has given us in writing, that within two months His Majesty shall gather together . . . the said princes, dukes and peers, crown officers and other subjects who were loyal servants of the dead king, in order that all together shall hold counsel and take decisions concerning the affairs of the kingdom, pending the decisions of the . . . Estates General, as is contained in the said promises of the said Majesty. [36]

In addition to this, we should hear how Henry IV, after his proclamation as king and still in the process of reconquering his realm, appeals to the heads of his native nobility of Perigord, 'to gather together and leave their houses to come and serve him', [37] how he summons 'his faithful nobility of the Île de France, Beauce, Champagne and Brie', how he instructs the governor of Picardy to bring him his 'good and affectionate servants'. [38] Yet he was the same man who took the last, decisive steps by which the old patriarchal ties between king and nobility, those of liege lord and vassal, were changed into the court-absolutist bond of king and courtier which reached its consummation under Louis XIV. And under Henry IV the necessarily contradictory attitudes of the kings and their representatives in this regime towards the nobility become quite clear. The bond with the nobility is still taken for granted by Henry IV. He lived in the midst of a noble society. [39] He lamented the situation which threatened many 'good and ancient families' with ruin, and sought to alleviate their debts by laws. [40] He did everything he could to

[35] However, we should not forget, in considering the continual uprisings of these *grands* against the king up to the time of Louis XIV that even their financial strength, and so their position in relation to both the king and the bourgeois strata, was sinking. Cf. Ranke, *op. cit.*, vol. 7, p. 98, n. 2.

[36] Quoted by Koser, *op. cit.*, p. 263.

[37] Avenel, *Lettres de Henri IV, Collection des documents inédits de l'Histoire de France*, vol. 4, p. 403.

[38] Avenel, quoted by de Vaissière, *op. cit.*, p. 217.

[39] '"The king knows that I am as good a noble as himself," says a minor nobleman in a novel of the time.' De Vaissière, *op. cit.*, p. 198.

[40] Mariéjol, *Henri IV et Louis XIII*, Histoire de France, vol. 4, p. 3.

reconcile his helpers of earlier days with the turn that things had taken, by which the leader of the Protestant nobility had now become a Catholic king over these nobles. But at the same time the immanent logic of his situation as king forced him to suppress all stirrings of protest in the declining nobility that often felt discriminated against. He first treated these rebellious stirrings mildly and humanely, bearing in mind their common struggles and the obligations under which they placed him. He demanded no more than that the rebels openly confessed their guilt, and if they repented he offered reconciliation and restored them to favour without further punishment. But in demanding subordination and confession of guilt he was implacable. He had to be. For example, he first requested the Duc de Biron, who was planning an uprising, to confess his intentions in a confidential meeting between the two, promising him certain forgiveness if he confessed and repented. But when de Biron refused to confess, despite the latter's repeated reminders of services rendered to the king,[41] he had him unceremoniously brought to justice and finally executed. But even though the king, faced by this conflict between his ties to the nobility and the inescapable demands of kingship, found his solution in the firm but fundamentally conciliatory attitude expressed in the Edict of Nantes, he was gradually but increasingly drawn towards the path of absolute monarchy, as if forced by the opportunities in his way. He never kept his promise to call the Estates General. 'Il voulait au maniement de ses affaires d'Etat estre creu absolument et un peu plus que ses prédécesseurs n'avoient faict', a gentleman of the *robe* said of him.[42]

19. If, despite all this, Henry IV remained as helpful and moderate towards the nobility as his royal task permitted, in one decisive matter he could have helped the nobility very little, even had he wished to, in its economic situation.

What the inflow of new finance, the growing commercialization of the social field meant for the nobility has already been explained.[43] This development meant economic ruin for a large section of them. It was all the more severe since the religious wars had had the same function for the nobility as civil wars often have for declining classes; they concealed from it the inevitability of its fate. The troubles and unrest, the trials in battle, the possibility of plunder and the facility of gain, all this persuaded the nobility that they could maintain their

[41] Ranke, *op. cit.*, vol. 7, 5, p. 64, quotes Biron's words: 'Without us, where would you be?' Cf. also Mariéjol, *op. cit.*, p. 43, 'If he had spoken ill, Biron said of himself, he had acted well.'
[42] Etienne Pasquier, quoted by Mariéjol, *op. cit.*

long-threatened social position and be saved from sinking into poverty. They had no understanding of the economic upheavals in which they floundered. They interpreted the new phenomena they encountered in terms of their previous experience, with their old concepts.

This aspect of the predicament of the nobility is brought to life when we hear how one of the victims interpreted the unexpected influx of precious metals and its significance for the nobility:

> Far from having impoverished France, this civil war has greatly enriched her, revealing an infinity of treasure hidden underground, and in churches, that served no purpose, placing it in the sun and turning it into good money in such quantity that more millions of gold were seen in France than there had previously been millions of pounds of silver, and more fine new silver coins forged from these hidden treasures than there had been coppers before. . . .
>
> That is not all: the rich merchants, usurers, bankers and other niggards down to the priests, kept their money locked in their coffers and neither enjoyed it themselves nor lent it except at excessive interest, or by purchasing or mortgaging land, goods or houses at a wretched price. So the noble who had been impoverished during the foreign wars and had pawned or sold his goods, was at his wits' end, without even enough wood to warm himself, the usurous knaves having pocketed everything. This fine civil war has restored him to his rightful place. I have seen gentlemen of high birth who, before the civil war, went about with two horses and a footman, recover so well that during and after it they were seen travelling the country with six or seven good horses . . . that is how the brave nobility of France has been restored by the grace or, one might say, the grease of this good civil war.[44]

In reality, however, the major part of the French nobility, returning from this 'good' civil war that was supposed to have restored them, found themselves debt-ridden or ruined. Life was expensive.[45] Creditors, as well as rich merchants, usurers and bankers, and above all gentlemen of the *robe*, crowded in, seizing noble estates wherever they could, and often enough noble titles as well.

The nobles who had kept their estates suddenly found that their income was no longer enough to cover the cost of living:

'The lords who had ceded land to their peasants against duties in

---

[43] See above, p. 000.
[44] Brantôme, *Oeuvres complètes*, publiées par L. Lalanne pour la Société de l'Histoire de France, vol. 4, pp. 328 – 30.
[45] Cf. de Vaissière, *Gentilshommes campagnards* (Paris, 1925), pp. 220ff.

cash, continued to collect the same revenue but without the same value. What had cost five sous in the past cost twenty at the time of Henry III. The nobles were being impoverished without knowing it.'[46]

As always with an upper class that goes into decline, what we see here is not a total deprivation of money but a reduction of it in relation to their social claims and the needs customary in society:

> If the nobles who have lost their income and are heavily in debt showed prudence and good management, there is no doubt that with the ease of life which they enjoy they could put their affairs right, at least in part if not completely; for, living normally in their domains, they could do so without putting their hands to their purses. There is none of them, indeed, who is without wood for heating, fields to harvest grain and wine, gardens and fruit, and beautiful green avenues to walk in, pens for hares and rabbits, the countryside for hunting, dovecotes for their pigeons, a farmyard for their fowls, etc.[47]

But just because many nobles did not wish to live in this way, just because they struggled to preserve their existence as nobles, they crowded to the court and made themselves directly dependent on the king. It is in this way that what from certain points of view is rightly called the struggle between the monarchy and the nobility was decided. The links in the chain binding the nobility interlock: they are impoverished because a certain class tradition and the social opinion corresponding to it require them to live from private means without professional work if they are to maintain their social prestige; with inflation they cannot keep pace with the standard of living of the money-earning bourgeois strata; the majority of them therefore have the choice of living like peasants or at least in a way bearing no relation to their pretensions as nobles, or of becoming prisoners of the court and so maintaining their social prestige on a new basis. Some succeed in this, others do not. The reconstruction of the nobility on the foundation of court distance, which comes to the fore clearly under Francis I, does not take place all at once. It is not completed even under Henry IV; for the influx of provincial nobles trying to rise into court circles from the despised country nobility never completely stops during the *ancien régime*, although acceptance at court becomes more and more difficult.

---

[46] Mariéjol, *op. cit.*, p. 2.
[47] Report by Pietro Duodo (1598) in Alberi, *Relazioni Venete*, Appendice, p. 99; quoted by de Vaissière, *op. cit.*, p. 226.

The money economy of the court, being in the process of evolution from the old barter economy, forms a kind of vessel collecting particular social streams. The fuller this vessel becomes, the fewer people can be carried into it by these streams from the camps of the provincial aristocracy and the bourgeoisie. So the pressure-relationships within the social circulation that develops, with the court as its highest organ, are gradually entirely changed, until finally the whole system is torn apart by its internal tensions.

20. It is no doubt, to begin with, the king's conscious policy to demand very sternly that members of the greater and lesser nobility should stay at court if they wish to enjoy the king's favour. Henry IV did not yet have sufficient means to finance a court machine on the scale, or to distribute court offices, favours and pensions in the abundance that was seen later under Louis XIV. It was not so clearly his intention as it was for Louis to make the court a noble formation, an institution supporting the nobility. The figuration is still in a state of flux. Noble families are sinking, bourgeois ones rising. The estates still exist, but the fluctuations between them are great, and the wall dividing them breached in many places. Personal ability or lack of it, personal good or bad luck, often have as much influence on a family's chances in this period as its original descent from one or the other social group.

Then slowly the roads leading from non-court strata into court society grew narrower. The royal court and court society were slowly transformed into a social formation whose customs, including the way of speaking, dressing and even moving the body when walking and in conversation, differed markedly from those of all non-court formations. It became more difficult than before for people who had not grown up in the 'court atmosphere', or gained early access to court circles, to develop the personal characteristics by which the aristocratic court people distinguished themselves from the non-court nobles and bourgeois, and by which they recognized each other.

With the increasing development of the French royal court into a sharply distinguished social elite formation, court society developed a special culture as a natural part of its special social existence. Early forms of this elite culture in gestures, speech, love-making and taste — to mention only a few aspects — had existed not only at royal courts but even, and especially, at the courts of territorial lords as early as the Middle Ages. If one took the trouble, one could trace precisely how what may be called 'court culture' gradually grows out of the social field as a distinct elite formation. Such a study could contribute much towards bringing the idea of 'culture', which is often used today as if it were a phenomenon hanging in mid-air independently of people, back into contact with social development, within which alone cultural phenomena or, to use a different term, social traditions can be studied and explained. Court culture gradually became influential in many countries in the sixteenth and seventeenth centuries because court society, particularly in France, was becoming the most influential social formation in the country with the increasing centralization of the state. The encapsulation of court society was more or less completed under Louis XIV. During his reign access to it by bourgeois as well as provincial nobles was considerably curtailed. Nevertheless, it was not yet completely blocked.

Very gradually the court acquired its character as both an organization supporting the nobility and an instrument for maintaining the king's rule against the nobility. This happened after the groups concerned had repeatedly tested their relative strength and mutual dependence in open or concealed conflicts. Louis XIV only seized, though with the utmost vigour and determination, the opportunities which his power position put in his way. We understand these opportunities perhaps better if we read an appeal addressed to Louis XIV's predecessor by the nobility with the heading 'Requestes et articles pour le rétablissement de la Noblesse' and dated 2 October 1627.[48]

This begins by saying that it is to the nobility, besides divine aid and the sword of Henry IV, that the king owes his crown, at a time when most of the other classes had been incited to revolt, but that nevertheless the nobility 'is in the most wretched state ever . . . racked by poverty . . . made vicious by idleness . . . and reduced by oppression almost to despair'.

Among the reasons now given for this state is the mistrust that a few members of this estate have aroused in the king by their arrogance and ambition. These, says the document, have convinced the kings of the need to curtail their power by elevating the Third Estate and by excluding nobles from offices and dignities they might have misused, thus depriving the nobility of the administration of law and taxation and expelling them from the royal councils.

Here the playing-off of one estate against the other, the exploitation of the equilibrium between them, is understood quite clearly as the traditional policy of the king.

The nobility then confronts the king with its demands in twenty-two articles including the following: apart from the military gover-

---

[48] Mariéjol, *op. cit.*, p. 390.

norships throughout the realm, the civil and military posts in the royal house — that is, the skeleton of what was later to make the court a mechanism supporting the nobility — should cease to be purchasable; they should be reserved to the nobility. In this manner, which appears here as a demand of the nobles, Louis XIV did indeed provide for the nobility, while also subduing them. He reserved the court posts for the nobility and distributed them by personal favour, although of course they had to be paid for when passing from one family to another, for they were, like every other office, a possession.

But the nobility demanded many other things in these twenty-two articles. They wanted a certain influence on provincial administration, and access for a number of specially qualified nobles to the parliament, at least in an advisory capacity and without emolument. They demanded that a third of the members of the councils for finance and war, and other instruments of royal rule, should come from their ranks. But of these and other demands by the nobility, apart from a few insignificant ones, only the first-mentioned was later fulfilled: the court offices were reserved to the nobility. All the other demands, as far as they entailed even the most modest participation by the nobility in government or administration, remained unfulfilled until Louis XIV's death.

21. We have, here again, a clear picture of the shift of equilibrium which led in France to the court manner of preserving sections of the nobility. The counterpart of this which perhaps comes most readily to the minds of Germans, is the Prussian solution to the problem.

'Frederick II,' writes Taine,[49] 'hearing about this etiquette, said that if he were king of France his first edict would be to create another king who would hold court in his place; and indeed these idle people who salute need another idle person to salute. There was only one way to free the monarch: to recast the French nobility and transform it, on the Prussian model, *into a laborious regiment of useful functionaries*.' This is indeed the exact opposite of the form of the nobility which the traditional attitude of the French kings did so much to maintain.

To raise the question why development took one direction in Prussia and the opposite in France is to pose the whole problem of the difference between these national developments. It could be shown how important it was for the formation of Prussia that the court had to be created anew under the first Prussian king, more or less on foreign models, whereas in France it took on a certain tradi-

---

[49] Taine, Les origines, 'Ancien régime', vol. 2, bk. 4, ch. 3, 2, p. 170.

tional form that needed to be developed but never really 'created', in a very gradual evolution lasting centuries. It could also be shown what the lack of a common court culture and traditional bonds meant for the relationship of nobility and monarchy in Prussia. The relative under-development of the urban bourgeoisie gave the balance of forces in Prussian society a different character. In this context only one of the numerous problems raised by the different development of the two figurations will be briefly mentioned, because it has direct relevance to courtization in France. In noble circles in Germany a tendency towards legal studies and official careers is evident even before the Reformation.[50] In France, by contrast, the nobility was traditionally a non-working warrior estate whose members generally went to university only if they intended to become ecclesiastics. At any rate, in the whole modern history of France we hardly ever come across names of lawyers who were nobles, i.e. members of the *noblesse d'épée*.[51] It can only be indicated in passing here that the difference in the way the German and French intelligentsias were formed and recruited is very closely bound up with this fact. In Germany the university became a decisive instrument of culture, while in France in the *ancien régime* it had hardly any live contact with the society actually creating culture, court society. In Germany the intelligentsia was composed largely of scholars, or at least of people who had attended university, while in France the selective mechanism was not the university but court society, the *monde* in the narrower or wider sense. In Germany, finally, despite all the social relationships between members of the in-

[50] Cf. e.g. A. Stolzel, *Die Entwicklung des gelehrten Richtertums in deutschen Territorien* (Stuttgart, 1872), p. 600. 'The majority of trained judges in the sixteenth and seventeenth centuries came mainly from the senatorial families of the larger and smaller Hessian towns. The higher official posts were reserved to the nobility; to attain them, the number of Hessian students from the nobility increased considerably after the Reformation.' That the bureaucratization of the nobility, usually as a career for younger sons, began relatively early in Germany is demonstrated by abundant evidence. The reasons for this development, however, remain an unsolved problem that has perhaps been given insufficient attention up to now, although it is of the utmost importance for the development of the German and French national characters and for an understanding of this development. At the present stage of research one can only offer conjectures on the reason why at least a part of the German nobility went to university and why this was clearly compatible with their honour as an estate, while that was certainly not the case in France. In particular, it is worth investigating whether this practice was confined to the Protestant nobility or is also to be found in Catholic states in Germany.

[51] Cf. Brantôme, *Biographische Fragmente*, vol. 13, section 2, p. 159: 'King Francis also filled his privy council with various ecclesiastics, being compelled to do so mainly by the circumstance that the nobles of his realm, at least the younger sons (the question of study only arose for them), had not studied or learnt enough to be appointed to his parliamentary courts or the major and minor state councils.'

telligentsia, the book was a particularly important, if not the primary, means of communication between people, while in France, however well-loved books might be, conversation was the foremost means. These are only a few of the phenomena directly connected to the special place of the university in Germany, and to the separation of university and court society in France.

22. Not only is the form of the nobility in France different from that in Germany or, more exactly, in Prussia; the form of officialdom also differs between the two countries. Both facts are closely interrelated; one cannot be understood without the other. This connection is also of importance regarding the evolution of the court as a support for the nobility. This can be briefly indicated. Characteristic of officialdom in the *ancien régime* was the institutionalized purchase of offices. Regardless of how this came into being, it was extended further and further, with some fluctuations, in the course of the sixteenth century, and in Henry IV's reign it could hardly have been abolished without massive upheavals in the whole social fabric. The entire structure of the court monarchy of the *ancien régime* was inseparably bound up with this institution.

The question whether the purchase of offices was 'good' or 'bad', measured by the values of our own later stage of development, is not only irrelevant but wrongly posed. For the values of the official ethos now prevalent originate, like the present form of bureaucracy itself, from earlier forms, including the values connected with the sale of offices. The legitimization of this institution by Henry IV had, on one hand, definite financial reasons. The sale of offices was an important source of income to the king. But in addition the legitimization was put into effect explicitly in order to make it impossible for the nobility to have any influence on the filling of official posts in the manner of feudal patronage. This institution too, therefore, was in some respects an instrument used by the kings in their struggle against the nobility, particularly the high nobility.

It would have been quite pointless and contrary to all the demands of royal policy to force the nobility to participate in the purchase of offices institutionalized by Henry IV and founded in part on the tensions between king and nobility. It would also have been quite impossible. For only the abolition of purchasability, for which the nobility fought often enough and which would have overturned the entire system, would have given the majority of the nobility, who had very limited means, renewed access to offices in administration, taxation and justice. Such a change would either have entailed enormous cost — for unless he were willing to confiscate property on a massive scale the king would have had to refund the price of the offices — or the rich bourgeoisie, whose property the offices were, would have been crippled. Moreover, the kings themselves had no interest in such a measure. Apart from the fact that the sale of offices was an indispensable source of income to them, the abolition of the institution would have gravely disturbed the social equilibrium within their state.

Every attempt to abolish the purchasability of offices during the *ancien régime* foundered partly on financial considerations and partly on the bitter resistance of the owners. It can also be said that at the decisive stage in the reconstitution of the French nobility no one seriously considered solving the problem by bureaucratizing the nobility. It lay outside the sphere of what was conceivable within the social field, and of what was desired by the various centres of interest — the *robe*, the nobility of the sword, and the monarchy. The appeal by the nobility in 1627 mentioned above, that considers all the possible ways of preserving the nobility, does not even mention this possibility. As we have said, the nobility itself demanded only *advisory* and limited participation in the high court of justice and parliament, without remuneration; that is, not in order to be provided for, but to occupy a position of power.

23. The means of support left to the nobility were, apart from their estates, and pensions and gifts from the king, primarily posts in court diplomacy and military offices. The nobility's demand that both should be reserved to noblemen therefore only had any success as far as this kind of office was concerned. But this only happened under Louis XIV. Under Louis XIII and Richelieu, the time when the appeal quoted was made, this stage had not yet been reached. The condition between the main groups had not yet been stabilized to the optimum advantage of the royal position. The 'great ones' of the realm, some of whom were at the head of the Huguenot movement, were still a danger to the absolute power of the monarchy.

If one tries to assess the figuration of the court and the condition of the social tensions through which it slowly formed in the period of Richelieu — tensions between the monarchy and its representatives on one hand and the nobility threatened by the rising Third Estate on the other — the following picture emerges:

The assemblies representing the nobility and therefore the majority of this estate had hardly any independent importance as political factors in the struggle against the monarchy. The Estates General of 1614, on the other hand, show unambiguously for the first time how strong and assertive the Third Estate has become and how the nobility, needing the monarchy's support and arbitration against the bourgeoisie, is unable to resist the demands of the royal position on a second front.

However, the group of the nobility closest to the king, the high nobles, led by the princes of the blood, the dukes and peers of France, still had considerable power as counterweights to the monarchy. The source of this power is fairly clear: it was based primarily on their function as *gouverneurs*, the military commanders of their provinces and fortresses. After being gradually driven out of all other areas of government, the nobility retained this last independent power position.

Moreover, the king, and Richelieu too, were at first fairly indulgent towards the closest members of the royal house, above all the king's mother and brother. Repeated evidence of the threat posed to the king and his rule by the interference of close relatives in government, and the suppression of all such attempts, was clearly needed to induce Louis XIV, in whom this tendency, too, culminated, to adopt a strict and conscious policy of excluding his closest relatives from government and centralizing all decisions in his own hands. In the development of the dynastic[52] phase of state formation this was a significant step. Under Louis XIII and Richelieu all uprisings by the nobility against the monarchy centred on the relatively intact military power position of men and women of the high nobility. Thanks to them, the court factions which always existed but which, without such power positions, would have remained more or less insignificant or at any rate would not have represented a danger to the king, still had a social power which was not to be underestimated.

It is highly characteristic that Louis XIII's brother, Gaston, Duke of Orléans, exactly like the hostile brothers of earlier kings, having decided to lead the party opposing the cardinal and having clearly assured the latter of his friendship, immediately leaves Paris for Orléans so that he can begin the conflict with Richelieu from a strong military position.

In a similar way a faction had already gathered around the bastard son of Henry IV, the king's natural brother, the Duke of Vendôme. His power base was Brittany. The duke was governor of this province and believed he had a hereditary right to it through marriage.

---

[52] From the early forms of dynastic states, which to some extent are still to be found in Africa today, a line of development leads, with many ramifications but a clear overall direction, to these late forms. In the early forms, despite the power of the single ruler, the ruler's 'house', his family and frequently his mother above all, have a decisive influence, usually laid down by tradition, on certain affairs of government. The choice of a successor in particular is often in the hands of the dynasty.

In this manner the old aspirations to power of the great crown vassals lived on in the high aristocracy under Louis XIII. Provincial particularism, in combination with a fairly extensive military decentralization with relatively autonomous military leaders in the provinces, gave such claims a real basis. The same structure shows itself in all the tensions and conflicts between the royal representative, Richelieu, and the high nobility. Now the governor of Provence was the centre of resistance, now the governor of Languedoc, the Duke of Montmorency. A similar power position also provided the basis for the insurrections of the Huguenot nobility. As the army was not yet completely centralized, as provincial governors could regard their purchased and salaried posts as their property, as even the commanders and captains of fortresses still had a high degree of independence, at least the high nobility had retained a last position of power that enabled it to resist the absolute monarchy.

It is certainly no accident that the assembly of notables selected by Richelieu in 1627 demanded above all that fortresses should no longer be left in the hands of the *Grands*, that all fortresses not essential for defending the country should be razed, that no one should own or cast canon without the crown's permission. After some arguments over the manner of collection and the amount of individual provinces' contributions, the cost of a standing army of twenty thousand men, which, apart from defending the country against external enemies, was to secure public order and respect for the king, was approved without opposition. In this way Richelieu launched his attack on the last power position of the high nobility. Those who resisted were defeated; some died in prison, some in battle, some in exile; Richelieu even let the king's mother die abroad. The power of the high nobility still made resistance to the monarchy possible; but now that a resolute personality had taken up the king's cause, the power of the mutually suspicious *Grands* was no longer enough to defeat the king. Even if Richelieu did not carry out his plan to replace the military governors of the provinces every three years, he kept them on a tight rein and dismissed them at will.[53] This was humiliation enough for them.

In his memoirs he says explicitly: 'To believe that as sons or brothers of the king or princes of his blood they may disturb the realm with impunity, is to be mistaken. It is far more reasonable to protect the realm and royalty than to respect any hereditary impunity in them.'[54]

[53] Mariéjol, *op. cit.*, p. 363.
[54] *Mémoires de Richelieu*, vol. 7, p. 177, quoted by Ranke, *op. cit.*, p. 293.

Thus he subordinated the 'birth' of the nobility to the necessities of royal power. This distribution of power between nobility and monarchy influenced the form which the court took on under Louis XIII. Through the inflow of deracinated nobles it had grown enormously. It was still, as in Henry IV's time, a kind of a crucible in which rising bourgeois elements, elevated primarily by the purchase of offices, recently ennobled people particularly from the camp of the *robe*, jostled with members of the old nobility and to an extent mingled with them through marriage.[55] The court had not yet become the permanent domicile of the great ones of the land and so the only social centre in France. But the free chivalrous life that gave the nobleman a country seat, a secure homeland and the roving army camp as his domain, and the noble lady at least the country household as hers, was for many nobles a thing of the past.

24. From now on not only was the material basis of a part of the nobility reduced, but their horizon and sphere of activity were narrowed. They were confined to their country estates in more or less straitened circumstances. The compensation of the army camp and the changing scene of war was at least partly removed. And the broader horizon, the self-fulfilment coming above all from prestige that now only court life could give, was closed to them.

The others found a new, more unstable homeland at the royal court in Paris or, to begin with, at the courts of other great ones of the land. But for the latter, as for the kings, their country estates were now no more than appendages of an hotel and court situation in the capital of their district. For the rest, they too, provided they were not banished or in disgrace, lived at least from time to time at the royal court, even though it had not yet become their permanent domicile. Society under Louis XIII was already a court society characterized by the importance of women — whom the men, bereft of their knightly function, now overshadowed socially far less than before; but it was still a relatively decentralized court society. The knightly mode of life and its specific ethos had not yet entirely disappeared; but these attitudes, which had once been the source of all the renown and success of the nobility of the sword, gradually became, in this changed situation, more and more unrelated to reality, condemning those holding them increasingly to failure.

No one will be impervious to the tragic aspects of this defunctionalization, whereby people whose existence and self-confidence are bound to a certain traditional attitude that has brought their

---

[55] 'Les nobles épousent, mais détestent', Mariéjol, *op. cit.*, p. 161.

fathers, and perhaps themselves in their youth, success and self-fulfilment, but which now, in a world that has changed for uncomprehended reasons, condemns them to failure and downfall. A scene described by Ranke gives such a vivid picture of the fate of the last noble representatives of the knightly tradition that we shall quote it here at length. The Duke of Montmorency, the son of a man who had made a major contribution to Henry IV's victory, had rebelled. He had a chivalrous, princely nature, generous and brilliant, courageous and aspiring. He too served the king; but that the king — or more precisely, Richelieu — should have the sole power and right to rule, he did not understand. So he rebelled. The king's general, Schomberg, faced him in a far from favourable position; but, Ranke says:

> That was an advantage to which Montmorency paid little attention; seeing the enemy army he proposed to his friends that they should attack without delay. For it was chiefly in terms of the daring cavalry charge that he understood war. An experienced companion, count Rieux, begged him to wait until the enemy formation had been weakened by a number of guns that were being moved into position. But Montmorency was already seized by impetuous lust for battle. He said there was no more time to lose, and his adviser, though fearing the worst, did not dare to oppose the express will of the knightly leader. 'Lord', he cried, 'I shall die at your feet'. Montmorency was recognisable by his battle stallion adorned with red, blue and dun feathers; it was only a small troop of men that went with him over the ramparts; they cut down everything that stood in their way; they pressed forward until they reached the real battlefront of the enemy. There they were met at close range by rapid musket fire: horses and men were wounded and killed; Count Rieux and most of the others died; the Duke of Montmorency fell from his horse, which was wounded like himself, and taken prisoner.[56]

Richelieu had him tried, being sure of the outcome, and, soon after, the last Montmorency was beheaded in the courtyard of the town hall of Toulouse.

In what is thought of as the large-scale course of history, this is a fairly minor event. But it has the meaning of a *typical* event, a symbol. The old nobility did not founder simply on firearms, but above all on the difficulty of severing themselves from modes of behaviour to which their whole self-respect, and so their joys and pleasure, were bound. We see here what it meant for a form of behaviour once ap-

[56] Ranke, *op. cit.*, bk. 10, ch. 3, pp. 315–16.

propriate to reality to become alienated from it in a gradually changing figuration of people in which opportunities are increased for some and reduced for others. We also see from a different side why the monarchy was victorious, and how a chivalrous warrior nobility became a relatively pacified court aristocracy.

When Louis XIV came of age and ascended the throne, the nobility's fate was already sealed. The inequality of the opportunities open to the king on one hand and the nobility on the other had made it possible to expel the nobility from all independent power positions, and the able and energetic royal representatives had made the most of this opportunity.

25. Despite the weakness of the nobility's position, the sense of a threat coming from the nobility and particularly from the high nobility closest to him, born of the experiences of his youth, had become second nature to Louis XIV. Unfailing vigilance towards the nobility — as towards all his other subjects — remained one of his dominant traits. The indifference towards economic questions that characterized him as it did court people in general, since the pressure from his sphere did not touch the root of their social existence, was completely set aside as soon as questions of power, rank, prestige and personal superiority were involved. In this sphere Louis XIV was anything but indifferent. Here he was intensely alert and quite implacable.

He neither wished to let the nobility decay nor was this a possibility that he could contemplate. It was not only the outward splendour and prestige of his reign, not only his own prestige as a nobleman, his need of distinguished company, and, lastly, not only tradition that made this idea inconceivable to him, but the structural tensions of his dominion itself. He was not free to decide whether to preserve the nobility or let it decay. He needed it, as has been shown, in many ways. When he said, on Saint-Simon's resignation from military service: 'One more who is leaving us', this is an example of his need.

For these reasons he very deliberately expanded his court on the pattern of the ambivalent relationship already mentioned so often, as an institution both supporting and subduing the nobility. In doing so, he based himself on the preparatory work and experience of his predecessors, but was now in a more favourable situation than they had been.

He wishes 'to unite under his observation all those who are possible leaders of uprisings and whose castles could serve as focal points . . . .'. [57]

[57] Lavisse, *Louis XIV*, p. 128.

How far the structure of the court was understood by the other side, the nobility itself, as expressing a conscious policy of domination, is shown by an account by Saint-Simon:

Court life, too, served as a tool of despotic policy. I have already shown how, with its help, the highest nobles were sullied, humiliated, mixed with the crowd; how the ministers overshadowed all others, even the princes of the blood, in influence and power. . . . Several considerations confirmed the king in his decision to move his court away from Paris and reside permanently in the country. The disorders that had taken place in Paris before he came of age had made the city distasteful to him. He also considered it dangerous to live there; he thought that by moving the court he would make cabals more difficult. Equally important in his decision was the number of mistresses he kept and his concern lest he give too much offence amid so large a populace. There was also a certain consideration . . . for his security. . . . Apart from this, he took more and more pleasure in the building itself; and he believed he would be more highly esteemed by the mass if he did not show himself every day.[58]

As we can see, there was a whole number of reasons for the final formation of the court at Versailles. But all these reasons were closely connected, they all revolved about the expansion of the king's power and prestige.

And indeed, the structure of Versailles corresponded perfectly to these intertwined tendencies of Louis XIV. At Versailles, and within the framework of etiquette, every person of rank was directly under his observation:

The king not only saw to it that the high nobility was present at his court, he demanded the same of the minor nobility. At his *lever* and *coucher*, at his meals, in his gardens at Versailles, he always looked about him, noticing everyone. He was offended if the most distinguished nobles did not live permanently at court, and if the others came only infrequently, and those who showed themselves never or hardly ever incurred his full displeasure. If one of these desired something the king said proudly: 'I do not know him', and such a judgement was irrevocable. He did not take exception to a liking for country life in his courtiers, but they should practice moderation in this and take precautions when leaving for long periods. When, in my youth, I made a journey on affairs to Rouen, the king wrote to me through his minister enquiring about my reasons.[59]

[58] Saint-Simon, *Memoiren*, vol. 2, p. 82.
[59] *Ibid.*, p. 85.

For understandable reasons Louis XIV kept a particularly watchful eye on the people closest to him in rank. The structural feature of dynastic states by which, overriding all personal considerations, related pretenders to the crown, and even the immediate heirs, are so often brought into open or concealed opposition to the ruling prince, manifested itself here. Louis XIV was extremely displeased when his eldest son kept a separate court at Meudon, 'dividing the court', as he put it. When this heir died, the king hastily had the furniture of his *château* sold, for fear that the grandson who had inherited Meudon would make use of it and 'partageât ainsi la cour de nouveau'.[60]

This anxiety, said Saint-Simon, was quite without foundation. For none of the king's grandsons would have dared to displease him. But when it was a question of maintaining his prestige and securing his personal power, the king's severity made no distinction between his relations and other nobles.

There are some rather horrifying examples of this which, however, help to make the coexistence of repulsion and attraction, of nearness and distance between the king and the nobility fully comprehensible.

The king was going, as was his custom, from his *château* at Marly to Versailles. The whole court, particularly his relations, had to follow him there. The Duchess of Berry, the wife of his grandson, was three months pregnant for the first time. She felt unwell and had a high temperature. The physician to the king and the royal family, Fagon, considered that the journey from Marly would be too much for the young woman. But neither he, nor her father the Duke of Orléans, dared to speak to the king about it. Her husband, mentioning it very timidly, was badly received. An attempt was made to influence the king through Mme de Maintenon, and although she thought it very risky she finally spoke to him about the matter, supporting herself on the doctor's opinion. But she met with no success. She and the doctor were not deterred and the dispute lasted three or four days. In the end the king simply became angry and capitulated to the extent that he allowed the sick duchess to travel by boat instead of the royal carriage. This made it necessary for the duchess and duke to leave Marly a day earlier, to spend the night at the Palais-Royal, to rest for a day and then continue the journey. While the duke was given permission to accompany his wife the king forbade him to leave the Palais-Royal even to go to the opera, although one could go directly from the Palais-Royal to the Duke of Orléans's box.

'I would,' says Saint-Simon, 'suppress this trifle occasioned by the journey, if it did not serve to characterize the king more and more exactly.'[61]

If the king acted in this way on matters that at least indirectly touched his prestige and authority in his intimate circle rather than his power itself, he was, of course, no less unremitting when his rule was directly concerned. Under no circumstances would he permit any of his relations to receive a post that might give him influence. He never forgot, for example, the importance which the post of governor had had under his father as a basis for resistance to royal power. And he always vividly remembered the difficulties which his uncle, Gaston of Orléans, had caused the king on this basis. So, when his own brother asked him for a *gouvernement* and a fortress, a *place de sûreté*, he answered: 'La meilleure place de sûreté pour un fils de France est le coeur du Roi.' And this answer is no less typical of his way of speaking than of his attitude in general.

26. The nobility is subdued. But how does it bear this subjugation, which is also a humiliation. How does it express its inner opposition now that every possibility of outward resistance is closed? The way the nobility is bound to and dependent on the king is directly expressed in the outward life of the court. Is the nobility inwardly broken and submissive, or does the ambivalence of its relationship to the king sometimes break through its pacified outward face even under Louis XIV?

There were very different ways in which nobles held captive at court could come to terms with the latent conflicts inherent in their ambivalent position vis-à-vis the king, within the scope left to them by this institution. They could compensate for the trouble and humiliation they had to endure in the king's service by consciousness of their influence at court, by the opportunities of gaining money and prestige that it offered them, to such an extent that their antipathy towards the king and their desire for release from his oppression receded even within their own minds; these were manifested only indirectly, in their relations to others. This attitude formed one pole on the scale of possibilities open to the court nobility. We find it rather strongly represented by the Duke of La Rochefoucauld, the son of the writer of the 'Maxims', *Grand-maître de la Garde-robe* to the king.

Alternatively, a man of the court nobility could give precedence to the negative aspects of the ambivalent relationship. In this case he might permit himself — perhaps in a trusted circle — to criticize the

[61] *Ibid.*, vol. 18, ch. 308, p. 57.

king's rule and make secret plans for the time after his death whereby the nobility, above all the high nobility, would be restored to its rightful position in relation to the king and his bourgeois ministers. During Louis XIV's lifetime a noble of this kind had only one realistic way of giving expression to this attitude, apart from leaving the court, which meant a renunciation of all prestige: to unite himself with the possible heir to the throne and try to win him over to his ideas. Open opposition had become completely futile. A representative of this possibility was the Duke of Saint-Simon. He himself describes the opposite type, a representative of the submissive nobility, the Duke of La Rochefoucauld, as follows:

> If M. de la Rochefoucauld spent his life in the most evident favour, it must be said that this cost him dearly if he had any feeling of liberty. Never was there a valet so assiduous and self-abasing — we must say the word: so enslaved. It is not easy to imagine another who would put up with more than forty years of such a life. The *lever* and the *coucher*, the two other changes of clothes each day, the king's daily hunts and walks, he was present at all of them, sometimes spending ten years on end without sleeping away from the court. He was on a footing where he needed to ask permission, not to sleep somewhere, for in forty years he did not sleep twenty times in Paris, but to dine away from court or not to be present on a walk. He was never ill, except rarely and briefly with gout at the end. [62]

Following the career of this man we find the following: his father had been prominent in the *Fronde*; afterwards he never went to court, for the king never forgave his rebellion.

The son appeared at court as a man without any chances. 'No one was afraid of him,' says Saint-Simon. He had neither offices nor honours. He had little prospect of inheritance; most of the family wealth had been lost in the troubles. Apart from this, his appearance was unprepossessing. In some way he managed to gain the king's favour. And now began his rise in the court hierarchy. He received the office of a *grand-veneur* and of a *grand-maître de la garde-robe*. He was on friendly terms with Mme de Montespan, the king's mistress. After she had left the court he had no support there except the king himself. This was undoubtedly what the king needed. We see how the interdependence is constructed. Since La Rochefoucauld had been in favour with Mme de Montespan, he could be sure in advance of the disfavour of her successor, Mme de Maintenon. He

[62] *Ibid.*, vol. 13, ch. 229, p. 71.

did not get on well with the ministers. And the rest of court society had little to do with him apart from the old circle of Mme de Montespan. The king, however, three times paid his debts, and gave him much — not all — of what he asked; and he asked for a lot. He could speak openly with the king, without regard for others. The king valued him; for this reason the others feared him. It was not by his decision or choice that he placed his life entirely in the king's service; rather, his social existence was wholly in the king's hands. As the impoverished Duke of La Rochefoucauld, the son of a rebel without contacts within court society, without a pleasing appearance to help him, he was nothing. From this nothingness the king had raised him up.

There is much that is typical in this development. The sons of rebels, lost unless the king restores them to grace, become the most devoted courtiers.

'This story of de La Rochefoucauld resembles that of Condé. The prince himself became a courtier; his son did not leave the king's side; his grandson married the king's illegitimate daughter. The La Rochefoucaulds and the Condés fell from revolt into servitude.'[63]

The exact opposite is the case with Saint-Simon. His father had been elevated by Louis XIII to high office and honour. He was the king's confidant and in all the troubles, even after the king's death, he remained unerringly loyal to the monarchy although the temptations to join the opposing nobility were sometimes very strong. In possession of an assured reputation and a considerable fortune, therefore, Saint-Simon, the writer of the memoirs, came to the court. He too was certainly dependent on the king, for the king's disfavour — as he sometimes said — meant the abolition of his social existence. Nevertheless he was not dependent on the king's favour to the same degree as La Rochefoucauld. He was far more the heir of office and honour than the latter. The king's obligation towards him as the son of a loyal supporter of the royal family sustained him; in his way he was relatively self-reliant. He demonstrated his independence early on when he left his regiment as a result of a slight. He sometimes hoped the king would entrust him with a diplomatic post but nothing came of this; and he lived at court without any court office, fulfilling only his duty as a duke and peer of France and what the king required of all men of the high nobility.

When, after the death of the first and second dauphins, everyone saw the future regent in the Duke of Orléans, Saint-Simon was for a

[63] Lavisse, *Louis XIV*, pp. 103–4.

time almost the only person who had anything to do with him, although Louis XIV disapproved of all contact with the duke, who was blamed for the death of the king's grandsons and was totally isolated at court. If we are to believe Saint-Simon's own words, he was the only one who stood beside him at court functions. Saint-Simon walked with him through the gardens of Versailles until the king threatened him with disgrace and demanded that he leave the court for a time if he did not wish to be banished for ever. Then Saint-Simon obeyed. Only within this framework was an independent stance possible.

But this independence had shown itself previously in his relationship to the second dauphin, Louis XIV's grandson. A description of the relations between these two people and the ideas that unfolded in their conversations is particularly important in giving us a direct insight into the minds of the nobility that secretly opposed the king.

Great caution was needed before people who did not know each other very exactly could open their minds to each other at this court:

> I thought it right [Saint-Simon tells us] to sound out the Dauphin in the first days of his new glory. . . . I took care to say a word about our standing. . . . I told him how right he was not to lose sight of the least part of his legitimate rights, and I seized the favourable moment to tell him that if he, who was so great and whose position was so secure, had reason to watch over it, how much more had we whose rank was often disputed and sometimes even withdrawn almost without our daring to complain. . . .
>
> Finally the conversation turned to the king. The Dauphin spoke of him with great tenderness and gratitude; I immediately expressed the same feelings, except that affection and gratitude should not become a dangerous admiration. I hinted that the king did not know of many things and had unfortunately placed himself in a position where he could not know of them, although with his kindness he certainly would not be insensitive to them if he knew.
>
> This string, gently plucked, immediately produced a full resonance. The prince admitted the truth of what I said and immediately began to attack the ministers. He spoke at length on the limitless authority they had usurped over the king, on the dangerous use they might make of it, the impossibility of anything reaching the king or coming from him without their interference. He did not name anyone, but clearly indicated that this form of government was entirely against his taste and his maxims.
>
> Then he came back to the king, lamented the bad education he had had and the ruinous hands into which he had successively fallen. In this way, since, on the pretext of policy and authority, all power and

advantages existed only for the ministers, his heart, by nature kind and just, had been constantly deflected from the right path without his noticing.

I took the opportunity to draw his attention to the arrogance of the ministers towards the duke and those of even higher rank. He was indignant that they denied us the title 'Monseigneur', while they demanded it of everyone who had no title, except the robe.

I can scarcely convey how much this impertinence shocked him, and this distinction of the bourgeoisie at the expense of the highest nobility. [64]

In the last words the central problem reappears. Under the surface of the absolutist regime the tension between nobility and bourgeoisie continued unabated. Regardless of the friendship uniting court nobles and even Saint-Simon himself with individual ministers, regardless of the marriages of ministers' daughters to court nobles, this central tension within the broader social field survived in modified form in the central group of the court. In one place Saint-Simon quotes with visible satisfaction the 'admirable' dictum of the old Maréchal de Villeroy:[65] 'Rather a hostile first minister who is a noble than a friendly bourgeois one.'[66] At the same time the ambivalent relationship of the nobility to the king finds clear expression in this conversation; it is no accident that in the same breath the court nobility's opposition to the king and to the bourgeois *parvenus* is expressed. These are the two fronts on which the nobility is threatened. And this situation becomes still clearer when we read the ideas published by Saint-Simon in his memoirs, and attributed to the dauphin after the latter's death; they express at least the ideas of Saint-Simon, and the situation and plans of the clandestine opposition among the court nobility under Louis XIV:

The annihilation of the nobility was odious to him [writes Saint-Simon of the dauphin] and the equal treatment of its members intolerable. This latter novelty, which gave way only to high dignitaries, and confounded the noble with the gentleman, and the latter with the *seigneur*, seems to him the ultimate injustice, and the lack of distinctions of rank a cause of imminent ruin to a military realm. He remembered that the monarchy had owed its safety in the perils under

[64] Saint-Simon, *Mémoires*, vol. 18, ch. 106, pp. 5ff.
[65] *Ibid*., vol. 17, ch. 299, p. 89.
[66] The term 'bourgeois', as we see, has taken on contemptuous undertones not only in the struggle between the middle classes and the proletariat, but in that between the middle classes and the nobility. From court society it gradually migrated to the theoreticians of the proletariat.

Philippe de Valois, under Charles V, under Charles VII, under Louis XIII, under Francis I, under his grandsons, under Henry IV, to this nobility alone which knew itself and respected its differences, which had the will and the means to march to the help of the state, in bands and by provinces, without embarrassment or confusion, because no one had left his station, or had difficulty in obeying one greater than himself. He now saw this help extinguished; everyone claimed equality with everyone else, so that all organization, command and obedience had disappeared.

As to means, he was touched to the bottom of his heart by the ruin of the nobility, by the course taken to reduce it and keep it in abasement, by the adulteration that poverty and the continual need for misalliances in order to eat had brought about in the courage of the nobles, their valour, their virtue and their feelings. He was indignant to see this so celebrated and illustrious French nobility becoming a people of almost the same sort as the people itself, distinguished from it only in that the people are at liberty to engage in any work or commerce, even to bear arms, whereas the nobility had become a second common people with no alternative to a mortal and ruinous idleness, the utter uselessness of which makes it a despised burden, except to be killed in war, insulted by clerks and secretaries of the state, by the secretaries of intendants. Not even the highest-born of the nobility, whose dignity places them above their class without their leaving it, can avoid this uselessness, nor the contempt of the masters of the pen while they serve in the armies. . . .

The prince could not accustom himself to the idea that the state could not be even partly governed unless one had control of the levies, and that the whole government of all the provinces had been put in the hands of the sons of the magistrature, each with his own province and infinitely greater power and authority than the governors of these provinces ever had.[67]

In this critical programme from a disaffected court circle the whole problem with which this study is concerned is again made visible.

It has been shown how a special tension existed between the groups and persons elevated by the king and those distinguished by hereditary titles within the court; by maintaining this tension the king manipulated the court. It has also been shown how, in the broader dominion, a similar balance of tensions was a condition of royal power in its existing form, enabling the king's representatives to attain the special degree of power that was realized in the system of the absolute monarchy. These two sets of tensions were structural

[67] Saint-Simon, *Mémoires*, bk. 18, ch. 322, pp. 222ff.

features of one and the same stage in the development of the French state as a whole — features of the total figuration.

Supported on the growing power of bourgeois classes, the king distanced himself more and more from the remaining nobility. And conversely, the king encouraged the bourgeois advance, opening to it economic opportunities and official prestige of many kinds, but also holding it in check. The bourgeoisie and the kings reciprocally elevated each other, while the remaining nobility declined. But if bourgeois formations, if the men of the high courts and administration to which Saint-Simon refers by the terms 'magistrature' and 'pen' went further than the king wished, he showed them their limits as implacably as he did to the aristocrats.

For the kings could tolerate the nobility's decline only up to a certain point. With the nobility they would have lost the possibility of preserving their own existence and its meaning; it was precisely in their struggle against the nobility that the advancing bourgeois strata needed the king. In this way the nobility step by step lost many of their previous functions in this social field to bourgeois groups. They lost their role in administration, in jurisdiction and even part of their military function to members of bourgeois strata. Even the most important part of the function of a *gouverneur* was in bourgeois hands.

27. But while on one hand the nobility lost some traditional functions, on the other it gained new ones or, more exactly, an additional function came into the foreground, the one it had for the king.

It is customary to refer to the nobility of the *ancien régime* as a 'non-functional' class. This is justifiable if we think of a functional system within which directly or indirectly each class or group satisfies the needs of every other group, that is, a system that is sometimes to be found within professional bourgeois nations. For the 'nation', the nobility of the *ancien régime* had no function.

But the system of functions, the mechanism of interdependence in the *ancien régime* was different in many respects from that in a bourgeois 'nation'. That the French nobility would have been able to survive without any social function is unthinkable. It had, certainly, no function for the 'nation'. But in the minds of the most influential functionaries of the society, the kings and their representatives, there was no such thing as a 'nation' or a 'state' as an end in itself. It has been explained above how, according to Louis XIV's concept, this whole social field culminated in the kings as its real purpose, and how he saw all the other elements of his regime only as means to this end of glorifying and maintaining the king. In this context it can be understood what is meant by saying that while the nobility may have had no function for the 'nation', it certainly had one for the king. A precondition of his rule was the existence of a nobility as a counterweight to the bourgeois classes, just as he needed the existence and strength of bourgeois classes as a counterweight to the nobility. And it is this function that to a large degree gives the court nobility its special stamp.

That this transformation from a relatively independent nobility into a court one changed the whole meaning and structure of its hierarchy can be readily understood. How much it resisted the overthrow of its traditional order in favour of one imposed by the king in his own interests even in Louis XIV's time, and still dreamt of a restoration of its old independence, is shown by the ideas of Saint-Simon just quoted. The nobility did not understand its position and could not understand it. It was more or less at the king's mercy. And just as the king took care in his wider dominion that the bourgeoisie and nobility balanced each other, his policy within the court was to compensate the conservative pressure of the nobility by bourgeois people or nobles who had risen within the nobility and owed everything to him and nothing to inherited rank.

This is the policy of which Saint-Simon complains, the situation in which traits are particularly developed that have here been called the characteristics of 'court people'.

28. Earlier we asked what kind of social constellation it was in which the court, as we see it before us, constantly reproduced itself as an institution lasting generations. Here is the answer: the nobility needed the king because within this social field only life at his court gave them access to the economic opportunities and prestige that enabled them to live as a nobility.

The king needed the nobility — apart from the many particular dependences that have been shown in the course of this study, e.g. the traditional dependence growing out of the relationship of liege lord and vassals, the need for the company of a society whose culture he shared, his need to distance himself from the people through being served by an estate of higher rank than all the others — apart from all this he needed the nobility above all as an indispensable weight in the equilibrium of classes that he ruled.

It is wrong to see in the king *only* the suppressor of the nobility; it is wrong to see in the king *only* the preserver of the nobility. He was both. It is wrong to stress only the dependence of the nobility on the king. To a certain degree the king was also dependent on the nobility — as every monopoly ruler depends on his subjects and particularly their leading groups. But although in maintaining his position the king was highly dependent on the nobility as a distant and separate estate, each individual noble depended on the king far more than the king on each individual noble. If a particular noble displeased the king there was always a 'reserve army' of nobles from which he could pick a replacement. It is this balance and distribution of dependence that gave the institution that we call the court its specific character, if we disregard the ministers and other officials coming from the bourgeoisie and the *robe* who, while belonging to the court, were usually very marginal figures in the court aristocracy. In this balance of tensions the two main protagonists held each other fast like boxers in a clinch: neither dared change his position for fear that his opponent might damage him; and there was no outside referee to break the clinch. All these mutual dependences were so carefully weighed and so ambivalent that mutual antagonism and mutual dependence were more or less in equilibrium.

29. We saw earlier how in the late stage of this regime even the people of highest status, the king and queen, the members of the royal house with their lords and ladies in waiting, became imprisoned by their own ceremonial and etiquette, obeying its commands however burdensome. They did so because each of their slightest actions represented a privilege of certain persons or families in relation to others, and because any change of traditional privilege in favour of one family or group aroused the displeasure and usually the active resistance of others, who feared that if one privilege were altered theirs might be the next. What can be observed here in the etiquette of court circles is symbolic of the relationships of the privileged elites of the *ancien régime* as a whole. Whether it was a matter of monopoly rights to certain offices, to sources of income or to rank and prestige, rights not only of the royal family and its courtiers but more broadly of the nobility of the sword and of office and of the tax farmers and financiers, who all remained separate groups with different privileges despite their cross-connections — all these graduated privileges represented a kind of property that every group and family sought with utmost vigilance to protect against all threats, including the threat of an increase in the rights of others. Louis XIV had still been powerful enough to increase or reduce privileges within certain limits, and so manipulate the mechanism according to the needs of the royal position. Louis XVI and the whole ramifying dynasty of the royal family were already prisoners of the mechanism. Instead of manipulating it, he was to a degree manipulated by it. Like a ghostly *perpetuum mobile* it forced all those making it up to defend the privileged basis of their existence by incessant competition, so

that everyone was running on the spot. On this deadlock, this social clinch, foundered every attempt at radical reform that came from within the ranks of the privileged elite. Such attempts were not lacking, indeed there was a surfeit of ideas on reform. But these ideas were seldom based on a realistic analysis of the figuration of privileges.

Awareness of the need for reform became more acute as the pressure of non-privileged groups on the privileged elite grew stronger. But to understand the situation correctly we should not forget how great, in a figuration like the *ancien régime*, was the social distance between the privileged elite groups and what they themselves called the 'people', the mass of the unprivileged, despite their physical proximity, for example to their own servants. The great mass of the privileged still lived in a closed world — the more hermetically closed the higher their rank. The idea that they could develop their own country, raise the living standards of their own people, was alien to most of them. It had no relationship to their values. The maintenance of their own privileged existence was for them an end in itself. What went on among the majority of the population lay beyond their horizon. It did not interest them. So they had hardly any idea of the forces building up there. As they could not themselves break the ice of the frozen social tensions between the upper classes, it was finally shattered by the flood beneath. This frozen posture or 'clinch' of the privileged elites of the *ancien régime*, which no one could break in a peaceful manner despite the obvious injustices, was undoubtedly one of the reasons why a revolutionary movement finally overthrew the social and institutional framework of the old order, so that after much oscillation a power structure with a different equilibrium was established. We have indicated in what has already been said — although a longer study would be needed to do justice to the problem — that the notion of the 'bourgeoisie' as the revolutionary rising class and the nobility as the class defeated in the Revolution somewhat simplifies the actual state of affairs. The privileged groups that the Revolution overthrew included privileged bourgeois elements, or strata that originated in the bourgeoisie. It would perhaps be useful to distinguish the bourgeois estate, with the nobility of officials as its pinnacle, more sharply from the rising professional bourgeoisie.

30. How and why people are bound together to form specific dynamic figurations is one of the central questions, perhaps even *the* central question, of sociology. We can only begin to answer this question if we define the interdependence of people. There is at pres-

ent a lack of models for systematic studies of interdependence. Not only do we lack detailed empirical models, but also a systematic examination of traditional concepts and categories in relation to this task. There is still a widespread lack of awareness that many of these traditional conceptual tools were developed to explore particular areas of knowledge — above all the area called 'nature' — and are therefore not necessarily suited to exploring other areas — for example the one we call 'society', often rightly or wrongly in contrast to 'nature'.

A lack of clear awareness of such tasks often leads to a peculiar confusion in thinking about social problems. A large number of categories and concepts derived from the natural sciences and diluted by popular usage are clearly inapplicable to sociological problems. The classical concept of unilinear causality is a good example. Sociologists therefore often feel free to invent concepts more or less at will, without testing empirically how suitable they really are as tools for a scientific investigation of social phenomena.

An attempt has been made here to test a basic theoretical framework developed in detailed sociological work by reapplying it in an empirical study. This approach therefore departs from the prevalent nominalist theories of sociology whose exponents, while paying lip service to the study of human societies, finally postulate only isolated, closed individuals as really existing, so that everything they have to say about societies appears as features abstracted from isolated individuals, or even as systems or metaphysical entities independent of particular individuals.

Unlike these nominalist tendencies, a study of social formations as figurations of interdependent individuals opens the way to a realistic sociology. For the fact that people do not exist as isolated, hermetically closed individuals, but as mutually interdependent individuals who form figurations of the most diverse kinds with each other, can be observed and demonstrated by particular studies. In such studies the genesis and evolution of specific figurations, in this case a royal court and a court society, can be determined with a high degree of certainty even though they are, of course, only a step on the way. One can ascertain the conditions under which people were mutually dependent in this specific way, and how these dependences evolved in their turn in conjunction with partly endogenous and partly exogenous changes in the total figuration.

Only some aspects of the transformation of interdependences that finally led in France in the sixteenth and seventeenth centuries to a shift in the delicate balance between the king and the rest of the nobility in the former's favour, and to the preponderant power of the French king within his dominion — only shifts relating to certain elites have been illuminated here. Many ramifications within the broader field of French social development as a whole in this period therefore remain in the background.

But even as a limited model, court society is well suited to test through practical application, and so to clarify the meaning of concepts that may seem unfamiliar, such as 'figuration', 'interdependence', 'balance of tensions', and the 'evolution' of a figuration.

31. Some sociologists may ask whether it is rewarding to immerse oneself in the study of details of the power distribution and dependence of dukes, princes and kings, since social positions of this type have long since become marginal to developed societies. But such questions are based on a misunderstanding of the task of sociology. This task is finally to make people in every kind of association better able to understand themselves and others. By studying how people are associated and mutually dependent at a different stage of social development, by trying to elucidate the reasons why the mechanism of human dependence takes on this specific form at this stage, we not only contribute to a better understanding of the evolution of our own figuration. We also discern, among people living in what at first appear to be alien figurations and who are therefore alien and incomprehensible as individuals, the key positions that enable us to put ourselves in the places of people living in a quite different society, and therefore quite different from ourselves. In other words, by revealing the interdependence in which people are enmeshed, we are able to re-establish the identification without which any contact between people — even that of the researcher with his subject, of the living with the dead — has something of the barbarity of earlier, more savage phases of human development when people of other societies were regarded as aliens and sometimes not even as human beings. We are able to penetrate below the level of social phenomena on which they appear simply as a chain of different societies or 'cultures', below the level that gives rise to the notion that sociological studies of different societies imply a relativistic position, to the deeper level where the differentness of other societies and the people forming them loses the suggestion of quaintness, and where people of different societies become recognizable and understandable as people like ourselves. To put it differently, a predominantly descriptive approach in sociology or history stops short at the point where the people one is trying to understand are perceived merely as people in the third person. Only if the researcher

advances further, to the point where he perceives the people he is studying as human beings like himself — the plane on which the actual experience of the people studied, their first-person perspective, becomes accessible — can he approach a realistic understanding.

An analysis of interdependence helps us to advance to this plane. Thus the study of one part of the network of interdependence embracing the royal position at the time of Louis XIV shows the king from the third-person perspective; but it also gives access to a very exact reconstruction of his own experience. Without studying the mechanism of interdependence of which he was a part it is not possible to put ourselves in his position and understand what choices he actually had when ruling, and how he took advantage of them in accordance with his personal development and his position. It is only when we have a picture of his behaviour, particularly his decisions, in the context of the alternatives open to him, his own scope for experience and decision within the mechanism of interdependence, that we can have an adequate perception of his person. Only then can we begin to see Louis XIV as a human being who tried, like you and I, to solve specific problems. Only when we understand how he came to grips with or avoided the problems that confronted him, can we determine his value or his greatness. For the value of a person is not measured by what he seems when considered as an isolated person independent of his relations to others; it can only be determined if he is seen as a person among people, coming to terms with the problems posed by his co-existence with others. Thus it is understandable but fundamentally wrong to say, as often happens, that Louis XIV was an insignificant man but a significant king. This is perhaps an attempt to say that while he exploited the possibilities of his royal career in an optimum way, he would not have been as successful in a different social career, as a philosopher, historian, intellectual or in any other career, as a 'human being as such'. But there is nothing verifiable that can be said about a 'human being as such'. The value of a human being cannot be determined if his career in interdependence with others, his position and function for others, are disregarded.

At present this approach is still frequently adopted. There is a tendency, in judging people of other periods or societies, to start from the values important in one's own time and to select significant facts in the light of these values. This approach blocks access to the special context of the people whom one is trying to understand. They are detached from the structure which they actually form with others and placed heteronomously in contexts determined by contemporary values, to which they do not belong. But they can only be really understood as people if we preserve the relationship, the figuration they form with others in their own time, and respect the relative autonomy of their values as an aspect of this figuration.

The analysis of figurations is simply a procedure aiming to secure greater autonomy for the people being studied in relation to the transient values arising from the great factions in which the researcher is involved in his own time. Only a concern for the greater autonomy of the object of research as a central criterion guiding the eye and hand of the researcher makes it possible to bring the influence of the heteronomous ideals of the researcher under control. If autonomous values replace heteronomous ones increasingly in research, we can hope to come into closer touch with the factual context of the people being studied and to develop models of this context that are not exposed to rapid decay with the changing ideals of our own time, models that can be further developed by later generations and so give greater continuity to the study of men.

On a small scale, the picture of court society that emerges in this study is such a model. We saw that the people forming this society were bound together in different ways — formed different figurations — from those of industrial society, and that they therefore developed and behaved in many respects differently from people forming industrial societies. We saw that this 'differentness' of people in other societies is treated by the study of figurations neither — relativistically — as something peculiar and quaint, nor is it reduced — absolutistically — to an 'eternal human essence'. As was shown, the tracing of interdependences makes it possible to preserve the uniqueness and differentness of people in other societies, while recognizing them as people whose situation and experience we can share, with whom we are bound by an ultimate identification as human beings.

This is true not only of the king, whose position all too readily gives credence to the notion of a totally self-sufficient individuality, but of members of the nobility as well, if we take pains to discern their individual profiles. It is true of the Duke of Montmorency. The manner of his downfall, chosen here as an illustration, vividly illuminates certain features of his person. It also illuminates the shift in the axis of the social pendulum in the struggles between the nobility and royal position, in favour of the latter. In the same way we can gain a better understanding of the person of the Duke of Saint-Simon or the Duke of La Rochefoucauld if we realize that within the scope left to the high court aristocracy under Louis XIV, they each tended towards opposite poles. The idea that sociological studies flatten and obliterate people as individuals has a certain justification as long as sociological theories and procedures are used that treat social phenomena as existing outside and beyond individuals, rather than as figurations of individuals. But it sharpens and deepens our understanding of individuality if people are seen as forming figurations with other people.

·VIII·

On the sociogenesis of aristocratic romanticism in the process of courtization

1. In the transitional phase when parts of the knightly French nobility, mingled with rising bourgeois elements, are transformed into a court-aristocratic nobility, in the early phase of the subjugation of the nobility through the court, we can already discern a number of phenomena which are often attributed solely to very recent developments, and particularly to industrialization and industrial urbanization. In the course of these latter processes the independent artisan loses importance. The factory organization holding many people in permanent interdependence comes to the fore. The sons of peasants and rural workers migrate to the towns, and in recollection, the artisan and peasant are idealized by some classes as symbols of a better past or of a free and natural life, contrasting to the constraints of the urban and industrial environment.

Such sentiments also arise during the process of courtization and later, repeatedly, in court society. In forming a picture of the court nobility under Louis XIV, we must remember that its structure, its organization and mode of life, were the result of a process in the course of which sections of the old pre-court nobility were faced with the choice of either continuing to live in straitened circumstances on their own land and being despised as backwoodsmen by the court nobility, or of succumbing to the constraints and entanglements of court life.

But the people who were drawn into the maelstrom of these great changes did not see their fate as resulting from a long-term social process. The idea of a change of figuration, the power of which far exceeded that of any individual, even the king or the mightiest elite of the country, was alien to them. Even today we still speak of the 'age of absolutism' as if the growing power of the central rulers in all countries were to be explained primarily by the great deeds of certain individual kings or princes. The question as to the nature of the general social transformation that sooner or later, in the majority of continental European states, made exceptional power available to the central rulers, if it is posed clearly at all, is regarded as insignificant beside questions relating to the achievements of particular great men. It is not surprising that the nobles, too, who were involved in the development of the court in the deepest possible way, perceived the gradual shift in the equilibrium of the state to their disadvantage as resulting from the intentions and deeds of particular people and groups. If we put ourselves in their place, we should not assume they have the same understanding of their fate as we ourselves may possess.

The turning of the warrior nobility into courtiers, the importance of which in the civilizing process in Europe has been treated at length in another place,[1] is part of the gradual move away from the places where food was directly produced, which is today somewhat romantically called the 'uprooting' or 'estrangement' from the land. And romantic undertones can be heard in the court nobility's own treatment of this experience. In the age of transition nobles who had grown up on the estates of their ancestors had to accustom themselves to the more refined and diverse court life, with its more complex relationships that demanded far greater self-control. Even in these generations, the country life and scenery of their youth became for many men and women of the court an object of melancholy longing. And later, when the assimilation of the nobility to the court was an accomplished fact, when court nobles looked down on the landed nobility with unconcealed contempt as uncivilized rustics, country life nevertheless remained an object of nostalgia. The past took on the character of a dream image. Country life became a symbol of lost innocence, of spontaneous simplicity and naturalness. It became an opposite image to urban court life with its greater constraints, its more complex hierarchical pressures and its heavier demands on individual self-control. Undoubtedly the transformation of sections of the French nobility into courtiers had already advanced so far in the course of the seventeenth century that the lords and ladies of the court would not have greatly enjoyed being transported back to the comparatively coarse and uncomfortable country life of their ancestors. But in their social conversation, their books and other diversions, they did not envisage country life, or 'natural' existence, as it really was. In keeping with their social convention it ap-

[1] N. Elias, *The Civilizing Process* (Oxford, 1982), vol. 2, pp. 258–70ff.

peared in idealized forms such as the life of shepherds and shepherdesses, which had little to do with the actual, laborious and often penurious life of sheep rearers. This too, like the preceding wave of modish chivalrous romances of the sixteenth century that Cervantes tried to kill off with his great satire, was a symptom of the increasing transformation of warriors into courtiers. The figure of the great Amadis and the whole chivalrous romance — the *roman* only gradually parts company as the novel with romanticism — shows the proud medieval warrior bathed in the sunset hue of nostalgia for the free and self-reliant knightly life that was already sinking from sight in the growing centralization of states and therefore of armies. Likewise the pastoral romanticism that is prefigured episodically in the chivalrous romances expresses the longing of nobles and ladies more or less assimilated to court life for a rural existence transfigured by distance. They give a first-person perspective of the nobility's experience of becoming courtiers. This perspective throws light on the feelings of nobles who, with the increasing integration of the state, were drawn into, and later born into, a tighter mesh of interdependence demanding much stricter self-control.

2. In studying these court-romantic tendencies we encounter the central problem of the attitudes and forms of experience that have become known by the word 'romantic'. There are many varieties of romantic movement. What is lacking is a central theory that states the common structural features of such movements in paradigmatic form and which can be tested by further research, and either extended, revised, improved or replaced by one more adequate to the facts. Whatever may happen, the prevalent tradition in the history of ideas, which describes the common ideas of certain groups and their development as if they were suspended in mid-air independently of people, without systematically studying these groups, their structure, their situation, their experience — in short without a systematic sociological study — this tradition lends the term 'romantic' the aspect of a somewhat vague, blurred and often arbitrary classification. Artistic and other cultural products of certain groups are diagnosed as 'romantic', as if 'romantic' attitudes were, as it were, borne to them on the wind and vanished again when the wind changed. They are described as unstructured moods and modes of thought that overcome groups of people at certain times without reason. Descriptions are regarded as sufficient, as if such shifts were neither open to nor in need of explanation.

What has been said previously on the process of courtization, on the increasing constraints — particularly self-constraint[2] — during the formation of larger and more tightly integrated states with an increasing division of functions and lengthening chains of interdependence, gives us a key to the explanation of this phenomenon. The courtly-romantic tendencies are a part of the relatively early shift towards increased state integration, and the urbanization that is one of its central aspects. These tendencies have certain peculiarities distinguishing them from the later bourgeois-romantic tendencies. But there is no lack of common structural features that show them all to be manifestations of one and the same long-term change of the total figuration of people, a change in a particular direction and with similar or recurring basic patterns at different stages. One of these recurring patterns is the attitude and the type of experience referred to by the term 'romantic'. Courtly-romantic tendencies show this attitude and experience at an earlier stage of development and bourgeois-romantic tendencies at a later one. There is a certain continuity of themes. The romantic knight is one of the more obvious examples. But the real connecting elements are the parallel shifts and structurally similar situations of certain social classes. The overall direction of this shift towards increasingly interdependent, larger and more complex human associations produces recurrent movements and situations of this kind. The development of more and more centralized states with an increasing division of functions, and of larger and larger royal courts or, at a later stage, larger and more comprehensive centres of government and administration, the growth of cities, increasing monetarization, commercialization and industrialization — all these are merely different aspects of the same overall transformation.

But a crucial structural feature of this long-term transformation of human society, which emerges very clearly in a study of the transformation of warriors into courtiers, frequently escapes theoretical attention. It is the permanent interdependence of rising and sinking movements, of integration and disintegration, of construction and decay in the course of this total process. At present a rather oversimplified model of this long-term social change is often used. The predominant sociological classification of social classes lags far behind the empirical knowledge we now possess — partly because sociologists and historians work separately, historians being insufficiently concerned with clarifying and sharpening their theoretical apparatus, and sociologists with interpreting historical information.

[2] *Ibid.*, pp. 229 – 47.

So we are often satisfied with a basic model of social stratification that provides the researcher with three — or at most four — concepts with which to investigate the development of social strata: nobility, bourgeoisie and proletariat, perhaps with the addition of the peasantry as a separate stratum. On this basis the convolutions of social development are presented in a highly simplified form. When the 'bourgeoisie' rises, this scheme suggests, the nobility declines; when the proletariat rises, the bourgeoisie declines. The material provided by observation is interpreted only insofar as there is a real or imaginary disappearance of one of the social formations referred to by these names. But the same name often covers social formations of different types or, in other words, different stages of the total social development. It is by no means always the case that the members of a later stratum identical with an earlier one by name are descendants of members of that earlier stratum. Thus, as has been said, the court-aristocratic nobility of the sixteenth and seventeenth centuries in France consisted in part of descendants of non-noble families. Nor is it by any means always the case that structurally and functionally related strata at a later stage are classified by the same terminology, like related strata at earlier stages. Bourgeois elite strata, such as a bourgeois patriciate, may have considerable structural similarities to noble strata, elite strata in proletarian states with bourgeois elites; the rigidity, the crudeness and the affective loading of traditional concepts for different social classes makes it difficult to do justice in research to what is clearly present before us.

As a result, understanding of the processes under discussion here is often inexact. The rise of a new type within a certain social class — in this case a noble formation — can, as we saw, go hand in hand with the decline of an older type within the same class, or at any rate a class for which the same term is used without a clear distinction between these rising and declining types of a nominally identical class. And the rise of the central rulers and their representatives as a social formation *sui generis*, a rise achieved in long struggles with representatives of other partial formations at the same stage of development, usually has no place in this traditional pattern. The development of the total figuration formed by the different interdependent social classes, with the co-ordinating central ruler or government exerting a force of its own in the balance of tensions between interdependent groups, is often concealed behind concepts like 'the development of the state', which are used without the relationship between changes in the internal tensions between groups and the development of the whole structure being clearly seen.

In France, as we have seen, the main outline of the shift in the power relationship between the leading strata and the emergent court-aristocratic noble formations at the end of the Middle Ages was fairly clear. Part of the older, seigniorial warrior nobility went into decline as the centralization and integration of the state increased, while the court nobility evolved from parts of the old nobility and descendants of bourgeois families as a distinct formation separated from the non-court nobility by increasingly high barriers. In other countries this line of development was often considerably more complicated. In the German Empire, for example, there were, even at an early stage, violent swings in the balance of power in favour of bourgeois formations and at the expense of the nobility. During the rise of the medieval towns a bourgeois estate of guilds and commercial elements evolved that was not only very prosperous in many cases, but often possessed a degree of political autonomy in relation to the princes and the surrounding rural nobility which — if we include in it the associated border-areas of Switzerland and the Netherlands — had, if at all, a counterpart only in Italy. In other words, this autonomy was characteristic of the development of the power structure in the medieval German–Roman Empire. In the late Middle Ages, in German regions, substantial parts of the warrior nobility were becoming impoverished in their castles. In the manner of warriors they often took by force what they could not obtain by other means and so passed into history as 'robber knights'. There are plentiful testimonies to the bitterness of the frequent feuds between burghers and the country nobility, to the scorn of the former for degenerate examples of the latter, and to the resentment of nobles for what they saw as the presumption of the townspeople who formally were far beneath them. Echoes of this sharp division between town and country, bourgeoisie and nobility, can be heard in many though not all German regions long after the fragile balance of power has shifted back somewhat in favour of the nobility in the course of further state integration on the plane of the numerous territorial dominions. But the balance now is between new noble and bourgeois formations, the former being a court nobility or, more generally, a nobility of officials and officers, while the bourgeoisie has been impoverished, consisting now of politically weak artisans and tradesmen, its leading groups no longer comprising merchants of the calibre of the Fuggers, but rather bourgeois and court state officials.

But however different the development of the multi-polar balance of tensions between noble, bourgeois and princely formations may have been in detail in different countries, the main outline of this long-term process, the shift in the total figuration of people towards a greater and richer differentiation of functions, coupled to a more complete and stronger state co-ordination and integration within a given dominion, can be seen clearly enough. But it may appear, if our attention is confined to this outline in its various aspects, as if we are concerned with a straightforward process devoid of conflicts. Only if we take account of the many discontinuities within this main line of development, the simultaneity of integration and disintegration, of rise and decline, of victory and defeat, does our picture of the process come closer to reality.

In the course of this transformation of human interdependence older social formations and positions are constantly losing their function. The people accustomed to them lose either their social basis, what gave their life much of its meaning and value in their own eyes, and are impoverished; or they adapt themselves to new rising formations. But the latter are usually part of a tighter and more comprehensive network of interdependence than the declining ones. Compared to those of earlier stages, the people in the succeeding, rising formations are usually organized into larger associations with more numerous, diverse and unstable contacts. The ways in which they are directly and indirectly dependent on others are also more numerous and diverse. The rising formations demand of their members a greater and more complex self-control if they are to maintain a high social position. Thus, in the form of the absolutist royal court, the court aristocrat and even the king, as we saw, forms with other people a larger, more tightly integrated figuration, with a greater range of contacts; they are directly and indirectly interdependent with more people than a medieval knight or ruler in a comparable structure. The same applies to the noble officer in the royal armies and regiments, compared to the feudal lord, who followed his liege lord's call to war with his own retainers wearing armour paid for by himself, and often returned home if the campaign lasted too long for him or exceeded the agreed time. It applies on a different level to merchants plying their trade in the ever-tightening network of a modern commercial and industrial state. In place of the relatively independent owners of small and medium enterprises, the more dependent directors and managers of large concerns are now the leading representatives of commercial enterprise. It applies also to the workers and employees of large industrial firms as compared to the pre-industrial artisans and traders. If the distribution of power between the rulers and the ruled is considered in isolation, one might easily conclude that the compulsions of interdependence to which pre-industrial traders and artisans were subjected in their small businesses were greater than those affecting the workers and employees of large industrial concerns. But to understand the long-term process under discussion, it is not enough to consider these compulsions in isolation. What matters in this context is that the total chains of interdependence formed by people at one stage of development, as compared to those of the succeeding stage, are shorter, less numerous and usually less stable, less strong. From a certain stage of development on, from a certain length, density and strength of the chains of interdependence, the nature of the compulsions which people exert on each other changes in a specific way. One of the distinguishing features is a marked shift towards a greater conversion of external into internal compulsions. In the genesis of romantic movements this transformation plays a decisive part.

3. It may be useful to point out at least in passing that we are here encountering some of the criteria of social development that can serve in the future as a basis for comparisons between different stages of development, and so for determining the direction of a particular development, and which therefore make possible measurement with the aid both of statistics and of figuration-series. One of the simplest of these criteria is the number of routine contacts which people of different classes, ages and sex have at one stage of social development as compared to another. Others are the number, length, density and strength of the chains of interdependence which individual people form with others within a time–space continuum at a certain stage as compared to earlier or later stages. A standard criterion that could be better calibrated than is the case at present is the central balance of tensions in a society: the number of power centres increases with a growing differentiation of functions; inequality in the distribution of power — without disappearing — is reduced. Lastly, these criteria include the level of the three fundamental controls of people in society — the control of extra-human Nature, the control of people over each other, and the control of each individual over himself. They too change in a characteristic manner from stage to stage, though certainly not by a simple increase or decrease.

The structural change in the compulsions that people exert on each other and on themselves, to mention only these, that can be observed in the development of modern European society — as when, for example, the situation of the late medieval nobility is compared to that of the court aristocracy in France, or that of the bourgeois guild strata of pre-industrial Germany with that of professional bourgeois strata in the same country in the course of increasing urbanization, industrialization and state integration — opens one of the doors to an understanding of the peculiar phenomenon of the romanticization of functionally declining or already extinct social formations by representatives of a later stage of development. These romanticizing impulses can usually be located in particular elevated classes, especially in their elites, whose own claims to power are essentially unfulfilled despite their high position, and cannot be fulfilled without destroying the regime which guarantees their high position. These elevated strata are exposed to stronger compulsions to interdependence and stronger civilizing self-constraints than earlier formations, so that for them the representatives of earlier stages of development become symbols of a freer, simpler, more natural or at any rate a better life, representatives of ideals that are longed for but have no hope of realization in the social life of the present or the future. The glorification of the wandering knight by a nobility being turned into courtiers or — in a more individualized form — the glorification of the free, autonomous, medieval guild bourgeoisie and, again, of medieval knighthood in the operas of Wagner — precisely when the German bourgeoisie's hopes of a greater share of power had been broken and the pressures of state integration in conjunction with those of industrialization were increasing — are examples of such a constellation. It is, in other words, one of the central symptoms of romantic attitudes and ideals that their representatives see the present only as a decline from the past, and the future — as far as they see a future at all — only as the restoration of a better, purer, idealized past. If we ask why the gaze of such romanticizing groups is turned backwards and why they seek relief from their present distress in a return to an earlier stage of social development of which they have, precisely, a romantic, an unrealistic picture, we come across a specific conflict that can be called the basic conflict of the romantic forms of experience. What generally constitutes the romantic character of human attitudes and the cultural products expressing them is the dilemma of elevated strata which, while they may pull at their chains, cannot throw them off without jeopardizing the entire social order that secures them their privileged position, and so the foundation of their own social values and meaning. No doubt there are usually other possible ways of coming to terms with such a dilemma. In the court society of France itself, at the very time in which the king was in a position to tighten the reins of government in the reign of Louis XIV, romantic tendencies — as far as can be observed — played a smaller part than at times when the ruler was not yet so strong or had again relaxed the reins, although mystical-religious tendencies at Louis XIV's court perhaps had a similar function. The possibility of identifying with the 'oppressor', and the emotional rewards offered by such identification at a time when the king's fame was great and his realm mighty, may have made the political and cultural compulsions of court life more endurable and the negative components of the ambivalent feeling towards it weaker.

However that may be, it must be enough here to sketch the main features of the structure of this basic conflict. It is a conflict in which the fundamental ambivalence of the feelings of people within a certain social formation finds expression. Positive feelings, pride in their own social superiority, their greater self-control, better manners, better families, better education, are coupled with negative feelings towards the existing social order, particularly towards constraints arising from the system of rule that are emotionally localized in certain higher-ranking persons or groups. Or, if their own feeling of powerlessness, of the inescapability of the compulsions is strong, it may find expression in a discontent that is not clearly localized, in the form of a romantic pessimism, together, usually, with negative feelings towards the civilizing self-constraints which are likewise inescapable. In many cases these negative feelings do not reach clear consciousness as such. They are socially dangerous if directed against higher and more powerful persons or groups, and wholly unrealizable if directed against self-constraints, against the social norms built into the personality which, as in the form of good manners, norms, values, ideals or a good conscience, form a highly valued component of the 'self' and of self-respect which is both personally and socially indispensable. One of the forms in which they can find symbolic expression is the projection of one's own ideals into the dream-image of a better, freer, more natural life in the past. The peculiarly romantic light in which this bathes the past, the light of an unrealizable longing, an unattainable ideal, a love that cannot be fulfilled, is the reflection of the conflict discussed earlier, the conflict of people who cannot destroy the constraints from which they suffer — whether they arise from the power structure or from civilization or a combination of the two — without destroying the foundation and the distinguishing mark of their high social position, what gives their lives meaning and value in their own eyes — without destroying themselves.

This tentative model of the connections between a specific form of experience and a specific figuration of the people who have this experience reveals, of course, only some of the actual factors involved in the social genesis of romantic tendencies. But even this limited model can contribute to releasing romantic undercurrents in the French court aristocracy from their isolation and to bringing them into clearer light through the comparison with structurally related undercurrents in social formations at a different stage of development. One should think, for example, of the bourgeoisie of Wilhelmine Germany. There, too, very pronounced romantic undercurrents are to be found. Like the French nobility in the course of increasing commercialization and during the rise of the court, the German bourgeoisie, from about the beginning of the nineteenth century, was very noticeably caught up, likewise in the course of increasing commercialization, industrialization and finally state integration, in a movement in which chains of interdependence lengthened and tightened, and social pressure towards the formation of more stable, uniform, comprehensive and complex self-controls within the individual was markedly increased. These two strata were in many respects, of course, extraordinarily different. But different as they were when viewed as a whole, the way in which they were incorporated in the total figuration of their societies shows certain structural similarities. In both cases we have elevated strata whose pride and desire for prestige went hand in hand with exclusion from the highest functions of rule and the political decisions linked to them. In both cases covert claims to power went hand in hand with an overt and very accentuated role as obedient subjects which became second nature to the people concerned. In both cases we have strata within which each individual found himself in an intense, incessant and inescapable competitive struggle which, physical violence being disallowed, had to be waged with utmost circumspection, with permanent control of the affects, and in which individuals who did not compete or lost their self-control and acted impulsively under acute affective pressure had to contend with social failure and often enough the loss of their position.

In these professional-bourgeois strata too, particularly among their artistic and academic elites, romantic inclinations were not lacking. But in their case the love for a more beautiful past and the yearning for its restoration were coupled with a certain sense of its historical reality. Unlike these later, more professional-bourgeois romantic tendencies, those of the court aristocracy lacked access to a rich store of historical knowledge and the resulting historical consciousness. The projection of unrealizable longings for liberation and other forms of interdependence, on to the image of groups of people belonging to an earlier, simpler, less complex stage of social development, makes these groups appear as embodiments of high values unattainable in the present; but at this stage of development the ability of people to distance themselves from the present was still too low to permit them to localize their wishful images clearly in a different historical epoch, as was the case in the nineteenth century with the image of medieval knights or master craftsmen. The knights of the romances of Amadis, or later the shepherds and shepherdesses into whom members of the French nobility project their fantasies as the court encroaches on their lives, are ideal figures of contemporary people in a somewhat different costume.

But whether with or without an historical perspective, what these romantic tendencies have in common is their character as symptoms of specific affective discontents bound up with the transition to a more comprehensive and complex network of interdependence and to corresponding external and internal constraints. Owing to these, affective outbursts, uncontrolled emotional acts, become increasingly dangerous for their perpetrators, being threatened more and more by social failure, and punishment by both the state and conscience. In both cases people seek to escape the pressure of these constraints — with an oppressed heart — through dream-images of people of earlier times who are thought to have lived more freely, more simply, more naturally, in short, in a way less affected by the compulsions and emotional constriction felt by the later people. Such movements therefore also have in common an inclination towards the specific valuations inherent in romantic perception: to romantically inclined people the negatively valued features of the present from which they long to escape appear magnified in the foreground; what their time has gained as compared to earlier stages appears much reduced in the background of their picture. In the image of the idealized people of earlier stages of development into whom they project their longings, conversely, everything that they desire, that they consider the antithesis of the unwarranted features of their own society is magnified in the foreground, while everything unwelcome to them, if they perceive it at all, is obscured in the background.

The role that ideal images of bucolic life play in the court society of the *ancien régime* illustrates this function of a lost past age as an antithesis to the pressures and deficiencies of the present. The idea of the simple rustic life is often linked to the wishful image of a freedom and spontaneity that were once present and have now vanished. Some motifs of this kind, especially the idealization of rural Nature, which reflect, first in the circles of the court aristocracy and then, in the eighteenth century, among some bourgeois intellectual elites, the tightening of interdependence in the course of increasing social differentiation and integration, were taken further in the nineteenth century as integral features of the bourgeois–romantic tradition.

The part played by the concept of 'Nature' in Rousseau's thought is sometimes interpreted simply as anticipating bourgeois romanticism because Rousseau himself was of bourgeois origin. But the dissemination of his fame and ideas owes not a little to the resonance which they had in court-aristocratic circles, in the *monde*. And this resonance is hardly to be understood without reference to the idealization of nature and its use as a counterpart to the compulsions of the court and social civility that are recurrent motifs in the tradition of court-aristocratic circles. If the romanticization of rural societies and their stereotype figures, their warriors, shepherds or peasants, is seen in relation to an increasing estrangement from the country in the course of advancing urbanization and the whole complex of changes of which urbanization is a part, it should not be forgotten that the transformation of warriors into courtiers, the formation of ever-larger and more populous princely courts with the advancing political integration of ever-larger dominions, belongs in this context as a preliminary stage of urbanization. Despite all the discontinuity, there are nevertheless lines connecting the court-aristocratic and the urban-bourgeois romanticization of country life and 'Nature'.

It would perhaps aid understanding of such problems if we add that from an early stage among elite strata, and very recently in other classes too, non-romantic ways of dealing with the problems of the increasing estrangement from 'country' life in the course of urbanization can be observed. Mountaineering, skiing, as well as many other sports and leisure activities, and above all the regular holiday trips of more and more urbanized circles, are relevant here. Just as the court lords and ladies of former times took their court make-up with them in their bucolic games, now the people of developed industrial societies take their urban make-up with them into the mountains, to the sea, into the country. But in the latter case they do not wear costumes, they do not dream they are part of a vanished world. This 'return to nature' lacks the note of melancholy and longing. It does not serve as a substitute for frustrated political activity, as a safe escape from oppressive political constraints, as a refuge for underlings without a political stake in the highest monopolies of power.

In the court society of French absolutism, the attitude to 'Nature' and the image that people have of 'Nature' are often the expression of a symbolic opposition to the constraints of royal rule and the royal court that have become inescapable — an opposition which during Louis XIV's lifetime and often later could be uttered only in a whisper and in symbolic disguise.

Saint-Simon, in describing the Versailles gardens which he thinks in bad taste, makes a remark that is very revealing in this context: 'There it gave the King pleasure to tyrannise Nature and to tame her by expending art and money. . . . One feels repelled by the constraint that is everywhere imposed on Nature.'[3]

Saint-Simon hardly belongs to the romantically inclined circles of court society. As we have seen, he plays an often risky, and actually futile, but highly deliberate political game as far as is possible at all in the framework of an autocratically ruled court. In addition he ventilates his frustration at the king's omnipotence and the constraints of the royal court by writing his memoirs, which were at first kept secret. In them he holds out a mirror to the king and court in his own way, and says much that he could not utter aloud during the great king's lifetime. The remark quoted shows the overall situation on a small scale; it illuminates the connection between the power structure on one hand and park design and feeling for nature on the other. The sensitivity produced by his own cramped social position sharpens Saint-Simon's perception of such connections.

He sees that in the king's taste, in the way he and his assistants lay out the gardens and park, the same tendency is expressed as in the king's attitude towards the nobility and his subjects in general. Just as Saint-Simon resists the latter, so too he resists the former. It suits the king's taste to group the trees and plants in his garden in clear forms that are easily overlooked, as the courtiers are grouped by ceremonial. The trees and bushes must be trimmed in such a way that no trace of disorderly, uncontrolled growth is visible. The paths and flowerbeds must be so arranged that the structure of the garden shows the same clarity and elegance as that of the royal buildings. Here, in the architecture of buildings and gardens; in the total subjugation of the material; in the absolute visibility and order of the subjugated; in the perfect harmony of the parts in the whole; in the flowing elegance of the ornamentation which matches the elegance of the movements of the king and the lords and ladies of the court in general; in the unparalleled size and extent of the buildings and gardens, which apart from all practical purposes, served the self-representation of royal power — in all this we find, perhaps, a more

[3] Saint-Simon, *Memoiren*, vol. 2, p. 89.

perfect approximation of the king's ideals than in his control and subjugation of people. It is understandable and also symptomatic that Saint-Simon, who was a duke and a member of the French high aristocracy and who, if we are to believe his own words, never accepted his treatment as a subject more or less like all others, abhors the king's garden design, this tyranny over nature. His sympathies lie rather with English landscape gardening which allows much freer scope to the growth of bushes, trees and flowers and which also reflects the taste of the upper classes in a society in which the kings and their representatives were not in a position to establish a lasting autocratic or absolutist dominion.

4. This connection between the figuration of people and their feelings for nature can be traced very clearly in the development of the French nobility from the sixteenth century on. In the early period of the development of the court the feeling of estrangement from rural life, of being torn from their native soil, and of longing for a vanished world, often matches a very real experience:

> And while, alas, we spend our lives
> Upon a foreign river's unknown bank
> Misfortune makes us sing these mournful lines . . .

These are the words of Joachim du Bellay, one of the great French lyric poets of the first half of the sixteenth century (1522–60). This 'deracination' from the country in the course of courtization and the melancholy it induces are seen still more clearly in the following verses of du Bellay that are better heard in his own language:

> Quand revoiray-je, hélas, de mon petit village,
> Fumer la cheminée, et en quelle saison
> Revoyrai-je le dos de ma pauvre maison?

> Plus me plaist le séjour qu'ont basty mes ayeux
> Que des palais romains le front audacieux . . .
> Plus mon Loyre gaulois que le Tybre latin,
> Plus mont petit Lyré que le mont Palatin
> Plus que le marbre dur me plait l'ardoise fine,
> Et, plus que l'air romain, la douceur angevine.[4]

We hear the lament of the nobleman condemned to live in the

---

[4] Lemonnier, *La France sous Henri II*, Histoire de France, vol. 5, p. 294.

capital, the longing of an oppressed heart that we gradually come to know as romantic yearning. It is a longing that can find no fulfilment. Life in the great world of the capital becomes increasingly indispensable. Its compulsions are oppressive; but even if the cage were opened it would be impossible to escape; for the ties holding the courtier prisoner in the great world are a part of himself. He could return to the home of his ancestors but would not be able to find there what he sought. The free country existence of his childhood has become a dream like his childhood itself. The greatest of this group of sixteenth-century poets, who knows very well how to live as a man of the court and has strong monarchist sympathies, Ronsard (1524–85), the central figure in the famous Pléiade, writes when describing his youth:

> Je n'avais pas quinze ans que les monts et les bois
> et les eaux me plaisaient plus que la Cour des Rois.[5]

This nostalgia for a lost rural and 'natural' homeland, the antithesis of urban court life with its constraint, from now on becomes a fixed motif. After Ronsard, and in stronger tones, a member of the next generation, Desportes, sings in his 'Bergeries':

> O champs plaisans et doux! ô vie heureuse et sainte!
> Où, francs de tout soucy, nous n'avons point de crainte
> D'être accablez en bas, quand, plus ambitieux
> Et d'honneurs et de biens, nous voisinons les cieux!
>
> O gens bien fortunez, qui les champs habitez,
> Sans envier l'orgueil des pompeuses citez![6]

The lament for what was lost in leaving country life behind becomes increasingly intense, the opposition of town and country more emphatic. The development of towns and court, the assimilation of country-born people to the 'pompeuses citez' has not yet nearly reached its height.[7] But we already see how a human situation

---

[5] *Ibid.*, p. 295.
[6] Desportes, *Oeuvres complètes* (publ. by A. Michieles, 1858), pp. 435/37.
[7] Cf. de Vaissière, *Gentilshommes campagnards de l'ancienne France* (Paris, 1903), p. 175, where a large number of examples of the nobility's disinclination 'à faire ès villes sa demeurance' is given, and where it is shown how the rising *roture* was first carried by an inverse movement; for, to lead a 'noble' life and to be entirely cleansed of plebeian elements ('se nettoyer de toute roture'), they took up residence in the country, only for many of them to be impoverished once again and to appear at court in their turn as down-at-heel nobles.

was slowly established that remains throughout the *ancien régime* a factor not always visible but always influencing both the make-up and experience of court people and court styles, from the time of Henry IV to that of Louis XIV and beyond. Here, where discontent with the pomp and honour of the court bought by one's own freedom, where the ideal growing from it, the wishful image of simple spontaneous life to which arms are stretched out in vain, are intensified; where this constellation is constantly being reproduced at a new level where it can be apprehended, as it were, *in statu nascendi* — here the connection between the change of the figuration and that of the mode of experience of the people forming it can be particularly clearly seen.

The evolution of the human image of what we experience as 'Nature' is one aspect of the overall development of human society. Here we see a segment of it. The great mass of medieval warriors and lords still lived amid fields, households and villages, rivers, mountains and woods. These things made up their everyday surroundings. They did not experience them at a distance as a 'Nature', as 'landscape' standing opposed to them. Only in the course of the development of the court and towns did the fields and villages, meadows and mountains become an antithetical image seen from a distance. And the more the absolutist court was consolidated, the more clearly the image of nature took on the character of a landscape in which the contemporary society was reflected. In the evolution of court painting — for example, from Poussin to Watteau — we can easily follow this role of nature as both a landscape and a background to people — its role as the counterpart and mirror-image of the situation of court society at the time. All the attitudes and moods aroused by court life, such as the measured artificiality of gesture demanded by social convention, whether it be a pompous gravity or frivolous grace, all this passes from now on into the image of rural nature, into the shaping of landscape. In the hands of court painters, as a background to court life impregnated with yearning, Nature becomes successively the Classical, the Baroque and finally the Rococo landscape as the court and court society develop.

In the sixteenth century there might still have been some doubt about the inescapability of assimilation to the court. Perhaps it still seemed possible to break out of the mechanism. But even at this time court life was for many people not merely a costume imposed from outside that could be cast off by living in the country: the mask has already become flesh and blood for many people, an essential component of their self-respect, their pride and their gratifications.

But the conflict, the ambivalent attitude to court life, are still close to the surface. They can be felt, for example, in Desportes, when he sings of the man who

> Ne vend sa liberté pour plaire
> Aux passions des princes et des rois . . .
> L'ambition son courage n'attise;
> D'un fard trompeur son âme il ne déguise,
> Il ne sa plaist a violer sa foi;
> Des grands seigneurs l'oreille il n'importune,
> Mais en vivant content de sa fortune,
> Il est sa cour, sa faveur et son roy.[8]

5. By the reign of Henry IV there was no longer any escape. The hero of a satire on the courtier, a Baron de Foeneste, is asked 'how one appears at court today'. The first thing he says in answer is that one must be well dressed in the fashion of three or four gentlemen who set the tone. Then he enumerates exactly how to deport oneself:

> You require a doublet made of four or five layers of different taffetas; stocking such as you see, frieze and scarlet, accounting, I assure you, for eight ells of cloth at least; then you need boots, the flesh-side outermost, the heel very high, and spur-slippers also very high . . . the spurs must be gilded. . . . When, thus attired, you have arrived in the Louvre courtyard, — one alights between the guards, you understand — you begin to laugh at the first person you meet, you salute one, say a word to another: 'Brother, how you bloom, gorgeous as a rose. Your mistress treats you well; that cruel rebel has no arms against this fine brow, this well-curled moustache. And then this charming river-bank, one could die of admiration.' This must be said while flinging the arms, agitating the head, moving from one foot to the other, painting with the hand now the moustache, now the hair.[9]

The expression 'a man *comme il faut*' is still sometimes used today. Here we come across its social origin in court society. To keep one's place in the intense competition for importance at court, to avoid being exposed to scorn, contempt, loss of prestige, one must subordinate one's appearance and gestures, in short oneself, to the fluctuating norms of court society that increasingly emphasize the dif-

---

[8] Desportes, *op. cit.*, p. 431.
[9] Agrippa d'Aubigné, *Les aventures du Baron de Foeneste*, Oeuvres complètes, ed. Réaume and Causade (Paris, 1877), pp. 395–96.

ference, the distinction of the people belonging to it. One *must* wear certain materials and certain shoes. One *must* move in certain ways characteristic of people belonging to court society. Even smiling is shaped by court custom.

This *il faut* that increasingly embraces the whole life of people at court reveals very vividly both the mechanism and the intensity of the compulsion to which the people congregating at the court are subjected. No doubt, a certain code of conduct was binding at earlier stages of development, for example, on the warrior nobility of the Middle Ages, particularly at the territorial and royal courts of the preceding centuries. But the constraints, like the whole organization of these earlier strata and courts, were not yet so tight or inescapable.

6. Nothing is more fruitless, when dealing with long-term social processes, than to attempt to locate an absolute beginning. If, as sometimes still happens today, history is treated as a chain of the ideas of book-writing elites, it is easy and no doubt very gratifying to play a learned society game in which the prize is won by the person who finds a quotation in a book that demonstrably expresses a particular idea earlier than was assumed by the other players on the basis of their quotations. The earlier book is then regarded as the 'beginning' of the idea and the author as its real originator. If the change of figuration formed by interdependent people is kept in view as the background and centre of the historical process, it can be better understood that the search for absolute beginnings, even of ideas recorded in books, is futile. In this continuum of individuals bound together in groups there is no point at which something — whether it be a particular group of people, a figuration, or the ideas of people or other individual products — emerges as an absolute beginning, as if from nothingness or, which amounts to the same thing, from the inexplicable creativity of an individual person. What, on the contrary, can be very well observed and substantiated by evidence are relative beginnings, that is, explicable leaps and discontinuities within the long-term, gradual and continuous transformation of human groups and their products. The development of the French royal court and the figuration of people living there is one example. It can serve as a preliminary model for further work on such problems, precisely because the figuration of people at court is functionally bound up in the closest possible way with the whole organization of rule, with the total figuration of people of which the royal court is *one* organ, and, increasingly, *the* central one. The organization of the French royal court under Henri IV is the result of a long, continuous development with numerous leaps, reforms and reorganizations

made by individual rulers from their relatively short-term perspectives. The figuration of people at court, the structure of interdependence in which they are enmeshed, the kind of constraints to which they are exposed, is a continuation of the figurations, interdependence and compelling structures of the preceding phases. But our linguistic means are so inflexible that often we have nothing but comparatives with which to express the differences of grouping, experience and conduct between people at different stages of social development — terms like 'more' or 'less', giving the impression that we are concerned solely with quantitative differences. Marx — following in the footsteps of Hegel — tried to resolve such problems by using expressions such as the leap from quantity to quality. For his time this was undoubtedly an important conceptual advance. The formulations of Hegel and Marx are a bold attempt to develop our conceptual tools towards a clearer and more precise formulation of the relation of continuity to discontinuity in the evolution of human groups, as it can be actually observed. But there is no reason why we should make do for ever with the provisional models that they elaborated. These models are still highly speculative. The empirical basis from which they were developed more than a century ago was narrow and uncertain compared to the empirical knowledge now available when constructing such models. And the more the gaps in knowledge are reduced, the more necessary and possible it is to seek answers to such problems that are in closest touch with the wide field of empirical knowledge.

Within its limits, the development of the French court and of court society in France serves very well as empirical material for such a task. This is partly because this development has no direct relation to the controversies of our own time, so that it can be more easily regarded without emotional involvement. In the development of the French court we are concerned with a single but central strand in the overall development of a particular national society. Like the latter, the development of the court, if pursued with sufficient detachment from about the time of the Valois to that of Louis XIV, proves to be a continuous process. The organization of the offices of the royal household and retinue becomes more complex in the course of centuries. Household and government functions, at first exercised without clear distinctions by the same people, are separated and become different types of offices. The hierarchy of offices has an increasing number of rungs. The number of offices grows. There are inverse movements, but the main line of development continues in one direction with short-term fluctuations until far into the seventeenth century. In this sense the continuity of the process is unmistakable.

We can attempt to express it by comparatives. But comparatives are apt to give the impression that we are concerned only with a quantitative change. And this impression is misleading. It results largely from the rudimentary nature of our linguistic and conceptual tools. What we are actually concerned with is a gradual change in the grouping of people at court or, if we wish to express it differently, in the structure of the court. Even though our language and concepts are at present such that, in order to express the change in the figuration of people forming the court, we are forced to abstract from this structure of human relationships those aspects which can be expressed by comparatives and so appear as purely quantitative, this limitation of our present language should not conceal that the process we are attempting to formulate by this type of abstraction is really a change in the figuration formed by people, in the structure of their interdependence. This figurational change can only be conceptualized as such. However many 'more' or 'less' aspects we may abstract from this structure, without a precise definition of the figurational transformation as such, these comparative aspects, though indispensable at present, can only be provisional approximations. The idea of a transformation of quantity into quality thus rests on a misunderstanding, insofar as what appears in long-term developments, through the limitations of existing language, only as 'more', as a quantitative accumulation, is always something other than this, namely a structural change, a change in the network of interdependence and so too in the balance of power within the structure of tensions forming the total figuration. The shift in the distribution of power between the royal group and the remaining nobility in the former's favour is one example. 'More or less' concepts, terms like 'the increase in royal power' or 'the advance of monetarization' are an auxiliary framework expressing the continuity of change. But what, at the time of Henry IV and after many oscillations, can be simply represented as a further increase in the power of the kings, is also a *metabasis eis allo genos*: from the continuous change of the evolving figuration a new type of figuration has emerged.

The notion of the transformation of quantity into quality therefore points to an important problem that deserves careful theoretical investigation. Its theoretical significance can be indicated only in passing. But the problem itself cannot be entirely avoided. Without a reference to it a study of court society in France would be suspended in mid-air.

The development of French court society in the seventeenth century is a continuation of the development of the preceding centuries. Despite this continuity of development the relationship between the people at court in the seventeenth century, like their gestures and general make-up, also constitutes something new. The question is how this *metabasis eis allo genos*, this transition to another genus, this process of sociological mutation, can be expressed without encouraging either the idea of an absolute continuity of the same kind as a numerical series, or of an absolute discontinuity of development — how this leap can be expressed in a phase of the evolution of knowledge when the development of comprehensive theoretical models of such processes lags far behind the unintegrated detailed knowledge of them. Whenever we encounter problems of this kind we are obliged to enlist the aid of metaphors from other, simpler areas, and to develop their literal meaning in social usage until they gradually lose their reference to the original area and even the character of metaphors. Adapted to the material to which they are now applied they finally become special terminology for this new area. The concept of development itself is an example of the conversion of a word originally used metaphorically into a specialized term. Recollection of its literal usage has almost disappeared. Echoes of this original usage are now evoked by the verb 'to envelop'; another originally metaphorical, then specialized branch of the evolution of the word leads into the sphere of photography, in which the idea of 'developing' film is commonplace. But one is hardly inconvenienced by the relative inappropriateness of the literal meaning to its special usage. It is hardly noticed. The specialized usage has become familiar and self-evident.

In the sphere of social development the transition to a different genus is often expressed by a metaphorical use of words such as that of reaching a new stage, rising to a new plane. And as long as we remember that these are the first steps in the elaboration of specialized terms to apply to our observations, such metaphors can do no harm. They remind us of the experience of mountaineers who on scaling one mountain range have reached a particular plateau commanding a specific view, and from there climb through forests to the next, higher plateau that opens a new prospect. That the mountaineers climb higher and higher is a quantitative, a 'more-or-less' aspect of the climb. That the view from the higher plateau is different from that from the lower one, that from the higher plateau connections are perceived that are concealed from view on the lower plateau, is an example both of the difference and of the relation between a change that can be expressed through comparatives — 'higher' and 'lower' — and a holistic change, a change of the total figuration — the relationship of mountaineer, plateau and view. The higher plateau may be a region hitherto unvisited, bringing into view connections previously unknown, but however that may be, the metaphorical use of concepts such as a 'higher stage' or 'new level' would not be difficult to develop further in such a way as to express not only the quantitative continuity but also the relative discontinuity of the figuration, the sociological mutation, the transition to a new genus.

It is a transition of this kind that is referred to when we say that in the course of the transformation of warriors into courtiers — a long-term process the early stages of which include the relatively small territorial courts of the eleventh and twelfth centuries — in the seventeenth century a court aristocracy definitively supersedes the knightly warrior nobility as the highest noble formation. Thereby the development of the central organ of the state attains, as it were, a new plateau. Here comparative and other quantitative terms no longer suffice. We see the precipitation of a new figuration of people, a court aristocracy, within the framework of a continuous development of the royal court and of the whole society of which the court is the central organ.

For centuries the multipolar balance of tensions in French society oscillated with the conflicts between bourgeois, noble and royal formations of different kinds. After the accession to the throne of Henry IV at the end of the long civil wars it became evident that the overall course of social development had bestowed on the occupants and representatives of the royal position — particularly in the form of the two central monopolies of taxation and of police and military organization — power that gave them an unassailable preponderance over all other formations in their dominion, as long as these did not set aside their mutual conflicts and form a lasting united front against the monarchy. This shift of the main axis of the balance of tensions in the kings' favour is central to what can metaphorically be called the transition to a new genus or to a new stage of development in French society. This central phenomenon certainly does not stand alone. It would be to misunderstand such statements to construe them as statements about 'beginnings' or 'causes'. In long-term processes of social development there are neither absolute beginnings nor absolute causes. We must seek other linguistic and conceptual tools to examine and explain the emergence of relatively new figurations within a continuous overall development of society. This is precisely the problem with which we are concerned at present. The continuous overall change of French society reaches a point at which, after many fluctuations, the central axis of tension shifts in favour of the social position of the central ruler. Hand in hand with this change in the central ruler's position goes a corresponding change in that of the elite formations of the nobility and the bourgeoisie. Parts of the nobility are now more heavily dependent on the central ruler and more tightly bound to his court than ever before. We might say that one door is locked behind them while new doors open before them. They are shut off more and more from rural life.

7. In the nearer or more distant future — who knows how long it may take? — it will perhaps be possible to trace more precisely and in greater detail the long-term process of courtization, urbanization and the gradual increase in longing for a non-court rural life through its different phases until the plateau was reached at which the separation had become firm and irrevocable. One might imagine a time when schoolchildren can understand a process of this kind, which is scarcely less important for an understanding of the evolution of European society than are wars and peace treaties, together with other long-term lines of development, in order to understand themselves. There is certainly no lack of documentary evidence. To give only one example from the fifteenth century, there is the complaint of Philippe de Vitry, Bishop of Meaux: 'How happy is the life of him who makes his dwelling in the fields', in his verses 'on the great disparity of rustic life with that of the court'.[10] There are the testimonies of the poets of the Pléiade in the sixteenth century, a few examples of which were quoted above. Today we often speak in such contexts of 'alienation'. The concept would be appropriate in this context too, if it were not so often used with a romantic evaluation, if its use were less bound up with the lament over 'alienation' and more with explaining its social origin, independently of its value.

In the seventeenth century the gradual differentiation between urban court formations and rural formations in France reaches a new plateau. The impetus of social estrangement between the court and the country, the court and rural nobility, is so great that the court nobility at the time of Louis XIV has the character of an almost, though never entirely, self-contained formation. At earlier times war-

---

[10] *Les Oeuvres de Ph. Vitry*, ed. G. P. Tarbé (Reims, 1850).

riors and lords had lived often enough at the courts of princes or kings. But in the preceding centuries the mode of life, interests, make-up, ties and constraints of people in court and non-court rural social groups were not so totally different as was the case in the seventeenth century with the definitive rise of the royal position to preponderance over all other social formations. Now the royal court overshadowed the rest of the social network as an organization of a new order not only of magnitude but of complexity, as compared to other secular social organizations of the time and particularly the manorial estates, villages and other organizations of rural groups.

It was above all this aspect of the social division between court and country, the discrepancy between the complexity of life at court and the relative simplicity of the life of country groups, that contributed among courtiers to the feeling of nostalgia for the country, estrangement from the simple life, in short, to the idealization of an imagined rural existence which, just because it was a fantasy, was quite compatible with their contempt for the rural nobility and the peasants, and with a certain revulsion from rural life as it really was.

In addition, habituation to the relatively high standard of complexity in all human relationships at the royal court placed special demands on the capacity of court people for self-discipline. Life at the court of kings whose power was incomparably greater than that of each individual court noble and even of the various noble groups at court, demanded incessant self-control, a complex and — as Saint-Simon's remarks show — carefully calculated strategy in all one's dealings with social equals and superiors. The sources of income of a considerable part of the court nobles were dependent on the favour of the king or his confidants. To the incumbents of court and military offices, to the recipients of pensions from the king's privy purse, royal disfavour, wrong steps in the competition between court factions, the enmity of a favourite, a mistress, a minister, all this could threaten their income, the standard of life of their families as well as their prestige, their market value within court society, their prospects and hopes for the future. Even for courtiers who possessed a considerable family income, a reduction in royal favour was a danger difficult to endure. And the king's disfavour, banishment from court, meant as we have said, more or less the end of a courtier's social existence.

The nobles of the periods in the development of the Middle Ages when there was primarily a barter economy had at their disposal, as the incumbents of fiefs, a kind of income that made them relatively independent, or at any rate reduced their dependence on their liege lord once the fief was in their hands. By contrast, the king's manner of recompensing his nobles' services by money payments in the form of salaries or pensions paid at fixed intervals created a lasting dependence. Particularly the mass of lesser and middle court nobility, but even many of the high nobles who drew their income from the king's purse, lived in the framework of the large court organization in a manner that, despite all the obvious differences, recalls that of workers and employees in a large industrial concern. In addition, the French court nobility had practically no chance of escape. At least under Louis XIV its members had no freedom of movement. They could hardly move from one place to another without loss of status. The almost total inescapability of the dependence in which the majority of court nobles lived, and the constraints to which they were thereby subjected, makes understandable what nature and rural life could mean for them as contrasting images. That these constraints of interdependence also affected the kings and the royal family, particularly in the late period of the *ancien régime*, has already been shown. The function of rural life as the antithesis of the constraint at court is seen clearly enough — as when Marie-Antoinette and her ladies in waiting dress up as milkmaids. A particularly marked shift in this direction can be observed at the end of the civil wars in the early seventeenth century, when many courtiers became fully aware, perhaps for the first time, of the inescapability of their situation.

But the peculiar undertones of longing, the specifically romantic undertones that so often attend the image of nature and rural life in court circles, cannot be understood if the court is seen merely as an external mechanism of constraint. The decisive factor producing the specific romantic tonality which dreams of the natural life as an ideal already unattainable, is the peculiarity of the constraints arising from interdependence at court that has already been mentioned: the constraints which court people impose on one another are social pressures demanding a high degree of self-constraint from each member, a self-constraint which is already very complex and comprehensive.

In this way, after the civil war, for example, membership of the court increasingly entails a pacification, a heightened control of warlike habits and pleasures, which in turn forces each individual courtier to exercise stricter and more permanent self-control as regards aggressive impulses. Henry IV is still relatively indulgent towards duelling by his nobles. Richelieu and Louis XIV, as the custodians of the monopoly of physical force, are much more severe when their nobles fight in accordance with the old warrior custom. Duelling at this time and long after has the character of an enclave that nobles and, later, other classes reserve for themselves within the state — often in defiance of the king or other authorities — as a symbol of individual freedom as understood in the framework of the warrior tradition, that is, the freedom to wound or kill each other if they are so inclined. This too, particularly after the civil wars and recurrently later, is a symbol of the revolt by elite strata against increasing state control that tends more and more to subject all citizens to the same law. A wave of duelling is brought to an end when Richelieu has one of the chief duellists of high family publicly executed. Restraint must be practised. Anger and hostility can no longer be given free rein.

The compulsion to deal peacefully with people, which often means to duel with words rather than with weapons, demands an especially complex self-control because each member of this numerous society is constantly coming into contact with people of different rank and power and has to graduate his behaviour accordingly. Courtiers have to know how to adjust their features, their words and their movements exactly to the people they meet and to the occasions on which they meet them. It is not only the compulsions of interdependence represented by other people that are relatively inescapable at court, but also the self-imposed constraints resulting from this type of interdependence. The phenomena referred to by words like 'alienation' or 'romanticism' remain incomprehensible in their structure unless we include in the theoretical elaboration of these concepts their connection to the development of specific mechanisms of self-compulsion as an integral element in individuals. It may be that in the life of court people the exact nuance of a smile, the various shades of good manners, the whole complex elaboration of behaviour to match the rank and status of a given social partner, originally has the character of a disguise learned by conscious practice. But the capacity for a conscious shaping of the self is developed in societies the specific structure of which demands an extensive and constant masking of momentary emotional impulses as a means of social survival and success, a masking that becomes an integral feature of personality structure. If a courtier looks into a mirror as an adult, he finds that what was first a consciously assumed mask has become a part of his face. The masking of spontaneous impulses, the armouring and transformation of primary emotions, has not the same form and structure in the framework of court society as it has in the pacified middle classes that are brought up to earn their living by work, or in all the other strata of industrial societies whose members are subject to the compulsions of work and career. In court society the armour is not yet as all-embracing and automatic as in these working societies, since the greater inequality of people, the subjection, dependence and submissiveness of the lower-ranking, particularly the poorer strata, always opens a broad social field to court people in which affective impulses of all kinds can be relatively openly expressed without being threatened by social failure or penalties, and within which, therefore, the development of self-constraint is only slightly demanded. For this reason the armour of the court aristocracy is by and large fairly loose. Court aristocrats are often well aware that they wear a mask in their dealings with other people, even though they may not be aware that playing with masks has become second nature to them.

About the turn of the century, in the last decade of the sixteenth century and the first of the seventeenth, we can observe very clearly how, with the firmer centralization of state controls, the sharper pacification of behaviour and — after Henry IV's victory, the more and more irrevocable cleavage between the aristocracy of the capital and the great courts and that of the country and the lesser provincial courts, has reached a new plateau in France. It is, above all, the people transformed into the great court aristocracy behind whom a door is locked and before whom new doors open. The increasing compulsion to self-constraint opens new pleasures to them, new enrichments and refinements, in short new values, together with new oppressions and dangers. At any rate, self-control becomes for them a high personal value. The specifically courtly way of being civilized, resting on self-constraint that has become second nature, is one of the things distinguishing court-aristocratic people from all others, an advantage they believe they enjoy. For this very reason their self-constraint is inescapable.

With the centralization of all controls and power at the royal court, the provincial nobility, from the simple country nobles to what remains of the country nobility at small courts, loses more and more of its social significance. French society is not the only and certainly not the first European society in which this structural change takes place. Strong tendencies towards a centralized court, in conjunction with the allocation of money by the central rulers and their representatives, can be observed earlier in other societies, particularly Spain and Italy. But in the French centralizing movement of the seventeenth century is formed the largest and most populous court unit in Europe which has effectively functioning central control. Certain structural features of the plateau of development that is thereby attained can therefore be very well observed in the example of France.

8. These features can perhaps be best formulated by the metaphorical use of the term 'distancing'. The term 'distance' was used earlier in connection with the increased differentiation of urban court life from rural life. Urbanization, monetarization, commercialization and courtization are parts of a comprehensive transformation that leads people at this time to experience 'Nature' as something standing opposed to them, as landscape, as the world of 'objects', as something to be explored and known. It would lead us too far afield to draw together the different threads here. At any rate, processes of this kind play as great a part as the increasing capacity to relate together observation and reflection with regard to natural phenomena. All these are aspects of a specific distancing, a detachment from what is still referred to today as 'nature' or 'objects'. This detachment is seen as clearly in the representation of nature as landscape in painting, as in the scientific exploration of natural processes or in the philosophical question whether and how man is able to know 'objects' as they really are, or whether 'objects' are really 'there'. These and other symptoms of the detachment from 'nature' emerged as evidence of the social attainment of a new plateau more or less simultaneously in the phase that we still refer to by the somewhat antiquated term 'Renaissance'. They can clarify what the metaphor of climbing to a new plateau refers to in this context. For European societies remain for a number of centuries with this type of distanciation. The problems that come into view on this basis are developed and expanded in the most manifold ways. But the kind of distancing of men in their human associations from what they experience as 'nature' that was attained in the centuries of the 'Renaissance', represented by concepts like 'subject' and 'object', has remained broadly the same up to the present. We can see the preliminary signs of a rise to a new plateau clearly enough in painting at present, where there is an obvious attempt to represent something other than 'objects' that stand opposed to the onlooker in three-dimensional space. But the process in which we find ourselves can be better understood if we are aware that the distancing during the Renaissance, in the course of which people came to understand the multiplicity of physical events as 'nature', is only part of a more comprehensive process of detachment.

The study of a court society reveals particularly clearly some of the other aspects of this all-embracing process. The armour-plating of self-constraint, the masks evolved by all members of the court elites to a greater degree than before as a part of themselves, distance people from each other more than before. As compared to the preceding period the spontaneous impulses of people in their mutual dealings at court — and certainly not only at court — are more tightly reined. The deliberate sizing up of a situation, the taking of bearings, in short, reflections intervene more or less automatically between the affective, spontaneous impulse to act and the actual performance of the action in word or deed. Often enough the people on this plateau are well aware of reflection as a component of their armour. Depending on their position, they evaluate it either positively as 'reason', or romantically and negatively as a fetter on feeling, a hindrance, a degeneration of human nature. But however they evaluate them, they perceive their self-constraint, their armour and masks and the kind of detachment corresponding to them, not as symptoms of a particular stage of human-social development, but as eternal features of unchanging human nature. For all time, it appears, man stands opposed as 'subject' to 'nature', the world of 'objects'. Theories of human society start either from the assumption that human beings, each of whom exists behind his masks and his armour as an isolated individual, come into contact with each other only in a secondary way. Or they reify 'society', exactly like 'nature', as a thing beyond all individual people. In both cases the view that one commands from a particular plateau of detachment reached through a particular process of distancing — a plateau the temporal conditions of which can be very exactly explored and explained empirically — is interpreted as an eternal, timeless, immutable 'human condition'. Reflection, as we saw, intrudes itself as a control made more or less automatic by habit and education between man and 'natural objects', between man and man, on the plateau that is slowly reached in the phase of the 'Renaissance' to a greater degree than previously in European history. This applies not least to the relation between men and women. Here too — first of all in certain elites — the scope for spontaneity and impulse, even for men who are physically strong, diminishes in the course of the advancing centralization of the state. Women, considered as social groups, have far greater power at court than any other formation in this society. Not only masks, but fans are symbols of their disguise. A characteristic symptom of this major advance in the development of self-constraint, this reduction in spontaneity, this civilizing detachment, as far as the relations between women and men are concerned, is the development of romantic love both as a real occurrence and perhaps still more as a cult and ideal. Whatever other factors may have been involved, the distancing of the sexes by the armour of self-constraint, manifested now in the form of good manners, now in that of conscience or reflection — in short, a postponing of the enjoyment of love and a melancholy satisfaction in painful joys — all these, with varying emphases, are integral elements in the complex of feeling called romantic love. They mark the transition from relatively simple and unmixed affects to more complex and often mingled ones, that can undoubtedly be related to the transition from the use of relatively unmixed colours to that of mixed, more complex tones in painting.

Finally, there is one other kind of distancing that is fundamental to this whole change in human interdependence. A central aspect of the new plateau to which the people of European societies gradually ascend at the end of the Middle Ages is an increased capacity for self-detachment. This capacity, too, is very closely related structurally to the development by the individual of an armour of more or less automatic self-control. This can be observed first in small elite groups, and then, in the course of the increasingly complex organization of human interdependence over centuries, in broader and broader classes.

Jakob Burckhardt, in his *Culture of the Renaissance*, drew attention to this shift towards a greater self-consciousness of the individual as an individual that can be observed in the Italian 'Renaissance'. He also pointed in his own way to connections between the process of state formation, the increasing centralization of states, and the increased individualization. But the theoretical models that he used — for like every historian he too used specific theoretical models — were somewhat arbitrarily chosen. He believed that these developments could be best understood with the help of the model of a work of art. He conceived the new phase of the development of the Italian states, and of the idea that people of the time had of this development, as an evolution like that of a work of art. And in a similar way — with the work of art as his pattern — he treated what may perhaps be termed an 'individualization shift', a new state of consciousness of human beings, as the rise to a new level of self-consciousness. This comparison with a work of art serves among other things to express a greater consciousness in the shaping of states or, put more realistically, the centralization of the decisive means of power, and in the shaping of the individual by himself, which, of course, is conditional on a greater capacity for self-detachment. But he conveys the idea of a harmonious shaping; he blurs the difference between human-social structural changes and ideals expressed as such, as ideals, in the books of the time. In Burckhardt's followers this confusion of statements about ideas and ideals expressed in prominent books of the time, and the total development of the figurations formed by people and of the people forming these figurations, of which the development of ideas and ideals is only a part, is often far more conspicuous. As far as was possible and necessary in this context, we have attempted to remove this confusion. The changes discussed earlier are not only changes of ideas which men write down in their books but changes of men themselves in the change of the figurations that they form with one another. Such transformations of people are referred to when we speak of increased individualization, stronger armour of the affects, greater detachment from nature, people and the self, and other connected transformations that have been touched on here. In becoming aristocrats and courtiers, it is not only in their ideas that the people of the nobility are transformed, but in their whole make-up.

When the word 'history' is used today, it is not always clear that people themselves can change in a specific manner in the course of historical change. In this case, too, existing terminology is not quite adequate to do justice to such observations. It is necessary very circumspectly to seek new metaphors better suited to formulate such transformations than the usual concepts. The latter are largely formed in such a way as to imply that historical developments always take place on one and the same plane. To be sure, one speaks of different stages of development. But the relationship this metaphor refers to, the relationship between the different steps, is seldom clarified. The observation of the ascent to a higher degree of self-detachment in a period of social development makes it possible to elucidate certain aspects of historical stages that usually remain unexpressed. It also offers a further opportunity to understand why social development, despite the use of comparatives, can be seen not only in terms of increase or decrease, of more-or-less processes. We can often only do justice to it by including the change in the figuration as such in our analysis. The advance of self-detachment in the sixteenth and seventeenth centuries is an example. To do justice to it, metaphors of lines or surfaces are inadequate. Time–space metaphors or, in other words, four-dimensional metaphors are needed to give appropriate expression to these aspects of development.

A very apt metaphorical expression for what is observed here is the image of climbing or descending a spiral staircase, that is, a multi-dimensional model. A person climbs by such a staircase from one floor of a tower to the next. Reaching the higher floor, he not only has a different perspective of the country overlooked by the tower, but looking down he sees himself on the lower level from which he has come. This corresponds roughly to what can be observed in this earlier advance of self-detachment: people are capable to a higher degree than before of observing themselves; but they are not yet in a position to observe themselves as people observing themselves. This is only possible by climbing to the next plateau, to the next stage of self-detachment, that opens quite different perspectives to those of the preceding stage. This is the further climb that we are making at present. We are already in a position to detach ourselves from the advance in detachment of the Renaissance, to observe ourselves, as it were, climbing to the previous platform, and so to gain a better understanding of the direction in which we ourselves can now move. This is precisely what is happening here.

9. The courts were not the only figurations in which the people forming them developed greater self-control, and with it an increased detachment from nature, from each other and from themselves. But they were among the first, and for a time were undoubtedly the most powerful and influential of these figurations. It may be enough here to elucidate at least some symptoms of this comprehensive transformation of human beings by a few examples.

In the first and second decades of the seventeenth century in France, there was published in successive parts a long novel that had much resonance in the circles of the evolving court society. For a time it formed the literary centre of a kind of cult, of social amusements, games and conversation. It is still regarded as one of the literary milestones of this epoch. It cannot today be read with the enjoyment it gave its contemporaries. But this is precisely the challenge which a prominent and once fashionable literary document of a past epoch offers us. If we stop considering such a book simply as a literary product and see it as documenting the kind of people who found a certain selection of their inclinations, feelings and ways of experiencing and behaving expressed in it, we gain a better understanding of these people themselves.

The novel concerned, *L'Astrée* by Honoré d'Urfé, is a product of the period in which even the nobles who had grown up in the tradition of independent warriors and *seigneurs* were beginning to realize that the shift in the balance of power in favour of the monarchy and its representatives — or, in other words, the increasing power of the central government at the expense of the previously independent regional and local ruling class — was irrevocable. Honoré d'Urfé had sided in the civil wars with the Catholic Ligue against the Protestant armies led by Henry of Navarre, later to become Henry IV. He was taken prisoner, released and recaptured, and finally spent some time in exile. He belonged to a family of the prosperous and locally prominent provincial nobility who had close links with Italy, with the court of Savoy and with high ecclesiastics. He was cultivated in the manner of the Italian and French Renaissance. He was not a courtier, but educated in court ways. He was of the camp of the vanquished, and he now made his peace with the king who finally brought peace to a people exhausted by the civil wars.

To him he dedicated *L'Astrée*: 'Receive her therefore, your Majesty,' he wrote, 'not as a simple shepherdess but as a work of your own hand. One can say truthfully that your Majesty is the originator, for to you the whole of Europe owes its peace and repose.'

We can see what is meant by saying that a door has been locked. The long process by which a landed warrior nobility founded on a barter economy is supplanted by a court aristocracy founded on a money economy has entered the phase where a new plateau or level has been attained. Perhaps such a breakthrough to a new figuration of people, given the language currently available, must be expressed partly with the aid of comparatives. But it must also be analysed as a figurational change that cannot be reduced to quantities, central to which is a clearly definable change in the distribution of power between people and within people themselves. Conceptual distinctions, like that established earlier between warrior 'nobility' and 'aristocracy', point to such a structural change in groups and persons. But concepts like 'feudal nobility' and 'aristocracy' are usually used without the backing of a sociological theory that makes it possible to place the different types of noble formation that can be observed in clear relation to each other and to the structural changes of society as a whole.

The *Astrée* gives access to an understanding of the situation — and to the experience of this situation — of members of the nobility who, while themselves embodying the transition from the older to the newer noble type, still identify in many respects with the older type, as they see it, in their values and ideals. These nobles oppose the increasing centralization of power in the hands of the king, and the accompanying binding of the nobility to the court, if not in their deeds — they are defeated and war-weary — then in their daydreams. Art serves not infrequently as a social enclave to which the politically defeated or disempowered can retreat. Here, in daydreams that have been given shape, ideals can be pursued even when harsh reality has denied them victory.

D'Urfé himself embodies to a high degree the civilized refinement corresponding, on the plane of individuals, to an increased capacity for self-control, and on that of figurations to the increasing centralization of state controls based on money income. An aspect of the fundamental personal conflict permeating his thought and feeling and finding expression in the court-romantic features of his novel, those that have earned it the designation of a *roman sentimental*, is the conflict between the affirmation of civilized refinement and self-discipline and the negation of structural social changes, particularly the growing centralization of control that, on a long-term view, is one of the conditions of the development and maintenance of this refinement and self-discipline.

The dedication of the novel to Henry IV is a chivalrous gesture of recognition by a defeated man of the royal victor as his lord and master. It is at the same time a gesture of resignation. Even the leading groups of the rural provincial nobility must now come to terms with the fact that the centre of power has shifted to the high lords and ladies of the court. *L'Astrée* shows one of the possible reactions of this half-courtly, unwillingly half-pacified nobility in the transitional period when the doors of the court cage were closing, when the people they closed on could perhaps hardly escape the feeling that they were closing for ever, and when a French noble really had only the choice between sharing in the glory within the golden cage or living ingloriously outside.

In this situation many nobles look back longingly on the vanishing world in which they possessed the freedom that is now lost. D'Urfé's *L'Astrée* expresses this longing in his own way. The novel is an Utopia of the increasingly aristocratized court nobility. The sword is put aside and the world of play created, a mimetic world in which people disguised as shepherds and shepherdesses can live out the unpolitical adventures of their hearts, above all the sorrows and joys of love, without coming into conflict with the constraints, the commands and prohibitions of harsher, non-mimetic reality.

The difficulty is, as we have said, that in men like d'Urfé certain values, certain commands and prohibitions of the non-mimetic world have become second nature. They too reappear in the mimetic world of their creation. Even in the mirror of the pastoral romance, society retains the structural peculiarities that the people of the nobility take for granted as a part of their world and of any desirable world. Differences of rank between people, the existence of the nobles as members of an upper class, however romantically transformed in the light of romance, are preserved. In the literary productions of the later, bourgeois romanticism, in keeping with the specifically bourgeois individualization and idealization of the isolated person, the social peculiarities of the individual and differences of rank between different social groups often appear in a half-ashamed way, suggesting that the authors are not conscious of them as indicators of social conditions. In many cases they find their way into the mimetic world only by the back door. For especially in German romantic literature the authors are concerned above all with the spiritual fates of individuals that are worked out in a non-social sphere free of ties to the complex chains of interdependence, the compulsions emanating from differences of power and rank and political conditions.

D'Urfé transplants differences of rank and the hierarchical order of the non-mimetic world almost unchanged to that of his creation. He takes them over as far as they are of interest to himself and his public. His world is made up of nobles. Apart from beings who serve, figures likewise taken for granted in good society, non-nobles play no part in his world. But differences of rank between nobles themselves taken over into the illusory world of the romance, do not serve merely as background. In the world of play they have exactly the same role and the same form as in the non-mimetic social world reflected in it. In French noble society, and especially in the rising upper society of the royal court, noble groups of differing ranks and individuals of differing rank are in close contact, without the differences in rank being effaced in the slightest. Everyone knows exactly who belongs to a higher or lower group than himself. Membership of a group of a particular rank, and in d'Urfé's time this usually means rank inherited by descent or presented as such, is an integral component of each person. In the definitive version of *L'Astrée*, though apparently not in all the preliminary drafts that have been preserved, the two decisive noble classes whose relationship clearly exercises d'Urfé after Henry IV's victory, often appear in very transparent disguises. There are knights, princes and kings. There are druids and magicians, doubtless representing members of the ecclesiastical nobility. Above all, there are nymphs who are drawn quite unmistakably as great ladies of the court. One of the nymphs, Galathée, is possibly modelled on Henry IV's first wife. The shepherds and shepherdesses represent a lower-ranking stratum of the nobility. They correspond to the stratum to which d'Urfé himself belonged, the half-rural, half-courtly upper section of the country and provincial nobility. But in their playful disguise as shepherds and shepherdesses they appear in the novel in a romantically idealized form. Nothing is more characteristic than this disguise. Even sections of the middle and lower nobility are already civilized, made courtly, aristocratized and urbanized, they are already so enmeshed in the growing network of interdependence and money chains, and their social and psychological detachment from country life is so far advanced, that they can give expression to their longing for a simpler, freer life by disguising themselves as shepherds and shepherdesses living in primitive huts with their flocks.

It is to this unmistakably lower section of the nobility that the chief role in d'Urfé's mimetic world falls. To it belongs the chief hero, the shepherd Celadon whose love for the beautiful shepherdess Astrée is one of the main themes of the book.

From the position of this lower stratum of shepherds and shepherdesses d'Urfé conducts a sometimes hidden and sometimes quite open polemic against the higher stratum, the nymphs and other figures representing the high court nobility, and above all against its mode of life and values. To them he opposes the ideals of a simple country life full of uprightness and innocence, as led by the shepherds and shepherdesses. The theme is not new. As early as the beginning of the sixteenth century Sannazar in his *Arcadia* — partly, no doubt, under the influence of models from antiquity. — had used the figures of shepherds and shepherdesses as a kind of counterpart and reflection of the court at Naples. A large number of other pastoral romances and plays continue this tradition in the sixteenth century. It would be a rewarding task to trace with their help the development of the 'alienation' of the court aristocracy from the country.

10. *Astrée* reveals certain aspects of the connection between this alienation and the increase in consciousness, the ascent to a new level on the spiral staircase of consciousness. It touches again and again on one of the central problems characteristic up to our own day of the level of consciousness first reached in the Renaissance. This is the question of the relationship of reality and illusion. It is one of the great paradoxes of this whole epoch that in its course the society of men has extended further than ever before the realm of their control over their world, particularly over what they call Nature, but also over the world of men and over themselves, while simultaneously, over and over again in the most diverse forms, as a standing *leitmotiv* of this whole period, the question has been raised as to what actually

is real, object-oriented or whatever else it may be called, and what merely a human idea, an artificial product, illusion, merely 'subject-oriented' and in this sense unreal. This whole problem is connected with a specific development of the self-control deeply inbuilt in human beings, the armour that makes them feel that their existence is separated from the rest of the world, so that they are not able to convince themselves that what penetrates to them through their armour is not a chimera, something invented or superadded by themselves, and so unreal. Only the ascent to the next level of consciousness — on which, as has been adumbrated here, one comes to understand oneself in one's armour and the nature of this armour as it has come to being on the preceding level — makes it possible to show the limited perspective that gave rise to the problem and convincingly to solve the problem itself.

It is enough here to show how this ascent to the plateau of the 'Renaissance' is represented in d'Urfé's novel. This is an example of the specific way in which noble people experienced life and themselves in this phase of the transition to a state in which the high French nobility were finally subjugated by the court. Their type of experience cannot be fully understood unless one is aware that what people experience as reality changes in the course of social development in a way that is open to very precise definition, and that in the transition from the period we call the 'Middle Ages' to what we call the 'Modern Age', a noticeable shift to a new conception of what is 'real' and what is not can be observed. At the preceding level of consciousness the social and personal basis of what was regarded as reality was still — as in all earlier phases of human development — a relatively spontaneous, affective basis. Ideas corresponding to the emotional needs of people, appealing powerfully to the affects, were evaluated as representing something that really existed in proportion to the strength of the feelings that they aroused. A simple example is the attitude of primitive peoples to their masks. In the right social situation, for example, a feast, a mask can be experienced as a powerful spirit that one fears or perhaps seeks to propitiate by certain rituals. It is quite possible that at the end of the feast the same mask is thrown unceremoniously into a lumber room or on to the rubbish heap. This is sometimes interpreted as expressing the fact that the powerful spirit has left the mask. But on closer consideration we become aware that it is the feeling of the people involved that has left them with the changing situation. At this stage, the identity of the object is not located primarily in its character as an object, but in the affective ideals associated with it. If the feelings are strong, the object is experienced as powerful, and this element of power is and remains a decisive factor in that which people consider 'real'. Objects from which the group concerned expects no effect in relation to themselves are, at this stage of development, meaningless to them and so not actually real.

From the end of the Middle Ages on we can observe a strong shift towards the idea that objects can possess an identity, an effective reality, independently of the affect-charged ideas associated with them here and now by the groups concerned through their traditions and situation. This shift towards an increased consciousness of the autonomy of what is experienced in relation to the person who experiences, towards a greater autonomy of 'objects' in the experience of 'subjects', is closely related to the thickening armour that is being interposed between affective impulses and the objects at which they are directed, in the form of ingrained self-control.

This shift makes it possible for people, in their search for wider knowledge of their world, to attain greater certainty of knowledge, a better approximation of concepts to their objects and so a greater degree of control over these objects, in certain areas of their lives. The transition from a theological to a scientific mode of acquiring knowledge is a move in this direction. From a level on which the emotional content of traditional social ideas is regarded as guaranteeing the reality of these conceptions, a plateau is reached on which people consider it worthwhile to explore the laws inherent in natural phenomena regardless of their direct affects in relation to these phenomena. The fund of relatively certain knowledge is thereby increased considerably.

But on this new level of ability to attain greater certainty about events, quite specific new sources of uncertainty are opened at the same time. And as long as the development of human consciousness has not surpassed this stage, the steady increase in certain knowledge is accompanied in countless variations by manifestations of this specific uncertainty. While in some areas, particularly that of 'Nature', the concepts and modes of thought used by people match the observable facts better than ever before, while in this sense the image that people form of natural phenomena becomes more adequate and reliable, at the same time people cannot convince themselves that everything they think about this 'reality' is not mere ideas, products of the human mind, in short illusions.

This uncertainty, the doubt concerning the relation of reality and illusion, pervades the whole period. The transition to a more realistic presentation of perceptions in painting is, to an extent, symptomatic of the peculiar oscillations and amalgamations of reality and illusion. Through the attempt to represent three-dimensional spatial phenomena on two-dimensional canvas, on one hand a more realistic artistic form is attained, and in this phase that is indeed the goal that is pursued. But what is projected on to the canvas is at the same time an illusion of three-dimensional space. It is a phantom. This possibility, this desire to give illusion the form of reality is the counterpart to the philosophical uncertainty over whether what appears as reality is illusion. The question: 'What is real, what is illusory?' preoccupies people over and over again at this stage of consciousness.

The reason why such questions are insoluble is fairly easy to perceive if we are in a position to ascend to the next level of consciousness and to consider the heights gradually attained from the end of the Middle Ages on from a greater distance. If we are able to do this, we see that the uncertainty over the meaning of 'reality', and the recurrent doubt as to whether all judgements relating to what are called 'facts' are not artificial products of the human understanding, arise from the fact that, from the Renaissance on, people reify the constraint on the affects, the detachment of emotions from the objects of thought. The act that has here been referred to as an act of distancing appears to them as a distance actually existing between themselves and the object of their thought. The armour of their ingrained self-control appears to them as an actually existing wall between themselves and the object of their thought. The uncertainty over the nature of 'reality', which led Descartes to the conclusion that the only certainty was thought itself, is a good example of the reification of an emotive idea corresponding to a structural peculiarity of people at a certain stage of social development, and therefore of human self-consciousness. The feeling that, even in scientific reflection and observation, one is separated by a void from that on which one is reflecting or is observing, may be entirely genuine. But the abyss itself no more exists — has no more reality outside this feeling — than the spirit-power that a group of primitive people attribute to a mask when they feel spontaneously that it possesses such power. The difference is merely that in the later case the civilized armour on feeling is far stronger and more all-embracing than in the earlier one.

So it happens that people in European societies, when they reach the new level of self-consciousness from, very roughly, the fifteenth century on — a self-consciousness whose symptoms include the scientific acquisition of knowledge as well as the Cartesian and then the recurrent nominalist philosophical standpoint — when they become conscious of their own consciousness and strive to understand their own efforts at understanding, fall perpetually into the same predicament. While the scientific use of their capacity for thought brings to light an ever-increasing store of knowledge that claims to be knowledge of something really existing, people are unable to convince themselves, on thinking about their own scientific work, that anything really existent, anything 'real', corresponds to this knowledge attained through a combination of systematic thought and systematic observation. In keeping with their feeling of an abyss between the 'subject' that knows and the 'objects' that are known, the idea of reality itself appears suspect and naïve. Is not perhaps all knowledge finally only an invention of human thinking or a picture influenced by the human senses? Are not the events that take place 'outside' the observer so changed by the mind or senses that the self apparently existing 'inside' the armour cannot perceive them as they really are, but only in a metamorphosis and disguise produced by thought and the senses? On this level of self-consciousness where people, when thinking about their thought processes, can already detach themselves enough from these processes to perceive objects as something independent of themselves, and especially from their affects, and in this sense as autonomous, but where they cannot yet distance themselves sufficiently from themselves and their own thought processes to include the structure of this distancing as itself a basic element in their conception of the subject–object relationship, such questions are ultimately insoluble.

As a result, this stage of consciousness is characterized by the constant recurrence of the problem of the relationship of 'subject-orientation and object-orientation', of 'consciousness and being', of 'illusion and reality', of what is revealingly designated by a spatial category as the 'inner world', the 'actual self' in its civilized casing, on one hand and the 'external world' existing outside this casing on the other. Descartes' doubt concerning the 'reality' of everything that takes place outside thought, the transition to illusionistic types of painting, the stress on the outward-looking facade in church and domestic architecture, these and many related innovations are manifestations of the same change in the structure of society and of the people forming it. They are symptoms of the fact that people, through the greater emotional restraint imposed on them, no longer experience themselves in the world simply as creatures among others, but more and more as isolated individuals each of whom is opposed, within his shell, to all other beings and things, including all other people, as something existing outside his shell and separated by it from his 'inner' self.

The symptoms of this once new but now long-familiar structure of self-consciousness include not only the specific uncertainty about the nature of 'reality' already mentioned, but also the conscious play with reality and illusion, the rapid transition from one to the other or the mingling of both, that from now on is found, in ever-changing variations, in art and literature. *Astrée* is one example. The exemplary figures in the novel not only curb their feelings and passions with the high degree of conscious reflection appropriate to the personal role the author gives them, they often disguise themselves quite deliberately. It then seems that they live for a time entirely in their other role; they appear as something other than what they 'really' are.

If we ask what is regarded as incontestably real in the society of *Astrée* and therefore in the society for which it was written, we are confronted, as in many other cases, with a peculiar mixture of what is and what ought to be, of fact and social norm. The undoubted foundation of what a person 'really' is appears in this novel as his line of descent, and the social rank determined by it. This exactly matches what appears in the society for which *Astrée* was primarily written as an unalterable and unquestioned component of human reality. Only if one knows the social origin and thus the social rank of a person, does one know who and what this person really is. At this point doubt and reflection stop short; one does not think further. One cannot and need not think further. For descent and social rank are keystones of the social existence of the nobility. *Astrée* is an aristocratic novel that puts variously disguised aristocrats on the stage for an aristocratic audience. That was — and is — the first question that interests nobles when they meet another noble: 'From what house, from what family does he or she come?' Then he can be classified. The novel indicates that we are already concerned here with a relatively extensive and immobile noble society. We are on the way to an aristocracy of the great courts, within which people come into contact who do not know each other and their families from childhood, as is the case in narrower noble circles. *Astrée* reflects a society whose members often do not know who the other person whom they meet 'really' is. Thus disguises and deceptions — even concerning rank — are possible.

It sheds much light on the stage of consciousness represented by *Astrée* that not only do people here disguise themselves or pretend to be, do or feel something that does not correspond to 'reality' — this happens often enough in literary products of the preceding period — but that disguise and deception by people become an object of reflection. The relation between 'reality' and 'mask' becomes a problem that is often debated explicitly and at length. The possibilities of masks are tried out quite deliberately. The questions that arise from the fact that people can mask themselves, their thoughts and feelings, are explored. In short *Astrée* is an example and a symptom of the ascent to a social situation and, as one of its dimensions, to a level of consciousness with specific new structural features.

These features include the level of reflection about people that is attained here or, in other words, the level of self-detachment. Compared to the figures in earlier romances of a similar *genre*, *Astrée* — and certainly not only *Astrée* — represents a stage at which people are already capable of self-detachment and self-confrontation. They have climbed to a higher floor on the spiral staircase of consciousness. From it they can see themselves standing and acting on the floor below, can contemplate and observe themselves interacting there with other people.

The type of love relationship that we encounter here is itself a manifestation of this heightened capacity for affect control, for detachment by people in their relations to each other, and for self-detachment, that corresponds to the transformation described earlier in the figuration of people, and particularly the change of interdependence in the course of increasing centralization and state power and the growing formation of aristocratic elites. Here it is not without significance that the ideal love relationship which is central to *Astrée* is not that of the highest and most powerful court aristocracy, but rather that of an aristocratic middle stratum. D'Urfé consciously opposes this ideal, as the nobler, purer, more civilized love ethos of the shepherds and shepherdesses, i.e. the representatives of a lower-ranking stratum of the nobility, to the looser and more sensual *mores* of the dominant court aristocracy. One can easily have the impression that *Astrée* is an entirely apolitical, 'purely literary' product. Problems of love are central to the novel. But even though d'Urfé, like many other people after the civil wars, having fought vainly against the man who is now crowned and at the centre of the court and probably against the growing power of the monarchy as well, lays down his sword and creates a dream image of peaceful and simple pastoral existence for war-weary people, nevertheless, on the ideological level he continues the struggle in his novel. The simple, good, free life of the lower-ranking shepherds and shepherdesses is contrasted again and again to the customs and morals of the higher-ranking lords and ladies of the court, the actual wielders of power in this world. And the repeated stress on the difference in the amorous behaviour of the two groups shows particularly clearly the continuation of the struggle on a different level, as a conflict between two different sets of values, a protest against the encroachment of the court that is becoming increasingly inescapable, a half-concealed polemic against the ruling court aristocracy. *Astrée* shows in an early but highly paradigmatic form the connection between two aspects of the powerful shift of civilization that, from about the fifteenth century on — earlier here, later there — can be observed in European societies: the connection between the more comprehensive transformation of external into internal constraints, the intensified formation of conscience, the so-called 'internalization' of social constraints in the form of an 'ethos' or a 'morality' on one hand, and movements aiming to escape civilizing constraint by withdrawal from civilized society into enclaves of simpler, usually rural life, half playfully and half in earnest — by retreating into a dream world on the other. We can see here why this civilizing dialectic of advances in the formation of conscience and morality, in the 'internalization' of civilized compulsions, and of attempted or imagined flight from the constraints of civilization, is to be observed most frequently in middle strata, in strata with two fronts, and scarcely at all in the highest and most powerful ruling strata. It is not only in the development of bourgeois middle classes, but already in the love ethos of the noble middle strata depicted in *Astrée*, that something of this dichotomy is seen.

11. The word 'love', as it is used today, often makes us forget that the love ideal that has been regarded over and again in the European tradition as a model of real love relationships is a form of affective bond between man and woman that is to a high degree determined by social and personal norms. In *Astrée* this affect-model is encountered as the ideal of an aristocratic middle stratum that is already half-assimilated to the court. The love of the hero Celadon for the heroine *Astrée* is not simply the passionate longing of a man to possess a particular woman. In an aristocratic articulation we find here a form of love relationship that is very closely related to the romantic love ideal of later bourgeois literature. It is a passionate reciprocal emotional bond between an unmarried young man and an unmarried young woman that can find fulfilment only in marriage and is to the highest degree exclusive. It is the desire of this man for this woman and no

other and, conversely, of this woman for this man. This ideal bond of love thus presupposes a high degree of individualization. It excludes any love relationship of one of the partners to a third person, however fleeting. But as it involves two people with strongly individualized self-control, with highly differentiated armour, the strategy of courtship is more arduous and protracted than previously. Here the young people are socially already so self-reliant that father and mother, even if they oppose the choice, can do little against the strength of the love bond. For this reason courtship is very difficult and full of peril. The two people must put each other to the test. Their amorous play is influenced not only by their half-involuntary, half-voluntary affect-masking itself, but also by awareness of the masks, by reflection on them. What is really happening behind the mask of their partner? How genuine, how reliable are the other's feelings? In less individualized, more confined groups there are usually traditional family controls and rituals, there is a kind of family opinion on young people who want or are expected to marry. Here the young woman and the young man must rely entirely on their own judgement and feeling. For this reason alone this kind of love bond can find fulfilment only after long personal trying out, after overcoming many misunderstandings and trials created partly by themselves and partly by others. And the difficult, often fantastic and always retarding strategy of courtship that fills a good part of the novel is itself, therefore, a manifestation of the growing distance between human beings.

As it is presented in *Astrée*, this bond of love between the principal characters is an ideal. It is a complex amalgam of desire and conscience. It is characteristic of this love complex that the heavier armour of civilization not only holds the more spontaneous animal manifestations of human passion in check for long periods, but that at this stage of the civilizing process, as a kind of secondary gain, a certain joy in the postponement of pleasure, a melancholy delight in one's own love pain, an enjoyment of the tension of unfilled desire comes into being. It gives this type of love relationship its romantic character. This protraction of love play and the secondary pleasure gain from the tension of unsatisfied desire are very closely related to a particular love ethos, with the strict subjugation of the lovers to social norms dictated to them by their own consciences. The chief of these norms is the lovers' unshakable fidelity to each other and particularly the fidelity of the man to the woman. However great the misunderstandings and temptations may be, absolute constancy of devotion is, in the ideal of love placed before us by d'Urfé in *Astrée*, the duty and honour of the man who loves. It is this love ethic which d'Urfé opposes as that of the shepherds and shepherdesses — that is, a middle stratum of the nobility which, though already in part a court nobility and civilized to a high degree, resists the encroachment of the court and the growing constraints of civilization — to the freer morality of the ruling court aristocracy.

A short scene makes this situation clear:

Galathée, a nymph in the novel, i.e. the masked likeness of a high court lady and probably of Margaret of Valois, reproaches Celadon, a simple shepherd and therefore representative of the lower-ranking nobility, for his ingratitude and coldness towards her. Celadon replies that what she calls ingratitude is simply the expression of his duty.

'By that you only mean,' replies the high lady, 'that your love is attached to someone else, so that your faith places you under an obligation. But,' she continues, 'the law of nature dictates something quite different. It commands that one should take thought for one's own welfare, and what could prosper you more than my friendship? What other person in this region can do as much for you as I? It is a foolish jest, Celadon, to persist in this nonsense of fidelity and constancy. These are words invented by old women or women who are growing ugly, to bind souls to them whom their faces would long have set free. There is a saying that all virtues are in chains. Constancy cannot exist without worldly wisdom. But would it be wise to disregard a certain benefit in order to escape being thought inconstant?'

'Madame,' Celadon replies, 'worldly wisdom will not teach us to seek an advantage by ignoble means. Nature will not command us by its laws to erect a building without having secured the foundations. Is there anything more base than to break one's promise? Is there anything more wanton than a spirit which, drawn like a bee by a new sweetness, flits from flower to flower? Madame, if there is no fidelity, on which foundation can I build your friendship? For if you yourself follow the law of which you have spoken, how long will this fortune smile on me?'

As we can see, the shepherd too is adept, just like the high court lady, in the art of court disputation, which, with the increasing civilization of the nobility at court, has in part replaced the physical conflict of the knights. We also see in this little scene the protest of a nobility being engulfed by the court against the ethos of the great

---

[11] D'Urfé, *L'Astrée*, new edn (Lyon, 1925), vol. 1, pp. 438–39.

court. This representative of a middle stratum of nobility upholds a love ethic that anticipates a widely disseminated ideal of bourgeois middle classes. The high lady represents the worldly wisdom of the great court as d'Urfé sees it. There is strong reason to believe that what she says comes very close to the actual thinking and behaviour in the ruling court upper class. A short narrative written by Margaret of Valois herself shows a very similar relationship between a high lady and a simple knight which, however, in this case has a happy outcome for the lady.[12] It is not without interest to see that the ethos of this court upper class anticipates the interpretation of natural law that is taken over and systematically developed by bourgeois social and economical philosophy, the interpretation of natural law as a norm commanding the individual to act in accordance with his own welfare, his own advantage. Celadon, the shepherd, upholds an ideal opposed to that of the dominant court upper stratum. Like pastoral romanticism it remains alive for a long period as an antithetical ideal of people suffering under the constraints of court rule and civilization.

Much the same applies to the nature ideal of the shepherds erected by d'Urfé. As in the case of the love ideal, we find here too the transfiguration by longing of what is growing distant, in this case the simple country life.

Celadon explains to the nymph Sylvie that no one knows who the shepherd Sylvandre is, that is to say that his family and lineage are not known. He appeared among them years ago, Celadon tells her, and as he knew much about herbs and the animals of our herds, everybody helped him.

> 'Today,' says Celadon, 'he lives very comfortably and can consider himself rich, for, o nymph, we do not need much in order to think ourselves rich. Nature herself is satisfied with little, and we who only strive to live by nature's example, are soon rich and content. . . .'
> 'You,' replies the nymph, 'are happier than we.'[13]

Here again we see the ideological strain in the novel. The artificial life of the court upper class is contrasted to the simple natural life of the shepherds. But the pastoral life is here already the symbol of a longing for a kind of life that is unrealizable. It is the longing of people split 'within': they perhaps remember rural life from their own youth. D'Urfé himself quite consciously situates the main action

---

[12] Marguerite de Valois, *Oeuvres*, ed. M. F. Guessard (Paris, 1842), p. 56.
[13] D'Urfé, *op. cit.*, vol. 1, p. 389.

of the romance in the region of France where he spent his youth. But these people are already so deeply involved in the process of aristocratization and so changed by civilizing court influences that they are too estranged from rural life to be satisfied with a simple existence among the peasants and shepherds. D'Urfé realizes quite clearly that the return to the countryside of his youth, which he now populates with court aristocrats disguised as shepherds, is a dream and a game. Only the yearning for it is genuine. And the ideological struggle against the morality, the artificial manners and the whole mode of life of the court is quite genuine. But the capacity for self-detachment and reflection has already attained a level at which one cannot conceal from oneself that the shepherds and shepherdesses, although symbols of a genuine longing, are only shepherds in fancy dress, symbols of a Utopia and not real shepherds. As has been said, it is a feature of this stage that while one can attain sufficient self-detachment to ask: what is reality, what is illusion? the question cannot be answered correctly. Often enough one merely plays with the possibility that what seems illusion is real and what seems real is illusion.

D'Urfé prefaces his novel with a dedication to the shepherdess Astrée in which he says:

> If you are reproached with not speaking the language of the villages, and if you and your herd are chided for not smelling like sheep and goats, answer, my shepherdess . . . that neither you nor those who follow you are of those needy shepherds who lead their flocks on to the meadows to earn their living, but that you have all chosen this form of life in order to live more gently and without constraint. Answer them that it would amuse them little to listen to you, if your ideas and words were really those of common shepherds, and that you would be ashamed to repeat them.[14]

The longing that d'Urfé expresses here, early in the great advance of civilization that began at the end of the Middle Ages, in the words *vivre plus doucement et sans contrainte*, appears as a recurring structural feature of the many romantic countercurrents that are characteristic of this movement of civilization. What has been said here about the early form of pastoral romanticism, embodied in *Astrée* as an example of the possible types of experience of court people, throws some light on the social structure of these romantic currents. Sooner or later a comprehensive theory of civilization will

[14]   *Ibid.*, p. 7.

no doubt achieve a theoretical clarification of the many romantic movements that are a constant feature of the civilizing process. Here we can see some pointers towards it. The period of *Astrée* is a time when civilizing compulsions in the form of voluntary or involuntary affect-controls exerted by people on themselves are noticeably intensified in the form of manners, conscience and many other phenomena. The processes of socialization, the transformation of young people in keeping with the rising standard of affect-control prevalent in society, become more difficult. The habitual ability to detach oneself on all sides, from 'objects', from 'nature', from other people and from oneself, is heightened. But while the capacity for reflection is thereby increased as well, at this stage of the civilizing process the nature of this change to which people are subjected remains largely concealed to the people concerned. They feel the pressure of the compulsions, particularly on the affects, to which they are exposed, but they do not understand them.

The coming and going of romantic movements which in one form or another express the longing for liberation from these compulsions in a Utopian, that is, unrealizable form, often partly with the consciousness that it is unrealizable — makes it probable that certain social structures, particular situations of human groups, favour the emergence of movements and ideals that promise people liberation from their constraints — sometimes from cultural and political constraints simultaneously — by retreat into enclaves of a simpler social life or by the restoration of the life of the past as a simpler, purer and better life. The conditions under which D'Urfé's *Astrée* was written enable us to perceive some of the connections between certain social structures and the specific conflict mentioned earlier that is characteristic of romantic products and movements. It can only be established by further research how far this connection between the romantic structure of ideas and ideals with specific social structures is repeated in other cases. What we see in the case of *Astrée*, the yearning for a simple life, is the yearning of an upper class that recognizes itself to be of second rank, dominated by a higher class, while at the same time stressing its own elevated and privileged position in relation to lower classes. In the case of bourgeois strata in this situation we usually speak of 'middle classes'. When speaking of nobles we can use this term only hesitantly. What such strata have in common can be best expressed by calling them dual-front classes. They are exposed to social pressure from above by groups possessing greater power, authority and prestige than themselves, and to pressure from below by groups inferior to them in rank, authority and prestige, but nevertheless playing a considerable role as a power factor in the overall interdependence of society. They themselves may well experience the compulsions to which they are subjected primarily as emanating from the greater power of the social class above them. This, as we saw, is the tenor of the ideological struggle d'Urfé wages in *Astrée* against the ruling stratum at court, the court-aristocratic upper class. The mode of life and the models of behaviour prevalent at court are the target implied by the presentation of simple pastoral life. When d'Urfé speaks of his shepherds seeking a gentler life without constraint, the constraint he means is that emanating from the victorious king and his court. He is not aware that the constraints weighing on himself and other members of his stratum are also constraints exerted by themselves in order to cultivate in themselves all the distinguishing marks that they value not only for their own sake but as symbols of their high social position, as instruments of their social superiority and authority over lower classes. Even by the refined play of love, the exalted love ethic, they distinguish themselves from the 'coarser' sexual relations of non-aristocratic classes. They are hardly aware of the paradox inherent in this combination of the desire for freedom and its symbol, the ostensibly free pastoral life, with the self-constraints of a refined love ethic.

In societies of the modern period, dual-front classes, whether noble or bourgeois, often find themselves exposed for long periods to particularly oppressive constraints, including cultural ones,[15] precisely because they live under the pressure of constant tensions and frequent conflicts on two fronts. The compensating social bonus of first-rank classes that feel no one above them and must only repulse the pressure from below is denied to them. They wish to discard the negatively experienced aspects of political and cultural constraints while preserving unimpaired the positive aspects of their own civilized culture, which are for them indispensable marks of their distinction, their raised social position, and are usually central to their social and personal identities. In d'Urfé's argumentation this conflict shows itself very clearly. His shepherds wish to escape the pressure of the court aristocracy without forfeiting the privileges and superiority which, precisely in conjunction with the civilized aristocratic culture, distinguish them from the uncultivated people, the real peasants smelling of sheep and goats.

---

[15] An interesting and far more extensive study of this problem from particular aspects (flight from the world, melancholy, *ennui*, escape to Nature, etc.) can be found in W. Lepenies, *Melancholie und Gesellschaft* (Frankfurt/Main, 1969).

We see here more clearly than before the character of the conflict which is responsible for the specifically romantic twilight quality of such creations, for the crystallization of genuine longing and real distress in unreal phantoms, in Utopian illusions which are often partly recognized as such and perhaps clung to the more stubbornly for fear of becoming fully conscious of their illusoriness. The more obvious conflict of high-ranking dual-front classes consists in the fact that they run the risk of undermining the ramparts protecting them from the pressure from below if they undermine those securing the privileged position of higher-ranking classes. They cannot free themselves from the oppressive dominance of others without calling into question their own domination over others. But that is only an aspect of a deeper conflict. The conflict of dual-front classes concerns not only the pressures arising from the hierarchical distribution of power and authority — in d'Urfé's case subjection to the victorious king and the court upper class — but also the cultural constraints on the affects that are self-imposed and form an integral part of the personality. The illusory character of the pastoral Utopia rests finally on the fact that its representatives, while wishing to lead a simple and natural shepherd's existence opposed to life for a court aristocrat, wish at the same time to preserve all the refinements of human intercourse and particularly of love that distinguished them as civilized aristocrats from the rough uncivilized shepherds. It is characteristic not only of this manifestation of romanticism but of many others that within it people seek to escape civilizing pressures and are unable to do so because these pressures are part of themselves. Probably the constraints of civilization, whether in the form of refined manners and the relation of the sexes, or in the form of conscience and morality, are particularly oppressive in dual-front classes because their position in the network of interdependence exposes them constantly to tension and conflicts on two fronts. From whatever side we consider the personal conflict at the roots of romantic tendencies in dual-front classes, seen both from the aspect of political and of cultural constraints it is a conflict that derives its character in large part from the very unequal distribution of power and differing levels of civilization in the society concerned. People wish to retain the advantages, the privileges, the distinguishing value they possess through their superior civilization — however this distinction may be conceived, as education, manners or culture — but wish at the same time to be free of the constraints to which they are subjected not least as a result of the civilized qualities to which they owe their advantages, superiority and distinction.

12. It is interesting to see that the problem and the goal which d'Urfé formulates in his pastoral romance in the words *vivre plus doucement et sans contrainte* has reappeared since his time in successive new movements. Even in the anarchistic and psychedelic tendencies of our day echoes of it can be heard. Their romantic Utopian character stems partly from the fact that people are trying to escape the painful pressures that they exert on each other through their interdependence, and are attempting to withdraw from or break through their constraints without possessing clear knowledge of their structure. The expression *vivre plus doucement* is not readily translated: a more peaceful, friendly, more pleasant and gentler way for people to live together than has existed previously; however it is translated, such a goal is undoubtedly within the realm of possibility. Social co-existence without constraint, however, is impossible and inconceivable. But this in no way means that these constraints must necessarily have the structure they have had in the development of society up to now, the structure that leads over and over again to endeavours which are Utopian and therefore condemned in advance by their own terms to failure. Whether they are constraints which people exert on each other, as political rulers and subjects, or constraints exerted by people on themselves, even at this early stage in the investigation of such constraints we can see that the especial severity of many previous forms of constraint that find expression in the recurrent romantic–Utopian movements and ideals is connected to specific structural features of the networks of interdependence existing up to now that are by no means unalterable. The unequal distribution of social power, and especially the extraordinarily wide discrepancies in the level of civilization, are undoubtedly factors contributing to the severity of compulsions, including the self-constraint of civilization. We generally have very little awareness of the peculiar boomerang effect of the constraints exerted in an interdependence network by more powerful groups on less powerful ones, by more civilized groups on those less civilized. We often close our eyes to the fact that in one form or another the constraints that more powerful groups exert on less powerful ones recoil on the former as constraints of the less powerful on the more powerful and also as compulsions to self-constraint.

Even the use of words such as 'rule' or 'authority' as sociological technical terms can block understanding of the relation of pressure and counter-pressure in human interdependence networks. They usually make visible only the pressures exerted from above to below, but not those from below to above. They tend to make us forget that in any form of 'rule', as the study of the 'rule' of Louis XIV showed, a more or less precarious balance, particularly the balance of power, is involved. As a more comprehensive analytical instrument the term 'constraint' is preferable, if it is used in the sense of a reciprocal but not necessarily equally strong constraint of people on each other, in the sense of a figuration constraint within the framework of an analysis of interdependence, but not in the sense of a constraint by apparently extra-human norms or principles.

It is understandable that up to now research has often concerned itself only with the constraint to which less powerful groups are exposed. But in this way we gain only a one-sided picture. Just because in every society, in every interdependence network, there is a kind of circulation of constraints, exerted by groups on groups, individuals on individuals, the constraints to which lower strata are exposed cannot be understood without also investigating those affecting the upper strata.

The preceding study of court society is a step in this direction. From the point of view of less powerful strata, princes and aristocratic groups are apt to appear as people leading a free and unconstrained life. Here, in the course of a more detailed investigation, it emerged very clearly to what constraints upper classes, and not least their most powerful member, the absolute monarch, are subjected. We saw that they are subjected to them in good part in the form of constant self-discipline, precisely because the preservation of their high position, their distinction, their superiority over others, has become an end in itself dominating their whole existence.

D'Urfé presented a relatively simple, indeed simplified picture of the constraints to which the nobility was subjected in the course of its transformation into a court aristocracy. Attention in his romance is limited almost exclusively to groups of the nobility. Bourgeois groups play hardly any part in this novel. In this ideological simplification there are on one side aristocratic lords and ladies disguised as shepherds and shepherdesses who all have the same rank. On the other, there are figures of higher rank many of whom represent the upper stratum of the court aristocracy. Even in the time of Henry IV the structure of the influential elite strata in France, and therefore the balance of tensions between them, was in reality a good deal more complicated. But the pressure from non-elite strata, from the predominantly peasant lower classes who even in many towns were scarcely able to read or write, together with the guild and official-bourgeois groups above them, the pressure of these groups on the influential elite classes, their social strength, their opportunities of power, as compared to those of the elites concentrated at the centre, were relatively slight, if we disregard the locally concentrated masses of the metropolitan population. The mere physical agglomeration of the latter represented a certain threat to the court elites and so — as a possibility — a factor in their social strength, their power potential, the pressure of which Louis XIV sought to reduce by moving his court to Versailles.

·IX·

On the sociogenesis of the French Revolution

In pre-industrial territorial states the inequality in the distribution of power, as compared to that in the more developed industrial nation states, is very great. Court society is an example of a pre-industrial monopoly elite. The greater inequality in the distribution of power was expressed among other things by the fact that the great majority of the French people were of interest to court aristocrats only in their role as servants. In the course of increasing modernization and commercialization, urbanization and centralization, the centre of gravity in the interdependence between the traditional monopoly elites and the masses of the population slowly shifted in favour of the latter. It is perhaps useful to point out that a shift in this direction can be observed not only in the period of manifest democratization in conjunction with advancing industrialization, but, in rudimentary form as a kind of latent democratization, in societies of the type of the *ancien régime*, above all in conjunction with the commercialization that preceded industrialization.

The attempt is sometimes made to explain explosive shifts in the distribution of power, like the French Revolution, in a short-term way from the events immediately before or within the revolutionary period itself. But often enough such violent outbursts can only be understood by paying attention to the long-term shifts in the centre of gravity of the society concerned, which proceed slowly over long periods in very small steps so that both the people concerned and later generations looking back usually see only isolated symptoms but not the long-term change in the distribution of power as such. The question is why this phase of latent, half-underground and very gradual transformation in the distribution of social power passes at a certain point into a different one in which the shift in power is accelerated and power struggles are intensified, until the monopoly in

268

the use of force held by the previous rulers is contested by physical force by the non-elite strata previously excluded from the state monopolies, is extended through participation of those previously excluded or is entirely abolished. In the last case the central state monopolies of physical force and taxation are not destroyed as such, though their destruction may for a time have been the goal of the combatants. What usually happens is that groups previously excluded from the control of the central state monopolies either gain a share in this control or replace the previous monopoly elites by their own representatives. A central problem that we cannot pass over in concluding a study on the court society of the *ancien régime* is the question: under what conditions does a long-term shift in power within a state lead to the attempt to overthrow the previous controllers of the monopoly of physical violence by physical violence?

The study of the court elites of the *ancien régime* gives some reference points for an answer to this question. It shows us that the idea that the use of physical force by strata previously excluded from the control of the monopoly of force in France is to be explained simply as the struggle of the bourgeoisie against the nobility as the ruling class, is at best a simplification. At the root of this simplification is a confusion of social rank with social power. The nobility, as we saw, was quite clearly the highest-ranking class in the *ancien régime*, but it was by no means as clearly the most powerful class. At the French royal court there was at any given time a fairly firm hierarchic order of rank, in accordance with which the members of the high court aristocracy, above all the members of the royal house, held the highest rank. But social rank and social power no longer coincided. The extraordinary power with which the royal position endowed its occupants and their representatives in the framework of the overall development of French society, made it possible for them, in order to strengthen their position or to satisfy their personal inclination, to reduce the effective power of people of high rank and to increase that of people of lower rank. Saint-Simon once complained that Louis XIV reduced even the peers of France to the level of subjects. He paid too little attention to the difference in rank between people and indulged in a kind of egalitarianism. In reality the king was very concerned to preserve and even to emphasize the differences of rank between different estates. But he was no less concerned to let the highest-ranking people feel that they were his subjects. In this way he cast down or raised up people and played off his bourgeois advisers and assistants against the members of his court nobility. A minister like Colbert, whose bourgeois origins no one, even himself, ever forgot, had at times incomparably greater power at his disposal than most members of the high court aristocracy. The king's mistresses were often far more powerful than higher-ranking court ladies, including the queen. For this reason alone, through the divergence of social rank and social power, the concept of a ruling class is questionable if it is limited, as sometimes happens, to the nobility in the absolutist regime, and if, in view of the legal status of the nobility as an apparently unified privileged estate, one forgets to enquire into the actual distribution of power within the society of the *ancien régime*.

The preceding studies have pointed, among other things, to specific types of concept needed in analysing so complex a structure of tensions. What we see before us is a figuration with a multipolar balance of tensions. It has a main axis about which many other greater or lesser tensions are grouped. The occupants of the highest governmental and administrative offices, who come directly or in-directly from the bourgeoisie, the official nobility, on one hand, and the members of the court aristocracy, mostly belonging to the no-bility of the sword, some of whom occupy high court, military and diplomatic offices on the other, form the two poles of the main axis of tension. All around them fly the sparks from other tensions, which are partly permanent and structural, and partly of a transitory and more personal kind. So there are recurrent tensions between noble groups of higher and lower rank; at Louis XIV's court there are specific tensions between the legitimate princes of the blood and the bastard sons of the king and one of his mistresses. What we see before us in considering the court, is a complex of interdependent elite groups competing with each other and holding each other in check, with the king at their head, and within the structure of which the precarious balance between groups of officials of bourgeois origin and groups from the nobility of the sword has a central pos-ition. This central balance of tensions in the court elites of Louis XV is the continuation of a balance of tensions within the camp of the elevated non-court strata. The court nobility of the sword forms the hierarchical tip of the pyramid of the nobility, the lower ranks of which are to be found for example in the officer corps of the army and the fleet, or in the country nobility scattered throughout the whole dominion. The incumbents of the highest governmental and administrative offices at court have contacts with the numerous owners of high and lower judicial and administrative offices in the country, from the old families of the nobility of officials down to the families owning lower offices and the representatives of the guilds. This bourgeois pyramid of the owners of hereditary civil offices, whose tip is formed in the eighteenth century by the *noblesse de robe*, also forms an opposed pole to the noble pyramid in society at large. In broader society as in the court elite society there are many other polarities of tensions grouped around this main axis. The clergy, the tax farmers and many other special cadres play a part. What was said earlier may be enough here to show why it is misleading, in trying to understand the structural development of the *ancien régime*, to consider the simple pattern of the hierarchy of the estates as identical with the power structure. In terms of the order of rank the nobility could perhaps be presented as the ruling class. But if we examine the distribution of power we find that centuries before the Revolution social formations of bourgeois origin and those of noble origin were struggling for supremacy without one being able finally to overthrow the other or gain the upper hand permanently. How closely the rise of the royal position as a power centre in its own right was bound up with the growing opportunities of the kings to play off groups of bourgeois origin against groups noble by birth, to distance themselves increasingly from both groups, to maintain the balance of tensions between them by very careful strategy and so to increase their own power, has been shown and need not be reiterated here.

But it is perhaps worth showing in more detail, by way of summary, what a study of this court figuration can contribute to an understanding of the end of the *ancien régime*, of the adoption of violence by groups previously excluded from control of the monopoly of force and from the power that went with this control. The explosion of violence cannot be properly understood if we consider only the constraints acting on the lower strata that finally revolted; it can be understood only if we also consider the compulsions to which the elites, the upper strata, are subjected, against whom the outbreak of violence is directed. Understanding of these compulsions and so of any revolution is blocked as long as one is uncritically guided, in searching for a structural explanation of the Revolution, by the pronouncements of the revolutionaries. In the eyes of many revolutionaries the aristocracy with the king at their head had indeed primary responsibility for the conditions they combated. From the point of view of the revolting masses the difference and the fluctuating balance of tensions between the kings and their representatives, the nobility of office and the nobility of the sword, were of little significance. Even bourgeois historians have often been misled regarding the autochthonal significance of the rivalry between these monopoly elites by the fact that cross-connections, for example by descendants of the nobility of office rising into the nobility of the sword or by marriages between the two cadres, were entirely possible. But such cross-connections in no way obscured to the members of these monopoly elites the differences in structure, in tradition and interests between them. The *robe*, including its noble leading group, owned the monopoly of the hereditary and largely purchasable civil offices; the nobility of the sword, apart from a kind of monopoly of seigniorial land ownership, held the highest and some of the middle military, diplomatic and court offices. Up to the last decade of the regime their representatives fought stubbornly, despite all attempts at reform, to preserve their monopolies and the privileges connected with them, and to fill the highest government positions, partly against the representatives of the king and partly against each other. The Revolution not only put an end to a certain stratum of the *ancien régime*; it not only destroyed a part of the aristocracy of birth, but annihilated perhaps far more radically and finally the privileged strata of the bourgeoisie and the nobility of office that originally came from the bourgeoisie and which, despite all cross-connections and temporary alliances, remained in the figuration of the *ancien régime* the antagonist of the king and of the various groupings of the nobility of the sword. At the same time as the aristocrats the parliaments disappeared, the bourgeois tax farmers and financiers, the guild offices and other manifestations of the older type of bourgeoisie. Many institutions of the *ancien régime* that now disappeared had been, long before the Revolution, without function for the nation state that was evolving under the cover of the old regime, if not without function for the king and the existing regime. There had not been a lack of proposals for reform. A main reason for the inefficacy of the reforms attempted was that the monopoly elites of the old regime themselves were not unified but internally split, forming a complex of rival leading groups holding each other in check. In the time of Louis XIV this structure of feuding elites with two main cadres of privileged elites of bourgeois and noble origins was still elastic. The king himself, thanks to his distance from all other groups and the skill of his strategy as a ruler, was able to keep the structure in motion and, within certain limits, to remedy abuses. If we compare this figuration at Louis XIV's time with that at Louis XVI's time we find a change that is perhaps best expressed by saying that the basic features of the structure were still the same but that it had become frozen in a form that allowed none of the three main power centres, the kings, the parliaments and the nobility of the sword, absolute preponderance. Intrigues, changes of ministers, fluctuations in the balance of power between the main groups and many subsidiary ones, were more frequent than in Louis XIV's time, because the king had less power, was himself drawn further into the struggle of factions and could no longer, like Louis XIV, direct the conflicts and tensions from outside as a kind of umpire. We meet here with a phenomenon that has some significance as a model. It is a figuration of ruling elites who are caught by their opposed tensions as in a trap. Their ideas, their values, their goals are orientated so much towards their opponents that every movement, every step taken by themselves or their opponents is seen in the light of the advantages and disadvantages that it might confer on either party. Even if it often happened, particularly in the various power struggles at the court in the last decades of the monarchy, that representatives of one of these main cadres attempted to limit the privileges and so the power of another, the means of power were really too evenly distributed, and the common interest in maintaining traditional privileges against the growing pressure from unprivileged strata was too great, to allow one side a decisive increase in power over the other. The even distribution of power between monopoly elites, the maintenance of which Louis XIV had consciously striven for as a condition for strengthening his own power position, now regulated itself. All parties kept watch with Argus-eyes to ensure that their own privileges, their own power were not curtailed. And as every reform of the regime threatened the existing privileges and power of one elite in relation to another, no reform was possible. The privileged monopoly elites were frozen in the equilibrium consolidated by Louis XIV.

Here, therefore, we meet on a larger scale the same figuration that was demonstrated on a smaller scale as a peculiarity of the last period of the *ancien régime* in the development of court ceremony. Even the highest personages, even the queen and princesses, are ineluctably bound, as we saw, to the tradition of court ceremonial that by and large was still in the form it had taken on in the reign of Louis XIV. Any change to a single step in this ritual threatens or destroys certain traditional rights of individual families or persons. Just because everyone here is competing intensely for rank, privileges and prestige, everyone vigilantly ensures that his own rank, privileges and prestige are not damaged by others. Since in this final phase none of the participants, not even the king himself, is in a position to distance himself from this structure of tensions and to use his power position to burst the constraints that the interdependent people within the figuration exert on each other, and, if necessary, to reform them at the expense of one or the other, the figuration is petrified. The constraints oppressing the people, leaving aside the wider compulsions imposed upon them by their elevated position and the pressure from lower strata, are constraints that they exert on each other and on themselves. But as no one can regulate or correct them, they take on a ghostly life of their own. People submit to them, even while criticizing them, because they accord with tradition, because this tradition guarantees their own privileged position and reflects the ideals and values with which they have grown up. While Louis XIV to a certain extent shaped and controlled the court tradition, now the tradition controls the people, none of whom is in a position to transform or develop it in keeping with the changes that are slowly taking place in French society.

This applies to the various ranks of the court aristocracy from the royal family downwards. It applies to the two privileged hierarchies of the nobility and the bourgeoisie. Like boxers in a clinch, none of the various privileged groups dares alter its basic position in the slightest because each fears that it might thereby lose advantages and others gain them. But there is no referee here who could intervene to break the clinch and release the parties from their petrifaction.

If in the course of the long-term development of a society the strength of its various strata and groups shifts in such a way that relatively weak groups previously excluded from access to the control of the central state monopolies, above all those of physical force and taxation, gain power in relation to previously privileged classes, there are basically only three possible solutions to the problems arising from such a change in the balance of power. The first is the institutionally regulated admission of representatives of the groups increasing in social power to the positions of power and decision giving control over the power monopolies, as partners of the previous monopoly elite. The second is the attempt to hold the rising groups in their subordinate position by granting concessions, above all economic ones, but not access to the central monopolies. The third arises from the socially conditioned inability of the privileged elites to perceive that the social conditions, and so the power relationships, have changed. In France, as later in Russia and China, the pre-industrial monopoly elites of the old regime took the third path. Concessions, compromises to accommodate the shifts of power that went with incipient industrialization, were inconceivable to them. The gradual transformation of society that gave all public social positions the character of paid professions, defunctionalized their privileged positions as holders of hereditary office and as nobles no less than as kings. To imagine this would have meant imagining the total defunctionalization and devaluation of their present existence. Apart from this their attention was absorbed by their non-violent skirmishes and struggles over the distribution of social opportunities. The stalemate of the competing monopoly elites also prevented them from taking account of developments in society as a whole that were increasing the social strength of hitherto unprivileged strata. In addition, despite their antagonism the privileged participants in such a constellation have a common interest in excluding unprivileged groups from sharing control of the central state monopolies of power. In this situation the probability is high that the groups that are gaining strength, who have previously occupied the position of outsiders, will seek to gain access to the state monopolies that are blocked to them, by the use of physical violence, that is, by revolution. In this case the probability is also especially high that in the course of such struggles the traditional privileges and the now functionless social groups will be destroyed, and that a society with a different type of social stratification, which was already evolving under the cover of the older stratification, will emerge.

This was at any rate, we may say by way of summary, the figuration that led to the violent outbursts of the French Revolution. In the course of the development of French society the latent social power of the different social cadres changed in their relations to each other. The actual distribution of power among them evolved in a way to which the manifest distribution of power anchored in the ossified institutional shell of the old regime no longer corresponded. The leading group, the monopoly elites of the regime, had become imprisoned by the institutions; they held each other fast in the privileged power positions they had once taken up. The rigid clinch of the monopoly elites and their incapacity to look their own defunctionalization in the face which, in conjunction with the inflexible nature of their sources of income, impeded concessions such as the voluntary limitation of their tax privileges — all these together prevented a non-violent transformation of the institutions in keeping with the changed balance of power. As a result the likelihood of violent transformation was very great.

Appendix 1

On the notion that there can be a state without structural conflicts

The promotion of rivalries and tensions, especially between elite groups, as an important instrument of government in non-charismatic, or no longer charismatic, monopoly rule is a very widespread phenomenon. It is to be found not only in absolutist, dynastic states but in a similar fashion in, for example, the dictatorially ruled National Socialist military and industrial state.

Traditional historiography frequently neglects the systematic investigation of power structures. If history is seen essentially as a complex of the clear and conscious plans and intentions of individual people or groups, the rivalries and petty jealousies of elites can easily appear as trivial background phenomena which are insignificant with regard to the course or 'interpretation' of history. Without sociological schooling both the difference between ideology and the actual distribution of power, and the function of ideologies as aspects of the actual distribution of power, do indeed remain unclear and undefinable. This can be observed only too often in historical research up to now.

The same is true of the possibility of gaining socio-historical insights by systematic comparisons between related social structures. The theory of the absolute uniqueness of what historians perceive as history blocks our view here as well. For this reason it is perhaps useful — in passing — to point out that a study of the governmental apparatus of absolute monarchs, and especially of the careful cultivation of the balance of tensions between leading groups in the case of Louis XIV, can also contribute something to an understanding of the strategy of the National Socialist ruler towards his leading groups in the transitional phase from charismatic to routine government (that he undoubtedly sought to prolong by the war). It is not possible here to elaborate the structural differences as well as the structural affinities. It will be enough to point to a publication that

276

deals with the rivalries of the National Socialist leading groups during the consolidation of power and the institutionalization of its distribution, and to the commentary of a young German historian who makes clear the fundamental importance of such studies. The clarification of the facts themselves, the investigation of conflicts and rivalries between the different leading groups in the German National Socialist state, has been much advanced by the work of the editor of the *Spiegel*, Heinz Höhne, which first appeared as a series of articles entitled 'Der Orden unter dem Totenkopf' (*Spiegel* (1966/67). The Heidelberg historian Hans Mommsen has vividly illuminated the problem that such conflicts pose to traditional historiography.[1] It is — *mutatis mutandis* — the same problem that arises if the structure of absolute rule and the function of the specific balance of tensions between leading groups with regard to the maintenance of the very wide scope to exert power enjoyed by an absolute monarch is made the object of study.

Just as the idea of a conflict-free state united under the absolute king turns out on closer examination to be incorrect, the notion of the monolithic National Socialist *Führer*-state proves a fiction. The picture dissolves, as Mommsen puts it, 'into an all but inextricable tangle of rival organizations, feuding cliques, struggles for power and position at all levels of the party and state apparatus'. The ostensible ideological unity also proves a fiction: under 'the empty formula of the "National Socialist *Weltanschauung*" there was a concealed struggle between heterogeneous ideological conceptions that agreed only in what they negated'.[2]

Höhne, in his introductory remarks, sets out the reasons why, in his opinion, traditional historiography is not really adequate to the task of taking account of such aspects of socio-historical reality. In conjunction with what was said earlier on the relation of historiography and sociology, these observations are very illuminating. Mommsen summarizes them briefly as follows:

> Höhne's introductory remark that the topic of the SS has been taboo for the mass of German historians, refers to the fact that such an object poses almost insuperable problems of exposition to an historiography orientated by the classical model. For any attempt to ascribe to the development of the SS a coherent purpose, an historical 'meaning' or at least the quality of a causal process, founders on the many contradictions in the SS machinery. . . . This is really true of

[1] *Der Spiegel*, vol. 21, no. 11 (Hamburg, 6 March 1967), pp. 71–75.
[2] *Ibid.*, p. 71.

the inner structure of the Third Reich in general. Not because questions about it were taboo, but because the model of totalitarian dictatorship made the problems of internal power distribution and the reality of organization appear secondary, research has been directed at other questions, the more so as insufficient sources were at hand.[3]

Properly understood, these words mean that historians have been prevented by the ideological model of totalitarian dictatorship from moving the sociological problems of the actual distribution of power from the background to the foreground of their studies, as Höhne did, and from discovering, like him, the sources that would have made it possible for them to study the actual distribution of power and the changing balance of tensions within the National Socialist state. This can perhaps be seen as confirming that, as was argued at the outset, an historiography orientated towards the classical model denies itself access, by its usually tacit and untested theoretical assumptions, to large areas of socio-historical reality.

Comparative analysis of consolidated monopoly governments in a relatively highly differentiated dominion sharpens our perception of the inescapable way in which unresolved rivalries and jealousies between leading groups make them all equally dependent on the monopoly ruler. Without such comparative analyses it is often difficult to recognize the strategy of the ruler and the pressure on his subjects.

Thus Hitler's toleration of the rivalries appears in Mommsen's account as hesitation, perhaps even indecision. He seems to ask why the dictator did not summarily put an end to them as required by the ideal image of the totalitarian state. But no scholarly books are needed to teach a powerful monopoly ruler that unanimity among his leading groups means a reduction of his power, perhaps even a threat to his personal rule, and that disunity, if it does not go too far, strengthens his power. As the case of Hitler shows, a strategy that carefully preserves rivalries and at the same time — with greater or lesser success — tries to prevent excesses, can be learned fairly quickly from practical experience. It is not even necessary for the ruler to be aware of his strategy as such or to formulate it explicitly in his mind.

But for a scientific exploration of these connections a clear formulation is essential. Without it one is confronted by riddles:

The nimbus and the personal charisma of Hitler [Mommsen writes] that held together at the top all the quarrelling institutions of the state

Ibid., p. 72.

and party sectors, and at the same time drove them into hostile
rivalries, do not offer a sufficient explanation of the fact that even the
leading cliques of the system, who had reason and opportunity to see
through the myth of the Führer's 'genius' and to perceive the
dictator's increasing remoteness from reality, were nevertheless
unable to sever themselves from him.[4]

There is no shortage of penetrating isolated observations pointing
to the structure of the interdependence between the rulers and ruled;
but there is a lack of theoretical schooling that would make it possible to draw these observations together through a clearly defined
model of the structure concerned. Consequently, negative evaluations and censure take the place over and again of a judicious account of the connections. Referring to these rivalries among National
Socialist elites, Mommsen speaks of the 'parasitic decay of a large
modern state'.[5] At the same time he very rightly sees the structure of
constraints whereby 'none of the rival groups was in a position to
form a new authority and so to lay claim with any legitimacy to
political leadership'.[6] It was exactly this possibility that the monopoly ruler by his strategy sought to prevent.

The most serious failing of the historiography based on classical
models manifests itself in the presentation of something which is an
integral part of a consolidating or consolidated dictatorship and a
basic condition of its continued existence in any complex society, as
something more or less accidental, a unique and fortuitous aspect of
this specific dictatorship, that can only be explained by the special
personal worthlessness or decadence of the individuals concerned.
This view follows from the basic theoretical assumptions of such
historiography. How much such assumptions lead to erroneous
judgements is seen particularly clearly in the idea taken up by
Mommsen that the 'groups competing for power and interests', who
are obliged to 'outdo each other in subservience to the dictator', and
therefore in 'political radicalism', that this whole 'escalation of an-
tagonistic, pluralistic wielders of power' on which — as Mommsen
himself says — the stability of the regime was founded, was 'a mere
caricature of totalitarian rule'.[7] Despite a clear awareness of the fact
that these rivalries of the leading groups formed part of the regime's
foundation, this commentator is prevented by his own assumptions
from seeing and stating clearly that these rivalries between leading

[4] *Ibid.*, p. 74.
[5] *Ibid.*
[6] *Ibid.*
[7] *Ibid.*, p. 75.

groups, far from being a caricature, were rather an integral part of totalitarian dictatorship.

We meet here with a further example of the difficulties that confront socio-historical research as long as it lacks scientific sociological schooling and thus has no clear theoretical idea of the relationship between social ideologies and social structures.

The ideology with which the National Socialist movement came to power was determined, as was stated above, by its opposition to the multi-party state of the Weimar Republic. The mass of the German people were strongly influenced in their attitude towards leadership in state affairs by the tradition of German, and especially Prussian, absolutism. There, state affairs were carried on essentially at the princely court. The rivalries, differences of opinion and conflicts of court-absolutist factions were confined to the inner circle. They were often conducted behind closed doors. At any rate, up to 1870 and in some cases up to 1918, the mass of the German people had little opportunity to participate in such arguments with a sense of shared responsibility. The personality structure of many citizens was adjusted to this way of dealing with public affairs. It is not saying too much to state that, in keeping with this socialization over a long period of autocratic rule by princely dynasties, many Germans felt distinctly uncomfortable when, after 1918, the arguments about the management of state affairs that had long been carried on largely behind the scenes at court, even after the establishment of parliaments, now took place far more in public view, and when they themselves were required to take part in these discussions. The public arguments between parliamentary parties demanded a specific kind of controlled aggressiveness, a measured hostility that was able to adapt itself to changing circumstances. It always takes a considerable time for broad sections of a population to become used to this moderate and controlled way of resolving differences. Usually — and undoubtedly in Germany — such populations are accustomed to very simple antitheses. A friend is seen as entirely a friend, and an enemy as entirely an enemy. Simple emotional fronts are desired so that one can give oneself up totally to friendship or enmity. To this basic disposition the parliamentary way of resolving differences, based on negotiation, changing alliances and fronts, moderate friendships, moderate enmities and frequent compromises, can easily become a source of annoyance. A form of rule entailing a measured and regulated settling of differences in public can be extraordinarily irritating to people who are not sure of controlling their own aggression, of resisting their own animosities. On one hand the party conflicts carried out in public negotiation constantly intensify these people's hostile feelings, and on the other the parliamentary system does not allow them to express this hostility by action. It remains on the level of words. The contemptuous reference to parliament by terms such as a 'den of gossip' shows the tendency of these feelings clearly enough. Such terms imply: They are only talking. They are fighting with mere words. But they do nothing. They are not really fighting at all.

Why it was precisely in Germany that this mixture of public verbal conflict without violent action, which is a peculiarity of a parliamentary regime, was felt by many people to be particularly irritating need not be discussed here. At any rate, the National Socialist programme very exactly matched the emotional needs of people who had a long tradition of being 'ruled from above' behind them and who still applied the wishful images of their private lives to the conduct of state affairs. Just as in private life one has, on one hand, friends whom one seeks ideally to regard as absolute friends, and on the other, absolute enemies whom one can simply hate and oppose, the National Socialist programme offered a wishful picture whereby the same emotional make-up could be transferred to the level of the state. Here, too, was to be found, on one side, the people united behind their leader, the ideal image of a community without friction, conflicts and differences, but no longer embracing a few hundred people like the pre-industrial village community that was elevated to an ideal, but many millions. On the other side were the absolute enemies. If it was one of the frustrations of parliamentary government that it required moderation and self-control even towards enemies, the National Socialist programme and the party's political strategy removed this irritating restriction at the outset. In keeping with the elementary polarization of the emotions, it confronted the absolute friends with their absolute enemies. But with enemies who could be freely and unconditionally hated and fought by action, not only with words.

As a wishful image, an ideal, an ideology, therefore, the idea of the total dictatorship, as of the popular community in which there are no opposed interests and no conflicts, is very understandable. But it implies a total misunderstanding of social reality to refer to the National Socialist regime as a caricature of totalitarian dictatorship on the grounds that it was riddled with conflicts and jealousies, particularly between the leading groups. This gives the impression that in a highly complex and stratified industrial state there could really be a dictatorship free of conflicts and opposed interests. It suggests that a consolidated dictatorship is possible in complex industrial societies without the dictator being obliged, like Louis XIV earlier, carefully to maintain the balance between rival elite groups and to prevent them forming alliances against him. It constitutes, as we said earlier, a confusion of propagandistic image with social reality. As far as conflicts and arguments between rival groups and classes are concerned, the difference between a parliamentary multi-party system and a dictatorial single-party system consists primarily in the fact that in the latter the conflicts between factions and interest groups take place in the closer circle of the dictator's leading groups, in his 'court', and so behind the scenes, while in a parliamentary regime they are resolved far more under public supervision and with the limited participation of broad classes in the form of recurring elections. Moreover, the National Socialist regime was only in the process of consolidation; the actual consolidation and routinization of the distribution of power among the leading groups was retarded by the war. These factors undoubtedly contributed to the unregulated and chaotic nature of the rivalries for power and prestige. But all that scarcely justifies the notion that such occurrences represented a decadence of the regime. Within the framework of a dictatorial regime the rivalries between ruling elites can never be regulated to the same extent as within a parliamentary regime. This is indeed the real essence of a parliamentary regime, that within it differences and arguments that are a normal part of any regime in the more developed and complex societies, manifest themselves fairly openly and can be regulated fairly extensively. We do not need here to discuss the question why, in Germany, the emotional habit of being ruled absolutistically or dictatorially from above, with the recurrent demand for a 'strong man', was so deep-rooted. The development of Germany society that led to it was very complicated. But undoubtedly a traumatic dread of the traditional disunity of Germans among themselves heightened the fear of not being able to hold one's hostility towards other Germans in check, a hostility that was constantly exacerbated by the normal party quarrels of parliamentary government in a way irritating to many Germans. The weakness of individual self-control where questions of state and politics were concerned then expressed itself in the demand for control from above by someone else, by representatives of state power to whom people in Germany had become accustomed in the long phase of princely absolutism from the period of the Thirty Years' War on. The social tradition of strong external control in matters of state, control by state and court authorities, left little scope for the development of a social tradition of individual self-control outside the narrow area of personal life. And the traditional weakness of self-control in matters of state and politics found expression, when the princely authorities disappeared, in the constantly renewed desire for external control by a non-princely strong man. He was expected to make the irritating party conflicts that contradicted the wishful image of a unified, brotherly German people disappear. But as differences of opinion and interests, with their attendant tensions and conflicts, are inevitable structural features of complex societies, even an exceptionally strong ruler could do no more than resolve the irritating arguments between Germans within the inner circle where he held his slowly developing court, and so remove them from the view of the majority of the people.

It is therefore an historical interpretation lacking a sociological foundation that presents the National Socialist dictatorship as something abnormal, a deviation from the ideal image of totalitarian dictatorship, on the grounds that it developed forms of satrapy and, as Mommsen puts it, of a 'lobbyism that has been incorporated in the state and is thus fundamentally anarchic'.[8] The competition between factions of the monopoly elites for prestige and economic and other power, the allocation of which is finally in the hands of a monopoly ruler, is a normal phenomenon in any monopoly government that is in the course of consolidation. It is a structural feature of the party elites of dictatorially ruled industrial nation states, as it is of the court-aristocratic elites of absolutistically ruled pre-industrial dynastic states. It is likewise determined by the structure of the regime that in this case *competition* and rivalries are regulated less by legal controls or public norms than by the personal decisions of the single ruler. Therefore, however much they may contradict the ideological facade of monopoly rule, they in no way represent, as supposed by Mommsen, a destruction of the state from within.[9] Such formulations really only mean that the ideological wishful image of the conflict-free united people is accepted as a potentially realizable standard of historical interpretation. As we see in this book, the competition of *elite groups* for *power* without a developed institutional framework and therefore with a strong personal colouring, is a phenomenon always found in monarchic monopoly regimes in pre-industrial dynastic states. The same thing undoubtedly applies, *mutatis mutandis*, to *dictatorial monopoly* rule in industrial *nation states*.

[8] *Ibid.*, p. 74.
[9] *Ibid.*, p. 75.

Appendix 2

On the position of the intendant in the estate management of the court aristocracy, with particular reference to the economic ethos of the court aristocracy

As a result of the historians' manner of selecting materials, the intendant, the man who was entrusted with the overall administration of the wealth of a court aristocrat and the general supervision of all his economic affairs, is seldom mentioned in historical studies. But for a sociological study, for understanding the figurations, the ties, the mode of life, the mentality of court aristocrats, the position of the house intendant is not without significance. Even a short glance at this social position gives us an idea of the subordinate role that the high lords and ladies of this society allocated to the side of their life that would today be called the 'economic aspect'. The whole routine of financial administration, including the overall supervision of estate and household, and a considerable part of the decision-making, were normally in the hands of a specially appointed servant from the lower classes — the intendant. There may have been exceptions. But usually the lords and ladies of the court had little interest in the details of their income and were little versed in the business aspects of their possessions and privileges. They were really only concerned that the income from leases and rents, pensions and other sources was regularly available to be spent in accordance with their requirements. It was the intendant's business to ensure that the money was there. For that he was paid.

The household of a high-ranking court aristocrat was a large organization. That should not be forgotten. But the ethos of status-consumption prevalent in this court society, the ethos that compelled the individual family to make its expenditure dependent not primarily on its income but on its status and rank, only seldom allowed this large organization centred on the consumption of goods to be given, over a period of several generations, what is today called a 'rational' and 'sound' economic basis, by constantly adjusting expenditure to income. The tendency towards an escalation of debts and finally ruin was therefore very great among members of this society. From immemorial times the warrior nobility, the nobility of the sword, had regarded economic calculation as penny-pinching, fitting for shopkeepers but not warriors. (The German language, which in certain areas very copiously perpetuates the values of noble circles, offers a fine selection of terms — e.g. *Krämer, Pfennigfuchserei* — expressing contempt for the bourgeois economic ethos.) Owing to the constant danger of mounting debts, we hear again and again of attempts at reform, and advice on good housekeeping.

There is much documentation on attempted rationalization in aristocratic households that usually remained abortive, largely because the absolutist structure of rule in the form it took on under Louis XIV positively forced court nobles to govern their expenditure primarily by rank if they did not want to forfeit prestige among their peers. Built into the personality by education, this social compulsion expressed itself in a distinctive noble pride in an attitude that did not subordinate expenditure to the constraints of income as in bourgeois economic calculations.

For example, a small treatise published in 1641 with the title 'Oeconomie ou le vray Advis pour se faire bien servir, par le sieur Crespin' (in E. Fournier, *Variétés historiques*, Paris, 1863, vol. 10, p. 1) reports how much the conduct of their lives and households by the high aristocracy had changed in the last twenty years. Crespin, who describes himself as 'maître d'hôtel de la Marquise de Lezaye', speaks of the bad housekeeping of earlier times:

People gave everything and had nothing afterwards. They bought themselves a favourable wind that often vanished in the merest rain shower. . . . If one is not to fall into such a trap, it is necessary to practise good, orderly housekeeping. For this reason . . . great lords and ladies must introduce good rules in their houses. But since not everyone can think or rule as is necessary, and since it does not accord well with their rank to concern themselves with the variety of their daily table, we consider it a priority for them to have a person who is loyal and experienced in housekeeping [bien expérimenté en l'oeconomie]. This person should be absolutely and in every respect the *chef d'hostel* and set over all the other servants. He should have to answer to no one except the lord of the house from whom he receives his authority.

The household, too, like the dynastic state, is seen as a hierarchical, personal unit of rule.

About two generations later, in 1700, Audiger, who for a period occupied a high-serving position in the house of a son of Colbert, published detailed instructions for the running and organization of a large aristocratic household, with the title 'La Maison réglée et l'Art de diriger la Maison' (Amsterdam, 1700). His instructions show something of the stricter housekeeping of the then young nobility of office, corresponding more to the bourgeois economic ethos, that had, we may assume, not yet disappeared from the households of Colbert's offspring despite their relatively quick passage into the nobility of the sword. It is possible that this pamphlet was written especially for families of the nobility of office, which at this time was evolving increasingly consciously into a new aristocratic social formation but aspired to the same rank and prestige as the old nobility of the sword.

In this pamphlet we find fairly detailed information on the range of tasks of the intendant, the 'manager' of a large noble household. It gives a good idea of the scope and, by bourgeois criteria, the importance of the tasks that the court nobility, in accordance with its own criteria, left to a servant. Since the majority of the court nobility, particularly the high court nobility with the king at their head as the prime example, regarded any occupation with bookkeeping as socially beneath them, and saw it as a sign of their privileges and the freedom befitting them to concern themselves only with the distribution of expenditure, these nobles were in fact far more dependent on their servants — were far more the prisoners of their intendants — than they liked to admit. Audiger states the matter quite bluntly:

So it is that Intendants, by their care and capacity, support and put back on their feet houses that are almost ruined, or that others damage by their fault and negligence, causing the total ruin of the most illustrious; we have twenty recent and notable examples of this in the houses of several princes and other great seigneurs well known in society.

A large number of social processes, including the French revolutionary process, only become comprehensible if we realize that the development of the economic ethos of the 'little folk', the bourgeois economic ethos that subordinates expenditure to income and aims where possible to achieve a surplus of income over expenditure to create capital and investment — the development of this ethos to the dominant economic ethic of a whole society, was tied to the rise of the 'little people' of that time to the position of a dominant class. This economic ethos was not, as it sometimes seems today, simply an expression of a 'rationality' innate in or at least acceptable to everyone. The different economic ethos of the court aristocracy — as we also see in the text above — was not an expression of the irrationality of these people, their lack of intelligence or even their social 'immorality'. All such explanations of the characteristic attitudes of a whole group of people, which are founded on the specific social structure of the group, in terms of concepts that make them appear as constituent and perhaps even innate peculiarities of particular individuals, lead us astray. The regularly recurring ruin of families of the nobility of the sword was just as inherent in the society of the *ancien régime* and in the structure of its upper classes, as the bankruptcy of firms is inherent in bourgeois society.

The social position of a domestic intendant as an institutionalized sphere of work is very characteristic of the specific pattern of the division of functions in this society and so, too, of the compulsions of interdependence that liberate men and women of the court aristocracy as far as possible from the economic management of the household. This is Audiger's account of the tasks of the house intendant:

> His duties and function generally concern all the possessions, revenue, and affairs of a great lord, of which he should know, point by point, the condition, the amount and the product, so that he governs expenditure accordingly, and attends to the most pressing debts of which, above all, he must have exact knowledge in order to avoid the embarrassment and chicanery that they can give rise to.
>
> As the majority of the largest estates of the nobility are in the country and because they have farmers or collectors on each of their estates, the intendant should pay attention to them and, on the renewal of leases, choose the best and most solvent; he should take care that during their tenancies they do not dissipate the revenue of the farms, do not damage the land or cut any wood or trees except those carried by their leases. He should also look after the lakes, woods, meadows, small farms, town houses and, especially, the seignorial rights, so that they are not lost or annulled through failure to perceive

them at the right time and place, or to carry out the necessary proceedings.

He should also keep a memorandum of the money he gives to the *Maistre d'Hostel* for the ordinary expenses of the house; see that he is usefully employed and have him report every week so that nothing escapes his knowledge; oblige him to provide every month a regular and general inventory of the expenditure that is made or could be made. He should show this to the *Seigneur* so that he can proportion everything to his revenues and not involve himself in untimely and superfluous expenses beyond his means. He should likewise keep a register of all the money he receives, and of his distribution of it, both to the *Seigneur*, the *Officiers* and other servants of the house, and to the merchants; he should list pension payments, repairs to property and houses both in the town and in the country, obtaining good receipts for both, to give valid justification of his use of money when he is obliged to do so.

It is also his duty to avoid confusion in affairs as far as is possible, and not to involve his master in unnecessary costs and expense; and when some new and difficult piece of business presents itself, before engaging himself in it he should take good counsel, and execute it well.

There follow the sentences quoted earlier on intendants who can restore to prosperity a house that is close to ruin and on those who by their mismanagement can bring about the decline and ruin of a mighty and prosperous house. Then come further details on the tasks and responsibilities of the intendant.

But the passages already quoted are enough to give a clear idea of what we would call, not quite appropriately, the 'economic' aspects of the court nobility's situation. The term is not quite appropriate because its meaning has become excessively fixed by its reference to the distribution of power, and so of functions, prevalent in the industrial societies of the nineteenth and twentieth centuries. This division gives people who act 'economically', i.e. who respect the primacy of income over expenditure, and save for capital investment, great opportunities of success and status. Social opinion, partly represented by economic theories ostensibly based solely on factual analysis, elevates such behaviour to a universal ideal. From the standpoint of such presuppositions, people at other stages of development, like the members of the court aristocracy, who do not behave in accordance with this ideal, or even acknowledge it as an ideal — who, in other words, do not act 'economically' or 'rationally' — such people appear from this standpoint as spendthrifts or fools. But in positing modes of behaviour generally regarded as normal at one's

own stage of social development, as normal behaviour for people at
all times and so, implicitly, as possible behaviour for all social formations at earlier stages of development, one denies oneself the
possibility of explaining and understanding why and how such
behaviour has risen, in the most recent, industrial phase of social
development, to the rank of the predominant, normal, ideal
behaviour of all people, how it has come about at all that
'economics' have become regarded as a separate, specialized area in
the total structure and development of society. For such a conception
certainly did not exist before the second half of the eighteenth century.

Censorious terms for people who habitually behave
'uneconomically' therefore hit the mark when they refer to people in
industrial societies. For within the framework of these societies such
behaviour represents an individual deviation from the social norm.
But they miss the mark when they refer to members of social cadres
which play the leading part at earlier stages of social development,
and particularly to members of earlier monopoly elites. For in those
contexts such behaviour does not represent an individual deviation
from the social norm but, on the contrary, normal
behaviour — behaviour by the individual in accord with the constraints of his socialization, with the institutionalized criteria of
membership of his society, in short, with the prevailing norm. In this
pattern of social constraints, what we call 'economic' constraints
have as yet no special role entailing a division of labour; and they certainly do not have primacy. Within court society, as we have seen,
honour, rank, the maintenance or improvement of the social position
of one's house, as well as physical courage and, often enough,
military success, quite definitely had precedence as determinants of
behaviour over what could be classified as 'economic' determinants
if they could have been isolated at all from the latter in this social
structure. This certainly does not mean that these people attached no
importance to enlarging their possessions and their income. What ran
counter to their status and their feelings was the increase of possessions or income by what we consider today as specific and
specialized economic behaviour. But they had not the slightest
objection to increasing their property by military plunder, presents
from the king, inheritance or marriage, and often enough sought
avidly to do so.

How uncongenial 'economic' behaviour in the present sense of the
word was to them is shown particularly clearly by the passages just
quoted on the sphere of functions of the intendant. As was seen at

the beginning of these quotations, it is the intendant who has to ensure that expenditure does not exceed income by too wide a margin. That there will be a deficit is usually regarded as inevitable and fairly normal, as is the whole deficit economy of the great aristocratic households. The difference between the 'normal' debts of business concerns in the form of credit for purposes of increasing the scope of production or trade, i.e. to assist capital formation, and the 'normal debts' of great court-aristocratic households, i.e. of consumer entities, needs no further explanation. The intendant is here made responsible for seeing to it that the lord of the house is spared any chicanery or unpleasantness from creditors. It is his concern that the state administrators and tenants on one hand and tradesmen on the other do not swindle his master. He must submit regular financial reports and protect his master from any needless expenses that he cannot afford. We can imagine that it was not always easy to restrain the lord and lady of the house from incurring expenses to which they felt obliged by their rank but for which they had not enough money.

That must be enough. It is sometimes useful to immerse oneself in details in order to see the great structural lines of development. We have become accustomed to covering up the problems of the court aristocracy by undiscriminating cliché terms such as 'feudal' or 'traditional'. What has been said here on court-aristocratic housekeeping and, in particular, on the position of the intendant, is merely a complement to the elucidation in the text itself of the special nature of court society as a specific, pre-industrial social formation. But it shows especially clearly that terms like 'traditional society' or 'feudalism' are too undifferentiated to make visible the distinctive peculiarities of this last great pre-industrial elite formation that was more or less entirely dependent on money income. It would be better to apply terms like feudalization, feudalism and feudal nobility to societies with a mainly barter economy type of interdependence, and terms like court society and court aristocracy to societies with a mainly monetary type of interdependence. This would leave sufficient scope for the gradual transition from one to the other.

This aristocrat – intendant sub-figuration was therefore so constituted that the persons in the more powerful position were bound to pursue an expenditure strategy governed by the primacy of rank and status, while persons in the less powerful, subordinate position had to adopt a strategy, as far as their weaker position allowed, where expenditure was governed by the income of the lord and master. This gives us an occasion to reflect on what is actually meant by speaking of behaviour that is well or ill adapted to society, more or less 'realistic'. In this context we can do no more than draw attention to the problems that are brought into view when we are confronted with such figurations and positions from an earlier phase of social development.

One of the terms that is sometimes used in trying to come to grips with these problems is that of 'relativism'. Applied to the situation under consideration, this term means roughly that it is not possible to speak of an absolutely valid 'economic ethos'. Which economic ethos, which type of behaviour is 'correct', the relativist position implies, depends on the differing structures of societies formed by people at different times. In a court aristocracy, one might then say, individual behaviour was 'well adjusted' or 'realistic' if the person in question spent his income primarily in accordance with his rank, his status, his honour and the customs at court. For that was the 'norm' prevalent in his society. In a bourgeois society, on the other hand, individual behaviour is 'well adjusted' or 'realistic' when a person makes his expenses dependent first of all on his income, since in this case the primacy of income over expenditure is one of the prevailing norms of the society concerned.

But this formulation shows that something is not quite right in this theory of sociological relativity. We encounter here a problem that is usually overlooked or at any rate not clearly posed in discussions of 'relativism'. This is the problem of the 'adaptation', the 'appropriateness', the 'realistic character' of social norms themselves. Is it not possible that 'norms' or 'behaviour standards' may be widely accepted in a social formation that were perhaps 'appropriate' and 'realistic' in an earlier phase of development, i.e. adjusted to actual social conditions, but which, although they continue to be maintained in the society concerned and passed on by its members by social education, by 'socialization', from one generation to the next, are conserved by the reciprocal controls and sanctions of the members, while becoming less and less useful or realistic in the course of social development? Is it not possible that these norms themselves may become increasingly inappropriate to actual social structures and in particular to actual power relationships? There is much discussion of the appropriateness of individual behaviour in relation to social norms, but very little of the appropriateness of social norms in relation to the developing structures of a society. Is it not possible that norms and their upholders can themselves become defunctionalized?

The observations on the status-consumption ethos of the court nobility, which has here been illuminated once more with the aid of the position of the leading servant in this cadre, suggest very strongly the possibility of such a defunctionalization of social norms, values, criteria or, more precisely, the possibility of a defunctionalization of the underlying social formation as a whole. For warrior elites in societies with little specialization, little use of money and little trade, modes of behaviour in relation to property or income related to those of the court nobility may be entirely appropriate to the figuration they form with each other and with other groups. Property here depends to a very considerable degree on military prowess and success, and military success, like one's position or rank in the army, can in turn depend to a certain extent on property. The entanglement of the individual in societies that gradually and with frequent fluctuations become commercialized and urbanized leads to a gradual defunctionalization of chivalrous norms, of the military values and attitudes that live on — often in a diluted and disguised form — in the norms, values and attitudes of the nobility of the sword transformed into a court aristocracy. The deficit economy of the warriors was not 'unrealistic' as long as the securing of contractual agreements by legal sanctions was relatively weak and ineffective, so that one could if necessary evade creditors by going on military campaigns or crusades, or perhaps kill them without undue danger, should they press too strongly for payment. But France in the seventeenth and eighteenth centuries was already in this respect a relatively ordered state. Particularly in the eighteenth century it was no longer easy even for high-ranking lords to escape their contractual obligations. Court nobles often complained that the growth of royal power had reduced the nobility to the position of subjects. That their rank was of little help even to high aristocrats when they tried to evade unpleasant or even ruinous contracts, for example debts, is an example of what they felt to be their reduction to the level of subjects, their loss of rank. This can be observed, although the nobility continued to possess specific legal privileges. This is one example of what is meant by saying that a behaviour standard, a social norm that encouraged people to give rank precedence over income as a criterion of consumption, became increasingly inappropriate, in the course of this specific social development, to the actual, changing figurations of people — that it became, in other words, less and less adequate to reality.

As successors to an epistemological tradition orientated primarily towards the cognition of nature, the contributions of sociologists to the theory of knowledge have for some time brought terms such as 'fact' or 'reality' into disrepute. Although it lies outside the scope of this study to examine such questions in detail, it is perhaps useful for an understanding of the matter with which this investigation is concerned to state clearly in conclusion that court society, and all other figurations formed by people, fully deserve to be referred to as 'facts', as 'realities' that exist whether or not anyone takes the trouble to make them the subject of scientific investigation. The distinctive characteristics, the structures of the figurations formed by people in conjunction with specific interdependences, can be explained with a high degree of certainty. It can be shown how and why this specific pattern of interdependence, the figuration of the great royal court and court society, came into being. This is by no means to say that the explanatory models of this development and this figuration given in this book represent the last word that can be said on their scientific diagnosis and explanation. That would wholly contradict the scientific character of this work, which is one step towards the elucidation of this particular piece of social reality. But the modality of these figurations, their existence as figurations actually formed by people that can be gradually revealed as such with growing certainty in the course of scientific research, are not changed in the slightest by the errors and deficiencies of the single step that has been taken here. To correct them is the task of coming generations.

For this very reason it is important to point at least in passing to the complexity of this specific reality formed by people. The behaviour and norms of the court nobility, we said earlier, became increasingly inappropriate to reality in the course of social development. What this means is not difficult to understand if we know the facts to which such statements refer. It is only the interpretation of such facts that still presents considerable difficulty at the present stage in the development of thought.

If we speak of 'social reality', this concept cannot be limited to a single partial figuration that can be examined here and now. The framework of reference for what is diagnosed as social reality is the stream of evolving figurations or, in other words, the total evolutionary process of the figuration formed by all interdependent people, by past and present humanity and that part of humanity that is at present advancing into the future. In relation to this, we can indeed observe that the norms, values and modes of behaviour of groups of people that were, in a certain phase of development, appropriate to the existing structures, at a later stage of development lose their appropriateness, their function in the total context of the interdependence now existing. Such processes of defunctionalization are among the phenomena that are repeatedly to be observed in the evolution of the figuration. They apply not only to the norms, values and modes of behaviour of individual sub-groups at a particular stage of development; they can apply to whole social formations. The court aristocracy as a whole, to mention only this example, suffered, with increasing differentiation, with the tightening and lengthening of chains of interdependence, with increasing commercialization and urbanization, a gradual deprivation of their function. The proof of this is the gradual disappearance of noble and princely positions as such in the societies that have attained a certain degree of differentiation, industrialization and urbanization. If the French Revolution is regarded simply as a struggle of the bourgeoisie against the aristocracy, justice will certainly not be done to the structural change in society that we are concerned with here. A defunctionalization not only of aristocratic norms, but of the court aristocracy as a social formation, already took place within the old regime. But the same applies to the norms and social positions of the pre-industrial bourgeoisie. The bourgeoisie of guildsmen and officials lost its functions in the course of increasing commercialization and industrialization in the eighteenth and early nineteenth centuries. Its norms, too, its values and ethos became increasingly 'unrealistic'. Rigid and unyielding as the values of privileged classes so often are, they contributed not a little to the failure of all efforts at reform by representatives of new and rising bourgeois positions. The loss of meaning and function by what the people of these power elites took to be the highest purpose and value of their lives was already in progress before the Revolution. But powerful elites are often unable to free themselves from the self-constraint of their defunct ideals without external compulsion. The violent elimination of the defunctionalized social positions and their traditional privileges finally came about because the old institutional structure was so ossified that a voluntary adaptation to changing social reality was not possible.

Index

absolute rule 22, 214 – 15, 276 – 7;
    established in France 164 – 5,
    180 – 3; in *ancien régime* 1 – 2, 3,
    61, 70, 127 – 8, 135, 146 – 8, 168;
    and charismatic rule 120 – 2;
    Prussian 146 – 7, 280; totalitarian
    dictatorship 276 – 83
action theory 141 – 3
advancement 123 – 4
alienation 237, 240, 250
animal societies 11 – 12
architecture: and economy 56;
    hôtels 43 – 5, 58 – 9;
    houses 54 – 7, 60; orders of 57;
    ornamentation 56n, 58 – 9, 74;
    palais 54, 59; prestige value 57;
    and social structure 41 – 65, 74;
    see also Versailles
aristocracy *see* nobility
armies: medieval 153 – 4; paid 149,
    154 – 5; Spanish 101 – 2, 164, 176;
    standing 193
art 247 – 8; work of 244; *see also*
    literature; painting
Audiger, 'La Maison réglée. . .'
    286, 287 – 8
Avignon, court at 39

beginnings 232, 236 – 7
behaviour: court 91 – 6, 100 – 1,
    231 – 2, 239 – 41; 'normal' 92,
    288 – 9, 291 – 2, 293 – 4
Bernis, Cardinal, memoirs 106n
Berry, Duchess of, illness 198
Biron, Duc de 183

books 105 – 6, 189 – 90, 245,
    246 – 7; romantic 248 – 9, *see
    also* d'Urfé
bouche (eating and drinking) 46 – 7
bourgeois classes 218, 219, 222 – 3;
    advancement open to 61 – 2,
    64 – 5; dealing with people 110;
    economic ethos 64 – 5, 66 – 8, 70;
    houses 57 – 8; 19th cent. 60n,
    114; and nobility 148, 157,
    167 – 71, 178 – 9, 203 – 7; prestige
    60n; professional 52 – 3,
    114 – 16; and revolution 208,
    294; *see also* professional classes
Brantôme, Pierre 162n, 166
Burckhardt, Jakob 244 – 5
bureaucracy 38

capitalist cities, early 160 – 1
centralization: court 161, 241; of
    state controls 1 – 2, 216, 241 – 2,
    247 – 8
ceremonial 29, 89 – 90, 273 – 4; *see
    also* etiquette
Chamillart, Minister 121n
change: biological and
    social 11 – 14; rate of 14; *see
    also* development; transformation;
    transition periods
charismatic rule 22, 121 – 6
Châtelet, Marquise de 48n
chivalry 148 – 9, 154
chronology 14 – 17
church and clergy 165 – 7, 169, 171
civilization, advance of 256 – 65

classes, social 48, 217 – 18; dual-front
262 – 4; *see also* estates; lower
classes
Classicism 112
Colbert, Jean Baptiste 270, 286
commerce and trade 55, 69 – 70,
72 – 3
competition 22, 88, 93, 100 – 4, 119,
207 – 8
Condé, Prince de 172n, 174 – 6, 201
conflict: of king and nobility
146 – 59, 162 – 74, 179 – 207,
209 – 10; in power structures 146,
167 – 9, 276 – 83; in social development 219 – 25; *see also* tensions,
balance of
conquest and rule 1 – 2, 128 – 9, 130
consciousness 244 – 6, 250 – 7
constraints 239 – 43, 257, 263 – 6,
273 – 4
consumer society 160 – 1
continuity and transformation
232 – 8
controls in society 221
couchée of the king 87, 89 – 90
country houses 43, 45, 194, 197
country life, longing for 215 – 16,
225 – 6, 228 – 30, 237 – 9, 248 – 50,
256 – 7, 260 – 1, 263 – 4
court of *ancien régime*:
accommodation 43 – 7, 49 – 54;
functions 1; income 37;
peripatetic 161 – 2; rule, structure
of 118 – 45; social structure
41 – 65; structure and
significance 35 – 40; 16th
cent. 159 – 61, 162 – 4; 17th
cent. 161 – 2
court society: conflict in 119 – 21;
culture 186 – 7; development of
158; figuration 66 – 77; and
'good society' 78 – 80, 99;
heritage of 113 – 14; individuals
in 17 – 18; multiplicity of 3;
and outsiders 162 – 3, 186 – 7; rise
of 2 – 3; as social form 8 – 9;
social study of 1 – 2;
structure 35 – 40, 118 – 20,
196 – 7; values 75 – 7; *see also*
nobility

Crespin, 'Oeconomie. . .' 285 – 6
Croy, Duc de 53, 66

d'Abigné, Agrippa, *Les aventures du
Baron de Foeneste* 231
d'Argenson, *Loisirs d'un ministre*
175n
dauphin (grandson of Louis XIV)
107 – 8, 109, 120, 202 – 4
dealing with people 107 – 10, 111
democratization 268
dependence *see* interdependence
Descartes, René 253, 254
Desportes 229, 231
despotic rule, and personality 23
development, social: art and 244 – 6;
and biological 11 – 14; conflict
in 219 – 25; continuity
in 232 – 8; criteria of 221 – 2; of
individual
244 – 5; and reality 251 – 2
dictatorial rule 23, 276 – 83; *see also*
absolute rule
display and prestige-consumption
62 – 4, 67 – 8, 72 – 3, 76 – 7,
284 – 92; in houses 56n, 58 – 9;
see also luxury
distance: class 48; of court 162 – 3;
and etiquette 100 – 2, 111,
117 – 18, 153; from nature
242 – 50, 153 – 4, 258;
spatial and social 48 – 53
drama, French classical 112
dress, court 231 – 2
du Bellay, Joachim 228 – 9
du Châtelet, Madame 106n
dual-front classes 262 – 4
duelling 239 – 40
d'Urfé, Honoré, *L'Astrée* 246 – 51
255 – 66
dynastic society 1, 2

economic affairs: of nobility 64 – 5,
66 – 73, 92; estate management
284 – 90; under Henry IV
183 – 6; prestige-consumption
see display; luxury
economic ethos: bourgeois 64 – 5,
66 – 8, 70; industrial 72

economy: and architecture 56;
  feudal 156 – 7, 238 – 9;
  land 151 – 3, 155 – 6, 159;
  taxes 37, 152 – 3, 155; *see also*
  money
Edict of Nantes 183
elite formations 17 – 18
Elizabeth Charlotte of the
  Palatinate 172n
Empire, French 79
Encyclopédie (1777): Diderot and
  D'Alembert 44, 46, 47 – 8, 49,
  50, 54, 56, 57n, 58, 59n, 61, 63,
  74, 92; Marmontel,
  'Grands' 43n, 171 – 3
England: courts 37, 68; 'good
  society' in 68, 96 – 7, 98; king of,
  in army camp 101 – 2; 16th
  cent. 165; 19th cent. historical
  study 5n
'Enlightenment', the 113
entrées to king's bedroom 83 – 4,
  85
Estates General 163, 169 – 70;
  and Henry IV 163 – 4, 182, 183;
  of 1614 191 – 2
estates 54 – 5, 60 – 2, 63 – 4;
  assemblies of 163 – 4;
  conflicts 70 – 1; *see also* Third
  Estate
etiquette, court 78 – 115; breaching
  87 – 8, 131 – 2; fetish
  character 85; function and
  significance 29, 84 – 96, 99 – 103,
  132; from king's standpoint 89,
  117 – 45, 197 – 8; and
  power, 117 – 20, 132 – 7,
  139 – 40; and privilege 207 – 8;
  value of studying 8
evolution, biological and social
  11 – 14, 293 – 4

family 49 – 51
feelings, expression or curbing of
  111, 112 – 13, 239 – 43, 251 – 2,
  255
feudal social forms 8; vassals
  153 – 4, 156 – 7, 163, 238 – 9, 290
figurations: analysis of 208 – 10,
  212 – 13; evolution of 293 – 4;

and individuals 18 – 21, 25 – 6,
  33, 141 – 5
financiers 64 – 5; tax farmers 61,
  69, 272
food 46 – 7
formalism 109
Francis I, King of France 148, 152
  158 – 60, 162, 163, 165 – 6, 189n
Frederick II, King of Prussia 141,
  146, 147, 188
freedom, individual 29 – 32, 144 – 5,
  240
Fronde, the 169, 170, 174 – 6, 200

gardens 227 – 8
Genlis, Countess 87
German: architecture 56n;
  bourgeoisie 222, 224;
  Classicism 112; courts 36n;
  Empire, shift in power relationships 219; historians 5n;
  National Socialism 276 – 83;
  nobility 97 – 9, 172n, 188 – 90
gloire 134 – 6
'good society' 62 – 3, 78 – 9, 94 – 6;
  English 96 – 7; German 97 – 9;
  survival of 106
Goethe, Johann Wolfgang von 112
grands 43, 171 – 5, 179, 181, 182n,
  192 – 3
Gratian, Hand Oracle 107n, 108,
  109n
greatness, human 15 – 17, 24,
  126 – 7, 168

Hegel, Georg 233
Henry II, King of France 161n
Henry IV, King of France: accession
  of 151, 164, 167 – 8, 177, 178,
  236, 247; and nobility 148 – 50,
  151, 155, 164 – 5, 180 – 3, 185 – 6,
  190, 239
Henry VIII, King of England 165
historiography 4 – 7, 9 – 11, 15 – 16,
  24 – 5, 141, 276 – 9
history: change in 11 – 14, 245;
  framework of reference 14 – 17,
  25 – 7; individual role in 4,
  14 – 21, 24 – 7, 29 – 33; knowledge
  of 33 – 4; lack of autonomy

history (cont.)
  6 – 9; meaning of   4 – 6; 19th
  cent. studies of   5n; rewritten
  constantly   33 – 4; and
  sociology   1 – 34, 217 – 18,
  276 – 80; uniqueness of events   4,
  9 – 12, 18 – 21, 25; values
  in   7 – 11, 28 – 9, 34, 38 – 9,
  211 – 12
Hitler, Adolf   278 – 9
Höhne, Heinz   277 – 9
honour   95, 98, 103
hôtels (town houses)   43 – 7, 49, 51,
  54; appartements privés   49 – 51;
  reception rooms   51 – 3; significance of   53 – 4; under Louis
  XV   79
households and houses   41 – 65;
  country   43, 45; different types of
  54 – 6; maisons particulières   54,
  57 – 8; management of   284 – 90;
  ornamentation   56n, 58 – 9;
  palais   54, 59; prestige value   57;
  royal   41 – 3, 80, see also
  Versailles; significance of   53 – 4,
  60 – 4; town see hôtels
Huguenots   164n, 191

'ideal types'   13 – 14
individual: change in   11 – 14;
  consciousness   244 – 6, 250 – 7;
  development of   19 – 21, 244 – 5;
  independence of   29 – 33, 141 – 5,
  209 – 13, 243 – 4; role in
  history   4, 14 – 21, 24 – 7, 29 – 33,
  168 – 9; uniqueness of   10 – 11,
  13, 18 – 19, 29
industrial societies   72, 113 – 14, 214
intelligentsia   189 – 90
intendant, house   46, 284 – 91
interdependence, network of   136;
  and building design   73 – 4; and
  constraint   265 – 6; court   73;
  and etiquette   86 – 8, 117 – 20,
  131 – 2; and individual   29 – 33,
  141 – 5, 209 – 13, 243 – 4; and
  power   158 – 9, trans-
  formation of   220 – 5; of
  values   75 – 7
Italy, courts of   39

Jansenism   62
Jurieu   133

king, position of   3, 4, 22 – 4, 41 – 3,
  70 – 2, 135 – 7; bedroom   82 – 4,
  85, 138; bonding of through
  etiquette   117 – 45, 197; conflict
  with nobility   146 – 59, 162 – 74,
  179 – 207, 209 – 10; couchée   87,
  89 – 90; favour of   71, 73,
  155 – 6, 238 – 9; income   152 – 3,
  154, 155 – 6, 159 – 61, 177, 186; as
  individual 18 – 21, 24 – 5, 168,
  211 – 12; legitimacy   177 – 8;
  levée   83 – 5; need of
  nobility   157 – 64, 179 – 81, 187,
  205 – 7; power   3, 4, 22 – 4,
  41 – 3, 70 – 2, 135 – 7, 146 – 9; see
  also Louis XIV; monarchy
knightly game   149
knowledge   252 – 4

La Bruyère, Jean de   104n, 105, 138
La Rochefoucauld, Duke of (son of
  François)   199 – 201, 212 – 13
La Rochefoucauld, François,
  Maxims   105
land: income from   151 – 3, 155 – 6,
  159; longing for see country life
Leopold, Ludwig, Prestige   103n
Levée: of the king,   83 – 5;
  queen   86
literature   105 – 6; drama   112;
  L'Astrée   246 – 51, 255 – 66;
  romantic   248 – 9
Louis IX, King of France   158
Louis XIII, King of France   181,
  182, 187, 191, 192 – 4, 201
Louis XIV, King of France: and court
  17, 78, 79 – 80, 82 – 5, 89 – 90,
  120, 150 – 3, 181, 202, 222 – 3,
  239 – 40; and family   198 – 9; and
  Henry IV   149 – 50, 177; as
  individual 18 – 20, 24, 126 – 7,
  211; memoirs   117 – 18, 128, 129,
  135; rule of   42, 68, 70 – 1,
  127 – 36, 139 – 40, 186 – 8,
  196 – 200, 269 – 70, 272 – 3; youth
  of   70, 126 – 7, 174

Louis XV, King of France 79, 87, 132 – 3, 138, 272
Louis XVI, King of France 79, 86, 87, 173
love 243 – 4, 256 – 60, 263
lower classes 61, 266 – 7, 268; revolting 271; servants 45 – 9; taxes 37
Luxembourg, Duke of 91
luxury 37 – 8, 38 – 9, 45, 53, 63; see also display

Maine, Duc de 78
Maintenon, Madame de 121n, 198, 200
Margaret of Valois 259 – 60
Marie-Antoinette, Queen 86, 87, 239
Marly (château) 138
Marmontel 171 – 3
marriage: aristocratic 49 – 51; bourgeois 58; German nobility 172n; romantic 257 – 8
Marx, Karl 233
masks 240 – 1, 242 – 3; primitive 251; and reality 256, 258
Mazarin, Cardinal Jules, 127, 136, 172n, 174 – 6
Meudon, court at 198
Middle Ages 60 – 1; see also feudal social forms
Mommsen, Hans 277 – 9, 283
monarchy: absolute 3, 135, 148, 165; development of in France 147 – 9; see also king
money economy 151 – 3, 155 – 6, 160 – 1, 164 – 5, 184, 186, 239
Montespan, Madame de 200 – 1
Montesquieu, Baron de 68 – 70, 71, 73
Montmorency, Duke of, downfall of 195, 212
morality, formation of 257

Napoléon I 146, 147
nation see state
National Socialism 276 – 83
Nature 225 – 30, 239, 242 – 3, 260
Necker, Jacques 79n

nobility: accommodation 74, see also hôtels; and bourgeoisie 148, 157, 167 – 71, 178 – 9, 203 – 7; and the church 165 – 7; conflict with the king see under king; constraints on 262 – 6; courtization of 214 – 67; culture 147 – 8; decline of 68 – 70, 71, 73, 194 – 6, 199, 203 – 6, 292, 294; dependence on king 71 – 2, 90, 99, 158 – 60, 176, 238 – 9; development of 147 – 9, 157 – 9; economic affairs 183 – 6, 191, 284 – 94, see also display; and etiquette 117 – 18; feudal 153 – 4, 156 – 7, 163, 238 – 9, 290; figuration at court 66 – 77; function for the king 205 – 7; grands 43, 171 – 5, 179, 181, 182n, 192 – 3; income 152, 153, 155 – 6; norms and values 66 – 72; offices 162, 181 – 2, 190 – 1; ossified 70 – 1, 273 – 4; power 97, 150 – 1, 192 – 4, 269 – 75; provincial 171, 241; Prussian 188 – 90; rank and titles 63 – 4, 71, 90 – 1, 159, 249, 255; of the robe see robe; 16th cent. 159; 1627 requests 187 – 8; split into groups 171 – 6; of the sword 61, 68 – 70, 71, 73, 171, 189, 191, 292; warrior, old 153 – 5, 157, 159 – 60, 292
nominalism 209

observing people 104 – 7
offices, court 17, 162; hierarchy of 233 – 4; purchase of 181 – 3, 190 – 1
opinion, social 91 – 2, 94 – 101; German 172n; see also prestige
Oppenheimer, Franz 37
organizations, large 139 – 40; bureaucracy 38
Orléans, Duchess of 78 – 9, 86
Orléans, Duke of (nephew of Louis XIV) 78 – 9, 120, 178n, 198, 201 – 2
Orléans, Gaston of 192, 199

painting 230, 242, 244, 252 – 3
palace, the king's 80 – 6, 138;
    see also Versailles
palais 54, 59
Paris 43, 45, 148, 161, 167; in 1590
    164n; in 1650 175 – 6; court
    moved from 197, 267
parliaments 61, 163 – 4, 169 – 71,
    174 – 5; see also Estates General
Parsons, Talcott 32
past, longing for the 214 – 16,
    222 – 3, 224 – 5, 248, 262
pastorales 224 – 5, 230, 239,
    248 – 50, 256 – 66
patrimonialism 21 – 2, 41 – 2
personality: and despotic rule 23;
    development of 19, 244 – 5; value
    of 211; see also individual
Pléiade, the 229, 237
poetry 228 – 9, 237
Potlatch, in N. American tribes 67 – 8
power: centralization 1 – 2, 161,
    216, 241 – 2, 247 – 8; and
    conflict 167 – 9, 276 – 82; and
    etiquette 117 – 20, 132 – 7,
    139 – 40; and independence
    144 – 5; and individuals 15 – 17;
    in large organizations 139 – 40;
    monopolization of 2, 22, 23, see
    also absolute rule; and National
    Socialism 276 – 83; reproduction of
    distribution 157 – 8; shifts
    in 146 – 213, 268 – 75; and social
    rank 96 – 7, 269 – 71; sociology
    of 21 – 4;
precious metals, influx of 151, 164n,
    184
prestige 60n, 85 – 9, 92 – 3, 99 – 104,
    131; 'good society' 62 – 3, 78 – 9,
    94 – 6; and houses 57; of the
    king 134 – 7; see also opinion
prestige-consumption see display
private sphere 52 – 3, 54 – 5,
    114 – 16, 138; appartements
    privés 49 – 51
privilege 76, 86, 88, 207 – 8, 273
professional classes 54 – 5, 58, 153;
    ethos 66 – 7; houses 56; and
    private life 114 – 16; visits by
    52 – 3; Third Estate 61, 65n

Prussia 146, 147, 188 – 90, 280

quantity, transformed to quality
    233 – 5

rank: order of 91 – 2; and power
    269 – 70; and titles 160
Ranke, L. von 4 – 6, 9, 149, 175,
    176, 177, 178n, 195
rationality 92 – 3, 110 – 14
reality 250 – 6, 292 – 4
reflection 243, 261 – 2
relationships: of court people
    90 – 104, 141 – 5, 238 – 41; dealing
    with people 107 – 10, 111;
    distance 242 – 4; observing
    people 104 – 7; between
    groups 178 – 9; see also feelings
relativism 291 – 2
religious wars 163 – 4, 183 – 4, 247
Renaissance, the 242 – 7, 250 – 1
Revolution 79, 208, 268 – 9, 271 – 2,
    274 – 5, 294
Richelieu, Duc de 37n, 87, 191 – 5,
    239 – 40; attitude to money 67
robe, noblesse de 62, 69, 169 – 70,
    179 – 80, 184, 191, 271 – 2
romantic attitude 216 – 17, 222 – 30,
    237, 239 – 40, 243 – 4, 247 – 50,
    256 – 66
Ronsard, Pierre de 229
Rousseau, Jean Jacques 113, 226
rule: absolute see absolute rule;
    charismatic 22, 121 – 6; and
    conquest 1 – 2, 128 – 9, 130;
    conserving 126 – 31; despotic,
    and personality 23; and etiquette
    132 – 40; and freedom 140 – 5; in
    large organizations 139 – 40;
    pressures in 265 – 6;
    routinized 22 – 3; structure
    of 118 – 26

Saint-Simon, Louis de Rouvroy,
    Duc de 80, 106n, 196, 269;
    career 17 – 18, 89 – 90, 201 – 2;
    and dauphin 107 – 8, 109, 120,
    202 – 4; and Louis XIV 120, 140,
    201, 227 – 8; memoirs 227; quoted
    83n, 91, 100, 104, 120, 121n, 127,
    131, 133, 197, 198 – 9, 200, 203 – 4

salons, 18th cent. 79
Sannazar, *Arcadia* 250
self-consciousness 244 – 6
self-control 238 – 46, 248, 251 – 3,
 258; in Germany 282 – 3
self-detachment 244 – 6, 254, 256,
 261 – 2
servants 45 – 9, 268; house intendant
 284 – 91; *see also* offices, court
'social conditions' 143
social forms, development of 11 – 14
sociology 141, 208 – 13; and biology
 12; and history 1 – 34, 217 – 18,
 276 – 80
Sombart, W. 39
Southern, A.W. 5n
Spanish armies 101 – 2, 164, 176
Staël, Madame de 106n
state (nation) 133 – 4, 137 – 40,
 205 – 6, 216 – 20; structural
 conflict in 276 – 83
status *see* prestige
stratification, social: and etiquette
 86 – 9; mobility and rigidity
 of 70 – 2
Stubbs, William 5n
style 79n; architectural 56n;
 Classicism 112
Sully, Maximilien 37n
Swiss Guards 47, 129
system theory 141

Taine, Hippolyte 188
taxes 37, 152 – 3, 155; tax farmers
 61, 69, 272
tensions, balance of 120 – 1, 221,
 236 – 7, 266, 270 – 5, 276 – 8
theft, punishment for 48
Third Estate 61, 65n, 181, 187,
 191 – 2
totalitarian dictatorship 276 – 83
towns 36, 45; and country 214 – 17,
 226, 228 – 30, 237 – 8;
 early 160 – 1; dwellings in 54,
 57 – 8; urbanization 214 – 17,
 222, 226
trade and commerce 55, 69 – 70, 73;
 routes 155

transformations: and continuity
 232 – 8; of people 244 – 5; of
 power balance 268 – 75;
 social 214 – 26
transition periods 158 – 60, 214 – 16,
 225, 235 – 7, 247 – 8, 251 – 2; of
 power distribution 155 – 7

universities 189 – 90
Utopianism 262 – 5

values: and architecture 56 – 7; in
 historical judgement 7 – 11,
 28 – 9, 34, 38 – 9, 211 – 12;
 interdependence of 75 – 7; of a
 person 211; prestige - 85
Veblen, Thorstein 38n, 63, 67
Vendôme, Duke of 192
Vendôme, Grand Prior of 78
Versailles 80 – 3, 138; court formed
 at 197, 267; front courts 81;
 gardens 227 – 8; king's bedroom
 83, 138; size 80 – 1;
 structure 43 – 4, 45, 197
Villeroy, Maréchal de 203
violence 268 – 9, 275, 294
Vitry, Philippe de 237
Voltaire, François 48n, 98, 106n,
 113
von Boehn, M. 42n

warfare 37, 135; chivalrous
 148 – 9, 154; medieval 153 – 4;
 mercenary 149, 154 – 5, 160; 16th
 cent. 154, 159 – 60; religious
 wars 163 – 5, 183 – 4, 247
warrior elites 153 – 5, 157, 159, 292;
 transformation to courtiers
 215 – 16
wealth, attitude to 72 – 3; 99; *see
 also* display
Weber, Max 13 – 14, 21 – 2, 37 – 8,
 41 – 2, 63, 85n, 110, 121 – 2
women 194, 243 – 4; married
 49 – 51
work, attitude to 72 – 3
writing 105 – 6

ABOUT THE AUTHOR

NORBERT ELIAS, born in 1897, studied medicine, philosophy (with Edmund Husserl), and psychology in Breslau, Freiburg, and Heidelberg. He did his postgraduate studies with Alfred Weber and taught at Frankfurt with Karl Mannheim. He went on to posts in Paris and at the London School of Economics, becoming Reader in Sociology at the University of Leicester and Professor of Sociology at the University of Ghana. He is still Visiting Professor at the University of Bielefeld, where he now lives.